ODYSSEYS
IN
PSYCHOTHERAPY

ODYSSEYS IN PSYCHOTHERAPY

JOSEPH J. SHAY, PH.D.
JOAN WHEELIS, M.D.
Editors

To Madeline & Ed —
To my beloved couple whose
friendship I cherish more
with each passing moment.
Love
Joe

PUBLISHED BY
ARDENT MEDIA INC.

Copyright © 2000 by Ardent Media, Inc.

Library of Congress Cataloging-in-Publication Data is pending.

Bulk Purchase Discounts: For discounts on orders of 25 copies or more, please fax the number above or write the address above. Please state if you are a non-profit organization and the number of copies you are interested in purchasing. Bulk discount orders are nonreturnable.

Note to Book Sellers: All book returns require written permission and label from the publisher. Write to the address above or fax the number above for permission.

Customer Service and Warehouse
1-800-218-1535
8:30 am – 4:30 pm EST

Design and production: Digital Impact Design

ISBN 0-8290-5215-1

1 3 5 7 9 10 6 4 2

Printed in the United States of America

The paper used in this publication meets the minimum requirements of American National Standard for Information Sciences – Permanence of Paper for Printed Library Materials, ANSI Z39.48-1984.

To Laura, Kevin, and my mother
and to the memory of my father
JS

For Pablo and Nicolas, Allen and Ilse
who together keep the road traveled well lighted
so that I can see ahead into the darkness
JW

CONTENTS

Editors   *i*

Contributors   *i*

Acknowledgments   *ix*

Chapter 1   **Psychotherapy at the Millennium**   1
             JOSEPH J. SHAY, PH.D. AND JOAN WHEELIS, M.D.

Chapter 2   **Interim Notes on a Career in Psychology**   18
             SIMON H. BUDMAN, PH.D.

Chapter 3   **An Ethnocultural Approach to Psychotherapy**   46
             and to Life
             LILLIAN COMAS-DÍAZ, PH.D.

Chapter 4   **Making the Professional Personal and the**   67
             Personal Professional
             RUTH G. DEAN, D.S.W.

Chapter 5   **Once Upon a Time**   96
             SOPHIE FREUD, LICSW, PH.D.

Chapter 6   **Swimming Upstream: Voyage of a Lesbian**   126
             Psychiatrist
             NANETTE K. GARTRELL, M.D.

Chapter 7   **A Model of Connection for a Disconnected**   147
             World
             JUDITH V. JORDAN, PH.D.

Chapter 8   **My Professional Journey: The Development**   167
             of Multimodal Therapy
             ARNOLD A. LAZARUS, PH.D.

Chapter 9   **A Quarter Century of Psychotherapy**   187
              RONALD F. LEVANT, ED.D.

Chapter 10   **Embracing Uncertainty and Complexity in**   209
              Psychotherapy
              CAROLYNN P. MALTAS, PH.D.

Chapter 11   **What I Have Learned: Growth Through**   236
              Disillusion
              JOHN T. MALTSBERGER, M.D.

Chapter 12   **Psychodynamic Therapy: Heading in New**   253
              Directions
              ELIZABETH LLOYD MAYER, PH.D.

Chapter 13   **Reflections of a Group Analyst**   282
              MALCOLM PINES, M.D.

Chapter 14   **Personal and Professional Life**   312
              OWEN RENIK, M.D.

Chapter 15   **The Individual in Context**   337
              EDWARD R. SHAPIRO, M.D.

Chapter 16   **Reclaiming the Disavowed: The Evolution**   359
              of an Integrative Point of View
              PAUL L. WACHTEL, PH.D.

Chapter 17   **The Path Taken**   393
              ALLEN WHEELIS, M.D.

Chapter 18   **Back to the Future**   403
              JOSEPH J. SHAY, PH.D. AND JOAN WHEELIS, M.D.

Name Index   409

Subject Index   418

EDITORS

JOSEPH J. SHAY, PH.D. is Director of Psychological Services & Training at Two Brattle Center in Cambridge, Massachusetts. He is an Instructor in Psychology in the Department of Psychiatry at Harvard Medical School, and Senior Attending Psychologist in the McLean/Massachusetts General Hospital training program. Dr. Shay has a particular interest in the nature of change in psychotherapy and the ways in which views about the nature of change have matured.

JOAN WHEELIS, M.D. is Clinical Director at Two Brattle Center and is an Assistant Clinical Professor of Psychiatry at Harvard Medical School. Trained as a psychoanalyst, she is a faculty member of the Boston Psychoanalytic Society and Institute and at the Psychoanalytic Institute of New England. She is also on the faculty of the McLean/Massachusetts General Hospital psychiatry residency program and has a particular interest in the intensive outpatient treatment of character disordered patients.

CONTRIBUTORS

SIMON H. BUDMAN, PH.D. is Founder and President of Innovative Training Systems and a faculty member at Harvard Medical School. He is the former director of the Mental Health Staff Training and Research Program at the Harvard Community Health Plan. Dr. Budman is the recipient of numerous awards and honors including the American Psychological Association Year 2000 Distinguished Professional Contributions to Knowledge Award. Author of more than 100 books, articles, reviews, audiotapes, and videotapes on individual, couples, and group therapy, his books, *Forms of Brief Therapy* (1981), *Theory and Practice of Brief Therapy* (1988), and *The First Session in Brief Therapy* (1992) have established him as a significant contributor to the field of psychotherapy. His latest book, co-authored with

Brett Steenbarger, Ph.D., is *The Essential Guide to Group Practice in Mental Health: Clinical, Legal, and Financial Fundamentals* (1997).

LILLIAN COMAS-DÍAZ, PH.D. is the Executive Director of the Transcultural Mental Health Institute, Clinical Professor in the George Washington University Department of Psychiatry and Behavioral Sciences, and a private practitioner in Washington, DC. The former director of the American Psychological Association's Office of Ethnic Minority Affairs, Dr. Comas-Díaz was also the director of the Yale University Department of Psychiatry Hispanic Clinic. The senior editor of two textbooks, *Clinical Guidelines in Cross Cultural Mental Health*, and *Women of Color: Integrating Ethnic and Gender Identities in Psychotherapy*, she edits the American Psychological Association Division 45 official journal, *Cultural Diversity and Ethnic Minority Psychology.*

RUTH G. DEAN, D.S.W. is a Professor at Simmons College School of Social Work. In addition to her academic appointment, she maintains a private practice in Boston and is currently engaged in volunteer work with children and families at the Solomon Carter Fuller Mental Health Center. Dr. Dean has served on the editorial board of *Smith College Studies in Social Work* and *Families and Society*, and has published a number of articles on social constructivism, narrative approaches with groups, and ethical-clinical dilemmas. A two-time grant recipient from the Marion and Jasper Whiting Foundation, Dr. Dean has recently served as a visiting professor at the School of Social Work at Curtin University in Perth, Australia. She is also the recipient of the 1998 Award for the Greatest Contribution to Social Work Education from the Massachusetts Chapter of the National Association of Social Workers.

SOPHIE FREUD, LICSW, PH.D., born in Vienna, Austria, is a clinical social worker. Her clinical practice has been primarily in the field of child welfare and parent guidance, which led to her pursuit of a Ph.D. in 1970 from the Florence Heller School for Social Welfare. Subsequently, she devoted her attention to teaching at Simmons College School of Social Work for 25 years. Dr. Freud has written many papers on social work education, feminism, and group work as well as a book, *My Three Mothers and Other Passions*, which reflects on her three identities of mother, therapist, and educator.

NANETTE K. GARTRELL, M.D. is a lesbian feminist psychiatrist who specializes in individual and couples work with lesbians. She is an Associate Clinical Professor of Psychiatry at the University of California, San Francisco. She has been involved in documenting sexual abuse by physicians since 1982, and conducting a national longitudinal lesbian family study since 1986. Dr. Gartrell is the author of more than 45 articles on medical ethics and lesbian mental health and has served on the editorial boards of *Women and Therapy* and the *Journal of Lesbian Studies*.

JUDITH V. JORDAN, PH.D. is the Co-Director of the Jean Baker Miller Training Institute of the Stone Center at Wellesley College where she is also Director of Training and a Founding Scholar. She is an Attending Psychologist at McLean Hospital and Assistant Professor of Psychology at the Harvard Medical School. She is the recipient of the Massachusetts Psychology Association's Career Achievement Award for Outstanding Contributions to the Advancement of Psychology as a Science and a Profession. Dr. Jordan founded the Women's Studies Program and Women's Treatment Network at McLean Hospital where she served as its first director. She is co-author of *Women's Growth in Connection*, editor of *Women's Growth in Diversity*, and has published many chapters and journal articles.

ARNOLD A. LAZARUS, PH.D. is the President of the Center for Multimodal Psychological Services in Princeton, New Jersey, and a Fellow of the Academy of Clinical Psychology. He holds the rank of Distinguished Professor Emeritus of Psychology at

Rutgers University and is the recipient of many awards and honors including the Distinguished Psychologist Award from APA's Division of Psychotherapy, the Distinguished Professional Contributions Award from APA's Division of Clinical Psychology, and the Distinguished Service Award from the American Board of Professional Psychology. He is also the first recipient of the prestigious annual Cummings Psyche Award for his significant contributions to tbhe field of behavioral health. Dr. Lazarus was the first to use the term "behavior therapy" and "behavior therapist," and is the founder of the broad-spectrum assessment and treatment approach he called "Multimodal Therapy." He has published 16 books and more than 200 articles and is widely recognized as an international authority on effective and efficient psychotherapy.

RONALD F. LEVANT, ED.D., a clinical psychologist, is currently Dean and Professor at the Center for Psychological Studies at Nova Southeastern University. Dr. Levant has served as president of the Massachusetts Psychological Association as well as president of the APA Division 43 (Family Psychology) and is the cofounder and first President of APA Division 51 (Society for the Psychological Study of Men and Masculinity). Dr. Levant has won numerous awards and honors, and has also authored, coauthored, edited, or co-edited over 150 publications including 12 books, which include *Between Father and Child, Masculinity Reconstructed*, and *A New Psychology of Men*.

CAROLYNN P. MALTAS, PH.D. is an Assistant Clinical Professor of Psychology in the Department of Psychiatry at Harvard Medical School as well as an Attending Psychologist at the Massachusetts Mental Health Center where she teaches family and couple therapy. She is a co-founder and faculty member of the Psychoanalytic Couple and Family Institute of New England and also President-elect of the Section on Couple and Family Therapy of the Division of Psychoanalysis (Division 39) of the American Psychological Association. Dr. Maltas was also the founder and co-director of the McLean Institute for Couples and Families and has authored and co-authored numerous articles on difficulties within intimate relationships as well as conflict amongst therapists in multi-therapist systems. She maintains a private practice in Cambridge, Massachusetts.

JOHN T. MALTSBERGER, M.D. is an Associate Clinical Professor of Psychiatry at the Harvard Medical School, from which he graduated in 1959. All his psychiatric training was at the Massachusetts Mental Health Center in Boston. He is an Attending Psychiatrist at McLean Hospital, a Clinical Associate in Psychiatry at the Massachusetts General Hospital, former chairman of the faculty at the Boston Psychoanalytic Society and Institute, and has published many papers and book chapters on the suicidal patient. The New York University Press has recently published *Essential Papers on Suicide*, a book he compiled and edited with Dr. Mark Goldblatt.

ELIZABETH LLOYD MAYER, PH.D. is an Associate Clinical Professor in the Psychology Department of the University of California at Berkeley and in the Psychiatry Department of the University of California Medical Center, San Francisco. She is also a Training and Supervising Psychoanalyst at the San Francisco Psychoanalytic Institute and a Fellow of the International Consciousness Research Laboratories at Princeton University. In addition to her numerous publications in psychoanalysis, she is the Founder and Artistic Director of the San Francisco Bay Revels and has directed and produced a series of award-winning films about making music with children. Her interests center on differences in early male and female development, the interface between science and spirituality, the nature of healing, and cognitive and communicative processes in intuition.

MALCOLM PINES, FRCP, FRCPSYCH, DPM, is a psychiatrist in London, England. Dr. Pines trained in psychiatry at the Maudsley Hospital in London and in psychoanalysis at the

British Psychoanalytic Society. He served as Consultant at the Cassel, St. George's and Maudsley Hospitals, and in the adult department of the Tavistock Clinic. He is a founding member of the Institute of Group Analysis in London, and has served as President of the International Association of Group Psychotherapy and of the Section of Psychiatry at the Royal Society of Medicine in London. Dr. Pines is the editor of *Group Analysis* and *The International Library of Group Analysis*. His most recent books include *Ring of Fire: Primitive Affects and Object Relations in Group Psychotherapy* (with V. L. Schermer) and *Circular Reflections: Selected Papers on Group Analysis and Psychoanalysis*.

OWEN RENIK, M.D. is a Training and Supervising Psychoanalyst at the San Francisco Psychoanalytic Institute. He is Editor-in-Chief of *Psychoanalytic Quarterly*, and Chairman of the Program Committee of the American Psychoanalytic Association. He is the author of over 60 articles on a variety of topics including self-disclosure, enactment, and the irreducible subjectivity of the analyst.

EDWARD R. SHAPIRO, M.D. is the Medical Director/CEO of the Austen Riggs Center in Stockbridge, Massachusetts, as well as the director of the Erik H. Erikson Institute for Education and Research. He is also Associate Clinical Professor in Psychiatry at Harvard Medical School, a faculty member of the Boston Psychoanalytic Institute, and a Fellow of the A. K. Rice Institute. Dr. Shapiro is the author of *The Inner World and the Outer World: Psychoanalytic Perspectives*, and the co-author of *Lost in Familiar Places: Creating New Connections Between the Individual and Society*.

PAUL L. WACHTEL, PH.D. is CUNY Distinguished Professor in the doctoral program in clinical psychology at City College and the CUNY Graduate Center as well as Founding Director of the Colin Powell Center for Policy Studies at City College in New York. He is one of the founders of the Society for the Exploration of Psychotherapy Integration and maintains a clinical practice in New York City. Dr. Wachtel's most recent books include *Race in* *the Mind of America: Breaking the Vicious Circle Between Blacks and Whites; Psychoanalysis, Behavior Therapy, and the Relational World;* and *Therapeutic Communication: Knowing What to Say When.*

ALLEN WHEELIS, M.D. is a psychiatrist and psychoanalyst practicing in the San Francisco Bay area. He trained at the Menninger Clinic in Topeka, Kansas, as well as at the Austen Riggs Center in Stockbridge, Massachusetts. He is the author of 13 books including *The Quest for Identity, How People Change,* and, most recently, *The Listener: A Psychoanalyst Examines His Life.*

ACKNOWLEDGMENTS

Is psychotherapy a science or is it poetry? Is this even a meaningful question to ask? Since our own childhoods, both of us—albeit for differing reasons—have been fascinated with the workings of psychotherapy. Each of us has sought out the "elders" of psychotherapy to teach us what they believe. As the millennium turned, it seemed an opportune time to transform this personal interest into a volume in which several luminaries of psychotherapy would tell their stories, would share what they used to believe and what they now believe.

Selecting these figures was a daunting task, for we had to find individuals willing to reveal themselves in the personal way we asked, and amenable to giving time to this more autobiographical project, even as they continued to shape the field. To each of our contributors, we want to express our profound appreciation and gratitude for their willingness to reveal a personal story, and for their candor and integrity in sharing their changing views of psychotherapy.

We also wish to express our abiding appreciation to our publisher, Irving Naiburg, for his faith in our project, Suzi Naiburg for her help shepherding this work through its various stages, and Gregory Gross of Two Brattle Center, who generously shared the resources at his disposal. Finally, we extend special gratitude to our partners, Laura Zimmerman and Pablo Guevara, for having supported our efforts lovingly and without complaint from the very beginning.

We shall not cease from exploration.
And the end of all our exploring
Will be to arrive where we started
And know the place for the first time.
  "Little Gidding," T. S. Eliot

Scientific discoveries are emotional discoveries.
  J. H. van den Berg

The creative imagination requires a certain abandon and disre-
gard for results, which often paradoxically generates the most
useful outcomes.
  Shaun McNiff

[A] new theory…is seldom or never just an increment to what
is already known. Its assimilation requires the reconstruction
of prior theory and the re-evaluation of prior fact, an intrinsi-
cally revolutionary process that is seldom completed by a single
man and never overnight.
  Thomas Kuhn

There is no creativity that is not based on tradition.
  Donald Winnicott

ODYSSEYS
IN
PSYCHOTHERAPY

CHAPTER 1

PSYCHOTHERAPY AT THE MILLENNIUM

JOSEPH J. SHAY, PH.D. AND JOAN WHEELIS, M.D.

I f an asteroid were arriving in the new millennium, soon to shatter our planet with the resulting loss of most human life and recorded thought, what would we wish to preserve in a time capsule for the immediate use of surviving generations of psychotherapists? Whose works would survive?

Does Freud enter the capsule or is this unnecessary prologue? Does Szasz's (1961) influential work merit a place or is his interpretation dead, replaced by Kramer's (1993) masterpiece? Do we choose *The Courage to Heal* (Bass & Davis, 1988) or *The Myth of Repressed Memory* (Loftus & Ketcham, 1994)? Would the works of Fiedler (1950), Frank (1973), and Norcross and Goldfried (1992) highlighting common factors across all psychotherapies warrant inclusion? Or do we include one of the dozens of recently appearing technical manuals of practice, or the recent *American Psychiatric*

Association Practice Guidelines (1996), or the *Psychologists' Desk Reference* (Koocher, Norcross, & Hill, 1998)? What about managed care guidelines for diagnosis and treatment? Do we try to be very modern and select such works entitled *Single Session Therapy* (Talmon, 1990) or *The 60-Second Shrink* (Lazarus & Lazarus, 1997)? Or are we post-modern and choose *Inventing the Psychological* (Pfister & Schnog, 1997)? We now know that even "historical" tomes reflect a bias. Do we then choose Shorter's (1997) history, which leans toward the welcome resurgence of the biological, or Freedheim's (1992) compilation, which is less disapproving of psychotherapy? Has Eysenck's (1952) often-cited questioning of the very effectiveness of psychotherapy been replaced by the *Consumer Reports* (1995) study?

Finally, what of the works of the authors in this volume, let alone this volume itself? Will the thoughts of these talented, wise men and women stand the unforgiving test of time, fashion, and social change?

From Freud's Spark to Main Street Psychotherapy

In 1900, Sigmund Freud published *The Interpretation of Dreams*, which, with the rest of his work, ignited the psychotherapy movement. This movement, however, has not been linear but has taken numerous detours, many of them unpredictable and surprising. At the beginning of this new millennium, the landscape of psychotherapy looks increasingly complex, diverse, and confusing. Expanding from a handful of schools early in this century to more than 400 at present (Freudenberger & Freedheim, 1992, p. 454), the world of psychotherapy has changed profoundly, at times unrecognizably.

Even at the beginning, Freud's work hardly took the world by storm. Although six hundred copies of *The Interpretation of Dreams* were printed initially, these took eight years to sell (November Time Capsule, 1998, p.7). Similarly, at the 1910 annual meeting of the then-young American Psychiatric Association, only three percent of those present were in private practice. But just five years later, psychoanalytic ideas began to appear in the mass circulation women's magazines (Demos, 1997a, p. 64) and by the early 1920s, an entire class of influential intellectuals in America had entered psychoanalysis. One of them wrote, "We began to have alarming dreams, or perhaps, as the Freudians might say, we stopped repressing our dreams and became conscious of them. We talked all day long; we analyzed each other's dreams, fantasies and slips of the tongue....New fears developed....We suffered from various 'complexes.' We concluded in turn that we were extroverts, introverts, schizophrenics, paranoiacs and victims of dementia praecox" (Joseph Freeman, cited in Pfister & Schnog, 1997, p. 170).

In the 1930s and beyond, "the world epicenter of psychiatry shifted to the United States....Under the influence of Freud's teachings, American psychiatry accomplished the switch from psychosis to neurosis as the object of study, and from the asylum to Main Street as the venue for practice" (Shorter, 1997, p. 160). Following Freud's 1909 visit to Clark University, several psychoanalytic training institutes and clinics were established in the United States, with these institutions housing a significant number of clinicians who were also prolific writers. As a result, the psychodynamic orientation to therapy dominated the literature and the consciousness of a growing body of therapists, and "psychotherapy [which was] still a little-known clinical activity in 1940...was synonymous with psychoanalysis in the public mind" (Vandenbos, Cummings, & DeLeon, 1992, p. 74).

Psychoanalytic ideas formed the cornerstone of therapeutic thought, and "[f]rom World War II through the early 1970s, these core ideas—repression, resistance, the centrality of sexuality, the Oedipus, transference—yielded a tremendous amount of power with the academy while gradually filtering into and becoming part of the psychological common sense of the American middle and upper classes" (Schnog, 1997, p. 5). As noted psychologist Seymour Sarason put it, "American psychiatry before World War II was biological psychiatry and within a few years after the war it was largely a psychoanalytical psychiatry" (cited in Shorter, 1997, p. 171).

With the need for psychiatric care exploding during World War II as a result of the many psychiatric casualties, followed by the development of Veterans Administration programs to care for these patients after the War, the push was on for increased training of mental health professionals. Combined with enhanced funding for training from the newly created (1948) National Institute of Mental Health, and federal funding of the community health center movement in the 1960s, VA hospitals, universities, counseling centers, psychiatric hospitals, and community mental health centers were engaged in massive training of psychiatrists, psychologists, and social workers from the 1950s through the 1980s. By 1985, it was estimated that there were 159,000 psychotherapists in the United States, compared to 72,000 ten years earlier (Goleman, cited in Vandenbos et al., 1992, p. 86).

As American consciousness was changing, there was an increasing focus on the inner self and the problems that could arise within this self. Jan van den Berg, a historian of psychology, argued, "Modern psychology became possible because of an interiorization of all human realities. The interiorization founded a new domain: the inner self; psychology is its science. And of this science, Freud is the undisputed master" (1961, p. 34).

And the problems of the inner self seemed to grow almost exponentially. In 1952, the first Diagnostic and Statistical Manual (DSM) of psychiatric disorders was published, listing 60 psychiatric illnesses (Begley, 1998). By the second edition in 1968, there were 180, some of them now labeled "neuroses." By the third version in 1980, the list had ballooned to 265, which then grew to 297 disorders in the 1994 DSM-IV, although the label "neuroses" had disappeared (Shorter, 1997). As Begley (1998) asked in a *Newsweek* cover story, "Is everybody crazy?"

Whether they are or not, there are now plenty of psychotherapists around to treat them, having grown from an initial handful to a multitude.

FADING INTO OBSCURITY

Even as more and more diagnoses and therapists appeared, however, influential ideas of previous leaders in the field were to disappear, or at least to lose their prominence. Here are three examples. Though it is commonly agreed that the most prominent psychiatrist in the United States in the first half of the 20th century was European-born Adolf Meyer, most readers of this volume will have no knowledge of his contributions to the field. Similarly, today, extremely few therapists identify themselves as Jungian, while just a handful more even know what Jungian beliefs are, yet in 1955, Carl Jung appeared on the cover of *Time* magazine. Finally, Carl Rogers, the creator of client-centered therapy, is either little known or referred to by therapists today, even with the current burgeoning of relational, intersubjective, and self-psychological approaches. Yet in the 1960s and 1970s, his work stood in marked contrast to the dominant psychoanalytic and behavioral models by emphasizing a humanistic, existential approach to clients (not to be called "patients"), and virtually all students of psychotherapy identified with one of these three approaches.

How did these changes occur? Who, if anyone, engineered them or supported them or fought them? How did psychotherapists modify beliefs held fervently during their training and early experience—or even overthrow these beliefs? Do the changes in this century reflect the gradual accumulation of information from one generation to the next, or are they paradigm shifts (Kuhn, 1962/1996) yet to be articulated? What has been the evolution of some of the prominent ideas of psychotherapy of the 20th century, particularly the latter half? What is "the social matrix of influential ideas" (Demos, 1997b, p.81)? Are we witnessing little more than the "inevitable historicity of human thought" (Berger & Luckmann, 1967)?

Almost entirely transformed is the psychoanalysis of Freud, the behavior therapy of Skinner, and the existential approach of Rollo May, as the field of psychotherapy has migrated toward integrative therapies. Is this relocation a statement of resignation or one of hope? Why did many therapists move away from an investigation of an individual's problems to an examination of the larger system in which these individuals lived?

Has there been a paradigm shift in the field of psychotherapy? Have there been any "extraordinary episodes in which [a major] shift of professional commitments occurs" referred to by Kuhn as a "scientific revolution" (1962/1996)? As the 21st century dawns and progresses, will such current developments as Dialectical-Behavior Therapy (DBT), Eye Movement Desensitization Reprocessing (EMDR), Thought Field Therapy (TFT), or the manualization of treatments augur revolutions, or will they be laid on the historic dust heap of outmoded therapeutic interventions? Such discarded methods today include the ice pick through the eye socket lobotomy, insulin coma therapy, convulsion-inducing therapies, cold packs, straightjackets, hallucinogens and psychosis-inducing medication trials, bleeding, trepanning, incarceration with snakes, artificially induced epilepsy, the malarial fever cure, and the bromide sleep cure. And will some of what we currently hold true find its way to the same graveyard as Fromm-Reichmann's "schizophrenogenic mother" of the schizophrenic or Bettelheim's "refrigerator parents" of the autistic child? Indeed, the question has recently been raised as to whether parents matter at all (Gladwell, 1998; Harris, 1998).

The very institution of psychotherapy has been barraged by forces inimical to its continuation. Shorter (1997) notes that by 1990 "more than 100 of 163 residency training programs for psychiatry in the United States had abandoned instruction in intensive psychotherapy" (p. 307). And in a recent survey, the most significant professional concerns of psychologist practitioners were about the incursions of managed care on their income, their time, and the clinical and ethical nature of their practice (APA Practice Directorate, 1996). Currently, one in five psychotherapists is leaving the profession (Bass, 1998).

Why, we ask, do certain models or practices "gain cultural authority and lose explanatory power at particular historical moments" (Schnog, 1997, p. 3)? As one critic states, "Practices that now seem reckless and sometimes downright cruel were hailed in their day as pinnacles of medical achievement. Which of today's lauded practices, one wonders, will stand to be condemned a few decades hence?" (Bickerton, 1998, p. 22)

In less than a century we have traveled from Freud's declaration that *The Interpretation of Dreams* "contains, even according to my present-day judgment [1931], the most valuable of all the discoveries it has been my good fortune to make" (Freud, 1900/1931) to Shorter's assertion that "Freud's ideas, which dominated the history of psychiatry for the past half century, are now vanishing like the last snows of winter" (Shorter, 1997, p. vii). Even famed psychologist Rollo May, a pioneer of existential analysis, laments that in a year of case presentations in the early 1990s by his graduating doctoral students, "not one student [last year] mentioned a dream or a free association of the client, and this year there was only one. Never was a free association brought up; indeed, I often had to explain what is meant by the term *free association*" (May, 1992, p. xxv).

Where did dreams go?

THE PERSONAL IS PROFESSIONAL

This book will grapple with these questions in a very intimate way. Rather than write a scientific text tracing either gradual changes or more abrupt shifts in theory and practice, we have solicited personal reflections by senior therapists across the country (and one from across the Atlantic). These autobiographical essays by stellar and internationally renowned therapists focus on specific issues and themes related to changes in their beliefs about psychotherapy. By describing what they thought at the beginning of their careers and what they think now—and the nature of that change process—this book gives the "inside" story of the psychotherapy movement in the second half of the 20th century. Using this autobiographical format, we hope to illuminate where the field of psychotherapy was yesterday, where the field is today, and where it may be headed tomorrow. The underlying metaphor of this book is that the change processes in the field are reflected in the very change processes of distinguished and thoughtful psychotherapists.

Not all therapists, of course, are represented in this book.

No volume of this kind can reflect all perspectives or schools of thought or belief systems, so some of the reader's preferred viewpoints may not appear in these pages. While we regret this inevitability, we hope that our selection is broad enough to illuminate a major thrust of the volume, namely, that a wide range of therapists share significant conclusions while at the same time diverging widely from one another. As you read these chapters, you will see the convergences and divergences in the personal stories, and also the surprising turns as many clinicians not only tried to locate themselves within the social context in which they were practicing but also aspired to a sense of personal comfort, relevance, and meaning.

We invited each contributor to describe both the evolution of his or her thinking about psychotherapy and their personal development, focusing on relevant aspects of upbringing, entry into the field of psychotherapy, early training, and early mentors. What were the central elements of their belief systems at the onset of their careers? Did these originate by identification with mentors or with their own therapists? Did self-examination lead to greater congruence with a particular school of thought? Did personal character structure propel a greater affiliation with certain ideas?

We also asked contributors to highlight formative moments in their careers, turning points, and instances of change that led to their current beliefs. In each chapter, you will be exposed to the heart of their current convictions, at times through illuminating vignettes, and will see how these elements derive, variously, from theory, practice, research, or personal experience. You are encouraged to search, as well, for the influences of the prevailing social ethos at the moments of change.

Finally, we asked our contributors to conclude with their reflections on the current world of psychotherapy. Do they see it as moving in any specific direction? From their vantage point, has it developed in a positive trajectory or are we tilting toward a Tower of Babel which will predictably fall? What do they predict for psychotherapy in the next century? Will it survive the medicalization of psychiatric conditions or the incursion of economic factors?

THE ARC OF WISDOM

When we conceived of this volume, we hoped that our contributors would examine these questions through personal anecdote informed by a contextual frame. To our delight, all contributors have described the changes in their views in relation both to their life histories and the social and institutional contexts in which these personal journeys occurred. In this way, the evolution of psychotherapy is made visible through the personal narratives of the individuals who helped to shape it. We believe there is a deep wisdom embodied in these narratives, forged by years of persistent effort to understand the nature of psychotherapy and to use that enhanced understanding to improve the lives of others.

To the extent that such uniquely personal odysseys may result in shared areas of agreement as the millennium begins, we are witness to vital understandings about psychotherapy at this point in its history. Kassan (1996), who interviewed 60 psychotherapists at varying levels of experience, writes despairingly about gaining such agreement: "I expected to get a lot of divergent opinions about matters of theory and metapsychology. I did not expect to see the total lack of agreement even about such seemingly concrete and straightforward questions as to whether to answer the phone during a session or what to tell patients about confidentiality. If as a field we can't even agree about such simple matters, how are we ever to settle the more difficult questions of how therapy works and how best to conduct ourselves with patients?" (p. 583)

Nonetheless, in the following chapters, numerous points of agreement among contributors point to a more optimistic conclusion. To discern these overlapping themes is to become aware of current verities about psychotherapy; to identify the disparities is to consider how much we still do not know. Arguably, divergences among clinicians will exist as long as independent-minded therapists engage creatively with uniquely distressed patients. In this context of expectable differences, then, significant convergences will prove all the more illuminating.

Not surprisingly, nearly all of our authors were significantly influenced early in their careers by psychoanalytic thinking and the work of Sigmund Freud. While almost all underwent a personal psychoanalysis, interestingly, Sophie Freud, granddaughter of Freud, did not. For several contributors, notably Renik, Mayer, Pines, and Shapiro, psychoanalytic concepts remained central to their understanding of psychotherapy and change. Even among these thinkers, however, the psychoanalytic leitmotif is accompanied by the new chords of context, intersubjectivity, and integration of other models. Maltsberger echoes the sentiments of many contributors when he reveals he was forced by experience to accept that "words are not all powerful, and ... interpretations often fall blunted on the floor." Interpretation is no longer king.

While Sigmund Freud may have been the historical father to our contributors, many of them speak more fondly of their great debt to their mentors. Wachtel, for example, describes his formative relationship with Sid Blatt and Seymour Sarason; Maltsberger reflects on the powerful influence of Elvin Semrad; Lazarus speaks of his important relationship with Joseph Wolpe, although this relationship ultimately foundered; Shapiro emphasizes his gratitude to Roger Shapiro and to David Reiss, for their sustaining faith and direction; Pines reflects on his profound indebtedness to S. H. Foulkes.

Not one of our contributors considers himself or herself a purist. Indeed, as Lazarus astutely notes, "Purists are still very much among us, but I will venture to predict that many of the contributors to this book will reveal how they had started out by adhering rigidly to one discipline and subsequently saw the error of their ways." Indeed, many point clearly to the dangers of adopting a single perspective. Wachtel speaks of not being "hemmed in by orthodoxy." Pines writes, "The temptations of certainty have to be resisted and we must remain aware of all the depths of hidden knowledge previously revealed and those yet to be revealed."

Sophie Freud declares with proud defiance, "I am deeply irreverent and will never be totally faithful to any one perspective."

This theme of "anti-purism" is especially noteworthy given that several contributors who argue against it are themselves closely identified with a particular school. Lazarus (1973), who actually christened the term "behavior therapy" in 1958, is the founder of Multimodal Therapy; Wachtel (1977) wrote the seminal text on integrating psychoanalytic and behavioral therapies; Jordan (Jordan, Kaplan, Miller, Stiver, & Surrey, 1991) is one of the original co-founders of the Stone Center Relational School; Pines (1998) is considered by many to be the pre-eminent group-analyst in the world; Levant (1986, 1990) wrote the book on the psychoeducational approach to therapy with men; Budman (Budman & Gurman, 1988) is explicitly associated with brief therapy; and Renik (1998; 2000) has been the voice of intersubjectivity. It is ironic that several of these individuals, while trying to preserve a flexible, open approach, had to fight off critics who insisted on compartmentalizing them. Jordan and Lazarus speak clearly to this.

Several other themes spring forth from these chapters. Many of these clinicians, notably Freud, Gartrell, Budman, Renik, Wachtel, and Wheelis write of their disillusionment with the prevailing paradigms of the day. Others, notably Comas-Días, Jordan, Dean, Maltas, Shapiro, and Mayer, decry the lack of attention in their early years to social issues or context. Virtually every contributor has critical words to utter about the managed care model which pervades the current therapy landscape. Shapiro states the point forcefully: "The power of the unconscious will not be obliterated by the current focus on the manifest."

Most of our contributors give pride of place to *flexibility* as a therapist. Budman adds that, beyond flexibility, "being a 'mensch' in treatment was essential." Focus on being present in therapy in a caring, respectful, more active, and more self-disclosing manner also permeates these chapters, with Jordan, Freud, Dean, Renik, and Wachtel each offering powerful clinical examples of the impact of self-disclosure in the office.

Fortunately, this self-disclosure is not limited to the

authors' clinical work, so the reader will find in these chapters many personal revelations about early history and current experiences, which demonstrate honest and courageous self-examination. Wheelis describes the centrality of his brutal childhood to his professional development. Jordan writes of her early experiences of inadequacy. Renik shares the impact of his mother's depression and of his resulting early embrace of independence. Pines reveals a deeply painful and self-destructive period in his personal and professional life. Budman tells of the impact of his near-fatal heart attack. Maltas shares her surprise at learning from her audiotapes that she was a more directive therapist than she had thought. Levant reveals the shame he felt in his role as a father. Freud describes the experience of being Sigmund Freud's granddaughter and of having everyone know it. Maltsberger discloses his deep-rooted fear of abandonment. Shapiro confesses to areas of personal weakness and vulnerability, revealing aspects of his early history, which help the reader understand his development. Gartrell makes vivid her numerous encounters with homophobia as she was trying to fashion a career. And Budman, Jordan, and Lazarus disclose that, at times, they concealed from supervisors what they were actually doing in the therapy office.

Throughout these chapters, personal themes interpenetrate with key societal themes of the time. Many contributors note the direct impact of such major events as the Vietnam War, the community health center movement, the growth of feminism, increasing focus on diversity, a new emphasis on effectiveness and accountability, and the recent hegemony of postmodern thought.

Another recurring theme, which has also captured modern attention, centers on what has been called the "strength perspective" or the focus on "positive psychology" (Seligman, 1995, 1998). Most of our contributors strive, in their clinical work, to identify, support, and enhance the already existing strengths of their clients or patients. This is especially evident in the contributions by Dean, Freud, Budman, Comas-Díaz, Mayer, Wachtel, Jordan, and Lazarus. In addition, most of our contributors are willing to scrutinize their own weaknesses and to enter into a more genuine therapeutic interaction. A central theme for many is collaborative dialogue, with both parties exposing themselves to self-examination.

Perhaps one final overlapping theme most clearly reveals the dynamic creativity and wisdom of our contributors. These men and women, who have contributed so much to our knowledge and understanding of psychotherapy, demonstrate again and again that they are *open to surprise*. Each reveals a "willingness to divorce oneself from the obvious" (Bruner, 1979, p. 23). Many describe how a chance event or encounter was powerfully influential for them. Budman speaks of his father's belief in serendipity— "People plan and God laughs"—and of an "epiphany" which resulted in his becoming a psychologist. Lazarus is similarly changed forever by an "epiphanous event" when watching a heretofore resistant patient improve at the hands of unorthodox interventions. Gartrell reorders her life priorities permanently after the death of her sister. Wachtel is astonished to discover that behavior therapy is not antithetical to psychoanalysis. Renik, faced with an impasse in treatment, devises a uniquely collaborative if unorthodox technique. Freud recognizes with great clarity the pervasiveness of randomness and chance, that "life hangs by a silken thread."

Each contributor has held strong beliefs, yet has been prepared to be surprised by life and thus to modify those beliefs. Such openness to novelty, to innovation, to following the untrodden path, characterizes these individuals. Reading through the chapters, you will witness the wisdom of Bruner's (1979) remark that "it is in the working out of conflicts and coalitions within the set of identities that compose the person that one finds the source" of surprise and creativity (p. 29).

As a final thought, we invite you to consider that you, too, might contribute to this inevitable evolution in psychotherapy as we enter the new millennium. If you are prepared to be surprised, one of you reading this volume, perhaps inspired by the profound thoughts, sustained creativity, and genuine compassion of our current contributors, will leave an identifiable footprint for generations to come.

REFERENCES

American Psychiatric Association. (1994). *Diagnostic and statistical manual of mental disorders* (4th ed.). Washington, DC: Author.

American Psychiatric Association. (1996). *American Psychiatric Association Practice Guidelines.* Washington, DC: Author.

APA Practice Directorate. (1996). *CAPP Practitioner Survey Results.* Washington, D.C.: Committee for the Advancement of Professional Practice.

Bass, A. (1998, October 16). Conditions turning harsh for therapists. *Boston Globe*, pp. A1, A35.

Bass, E., & Davis, L. (1988). *The courage to heal.* New York: Harper & Row.

Begley, S. (1998, January 26). Is everybody crazy? *Newsweek*, 50-55.

Berger, P. L., & Luckmann, T. (1967). *The social construction of reality: A treatise in the sociology of knowledge.* Garden City, NY: Anchor Books.

Bickerton, D. (1998). Talking cure? [Review of the book *Madness on the couch: Blaming the victim in the heyday of psychoanalysis*]. *New York Times Book Review*, p. 22.

Bruner, J. (1979). *On knowing: Essays for the left hand.* (Expanded ed.). Cambridge, MA: Harvard University Press.

Budman, S. H., & Gurman, A. S. (1988). *Theory and practice of brief therapy.* New York: Guilford Publications.

Consumer Reports. (1995, November). Mental health: Does therapy help? 734-739.

Demos, J. (1997a). Oedipus and America: Historical perspectives on the reception of psychoanalysis in America. In J. Pfister & N. Schnog (Eds.), *Inventing the psychological: Toward a cultural history of emotional life in America* (pp. 63-78). New Haven and London: Yale University Press.

Demos, J. (1997b). History and the psychosocial: Reflections on "Oedipus and America." In J. Pfister & N. Schnog (Eds.), *Inventing the psychological: Toward a cultural history of emotional life in America* (pp. 79-83). New Haven and London: Yale University Press.

Eysenck, H. J. (1952). The effects of psychotherapy: An evaluation. *Journal of Consulting Psychology, 16,* 319-324.

Fiedler, F. E. (1950). Comparisons of therapeutic relationships in psychoanalytic, nondirective, and Adlerian therapy. *Journal of Consulting Psychology, 14,* 436-445.

Frank, J. D. (1973). *Persuasion and healing* (2nd ed.). Baltimore: Johns Hopkins University Press.

Freud, S. (1931). *The interpretation of dreams.* New York: Carlton House. (Original work published 1900.)

Freedheim, D. K. (Ed.). (1992). *History of psychotherapy: A century of change.* Washington, DC: American Psychological Association.

Freudenberger, H. J., & Freedheim, D. K. (1992). The practice of psychotherapy. In D. K. Freedheim (Ed.), *History of psychotherapy: A century of change* (pp. 453-455). Washington, DC: American Psychological Association.

Gladwell, M. (1998, August 17). Do parents matter? *New Yorker,* 54-64.

Harris, J. R. (1998). *The nurture assumption: Why children turn out the way they do.* New York: Free Press.

Jordan, J., Kaplan, A., Miller, J.B., Stiver, I, & Surrey, J. (1991). *Women's growth in connection.* New York: Guilford.

Kassan, L. D. (1996). *Shrink rap: Sixty psychotherapists discuss their work, their lives, and the state of their field.* Northvale, NJ: Aronson.

Kramer, P. (1993). *Listening to Prozac.* New York: Viking.

Koocher, G. P., Norcross, J. C., & Hill, S. S. (Eds.). (1998). *Psychologists' Desk Reference.* New York/Oxford: Oxford University Press.

Kuhn, T. S. (1996). *The structure of scientific revolutions* (3rd ed.). Chicago & London: University of Chicago. (Original work published 1962)

Lazarus, A. A. (1973). Multimodal behavior therapy: Treating the BASIC ID. *Journal of Nervous and Mental Disease, 156,* 404-411.

Lazarus, A. A., & Lazarus, C. N. (1997). *The 60-second shrink.* San Luis Obispo, CA: Impact Publishers.

Levant, R. F. (Ed.). (1986). *Psychoeducational approaches to family therapy and counseling*. New York: Springer.

Levant, R. F. (1990). Psychological services designed for men: a psychoeducational approach. *Psychotherapy, 27,* 309-315.

Loftus, E., & Ketcham, K. (1994). *The myth of repressed memory*. New York: St. Martin's Press.

May, R. (1992). Foreword. In D. K. Freedheim (Ed.), *History of psychotherapy: A century of change* (pp. xx-xxvii). Washington, DC: American Psychological Association.

McNiff, S. (1998). *Trust the process: An artist's guide to letting go.* Boston: Shambala.

Norcross, J. C., & Goldfried, M. R. (Eds.). (1992). *Handbook of psychotherapy integration*. New York: Basic Books.

November Time Capsule (1998, November). Landmark events in psychology's history. *APA Monitor*, p. 7.

Pfister, J., & Schnog, N. (Eds.). (1997). *Inventing the psychological: Toward a cultural history of emotional life in America*. New Haven and London: Yale University Press.

Pines, M. (1998). *Circular reflections: Selected papers on group analysis and psychoanalysis*. London & Philadelphia: Jessica Kingsley.

Renik, O. (1998). Getting real in analysis. *Psychoanalytic Quarterly, 67,* 566-593.

Renik, O. (2000). The future of psychoanalysis: Getting real as a profession. In R. Prince (Ed.), *The death of psychoanalysis: Murder, suicide, or rumor greatly exaggerated?* New Jersey: Jason Aronson.

Schnog, N. (1997). On inventing the psychological. In J. Pfister & N. Schnog (Eds.), *Inventing the psychological: Toward a cultural history of emotional life in America* (pp. 3-16). New Haven and London: Yale University Press.

Seligman, M. (1995). The effectiveness of psychotherapy: The Consumer Reports study. *American Psychologist, 50,* 965-974.

Seligman, M. (1998, December). Why therapy works. *APA Monitor*, p. 2.

Shorter, E. (1997). *A history of psychiatry: From the era of the asylum to the age of Prozac*. New York: John Wiley & Sons.

Szasz, T. (1961). *The myth of mental illness*. New York: Horber.

Talmon, M. (1990). *Single session therapy: Maximizing the effect of the first (and often only) therapeutic encounter*. San Francisco: Jossey-Bass.

van den Berg, J. H. (1961). *The changing nature of man: Introduction to a historical psychology*. New York: Norton.

Vandenbos,. G. R., Cummings, N. A., & DeLeon, P. H. (1992). In D. K. Freedheim (Ed.), *History of psychotherapy: A century of change* (pp. 65-102). Washington, DC: American Psychological Association.

Wachtel, P. L. (1977). *Psychoanalysis and behavior therapy*. New York: Guilford Press.

CHAPTER 2

INTERIM NOTES ON A CAREER IN PSYCHOLOGY

SIMON H. BUDMAN, PH.D.

The man who finds a job he loves never works a day in his life.

Confucius

In 1990, I began to introduce myself at workshops as a "recovering brief therapist." For many years before, I had struggled with what to call the clinical work that I do, teach, and present. Having never been fully comfortable referring to my work as brief therapy, the term that I created was time-effective therapy. Al Gurman and I actually first used the term in our book, *Theory and Practice of Brief Therapy* (Budman & Gurman, 1988). However, if we had used the term for the title of our book at that time, few people would have had any idea what it was. I now describe myself as a "time-effective" therapist, and see brief therapy as a misnomer for my work. There may be some clinicians out there who are actually doing planned brief therapy much of the time, but I doubt there are many. Unless pressed into doing short-term, time-limited treatment, therapists themselves are unlikely to assume such a rigid position for the majority of their work. The time-effective model described later in this chapter is much more realistic, practical, and compatible with patient and therapist realities.

My original desire to become a therapist probably dates back to my experiences growing up in Rockaway Beach, New York, in the early 1950s. Even though Rockaway is officially part of the borough of Queens, and Queens is on most maps part of New York City, few from Rockaway at that time would have identified themselves as New Yorkers. The distant, forbidding island of Manhattan was described in almost reverential (or perhaps ominous) tones as The City. For my parents and many of their friends, going to The City via the subway or, God forbid, by car, was an act of great courage and adventure and not to be undertaken lightly. The length of the subway trip to Manhattan was also significant, sometimes taking 90 minutes and three train line changes. Rockaway Beach, at that time, still felt like a very small town. In later years, when I compared my growing up to those from big cities and those from smaller towns, by every measure Rockaway was at the smaller end of things.

We had two elderly doctors in Rockaway—Dr. Wallach and Dr. Langer. Wallach was, like my parents, a survivor of the Holocaust, who had lost his family in a concentration camp. I imagine that he must have arrived in this country in the late 1940s and opened up what became a thriving practice in Rockaway. Many of his patients felt comfortable with him because he too was European, Jewish, and spoke a mixture of Yiddish and English (Yinglish) to them. Langer was born and raised in the United States. He was large, heavyset, and jovial, kept his pants up with suspenders, and looked a lot like pictures of Winston Churchill. Both of these physicians had practices in their homes. Their living rooms doubled as their waiting areas and a couple of smaller rooms were the spaces in which exams were done.

There were several characteristics of both of these doctors that will always remain with me. First, they were never on time. Going to the doctor in those days was an outing. They did not even have appointments! It was more like "sick call" in the military. People began to show up in the early afternoon for daytime hours and around seven for evening hours. Once they began to arrive, you could have mistaken the waiting area for the third-class compartment of the Titanic shortly after it hit the iceberg. Babies cried in their mothers' arms. Older kids fidgeted and complained. Adults just sat around looking worried and miserable. The rickety table in the middle of the waiting area was covered with frayed copies of *Reader's Digest*. (I still remember enjoying the regular features like You Be the Judge and The Most Unforgettable Character.)

For these doctors, mornings were for home visits. Although I did not realize it at the time, the other important characteristic shared by Wallach and Langer, and most of their brethren, was that there were few tools with which they could work. They both had stethoscopes and those silver and red rubber hammers to hit your knees with, of course, but aside from penicillin and a handful of other drugs, they had relatively little effective medicine at their disposal. The routine for most illnesses was the same. "Breathe in deeply; now breathe out." Next, listen to the patient's chest with the stethoscope. Get their temperature taken. Then, sit at the edge of the exam table and tap each knee with the hammer. Roll over, pull down underpants, and get a shot of penicillin in the upper part of your buttocks. It was what came next, however, that probably had the most impact on my life. Once the doctor finished going through these standard, ritualized medical procedures, he spoke to you! (I don't remember meeting or having contact with a female physician until college. In my memory they seem to have been pretty rare during the 1950s.)

These doctors had trained at a time when the physician's armamentarium was quite measly. Penicillin had only just come into widespread usage when I was a kid. Physicians who trained before World War II (and these men were trained long before the war) may have been taught to use sulfa drugs, but there were slim pickings after that. With the benefit of hindsight, I wonder if part of the reason that all prescriptions were written in Latin at that time (this was the case during much of my youth) was because doctors felt so self-conscious about their paltry arsenal of medications. Latin names at least made them feel as though they had somewhat more knowledge than their patients.

This lack of options meant that often doctors did what they could with hope, support, and encouragement. My recollection is that most visits to either of these doctors was spent talking about something. The content is now completely forgotten. However, both Langer and Wallach were generally soft spoken, kind, elderly gentlemen who would ask questions and actually listen to the answers.

At about five or six years of age, I decided to become a physician. Just before that time I became sick with a mysterious illness (which was never actually diagnosed). I developed a persistent high fever, sore throat, and general malaise. After spending two weeks in the hospital and being isolated from my parents except for very brief evening visiting hours, I completely recovered and was discharged. The terror and homesickness of that experience will always remain with me; it made a significant contribution not only to my desire to be a doctor, but to "do it right."

It Happened at College

My image of what a physician did was totally shaped by Drs. Langer and Wallach and would remain intact until I went to Queens College (part of the City University of New York) as a premed major. In 1963, at age 16, I started college. Taking biochemistry and calculus in my freshman year, I realized that being a physician (from the perspective of the Queens College pre-med program) had nothing to do with people. It had to do only with memorizing formulas and parts of the body. Original thinking was eschewed. Creativity was out. There seemed to be nothing that related to human interaction in the pre-med curriculum. By the middle of my freshman year I was in crisis.

I had to get out of the pre-med program, but felt that I was going to let my father down if I did so. My dad was from a large and extremely poor family. Before the Holocaust he had grown up in Poland. In order to help his widowed mother, Dad had to drop out of the fifth or sixth grade. At 11 years old, he had become an apprentice barber/hairdresser and did that work for the rest of his life. Although he never enjoyed the career that fate had forced him into, and always wished that he could have become a doctor, he was a persistently hopeful and optimistic man. All of his family and all of my mother's family were killed in the Holocaust, but my father was never bitter or depressed. He was one of the kindest and most generous people I have ever known. He hoped for better careers and better lives for his children, and my decision to become a physician was something that delighted him.

In the second half of my freshman year I stopped taking pre-med courses (I thought temporarily), and started taking as many art courses as possible. The art courses were terrific fun, and I was not a bad artist. When I thought about my future, however, I could not imagine how I would survive with art as a career. When I returned for my sophomore year, it was clear that I could no longer stay in limbo as an art student and briefly (very briefly) considered becoming a sociologist but I quickly became bored with sociology.

BRIEF THERAPY (OR MAYBE IT WAS TIME-EFFECTIVE THERAPY) CHANGES MY LIFE

Uncertain about what my major should be, and concerned about how best to break the news to my father that I was no longer planning to become a doctor, I made the decision to go to the Queens College student counseling center. It was there, in 1965, that I had my first experience with brief therapy.

I remember very little about the experience, other than the friendly and sympathetic female career counselor with whom I had two meetings. These sessions were focused on my areas of interest and why I was concerned about my father's reactions to a new career direction (whatever that might be). At the end of the second meeting the counselor said, "With your interests you would probably make a good psychologist." She went on to say, "We have a man here who just got his Ph.D. from the University of

Colorado. Why don't I have you meet with him once and he can tell you about clinical psychology?" I had never even heard of clinical psychology before, but I was open to anything. My meeting with the psychologist occurred soon afterward (I have no recollection of his name either). He was young and enthusiastic and spoke effusively about psychology and what clinical psychologists did. In that meeting I was sold. In that single session I became committed to psychology, and it was clear that this was what I had always wanted to do. From that day, I have never wavered in my interest in psychology as a career. What happened to me in that session can only be described as an epiphany. It all "came together."

Brain Waves and Bob Dylan

Once I decided to become a clinical psychologist the path was clear. I started taking psychology courses and read everything related to psychology that I could get my hands on. I was fortunate that in one of my first psychology courses my professor was a young, enthusiastic psychologist, Lloyd Gilden. The late 1960s was a very exciting period for the field. Working with Lloyd and a small group of students and professors, I began doing research studies in a variety of areas in which my interest (although expressed differently over time) would endure for the next thirty years. We did studies on biofeedback, brain waves, and the use of (what can only be described now as slow and primitive) computers in relaxation and the mind/body connection. Our research team was interested in Eastern Mysticism, and whether computers could help teach people to "get in touch with themselves without drugs." We also did studies in group dynamics and social systems. Many of our studies were done with us as subjects. We also formed a small, leaderless encounter group that we taped and then tried to analyze.

The study I remember most vividly was one that served as my senior honors thesis. In this project, I had small groups of undergraduate students get together and watch a short film called *Two Men and a Wardrobe* by Roman Polanski; it was made by him prior to coming to the United States (and well before the murder of his wife by Charles Manson's gang). I removed the soundtrack of the film and replaced it with Bob Dylan's then popular song *Desolation Row*. After watching the film, groups of students would discuss it for a half-hour. They would then make ratings of whom they liked best and whom they liked least in the group. We later had best and least pairs get together and have a general discussion about some other topics—now forgotten. After this, we did an analysis of the conversational patterns of people who liked one another and those who did not like one another. I describe this study in detail because my doctoral dissertation was about conversational patterns of counselors and clients (Budman, 1972); a number of the research studies I did during the 1980s focused on patterns of conversation in group therapy as well. The work I did while at Queens College with Lloyd and our research team has proved influential throughout my career.

WHAT TO DO IN PITTSBURGH AND BEYOND

I graduated from college (as an A+ student in those courses I really liked such as psychology, sociology, English, history, and art, and a C+ student in those courses I could not stand) and went on to graduate school at the University of Pittsburgh. The atmosphere at Pitt was open, fresh, and exciting. There were people on the staff who were psychoanalytically oriented and others who were Rogerian, or behavioral, and even some newly minted Ph.D.s who were family systems people. There was no implication that there was a "true road." The diversity and openness of the faculty allowed me to think broadly and not become identified with any school of thought.

One of the biggest sources of influence in my career as a graduate student was the Vietnam War. There were repeated efforts by my draft board to force me into the service, and repeated efforts on my part not to go. Although I had a well-paying traineeship from NIMH, which paid for graduate school and left me free not to work, I chose to spend 20 hours per week working at the VA Hospital in Pittsburgh. In part this was done for the experience and in part because I believed this would keep me from being drafted.

The work turned out to be fascinating. I developed a short-term group therapy program for returning disabled and disturbed Vietnam vets. The men I saw at the hospital were primarily suffering from what we now term post-traumatic stress disorder (PTSD). This diagnosis did not exist at the time. It was clear, however, that these young men, many of them my age or even younger, had been traumatized by their experience in the place they called "Nam." Most of the men I worked with had lost limbs, parts of their faces, or parts of their minds in Nam. They were scared, angry, and confused as to why they spent time in a place risking their lives and taking other people's lives for what they thought was a good cause, and then returning to the United States to be heckled, protested against, and spit upon. Their emotional turmoil was enormous. Another graduate student and I ran groups of vets for almost three years. These groups were short-term and intensive because most of the men we saw spent a maximum of twelve weeks in the VA hospital before being discharged back to their home community.

Working at the VA taught me to be flexible. The supervisor I had for the VA group was a young psychologist who had trained at the Menninger Clinic in Topeka, Kansas, at that time an extremely psychoanalytic place. This supervisor's recommendation was that we run the group in a psychoanalytic supportive-evocative way. This meant that we introduced ourselves when the patients came into the group (the supportive part), and we said nothing after that (the evocative part). After trying this approach in our first session and nearly getting killed by the members who became very evoked, my co-therapist and I took a new approach. We became much more active and participatory in the treatment. We also presented the group sessions to our supervisor in a way which made us sound passive, silent, and supportive-evocative. This experience helped me to understand that (1) supervisors didn't always know what they were talking about, and (2) that flexibility and being a "mensch" in treatment was essential. It never felt to me that the "blank screen" therapists that I read about in graduate school and would meet later in my training were particularly helpful to people.

There is some interesting research to support this point from David Malan, a psychiatrist and early brief therapist who worked at the Tavistock Clinic in London. In doing a follow-up study on patients who had been in rigidly analytic "Tavistock therapy groups" where the therapist said very little over the course of the sessions, Malan (1976) found that, for the most part, patients profited little and many got worse. Such an approach also felt to me like a contrived attempt to get the patient to focus on the therapist to the exclusion of the patient's real world issues. I have always been a very outcome-oriented, practical person and someone who enjoys engaging with people, rather than just frustrating them.

Next, at my internship in Connecticut at Connecticut Valley Hospital and Yale's Connecticut Mental Health Center, I was finally exposed to numerous people (at Yale) with rigidly analytic views. At the same time, however, I met people with rigidly behavioral views. My conclusion was that I neither enjoyed nor felt any affinity for those who were "true believers." There is a book by Sheldon Kopp, a psychologist, named *If You Meet the Buddha on the Road, Kill Him* (1988). I have met many people over the course of my career who met the Buddha (or someone they thought was the Buddha) and embraced him rigidly and mindlessly. This was particularly true at the University of Rochester Medical School where I did my post-doctoral training. Many of the psychologists and psychiatrists on the staff at Rochester at that time appeared to wish that they could have sat at the feet of Freud; some seemed to think that they had. Although there were some new faculty members who were trying to modernize the department, much of my time there reinforced my concerns about rigid idolatry in any psychological model.

GROWING IN BOSTON, ALMOST DYING, AND GROWING AGAIN

When I came to Boston in 1972, I started working at a community health center in Roxbury, an area which at that time was largely African-American. Although the job was often difficult and frustrating because of inadequate funding and poor leadership, the learning opportunities were exceptional. I began to consult to the school system and churches, developed programs for primary care doctors and nurses, and made home visits to clients. Once again, it was clear to me that I could not rigidly adhere to any theoretical model and hope to be helpful to the many clients with whom I was working.

While in graduate school I had gotten married. My wife, Susan, and I had our first child in 1973. Parenthood also taught me about the need for flexibility and the unlikelihood that books or teachers can fully prepare anyone for life. As ready as I felt to be a parent, and as much psychological training as I had, my one child and then my two children, Gabrielle and Shari, inevitably taught me about the need to be practical and open-minded.

In the mid-1970s, I began to work at the Harvard Community Health Plan (HCHP). At that time the Plan was a small 30,000-person HMO in Boston and Cambridge, Massachusetts. In those days, no one knew what HMO stood for, and only a few hardy souls were interested in finding out and joining. My major professional growth took place at HCHP over the 21 years that I remained there. In the early years, HCHP was an extremely interesting and innovative place to be. We viewed ourselves as pioneers, and what we were doing as "The Great Experiment in Health Care." Every day presented a new challenge. I developed numerous clinical programs, saw hundreds of patients, ran conferences and workshops, did teaching, got grant funding, and wrote dozens of articles addressing questions such as: could we reduce the length of group therapy and still have it be useful to people? (Budman, Bennett, & Wisneski, 1980); was short-term individual therapy as helpful as short-term group treatment? (Budman, Demby, Feldstein, & Gold, 1984); how could we best help those going through the stress of marital separation? (Wertlieb, Budman, Demby, & Randall, 1982); what led to the medical offset effect? (Budman, Demby, & Feldstein, 1984). The Plan was flourishing, as was I. Every day was more interesting and exciting than the last. I began to present at workshops and conferences around the country. It was a wonderful time.

Then with little warning, I came very close to dying. On Sunday November 4, 1984, I had just driven my older daughter, Gabrielle, then 11 years old, to the club where she trained in gymnastics. As I got into my car to go home, I had a stunning pain in my back. My right side became numb and I thought I was having a heart attack or stroke. I reached my home, told Susan, and called the Harvard Plan, where my family got their health care. I was told to go immediately to the Beth Israel Hospital (the BI). Associated with Harvard, the BI is one of the finest teaching hospitals in the country. When Susan and I reached the BI, a nurse greeted us and ushered us into an examining room where I was soon scrutinized by a medical intern. The intern did some tests and looked me over. After a few minutes she smiled and reported to me that I was fine and was suffering from a strained back. It was something that I wanted to believe and I felt slightly better after her reassurance. I had been doing a lot of running and training for the Boston Marathon, still several months off. I thought that perhaps I had been running too much and had somehow pulled a muscle or, in some other way, injured my back. We left the hospital and went home. Although I tried to go to a soccer practice with my younger daughter later that day, I began to feel myself in intense pain. I couldn't eat, felt fatigued, and very ill. I told Susan and my kids that I probably had the flu and went to bed in the afternoon. Throughout that night I woke up periodically and could hear my pulse beating in my ears. The next day, Monday, I called in sick for one of the few times in my entire career. As I felt worse throughout that morning, I called my friend Gene Lindsey. Gene was also my cardiologist and I had seen him several times in the prior year because of palpitations I was having. When I went to see Gene later that day, he did an echocardiogram and was shocked at what he found. He turned very pale and somber, and told me that I was having an aortic aneurysm which was dissecting. This meant that my aorta, the largest blood vessel in the body (it emerges from the heart and supplies the body with blood), was tearing and close to ripping itself apart. I needed to be operated upon without delay. Because of the aneurysm, my aortic heart valve was also failing.

I was sent to the Brigham and Women's Hospital, another Harvard teaching center, and two hours later underwent emergency surgery to repair my valve and aorta. The operation was done by one of the dozen most prominent heart surgeons in the world. It was, however, done wrong. The repair to my aorta and heart valve were insufficient for the nature of my problem but the surgeon was convinced that he had done the right repair. My condition deteriorated over the next month. I had a hard time breathing. I felt enormous fatigue and slept most of the day and night. Although I had been running 30 to 40 miles per week prior to the aneurysm, it now took what felt like super-human effort to get in and out of the shower. Although my doctors said that I was improving and that this was all associated with the trauma of the surgery and subsequent depression, I became convinced that I was dying. I withdrew from my children, my wife, and my friends and became very subdued and quiet. Most of my waking time was spent lying on the couch or in bed. One month after the initial surgery a close friend, who was a physician, was visiting me during the day. He saw how hard it was for me to catch my breath and noticed my awful pallor. He called my doctor at Harvard Health and said that he was bringing me in to the emergency department. When we arrived, an echocardiogram was done and this time it was clear that the aorta had again dissected and that I was in heart failure. I was rushed by ambulance back to the Brigham and Women's Hospital. Fortunately, the heart surgeon who had operated on me was out of the country at a conference and I saw the chairman of the thoracic surgery group, Dr. John Collins.

Collins and his residents examined me and he looked very concerned. He told me that whereas the first surgery I had was relatively "easy" to perform, this surgery would be much harder.

Collins said that doing the re-surgery was akin to trying to "redecorate your house when it is filled with cement." I asked him what my chances of survival were and he told me that they were about 70 percent. All I could see was a big *30 percent* flashing in front of my eyes. Dr. Collins also said that the thoracic surgery team was totally exhausted having just completed a heart transplant. He asked me whether I wanted them to operate immediately, or wait until early the next morning when they were all rested. It may sound strange that this is what he did. Why did he choose to give me the choice—especially under such dire circumstances? Later, looking back on this, I concluded that Dr. Collins had shown me the respect of allowing me to help make this crucial decision. Even though I was critically ill and could be dying, he chose to take my preferences and ideas into account. This event drove home to me that even the most impaired patient has preferences and ideas. Taking these away removes the patient's dignity and personhood. I chose to wait until morning.

After the surgery, when I awoke, I had a new mechanical heart valve and the problematic part of my aorta had been replaced with a Dacron tube. From almost the day after the second surgery I began to recover quickly. Although I was significantly weakened, I now felt as though I had some life ahead of me. After several weeks I began to see patients again in my home, and soon after that returned to work at the Harvard Plan. By April of 1985, I was doing a few workshops in the Northeast.

I learned an enormous amount from my illness; it was a pivotal event for me. My life, my world, my family, my work, my attitudes—all were indelibly altered by this illness. Some of these alterations were probably never apparent to those around me as they were internal. The immediate short-term change was that I became extremely anxious and depressed. I was also hypervigilant to perturbations in my body states. I worried about another event reaching out of the blue and this time killing me. I wondered how I had managed to survive, when some people I knew when I was younger, including one of my best friends, had died in young adulthood from medical illness. I also started having flashbacks.

Certain smells, sounds, and places would trigger an odd, terrifying, deja vu-like experience. After suffering with numerous painful and uncomfortable psychological/physiological incidents, I sought treatment with a senior psychologist whom I had met when I first came to Boston. Although he was well known in the psychoanalytic community as an analyst, he was flexible, open, and self-disclosing. I found him after several false starts with other psychologists who had excellent reputations, but were inflexible, rigid, or inept. One of the most useful parts of my therapy was that this therapist allowed me to structure the frequency of sessions and when, after a year, I felt that it was time to stop, he did not try to indicate that I was foolish for wanting to do so, or that we were just starting to get to the good stuff, or that this represented a "flight into health."

I think that I have always been a very compassionate and insightful therapist. My illness, however, gave me the additional compassion and insight that comes from "looking into the abyss." Before this, I don't think I ever fully understood what patients meant when they said that they had "flashbacks" of traumatic events. I never before understood the total despair that suicidal patients talk about. I had always had a substantial appreciation of the value of supportive family and friends, but this appreciation increased dramatically after my aneurysm.

Several months before my illness, I had started writing *Theory and Practice of Brief Therapy*, the book I co-authored with Alan Gurman. I had, by November of 1984, finished several chapters. After I began to recover, I threw out my initial drafts of the book. Those drafts did not reflect the changes which occurred as a consequence of my illness. Those first versions of the book were too cocky and too certain. They also failed to reflect issues like serendipity and chance events which occur in people's lives. My father would use a Yiddish expression which, loosely translated, means "People plan and God laughs." Most psychological theories largely rely on the premise that we are the masters of our own fates. If things are going badly, we are responsible. If things are going well, we have responsibility for that as well. There is certainly some merit to this argument. However, unexpected events befall people who had no part in these events occurring. In a similar vein, some nasty, inept, and unappealing people end up doing quite well in their lives. Though these comments may appear self-evident, they are, nonetheless, often given short shrift in the psychological literature. My experience left me thinking much more about existential and spiritual issues in psychotherapy. Many of these were reflected in the later drafts of *Theory and Practice*. The book ultimately did extremely well, and became a very widely used text in graduate schools as well as by clinicians around the country and around the world. I do not believe that this would have been true (or at least not as true) without what I learned from the personal crisis of my illness. I did not change in any dramatic way, and people around me probably did not notice anything different, but I began to more fully understand some issues which I either ignored or had only superficial understanding of prior to that time.

THERE IS LIFE AFTER ALMOST DEATH AND SURVIVING A CRISIS IN THE PROFESSION

The years since my aneurysm have been tremendously fruitful in a variety of ways. After the illness I increased my writing, training workshops, clinical practice, and research. I also moved to a variety of positions at Harvard Community Health Plan. In the late 1980s, HCHP began to change dramatically. It grew increasingly larger, and became much more of a business enterprise than it had been earlier. Changes at HCHP (which later went through a variety of names and iterations) influenced clinical work. The Plan, which at one time had been a model of how to do time-effective, ethical, caring, mental health treatment, became a place which was focused mainly on its survival. The broader healthcare and behavioral healthcare environment began to change as well. One after another, behavioral health settings which I had been enthusiastic about, or at which I had done training or consulting, were closing or downsizing. The overall environment went from one of excitement and exploration looking for newer efficient and effective ways of helping people change, to one where clinicians and systems were "hunkering down." Long-experienced therapists were changing careers or losing their positions and having to aim their goals low. Salaries for mental health professionals, and psychologists in particular, were getting hammered—for some they dropped 30 to 40 percent. For years I had been warning clinicians at my workshops that behavioral healthcare was about to go through a crisis, but I did not completely recognize the magnitude of that crisis nor how extensive the impact would be.

In 1996, I decided, after 21 years, to leave the Harvard Community Health Plan. I was not enjoying my work there, and felt the organization lacked the clinical and intellectual vision it had once had. Previously there had been an emphasis upon seeing patients rapidly and efficiently, and developing new programs and seeing if they worked. Now the emphasis was upon seeing patients rapidly, and as many as possible in the shortest amount of time. I had for many years been developing my own company outside of the Plan. Innovative Training Systems (ITS), which I founded in 1988, was a small consulting firm. It slowly was becoming a vehicle to bring other people into the workshops and consulting business I was getting, allowing me not to have to do all of the workshops myself; it was also developing some "brand recognition" as a company. While I was almost full-time at HCHP, Innovative Training Systems remained a relatively small "virtual" company run out of a room in my home. As I began to cut back my time, and brought others into the company, ITS grew dramatically. By 1999, we had more than twenty full-time employees including seven doctoral-level psychologists. ITS still does training and consulting in time-effective therapies to various organizations around the United States and in other countries. We have also broadened the populations we focus on to include substance abusers and those with severe mental illness. The largest part of ITS revenues, however, comes from the development of products and programs in various areas of healthcare and behavioral health. We are currently working on about 30 major products including: a multimedia, computerized version of the Addiction Severity Index (ASI)—the most widely used measure of initial severity and change in the substance abuse field; a handheld compliance tool for AIDS patients to help them adhere to their medication regimens; a computer game for adolescent smokers to help them quit; a video program and book for families in which a parent has cancer; a multimedia eating disorder prevention program for college freshman women; self-help materials for incarcerated substance abusers; and videos and books focused on helping patients in the health system become "empowered." We are also writing the pilot for a very funny and engaging TV show for children ages seven through ten with a focus on child health and nutrition.

The entire list is enormous and reflects yet another fundamental change in my thinking. I now believe that public health, population-based interventions are essential. I also feel that there are a large number of people who either will not come to see a therapist, do not see their problems in psychological terms, or could be better helped in a variety of other ways. This is in no way to say that I do not believe in psychotherapy or the kinds of things that I have written about, practiced, and taught over the years. It is to say that the world is changing dramatically, and that there will be diverse ways that people achieve change. We must be flexible and understand that not everyone will want to get treatment in the traditional ways that it has been delivered.

MEANINGFUL MENTORS AND MAXIMIZING MEANING

Throughout my career I have had mentors and friends who helped me think through ideas and develop creative directions for my work. My mentors have generally been people with strong, well-conceived opinions from whom I could learn; I would then modify their thinking to better fit my own ideas. People like Nick Cummings (Cummings, 1986; Cummings, Budman, & Thomas, 1998) and the late Gerry Klerman (Klerman, Budman, Berwick, Feldstein, & White, 1987; Klerman, Rounsaville, Chevron, & Weissman, 1984) have had an important impact on my thinking. Their positive quality was that they were very smart, generous, and thoughtful teachers who did not seek slavishly devoted followers. Nick's thinking on brief therapies and medical/behavioral healthcare integration has strongly influenced me since we became friends in the mid-1970s. Gerry Klerman was a brilliant psychiatrist with whom I wrote, taught, and did research through much of the 1980s. Gerry also had a strong interest in a flexible model of brief therapy and, similar to Nick, was strongly interested in the integration of medical and mental healthcare.

As important as mentors, my friends and peers have had a major impact on my work. I have been blessed with close professional and personal friends with whom I have been able to share ideas, and think more expansively and creatively. People like Michael Bennett, Steve Butler, Emil Chiauzzi and Al Villapiano have all been important in helping me think creatively and originally.

My wife, Susan Budman, CEO of ITS, has been able to help me think through and work out most of the big issues and concerns in my professional and personal life, and my children, Gabrielle and Shari, have helped to pull me back over the years from pure work to having fun with them in non-work ways. I have always felt that being a parent is one of the most important roles that one can play. Parenthood has also profoundly affected my clinical practice. Before becoming a parent I always believed that "this person's problems are a function of his or her parents." I have long ago given up that belief. (I now occasionally think "this person's problem is a function of his or her children.") The behavior of an adult or a child is not just a function of how his or her parents treated that individual. As a parent, I now see an individual's problems as a complex combination of parental, environmental (peers and siblings, community), and temperamental issues. Without the kinds of supports and input that I have gotten over the years from these, and numerous other, significant people in my life, I would never have been able to develop and implement my ideas or do the work I have done.

IDEAS NOW AND IDEAS FOR THE FUTURE

In the earliest years of my career I saw my work as brief therapy. I tried to emulate people I had the fortune of knowing, like James Mann and Peter Sifneos—some of the early brief therapists based in Boston. After several years of being a brief therapist, I became and have remained a time-effective therapist. My view is that time-effective therapy has to do with thinking about efficiency and effectiveness, not brevity. For the patient with a severe personality disorder, time-effective therapy may go on for months or years. The therapist, however, is always trying to think about the issue of time and cost. Thus, the patient with a severe personality disorder may be seen as part of a group therapy with others who have such personality problems, rather than in long-term individual treatment on a weekly or multi-times per week basis (Budman, Demby, Soldz, & Merry, 1996).

Time-effective treatment also focuses on Prochaska's stages of change model (Prochaska, Norcross, & DiClemente, 1994). Jim Prochaska is another colleague who has greatly influenced my thinking. His stages of change model helps the clinician think about how ready the patient is to make changes, and allows the therapist to structure his or her interventions so they are best suited to the patient's level of readiness. Jim is also a "big thinker," and is extraordinarily able to take broad theoretical perspectives when looking at the field of behavioral intervention. Much of the therapeutic work that I write about (Budman & Steenbarger, 1997), and many of ITS' products, have been strongly impacted by the stages of change model and Jim's overall views.

I also continue to believe that the therapeutic relationship is key in helping people change. I use Control Mastery Theory (CMT) (Weiss & Sampson, 1993) to better understand the therapeutic alliance. Control Mastery is an approach that I have trained in and written about in the past (Budman & Gurman, 1992). Based, in part, on the outstanding work of Alexander and French (1946/1972), CMT assumes that the patient comes into treatment with particular expectations regarding the behavior of the therapist. The patient expects that he or she will be treated by the therapist in much the same way that he or she has been treated by parents and significant others in the past. Thus, the patient who has had a controlling parent expects the therapist will try to control him or her and the patient who has been neglected expects neglectful behaviors. According to CMT, it is the therapist's task to ascertain the kind of fearful expectations with which the patient comes to treatment and then to behave in ways which contradict these expectations. The model is similar to the psychoanalytic concept of transference but the difference in CMT, and from the Alexander and French perspective, is that the therapist consciously attempts to contradict such irrational expectations and provide the patient with a new and therapeutic experience. Alexander and French describe this contradiction, when it occurs experientially for the patient, as "the corrective emotional experience."

The example which Alexander and French use to illustrate the corrective emotional experience is that of Jean Valjean from *Les Miserables*. Valjean, a good and honest man, is thrown into prison for 20 years for stealing a loaf of bread to feed his sister's starving children. After Valjean is paroled, he again falls into trouble for theft and, consistent with his experience in prison, expects that everyone will be cruel and punishing to him. To his surprise, however, he is rescued by the unexpected benevolence of a bishop, which transforms Valjean into a man who then performs extraordinary deeds of generosity and kindness. The bishop's ability to contradict Valjean's expectations is Alexander and French's "corrective emotional experience."

CMT researchers believe that, over the course of treatment, the patient will "test" the therapist many times to see if he or she behaves in the ways the patient fears. If the therapist does not behave in the expected manner, the test is "passed." If the therapist does engage in the problematic and feared way with the patient, the test is "failed." Immediately after a passed test, the patient, within the session, becomes more open, comfortable, and self-disclosing; following a failed test the opposite occurs. In their studies, CMT researchers have videotaped and transcribed hundreds of sessions, and raters have found the kinds of behaviors described above.

CMT is an approach that encourages therapist flexibility. Similarly, one of the central elements of time-effective therapy is flexibility. The model is flexible about the length of time between sessions; it is flexible about the involvement of significant others in the treatment; it is flexible about the integrative use of different theoretical models. One of the areas in which it is most flexible is in the belief that therapy is not a fixed process taking place over 10 or 12 sessions, or even two or three years. It is not a situation where someone comes to treatment, spends X number of sessions, and is never seen again. Rather, the treatment (like the work of Drs. Langer and Wallach in Rockaway Beach) is based on the family practice of medicine. People come to treatment at different points in their lives; they may leave and then return at other points when they have the need or desire. The fact that someone comes back to treatment does not indicate failure on the part of the therapist or of the patient. Indeed, I have, since early in my career, felt as though returning patients were an indication that the relationship with me had endured and that these individuals felt comfortable enough with the work we had done together previously to return and work with me again. This may be an example of going "back to the future," and may be what good therapists have done all along. When I started to practice and write about my work, however, the prevailing view was that you needed to do a piece of short or long-term work with the patient, doing it well enough that the patient would never need to return.

Arising from the flexible use of time, and the fact that many patients are not seen on a regular weekly basis, time-effective therapy helps the patient make maximal use of time between sessions. It is imperative that therapy continues outside the session. This is done by actively engaging the patient in continuing to think about and work on treatment between visits through the use of homework. I make use of a variety of different types of homework with patients and tailor the assignments to their stages of change. One would not ask a patient who was uncertain that he or she even wanted treatment to do very much between visits. With such a patient, the therapist could, however, ask him or her to think about what the visit was like, and what they would like to focus on the next time they came in. On the other hand, for a patient who was highly motivated and wanted to do as much as possible to facilitate change, homework would be more active and would require a good deal more participation on the part of the patient. The latter patient, for example, might be asked to send the therapist an e-mail describing her reaction to the visit, what she found most useful, and what she would like to be different in the next session.

It is also essential that in time-effective therapy there be a focus to the treatment. Without such a focus, there is a lack of clarity about goals and therefore about how to reach the desired outcome. It is remarkable how much treatment exists in which there is little clarity on the parts of the participants as to what it is that the treatment is aimed at changing or improving.

The components of time-effective treatment come together in the person of the therapist who must be willing to flexibly apply components of psychoanalytic therapy, behavioral, and strategic approaches. These come together not as a "little of this and a little of that," but in a thoughtful and theoretically driven yet, at the same time, practical way. Analytic theory, and in particular CMT, for example, may be helpful in understanding some aspects of therapeutic alliance. If the therapist becomes "stuck"—rigid and inflexible in his or her thinking—it often bodes poorly for the outcome of the treatment. Therapy must be tailored to the patient, rather than forcing every patient to comply with our model of treatment. A Zen master named Suzuki (1972) said that, "In the beginner's mind there are many possibilities, in the expert's mind there are few." The time-effective therapist attempts to think with a beginner's mind, and avoids forcing patients into categories which negate their unique qualities, needs, strengths, and deficits.

THE CURRENT HEALTHCARE ENVIRONMENT AND THE IMPERILED
FUTURE OF PSYCHOTHERAPY

Never has the future of psychotherapy been as imperiled as it is at present. Although I have little doubt that psychotherapy will remain a viable form of treatment and that millions of people will seek such treatment in the future, I do have major concerns about the future economics of the field. Managed care companies appear to believe that "talk is cheap." Whereas psychologists and other mental health professionals were at one time able to rapidly develop practices which provided them with a reasonable income, this is becoming more and more difficult. Some estimates are that income for solo practice psychologists has fallen 40 to 50 percent (*American Association of Practicing Psychologists Newsletter*, Fall, 1998).

What implications does this have for the practice of therapy? Several are probable: Many people who would have become psychologists or social workers or psychiatrist/therapists will not choose this field. There will be a deprofessionalization of providers of psychotherapy. If doctoral level psychologists are too expensive, organizations will hire master's level social workers to fill their positions. If MSWs cost too much, then bachelor's level counselors will fill the positions. At some point, those with two-year associates degrees could well become the norm at clinics and health centers. Of course, there will always be psychologists, social workers, counselors, and other more highly trained individuals doing therapy; these people, however, will be fewer in number and will probably fill more senior and supervisory positions. This is not a vision of the field that I see as desirable; rather it is one that may be inevitable for a period of time. In today's healthcare environment, there are more mental health clinicians than can or will be sustained.

What type of psychotherapies will be practiced as we move into the 21st century? I think the types of changes describe above will lead to a number of significant modifications of practices.

What types of psychotherapy will be done? There will be fewer individuals than ever practicing in an orthodox way and sticking to one model. This is already true and will become even more the case. Hybrid mixtures of psychoanalytic, behavioral, cognitive, and solution-oriented therapies will be the norm. I believe that time-limited therapies and short-term therapies will be displaced by time-effective treatment models. A primary care-like model of treatment, with patients coming back to therapists periodically over the course of their lives (already the reality), will become the accepted norm.

I believe, too, that there will be much greater use of technology in behavioral change approaches. It is remarkable that the "technology" of behavior change, for the most part, has little changed since Freud's day. Along with face-to-face treatment, psychotherapists will make use of other intervention tools such as computers, hand-held portable data devices, virtual reality glasses, and the Internet. These tools can be used to assist patients outside of sessions to test behavioral changes or observe changes that are taking place, to learn new skills, and to be exposed to difficult environments or situations. Large populations which might not obtain behavioral treatment could well get their first taste of psychotherapy using self-help computer or Internet programs for behavioral change. It is highly likely that 10 or 20 years from now the field of behavior change will look extremely different from the way it looks today, from the professional makeup of practitioners, to the goals, approaches, technologies, and models used in treatment.

Toward the Future

In closing this chapter I would like to answer some final questions from you, the reader. Since I can not yet (this will probably happen in a few years as books become interactive) speak with you directly about what you are left wondering at this time about me or about time-effective therapy, I will take the liberty of developing some of my own hypothetical questions from you.

Reader: Is it necessary to nearly die in order to have real

empathy for patients going through difficult circumstances?

SHB: I certainly hope not. However, when we work with patients and distance ourselves from their experience because it feels too uncomfortable for us to let ourselves get closer to that experience, therapy fails. The patient is objectified, and is pitied or disdained. These feelings lead us to become tangled up in technique and often we are unable to really hear what the patient is asking for—what he or she wants out of the treatment. I think the major impact of my brush with death was that I no longer set myself above or apart from patients in a way that I had done before this experience.

Reader: Even though you say it is not, it sounds to me as though time-effective therapy is just "woolly eclecticism." Level with me. Is that the case?

SHB: It all depends upon what the meaning of "is" is. Just kidding. It's really not. I try to have my interventions informed by Prochaska's stages of change model, and to think about the relationship in the context of control mastery. This is very different than my understanding of eclecticism, which has always felt like a mishmash of taking a little from here and little from there. When I intervene in a particular way, I try to know why I am doing so.

Reader: How can you talk at one moment about the therapeutic alliance, and the importance of the relationship in therapy, and the next about the use of computers in therapy? Isn't that a contradiction?

SHB: I don't think so, for a variety of reasons. First of all, I think that computers can be outstanding treatment and relationship enhancers. We know from research done at ITS and other places that many times people may be more honest with a computer than with another person. For some people, there may be real benefit to beginning to think about certain issues in their lives by using a

computer or the Internet. These people may later be able
to make use of a therapist in the change process. There
are also people who may prefer to use computers in an
ongoing way for self-change. This goes back to a point I
made earlier about flexibility and thinking with a
beginner's mind. Just because it is not our preference to
work on self-change with only a computer, for some
people this may be desirable. Finally, computers can be
extremely valuable in enhancing the treatment process.
The clinician may have the patient participate in various
kinds of experiences and learning activities, and report
on these in face-to-face therapeutic sessions. The
computer will not, for most people, replace human
contact as a part of psychotherapy; it can, however, if
used well, be an important adjunct for many people.

Reader: Geez, what a pessimist you are! All that doom and
gloom about the direction that things will take for mental
health professionals got me depressed. Do you really
believe that stuff?

SHB: I wish I didn't. I just do not see things getting better
quickly. There are some basic supply and demand issues
at work, and they are not looking good. I do think that
some people will be able to do well, thrive, and survive.

Reader: How will they do that?

SHB: Flexibility, flexibility, flexibility. If you have one goal,
and one way of getting to that goal, you are in big
trouble. If you intend to be a private practice therapist—
and see one patient after another—and live a comfortable
life, you may be shocked. You have got to think about
other areas for behavioral interventions. You have got to
think of other ways to deliver such interventions. You
need to be creative and look at all of the changes going
on in our society and in healthcare for exciting and
interesting opportunities where you can apply your
behavioral skills.

Reader: I don't know whether to thank you or to shoot

the messenger.

SHB: Best not to shoot the messenger.

Reader: Then thanks.

SHB: Don't mention it.

REFERENCES

American Association of Practicing Psychologists. (1998). Psychologist incomes plummet while mental health care continues to erode., *AAPP Newsletter*, *1*, 5.

Alexander, F. & French, T. M. (1972). *Psychoanalytic therapy*. Lincoln, NB: University of Nebraska Press (Originally published in 1946).

Budman, S. H. (1972). Clients' lexical organization and its effect upon therapists' empathy level. *Psychological Reports*, *31*, 77-78.

Budman, S. H., Bennett, M. J., & Wisneski, M. J. (1980). Short-term group psychotherapy: An adult developmental model. *International Journal of Group Psychotherapy*, *30*, 63-76.

Budman, S. H., Demby, A., & Feldstein, M. (1984). A controlled study of the impact of mental health treatment on medical care utilization. *Medical Care*, *13*, 216-222.

Budman, S. H., Demby, A., Feldstein, M., & Gold, M. (1984). The effects of time-limited group psychotherapy: A controlled study. *International Journal of Group Psychotherapy*, *34*, 587-603.

Budman, S. H., Demby, A., Soldz, S., & Merry, J. (1996). Time-limited group psychotherapy for patients with personality disorders: Outcomes and dropouts. *International Journal of Group Psychotherapy*, *46*, 357-377.

Budman, S. H., & Gurman, A. S. (1988). *Theory and practice of brief therapy*. New York: Guilford Publications.

Budman, S. H., & Gurman, A. S. (1992). A practical approach to brief psychotherapy: The I-D-E model. In S. H. Budman, M. Hoyt, & S. Friedman (Eds.), *The first session in brief therapy* (pp. 111-134). New York: Guilford Press.

Budman, S. H. & Steenbarger, B. N. (1997). *The essential guide to group practice in mental health*. New York: Guilford.

Cummings, N. A. (1986). The dismantling of our health care system: Strategies for the survival of psychological practice. *American Psychologist, 41*, 426-431.

Cummings, N., Budman, S. H., Thomas, J. L. (1998). Efficient psychotherapy as a viable response to scarce resources and rationing of treatment. *Professional Psychology: Research and Practice. 29*, 460-469.

Klerman, G. L., Budman, S. H., Berwick, D. M., Feldstein, M., & White, J. D. (1987). Efficacy of a brief psychosocial intervention for symptoms of stress and distress among patients in primary care. *Medical Care, 25*, 1-11.

Klerman, G. L., Rounsaville, B., Chevron, E. & Weissman, M. (1984). *Interpersonal psychotherapy of depression*. New York: Basic Books.

Kopp, S. B. (1988). *If you meet the Buddha on road, kill him*. New York: Bantam Books.

Malan, D. H. (1976). *The frontiers of brief therapy: An example of the convergence of research and clinical practice*. New York: Plenum Press.

Prochaska, J. O., Norcross, J. & DiClemente, C. C. (1994). *Changing for good*. New York: William Morrow.

Suzuki, S. (1972). *Zen mind, beginner's mind*. San Francisco: Weatherhill.

Weiss, J., & Sampson, H. (1993). *How psychotherapy works*. New York: Guilford Publications.

Wertlieb, D., Budman, S. H., Demby, A., & Randall, M. (1982). The stress of marital separation: Intervention in a health maintenance organization. *Psychosomatic Medicine, 44*, 437- 448.

CHAPTER 3

AN ETHNOCULTURAL APPROACH TO PSYCHOTHERAPY AND TO LIFE

LILLIAN COMAS-DÍAZ, PH.D.

Each man speaks with his father's tongue; ask a man who he is and he names a race.

Leonard Cohen, *The Favorite Game*

Like many working-class migrants, my Puerto Rican parents searched for the American dream on an empty stomach speaking broken English. Born in Chicago, I have always lived in two cultures at once, my parents' and that of my birth country. At the age of six I experienced another kind of culture shock when I "journeyed back" to live with my family in Puerto Rico. Leaving the frigid winter for the tropical Caribbean did not alleviate my adjustment crisis. Becoming a stranger in my own land left me feeling fragmented, longing for integration, and poignantly aware of the pervasive influence of culture on behavior. My need for belonging was intense because my young life was such a mixture of the strange and the familiar. Developing an ethnocultural approach to doing psychotherapy was a natural extension of these experiences.

My ancestral story begins more than 500 years ago with the creation of a new race in Latin America through *mestizaje* or the mixing of Iberians with indigenous people and African slaves. As a consequence, a plethora of colors paints Puerto Ricans' identity as a racial rainbow. Product of a mulatto Puerto Rican father and a "White" Puerto Rican mother, I was nurtured by fusion art such as salsas, Afro Caribbean literature, and NuyoRican poetry. Thus, my multiracial background sensitized me to the centrality of race in human development.

Colonialism is also an integral part of my cultural heritage. The legacy of Puerto Rican colonial status made me aware of the historical effects of oppression on behavior, prompted my interest in the psychology of colonization, oppression, and liberation, and heightened my appreciation for seeing individuals in relation to their culture, race, gender, sociopolitical, and historical contexts.

Migrating and becoming the other may well have contributed to my developing an interest in clinical work at an early age. As a parentified child, my relatives confided their problems in me. Classmates also trusted me with their difficulties and were appreciative of my "help." I became so popular as a "counselor" that teachers asked me to mediate conflicts between students. Physical disability may have well solidified my role as a wounded healer. Born with a cleft palate, which was repaired at age four, I stammered until high school. Of course, I became a good listener.

Growing up in a culture full of magical realism that emphasized the permeable boundaries of reality familiarized me with ways of knowledge other than the intellectual. My education was enriched by exposure to Latin American, Caribbean, and European as well as North American influences. Searching for my own voice, I read voraciously, finding healing in art. Being interested in humanities and science, I saw psychology as a natural answer to my dilemma of whether to become a scientist or an artist. By the time I entered college I had decided to become a clinical psychologist.

PERSONAL AND HISTORICAL PASSAGES

People are trapped in history and history is trapped in them.
James Baldwin, *Notes from a Native Son*

I entered college in the late sixties and was immersed in *independentismo* (Puerto Rico's pro-independence movement). As a liberation approach, the *independentista* movement integrated socialist and emancipatory influences within a cultural context. These influences nurtured my interest in psychotherapy's role in oppression and liberation, while issues of agency, mastery, and self-determination found their way into my conceptualization of clinical work.

Searching for psychotherapy's role in alleviating oppression, I discovered liberation literature. Albert Memmi's (1965) classic book, *The Colonizer and the Colonized*, and the work of Frantz Fanon (1967, 1976), a Black psychiatrist from a colonized Caribbean country, brilliantly exposed me to the psychology of colonization and oppression, validating psychotherapists' participation in the liberation process.

After college I returned to my hometown, Yabucoa, to teach science. My students—transplanted Ricans (second or third generation continental Puerto Ricans)—exhibited difficulties adapting to the island while carrying the emotional scars of racism from North Americans as well as from Puerto Ricans. Issues of internalized oppression plagued the national identity debate, pitting island Puerto Ricans against continental Ricans. This conflict further sensitized me to the plights of marginalized populations with multiple minority status.

During the early 1970s I enrolled in a masters degree program in clinical psychology at the University of Puerto Rico. Professing eclecticism, this program trained students with dynamic, behavioral, and humanistic approaches. One of the most profound formative training experiences was my practica at community mental health centers focusing on the seriously mentally ill. This experience convinced me of the importance of the person and environment fit, or the belief that individuals' functioning is enhanced when placed in the context that fits their strengths. This concept is crucial to my way of doing psychotherapy.

Because Puerto Rican culture is generally sociocentric, the psychotherapeutic services were offered within the client's environment. Individual work was always conducted within a systems approach. Characteristic of colonized situations, however, I confronted contradictions in my training. Although the psychology department was politically liberal, it lacked gender, racial, and class analyses. Even though the program provided a rich perspective in cultural context, I felt that I needed more clinical training.

After completing my masters degree, I moved to Connecticut to direct a Latino community mental health program. This translocation was part of my plan to obtain English proficiency and become acclimated to a different cultural environment, so I could eventually apply to a doctorate program in clinical psychology. The aftermath of the Civil Rights movement found me offering outreach psychological services in the schools, churches, ghettos, and barrios. Delivering psychotherapeutic services in this historical period also involved community activism and involvement with community leaders, business people, politicians, clergy, and others. Within this context I began to work with folk healers in cross referrals. Collaborating with the healers was a humbling experience that changed my assumptions about psychotherapy.

At that time I was a cocky clinician armed with scientific tools to "help" people. Although familiar with folk healing through cultural osmosis, I did not respect this model, secretly labeling it superstition. Consequently, I thought that my professional role was "superior" to that of an *espiritista's* because of my formal schooling. This elitist insensitivity was promptly challenged when I began to work with folk healers as equals. Listening to them, I learned that so much of what clients say is about spiritually—the meaning of life, pain, and death—areas that I was not clinically trained in. The folk healers provided me with a different paradigm, one that embraces holism in a culturally relevant manner. Respect for what was indigenous to culture helped me to conceptualize and develop a model of working within two healing orientations (Comas-Díaz, 1981a). Consequently, my view of psychotherapy comprises a spiritual component.

Back in the 1970s, I realized that psychotherapy cannot be isolated from the sociopolitical context. I still remember a freezing winter morning when, delivering psychological services, I had to literally run for my life because the police were raiding Mount Pleasant, a Puerto Rican barrio, attacking residents under the excuse of controlling a "revolt." Communities of color, particularly African Americans and Latinos, have accused the police of violating their human rights. In 1999, indeed, Amnesty International (1999) released a report charging the U.S. police with human rights violations against ethnic minorities. I presented the Mount Pleasant incident to the clinic's administration—hoping it would take an active stance against the systematic discrimination. Needless to say, I was disappointed. While trying to convey the importance of combating racism for improved mental health, I was shocked to hear my fellow clinicians advocate for a "neutral apolitical psychotherapy" while blaming the victim.

Working with ethnic minority populations experiencing racial discrimination, socioeconomic problems, and cultural adaptation difficulties made me question the role of the therapist as a change agent. Endorsing a comprehensive model including psychosocial services, at times I felt like Sisyphus, carrying the therapy uphill only to see my clients' lives slide to the bottom weighted down by the reality of their problems. During that period I participated in a Puerto Rican psychological association, where I met Julia Ramos-McKay, a doctoral psychology student at the University of Massachusetts at Amherst. Although I was familiar with Brazilian educator Paulo Freire's (1967, 1970) pedagogy of the oppressed, Julia, having worked directly with him, ignited the group with a fervor to apply his model to our clinical work.

Involving the awareness and critical analysis of oppression, this liberation paradigm helped us change our mentality and engage in transformative actions. Like cultural warriors, we rescued our identity working with Latino communities in order to improve their psychosocial condition. Viewing colonization as a special type of oppression, I envisioned liberation psychotherapy as promoting empowerment, reconciliation, and healing while advancing the integration of a fragmented colonized identity. This approach seemed to restore my hope in the clinician's impact at the individual, family, group, and even societal levels (Comas-Díaz, 1994; Comas-Díaz & Griffith, 1988; Comas-Díaz, Lykes, & Alarcon, 1998).

Because a clinician of color without a doctoral degree is impaired in her ability to be effective in the broader society, I made concrete plans to obtain my Ph.D. in clinical psychology. I applied to the University of Massachusetts because it was receptive to diversity and ethnic minority issues.

Turning points: "The Enigma of Arrival"

My diverse cross-cultural transitions showed me that the enigma of arrival involves the transformation of identity. Arriving at the University of Massachusetts in 1976, I began to work with Castellano Turner, an African American professor who honored his name (castellano or Castilian Spanish language) by bravely supervising a team of Latino clinicians. This supportive experience heightened my aspirations for pan-racial and pan-ethnic work. Wanting to integrate more technical knowledge, I studied with professors who espoused cognitive and behavioral approaches, later conducting my dissertation under Bonnie Strickland's supervision on the applicability of cognitive-behavioral approaches to depressed Latinas (Comas-Díaz, 1981b). Having found this orientation helpful in reducing presenting symptoms and as a result increasing my credibility with clients of color, I currently integrate it into therapy.

The Women's Movement was in full force during those exciting times and, like many female clinicians, I was swimming in the sea of feminist psychotherapy. I continue to find a home within this movement. Its emphasis on empowerment, cultural context, therapist's self-examination, and the personal-is-political dictum are congruent with my liberation beliefs. However, I am also aware that the mainstream feminist movement has been a White middle-class phenomenon and have critically articulated its limitations with respect to women of color (Comas-Díaz, 1991).

Another move landed me in New Haven to complete my clinical internship at the Yale University Psychiatry Department. Continuing my involvement with feminism, I became active in women's organizations and developed culturally relevant assertiveness training for Latinas (Comas-Díaz & Duncan, 1985) and inner city women. During that time, a feminist researcher Myrna Weissman trained me in interpersonal psychotherapy, an approach that I integrate into my ethnocultural work.

After completing my internship I was offered and accepted a faculty position in the Yale Department of Psychiatry. Delivering services to inner city populations, I sought training in alcohol and substance abuse rehabilitation. This experience provided an additional model to traditional dynamic psychotherapy, one that has been valuable while working not only with adult children of alcoholics but also with clients who abuse substances secondary to emotional difficulties (Comas-Díaz & Minrath, 1985).

During this period I trained in trauma work, particularly the trauma of sexual assault. Once more I struggled with translating monocultural clinical approaches from one culture to another. This time I was "lost in translation" because sexual abuse is a taboo topic in the Latino community, and many techniques congruent with individualistic societies are counterproductive in sociocentric ones (Comas-Díaz, 1995).

During my tenure at Yale, Stephen Fleck, a psychoanalytically trained psychiatrist, supervised me for several years. This experience was crucial to my development as a therapist. Stephen Fleck was a superb clinician, and I felt blessed to be around him and benefit from his psychotherapeutic wisdom. Moreover, he was a cross-culturally translocated individual—a German Jewish refugee who escaped the Nazi regime and settled in the United States. Fleck had the rare combination of clinical knowledge, systems approach, sociopolitical and historical contextualization, and "otherhood" that worked miracles for me as his apprentice. At a minimum, I owe him my clinical acumen.

During the same period, the ethnicity and family therapy movement was gaining momentum, and I trained with Behnaz Jalali, an Iranian woman psychiatrist whose competence, grace, and compassion were instrumental models for me. This experience was empowering because it validated my beliefs in the centrality of culture, ethnicity, and gender, and their interaction in psychotherapy.

A crisis prompted my own need for psychotherapy. I was apprehensive about finding a therapist, because I feared that dominant, dynamically oriented psychotherapies were too dogmatic for my multicultural reality. As a Puerto Rican, I had encountered ethnic discrimination among dynamically oriented psychotherapists and was suspicious of a therapeutic orientation that did not examine itself along those lines. I chose a Jungian analyst instead, finding this orientation less dogmatic and more receptive to cultural diversity. Instead of pathologizing my being raised by grandparents, this perspective accentuated the benefits of having multiple parents—a situation prevalent among collectivistic societies. The psychotherapeutic journey was nurturing, liberating, and actualizing. Combining my longstanding interest in mythology and tradition, it helped me to further integrate spirituality principles into my psychotherapy practice.

In 1983, I married Frederick M. Jacobsen and formed a union that became a full partnership in both my personal and professional life. A neuropsychopharmacologist who experienced cross-cultural translocation, Fred collaborates with me in writing and conducting research. In 1984, we left New Haven for Washington, DC., where I would direct the American Psychological Association Office of Ethnic Minority Affairs. This experience further immersed me in the political realities of being a professional psychologist. Although I did not practice clinical work, I realized that in many ways political work is similar to psychotherapy. Whereas directing the Office of Ethnic Minority Affairs was fulfilling, I lacked opportunities to refine my clinical skills, with one exemption. Due to my interest in international issues, I participated in a joint venture between the American Psychological Association and the American Psychiatric Association in a fact-finding delegation to Chile, investigating human rights abuses and their mental health implications. This investigation was an act of professional heroism in an attempt to support clinicians risking their lives by providing professional services. We met with clinicians developing therapeutic approaches to repair the individual, familiar, and societal wounds inflicted by political repression (Comas-Díaz & Padilla, 1990). Journeying into the abyss of repression and terror, we interviewed torture victims and their families (Padilla & Comas-Díaz, 1987). We emerged as transformed individuals.

Back in the United States, I became involved with several organizations—assisting victims of torture and political repression—and delivered clinical services to these victims. Under the aegis of the APA Committee on the International Relations in Psychology, I visited a clinic in Toronto specializing in services to victims of torture and political repression. My combined interest in psychotherapy and social action found a nexus in the field of ethnopolitical trauma. In 1986, I entered full-time private practice, founding the Transcultural Mental Health Institute with Fred.

CREDO

Instead of concentration on a transcendental ideal, sustained attention to diversity and interdependence may offer a different clarity of vision, one that is sensitive to ecological complexity, to the multiple rather than the singular.

Mary Catherine Bateson, *Composing a Life*

Ethnocultural psychotherapy considers ethnicity and culture as interacting paradigms requiring culture-specific as well as transcultural interventions. Without negating individuals' uniqueness, addressing ethnicity, race, and culture helps to catalyze major therapeutic issues such as trust, ambivalence, anger, and acceptance of disparate parts of self and other. Being on both sides of the couch taught me that therapists and clients negotiate clinical realities not merely in theoretical terms but also in terms of ethnic, racial, and gender meanings. These meanings influence both the process and outcome of psychotherapy. Given that virtually all psychotherapy is cross cultural in nature (Comas-Díaz, 1987), therapy is similar to a journey into foreign lands, where cross-cultural encounters identify connections and disconnections. During the healing voyage, therapists and clients inherently bring along diverse maps, each one with its unique ethnocultural, historical, and sociopolitical antecedents. As pathfinders, therapists help clients find their particular road to Rome.

A syncretic and holistic perspective, ethnocultural psychotherapy emphasizes context specificity, adaptation to the environment, plus cognitive, behavioral, biological, and spiritual plasticity. As a liberation approach, it promotes awareness of oppression and restoration of dignity through mastery, agency, and transformation. The ethnocultural liberation paradigm facilitates clients' critical consciousness, helping them to (1) become aware of the oppressed and colonized mentality; (2) recognize the historical and societal context of colonialism, oppression, sexism, racism, and classism; (3) correct dynamic and cognitive errors that maintain the colonized mentality; (4) increase mastery and achieve autonomous dignity; (5) reformulate an ethnocultural identity; and (6) develop an inclusive sense of an individual and collective self (Comas-Díaz, 1994; Memmi, 1965).

In order to examine the development of ethnic identity, Fred and I (Comas-Díaz & Jacobsen, 1987; Jacobsen, 1988) developed the ethnocultural assessment. As a diagnostic and treatment tool the ethnocultural assessment considers several stages. The first stage, the ethnocultural heritage, involves obtaining a history of the client's ethnocultural heritage, including genetic and biological predispositions. The second stage, the family myth, focuses on the circumstances that led to the client's (or his or her multigenerational family's) decision to move to another culture. The family niche or the post transition analysis stage is based on the client's intellectual and emotional perception of his or her family's ethnocultural identity in the host society after the translocation. The next stage, self-adjustment, concerns the client's own perceived ethnocultural adjustment in the host culture as an individual distinct from the rest of the family. The last stage, self and other, examines client-clinician relationship through the ethnocultural factors of transference and countertransference (Comas-Díaz, 1994, 1996; Comas-Díaz & Jacobsen, 1987; Jacobsen, 1988).

Ethnicity, race, and culture touch deep, unconscious feelings and become targets for projection by both client and therapist, making this material more available in therapy. As the other, culturally diverse people frequently become objects of defensive projections. We have identified a number of ethnic and racial transferential and countertransferential reactions occurring within intra-ethnocultural and inter-ethnocultural therapeutic dyads (Comas-Díaz & Jacobsen, 1991), as well as within the White client/therapist of color dyad (Comas-Díaz & Jacobsen, 1995). An American Psychological Association training video (Vandenbos, Frank-McNeil, Norcross, & Freedheim; 1995), in which I conduct a session, illustrates the management of ethnocultural transferences. The following case discusses ethnocultural transference and countertransference dynamics in an intra-ethnic and gender dyad.

> *Amalia Batista—a 35-year-old Mexican-American woman—presented to therapy after watching the TV show Cristina (the Hispanic Oprah). "I have the same problem that Ana was discussing with Cristina. My mood está caído (down) and I think I am depressed. I guess I have always been depressed, without recognizing it." College educated, Amalia worked part time in a museum in order to be more available to her family. Married to Rafael, a Mexican-American accountant, the couple had two daughters, ages eight and five. A clinical evaluation revealed that Amalia was moderately depressed because her husband took a co-worker on a date. Rafael confessed, but denied having sex. "He is just like Bill Clinton, smoking pot*

without inhaling and having sex without impaling," asserted Amalia, referring to a national scandal involving the U.S. President's affair with a White House female intern. Obsessing about the incident, Amalia acknowledged that Rafael previously had been faithful and that she married him because he was an honest man.

Amalia's moderate depressive symptoms appeared amenable to psychotherapy with an emphasis on ethnocultural and interpersonal factors. The ethnocultural assessment disclosed that both paternal and maternal lineages were Mexican and or Mexican-American. Her maternal grandfather left Mexico at age 15 and married a Mexican-American while her paternal family had been in New Mexico since the territory belonged to Spain. Thus, the Batista family myth not only involved a history of immigration but also a heritage of displacement in their own land. Her family niche included cross-cultural and sociopolitical translocations. The family lore rumored that the Batista family lost their ranch to dishonest American businessmen. Fully bilingual, Amalia's paternal family carried an ethnic pride as Hispanos and a historical disdain for "the invading gringos."

Amalia's identity involved a mixture of Mexican, Mexican-American, and Latino pride. As an avid reader, she identified with many Latin American as well as Mexican-American female authors. The ethnocultural assessment revealed that both her family and personal histories involved being betrayed in intimate relationships and by personas de confianza (people of confidence). Thus Rafael's betrayal touched intimate personal and historical roots, in that Amalia's personal family history included abandonment by significant others. She was particularly weary of romantic relationships. Describing her parents' marriage as espousing traditional gender values, Amalia asserted that her father was a womanizer. "Mami was a typical sufrida (sufferer) and I swore never to become one," she *declared.*

The ethnocultural assessment brought our attention to the historical material woven into Amalia's current clinical situation. Her parents' traditional marriage became a dreaded self-fulfilling prophecy: "Papi used to travel for business and he had a woman in every town. Mami knew about the affairs, but she refused to leave him, suffering in silence."

Amalia's cultural gender script appeared mirrored in her husband's affair. "He lived a cheap novella and then accused me of being jealous," Amalia complained. Rafael stopped dating his co-worker, although never admitted to his inappropriate behavior. "To top it off, he went out with a gringa! *Again,* norteamericanos *are trying to steal what belongs to us."*

The Batista family had a history of sudden dramatic deaths— "It is just like Gabriel García Márquez' novel One Hundred Years of Solitude," *Amalia asserted. Her reaction to Rafael's infidelity was further augmented by a complicated grief reaction. When she was 20, both of her parents died dramatically during her honeymoon. Becoming sick during the wedding, Amalia's father later suffered a heart attack, while her mother died on the day of his funeral. Amalia blamed Rafael for not leaving their honeymoon soon enough to properly grieve with her family of origin.*

During therapy, Amalia felt supported and reassured: "Telling you my story makes me realize that I have not buried my dead ones." She developed an idealized and ambivalent transference facilitated by the ethnic and gender similarity between us. She saw me as the good mother, succoring and nurturing her. The other side of her ambivalence contained her fear that I would not protect her and eventually abandon her. Moreover, she did not reveal the negative side of her ambivalence, following the cultural script of not confronting your sufrida *mother.*

Working through this transference entailed helping Amalia to become emancipated in a culturally congruent manner. I realized that she needed to complete her bereavement and transform herself from the grieving adolescent daughter into a mature woman. In order to take this journey, she also needed to break the Batista female chain: "I don't want my daughters to become sufridas.*"*

Utilizing an ethnocultural approach helped me to overcome my overidentification with her. During the ethnocultural assessment, I realized that my Puerto Rican heritage was very close to the Batistas' experience of becoming strangers in their own land. This reaction led me to stay too long with Amalia's sense of victimhood. Realizing this limitation, I addressed my countertransference by focusing on Amalia's ethnocultural differences from mine. I used the celebration of Día de los Muertos *(Day of the Dead), one of the most important Mexican holidays and a defining factor of the essence of Mexicanidad (Paz, 1950). Asking Amalia about her family's observance of this holiday helped us to culturally address her grieving. Properly examining her loss freed Amalia from the Batista* Maldición *(curse)—betrayal and abandonment.*

Accompanying Amalia through her transition into emotional adulthood entailed becoming her own parent given that she was an orphan. To help her in this journey, I suggested Mexican art. Because Amalia was a Frida Kahlo fan, I selected one of Frida's paintings—her depiction of the artist giving birth to herself as an adult, while Frida the mother is dead. The metaphor of a dead mother giving birth to a mature woman was consistent with Amalia's situation. She reconciled her parents' death with the acceptance of maturity, self-parenting, and parenting of her two daughters.

Amalia's vignette illustrates how ethnocultural tools reveal rich information and address the issues of identity and circumstances. Ortega y Gasset's (1958) classic saying: "I am me and my circumstances," emphasizes situating the individual in a cultural context. Following this principle, ethnocultural therapeutic tools include multigenerational genograms, transitional maps, narratives, testimonies, mythologies, and inventories, among others. The multigenerational genograms diagram extended family relationships, kinship networks, and historical links, emphasizing the family and ethnocultural group identity by strengthening clients' connection while identifying disconnections (Boyd-Franklin, 1989).

The ethnocultural transitional map assesses personal, familial, and community dislocations in clients and their families, involving the collection of psychological, social, and ethnocultural data in addition to the assessment of individual and family developmental stages (Ho, 1987). Along with the standard clinical interview format, the transitional map uses photographs, folklore, art, music, and other ethnic data as clinical tools.

Ethnocultural tales address the development of ethnic, racial, and gender identity as a life-story construction and reconstruction (Howard, 1991). Cultural stories tell the group's collective story of coping with life and responding to pain and problems (McGill, 1992). Family narratives tell where the ancestors came from, what kind of people they were, what issues are important, and what lessons have been learned from their experience (Stone, 1988). These narratives unfold messages regarding expectations, values, roles, identity (personal and collective), family and cultural scripts, self-fulfilling prophecies, prescriptions for success and failure, meaning of life and death, and other relevant information (Comas-Díaz, 1994). They also teach how to cope with oppression, racism, sexism, and trauma (individual, collective, and cultural).

Because oppression silences people's voices, the main purpose of the narrative is to validate clients' reality by listening to their story. A special type of narrative, *testimonio* (testimony) emerged in Chile as a treatment modality for victims of political repression and trauma. Testimony validates personal experience as a basis for subjective truth and knowledge in an affirming and empowering manner (Aron, 1992). It is a first-person account of one's traumatic experiences and how these have affected the individual and the family (Cienfuegos & Monelli, 1982). Consisting of a verbal journey to the past, testimony allows the individual to transform painful experiences and identity, creating a new present, and enhancing the future (Cienfuegos & Monelli, 1982). This empowering approach is helpful to people who have suffered individual, multigenerational, and collective trauma, dislocation, and oppression.

Ethnocultural psychotherapy acknowledges spirituality. For many people of color, psychological health demands balance, harmony, and spiritual development. Illness, then, is perceived as an alienation from body, mind, community, and spirit. Moreover, imbalance and neglect of spirituality could cause psychological distress. As an illustration, I used the celebration of *Dia de los Muertos* for grief work with Amalia.

PSYCHOTHERAPY, PROPHECIES, AND PLURALISM

A wonderful harmony arises from joining together the seemingly unconnected.

Heraclitus

From an ethnocultural perspective, the future of psychotherapy appears certain. In the early 1990s, I prophesied that ethnic minority psychotherapy and general psychotherapy will become one (Comas-Díaz, 1992). Recognizing the centrality of cultural diversity, clinicians will incorporate pluralism as a healing blueprint. Eurocentric models of psychotherapy will be augmented by more inclusive orientations, in an "East meets West" fashion integrating alternative and indigenous healing into mainstream therapeutic approaches. Values prevalent in egocentric societies, such as individuality, independence, freedom of choice, and insight as a therapeutic method will be challenged as ethnocentric goals. Conversely, sociocentric values like interdependence, familism, (an emphasis on the centrality of family), connectedness, conviviality, and communion (union with the environment) will be aspired as a desirable traits. Psychological determinism, such as destiny, karma, dharma (duty, code of behavior, and cosmic responsibility) (Tharoor, 1989) will complement internal locus of control and free will. This syncretism—best described by Jawaharlal Nehru—views life as a game of cards where the hand you are dealt represents fate and the way you play it is free will.

Collectivism and interconnectedness will become mainstream values. The concept of family will be expanded to include an extended, communal, spiritual, and cosmic family. Eastern concepts such as *giri* (social obligation) (Shon & Ja, 1982), *hsiao* (filial piety), and *pao* (reciprocity in social relationships) (Kleinman, 1980), will facilitate the meeting of a global family. As part of this collectivism, clinicians will systematically examine how their cultural and ethnopolitical background, experiences, attitudes, values, and biases influence their role as practitioners. Aiming for an inclusive psychotherapy, they will experience a process similar to cross-cultural translocation in the reformulation of their identities. While preserving their characters as scientists and healers, psychotherapists will develop a multicultural identity integrating their ancient roles as shamans and visionaries with modern ones that will include technology and psychopharmacology. We may even witness the emergence of the therapist-shaman–psychopharmacologist-psychotechnologist. Working in real and virtual realities, future psychotherapists will use cultural diversity as the psychological Rosetta Stone.

Psychotherapy will increase our sense of centrality in time and space. The historical and political context will acquire salience in treatment. As ethnic and racial demographics change, psychotherapists will deal with intensified tensions emerging from distinct groups' demands for greater access to resources. As our world village becomes smaller and interconnected, global politics will permeate the therapeutic hour. Future North American clinicians will highlight individuals' and groups' cultural adaptations and modifications to an evolving "nation of migrants." Ethnopolitical tensions and conflicts involving national and international politics will become part of therapy. Psychotherapy will require the skills of artisans, weavers, and quilters in composing lives. A wonderful psychotherapeutic harmony will arise from valuing diversity and connecting the seemingly disconnected.

Of course, these predictions reflect my life and situated experience. I have learned that identity is personal transformation and that transformation entails a critical examination of ourselves in a context-specific environment. If psychotherapy adheres to this principle, it will not only survive, but will thrive in the new millennium.

REFERENCES

Amnesty International. (1999). *United States of America: Police brutality and excessive force in the New York City Police Department* (AI Index: AMR available from International Secretariat, 1 Easton Street, London WCX 8DJ, United Kingdom.)

Aron, A. (1992). Testimonio, a bridge between psychotherapy and sociotherapy. In E. Cole, O. Espin, & E. D. Rothblum (Eds.), *Refugee women and their mental health: Shattered societies, shattered lives*. New York: Haworth Press.

Baldwin, J. (1955). *Notes of a native son*. Boston: Beacon Press.

Bateson, M.C. (1990). *Composing a life*. New York: Penguin Books.

Boyd-Franklin, N. (1989). Black families in therapy: A multisystems approach.

Cienfuegos, A., & Monelli, C. (1983). The testimony of political repression as a therapeutic instrument. *American Journal of Orthopsychiatry, 53*, 43-51.

Cohen, L. (1963). *The favorite game*. New York: Viking.

Comas-Díaz, L. (1981a). Puerto Rican *espiritismo* and psychotherapy. *American Journal of Orthopsychiatry, 51*, 636-645.

Comas-Díaz, L. (1981b). Effects of cognitive and behavioral group treatment in the depressive symptomatology of Puerto Rican women. *Journal of Consulting and Clinical Psychology, 49*, 627-632.

Comas-Díaz, L. (1987). Feminist therapy with Hispanic/Latina women: Myth or reality? *Women & Therapy, 6*, 39-61.

Comas-Díaz, L. (1991). Feminism and diversity in psychology: The case of women of color. *Psychology of Women Quarterly, 15*, 597-609.

Comas-Díaz, L. (1992). The future of psychotherapy with ethnic minorities. *Psychotherapy, 29*, 88-94.

Comas-Díaz, L. (1994). Integrative approach. In L. Comas-Díaz, & B. Greene (Eds.), *Women of color: Integrating ethnic and gender identities in psychotherapy* (pp. 287-318). New York: Guilford.

Comas-Díaz, L. (1995). Puerto Ricans and sexual child abuse. In L. Fontes (Ed.), *Sexual abuse in nine North American cultures* (pp. 31-66). Thousand Oaks, CA: Sage.

Comas-Díaz, L. (1996). Cultural considerations in diagnosis. In F. Kaslow (Ed.), *Handbook of relational diagnosis and dysfunctional family patterns.* New York: Wiley.

Comas-Díaz, L., & Duncan, J. W. (1985). The cultural context: A factor in assertiveness training with mainland Puerto Rican women. *Psychology of Women Quarterly, 9*, 463-475.

Comas-Díaz, L. & Griffith, E. H. (Eds). (1988). *Clinical guidelines in cross-cultural mental health.* New York: John Wiley.

Comas-Díaz, L. & Jacobsen F. M. (1987). Ethnocultural identification in psychotherapy. *Psychiatry, 50*, 232-241.

Comas-Díaz, L. & Jacobsen, F. M. (1991). Ethnocultural transference and countertransference in the therapeutic dyad. *American Journal of Orthopsychiatry, 61*, 392-402.

Comas-Díaz, L. & Jacobsen, F. M. (1995). The therapist of color and the White patient dyad: Contradictions and recognitions. *Cultural Diversity and Mental Health, 1*, 93-106.

Comas-Díaz, L., Lykes, B., & Alarcon, R. (1998). Ethnic conflict and psychology of liberation in Guatemala, Peru and Puerto Rico. *American Psychologist, 53*, 778-792.

Comas-Díaz, L., & Minrath, M. (1985). Psychotherapy with ethnic minority borderline clients. *Psychotherapy: Theory, Research and Practice. 22*, 418-426.

Comas-Díaz, L. & Padilla, A. (1990). Countertransference in working with victims of political repression. *American*

Journal of Orthopsychiatry, 60, 125-134.

Doi, T. (1962). *Amae*—a key concept for understanding Japanese personality structure. In R. J . Smith, & R. K. Beardsley (Eds.), *Japanese culture.* Chicago: Aldine.

Fanon, F. (1967). *Black skin, white masks.* New York: Grove Press, Inc.

Fanon, F. (1976). *The wretched of the earth.* Middlesex: England.

Freire, P. (1967). *Educaçáo como prática da liberdade.* (Education as a practice of freedom). Rio de Janeiro: Paz e Terra.

Freire, P. (1970). *Pedagogy of the oppressed.* New York: The Seabury Press.

Ho, M.H. (1987). *Family therapy with ethnic minorities.* Newbury Park, CA: Sage.

Howard, G.S. (1991). Culture tales: A narrative approach to thinking, cross-cultural psychology, and psychotherapy. *American Psychologist. 46,* 187-197.

Jacobsen, F. M. (1988). Ethnocultural assessment. In L. Comas-Díaz, & E. H. Griffith (Eds.), *Clinical guidelines in cross-cultural mental health* (pp. 135-147). New York: Wiley.

Kleinman, A. (1989, May 19). Culture, suffering and psychotherapy. Presentation made at the conference *Psychotherapy of Diversity: Cross-cultural Treatment Issues,* sponsored by the Harvard Medical School, Boston, MA.

McGill, D.W. (1992). The cultural story in multicultural family therapy. *Families in Society, 73,* 339-349.

McGoldrick, M., Pearce, J. K., & Giordano, J. (Eds.), *Ethnicity and family therapy.* New York: Guilford Press.

Memmi, A. (1965). *The colonizer and the colonized.* Boston: Beacon Press.

Gasset , J. Ortega y (1958). *Man and crisis.* New York: Norton.

Padilla, A. M., & Comas-Díaz, L (1987). Miedo y represión en Chile (Fear and repression in Chile). *Revista Latinoamericana de Psicologia, 19* (2), 135-146.

Paz, O. (1950). *El laberinto de la soledad* (The labyrinth of solitude). Mexico City: Fondo de Cultura Economica.

Shon, S. & Ja, D. Y. (1982). Asian families. In M. McGoldrick, J. K.

Pearce, & J. Giordano (Eds.), *Ethnicity and family therapy*. New York: Guilford Press.

Stone, E. (1988). *Black sheep and kissing cousins: How our family stories shape us*. New York: Penguin Books.

Tharoor, S. (1989). *The great Indian novel*. London: Viking Penguin.

Vandenbos, G. R., Frank-McNeil, J., Norcross, J., & Freedheim, D. K. (Eds.). (1995). *The anatomy of psychotherapy* (pp. 19-31). Washington, DC: American Psychological Association.

I thank Joseph Shay and Suzi Naiburg for their contributions to earlier versions of this chapter.

CHAPTER 4

MAKING THE PROFESSIONAL PERSONAL AND THE PERSONAL PROFESSIONAL

RUTH G. DEAN, D.S.W.

I n the middle of a career, it is hard to see the trajectory being created by individual decisions. One follows interests, creates opportunities, accepts invitations, and moves along bit by bit, often too busy to think of the ways the pieces will fit together and ultimately define a professional life. It is necessary to become disembedded from the process in order to comprehend it in its entirety. Looking back, one wonders how these pieces came together. Is there a story line or plot through which the professional life became the person having it? How has the personal become professional and the professional personal?

In considering the evolution of my career, I note that several major shifts have occurred in my belief system. At the beginning, the paradigms that informed my work were drive theory and ego psychology and I was mainly focused on intrapsychic phenomena. Once I concluded my social work training, I was only minimally aware of the contexts in which clients lived their lives, including the diverse circumstances of their backgrounds. I held a modernist orientation to knowledge that conceived of theory as truth and the therapist as neutral and expert. I was more interested in "historical truth" (Spence, 1982) than in clients' narratives.

The belief system that currently underlies my teaching and clinical work derives from a relational perspective strongly influenced by feminist theory and consciousness. It is based in a postmodern orientation to knowledge that states that all knowledge is personal, partial, and contextual, and that we can not know reality apart from our constructions of it. I no longer believe that neutrality is possible or even advisable, and I consider myself more of a collaborator in the therapeutic process. I am interested in the circumstances of clients' lives and in the meaning they make of these circumstances. I am more likely to take clients' comments at face value and am not always interested in possible underlying meanings and symbolism. I see narratives as central forms through which people create and make sense of their lives and so I am very interested in the stories clients tell. Sometimes I tell stories if I think they will help move the therapy along. I am less reserved, more active, and more myself.

How did these changes come about? The answer to that question requires going back at least to the beginnings of my professional development and my choice of social work as a career. As I trace the evolution in my thinking, I am aware that this story is recreating and making sense of the past through the lenses of my current thinking. According to E. Bruner, "Stories give meaning to the present and enable us to see that present as part of a set of relationships involving a constituted past and a future. But narratives change, all stories are partial, all meanings incomplete. There is no fixed meaning in the past, for with each new telling the context varies, the audience differs, the story is modified..." (1986, p. 153). Here, then, is my current story.

When I went to college in the mid-1950s, unlike my friends who wanted to be teachers, I knew that social work was a possible career because my mother was a social worker. Not that my female friends and I were particularly career minded—we simply thought we should be able to support ourselves if that became a financial necessity. Our focus was on marriage as the desired outcome of a college education and we harbored our parents' concern that too much education could interfere with a "girl's" marriageability. These attitudes typified the cultural surround that went with growing up white, Jewish, female, and middle class in Pittsburgh in the 1950s. I inherited my family's political liberalism, along with the stereotypes and prejudices that were common in their community, and I had little contact with people who were not like me.

The only experiences that took me outside of this sheltered environment, and furthered my interest in social work, involved working as a camp counselor and club leader at community centers and settlement houses while I was in high school and college. These part-time and summer jobs brought me into contact with social workers whose understanding of human development and behavior impressed me. I also discovered that I loved working with children.

This discovery began with a group of eight preadolescent Black girls who were members of the cooking and volleyball club that I led at the settlement house. Funds at the settlement house were limited as were the "dues" the girls could pay, so we could seldom afford to buy all the ingredients required in the recipes we wanted to make. We settled on cake mixes, which fell within the limited range of my cooking skills at the time and seemed to provide as much instruction in cooking as the club members desired. We would quickly prepare the mix and then, while it baked, move into the gym and the volleyball game. When the game ended we would devour the cake and decide on the kind of mix to use the next week. Around the edges of these activities, the girls discussed their lives and fought and laughed with each other as I tried to help them talk about their problems. They brought an energy and enthusiasm to every meeting that was contagious and I worked to help them sustain this vitality as they maneuvered the challenges of adolescence and the pressures of poverty. Frustrated by the oppressive forces in their lives and my own limited skills, I imagined that if I were professionally trained my efforts would be more effective.

Social Work Education

My supervisors at the settlement house encouraged my interest in social work and so, upon graduation from college, I applied and was admitted to the University of Pittsburgh School of Social Work with the vague expectation that I would specialize in work with children. I was quickly diverted from this goal when, during an admission interview, I was offered a generous fellowship that required a medical specialization. Working in a hospital seemed like it might be interesting and so, with nothing more serious than a fantasy about having lunches in hospital cafeterias with my medical student boyfriend, I took the fellowship and refocused my career.

At the University of Pittsburgh, along with studying social policy and research, I learned Freudian theory in courses on human development and in clinical practice classes. One of my favorite readings was Erikson's *Childhood and Society* (1963), which offered some social context along with developmental theory while staying within the classical mode. Although we were taught to study the client-in-(the client's) situation, Freudian theory and an intrapsychic focus held sway. In casework class, we pored over case transcripts interpreting human behavior according to psychoanalytic concepts. We wrote diagnostic assessments of clients based on an integration of social and psychological factors and considered interventions that ranged from "environmental manipulation" to "supportive treatment" and, for some, "insight oriented treatment." This last option was the one that held the most interest for me and many of my classmates. My teachers taught analytic theory with reverence. This was the canon and I absorbed it as "truth."

However, I soon discovered that psychoanalytic theory did not enable me to appreciate the oppressive realities of clients' lives. My first field placement was with the welfare department. Carrying the black notebook that identified me as a "welfare worker" and feeling relatively safe, I walked up and down the streets of the Hill District, a poor, mostly Black ghetto adjacent to downtown Pittsburgh. One of my first clients, a middle-aged Black woman who lived on the top floor of a tenement with her boyfriend, provided a challenge to my efforts to be analytic. On my first visit, I climbed four flights of dark, narrow, foul-smelling stairs and hesitantly entered a small, clean and neatly arranged apartment while she and her boyfriend eyed me suspiciously. My job was to re-determine her eligibility for welfare and there was certain information I had to obtain.

As I nervously hurried through my questions, making every effort to use her answers to support her eligibility, she suddenly took her shoe off and slammed it against the wall, killing a cockroach that landed on the table between us. I jumped, and we all laughed and then relaxed together as the interview proceeded. When it was time for me to leave, it was beginning to get dark and her boyfriend walked me down to the streetcar stop, sensitively showing me a place to wait next to the only other white person on the street.

What were the lessons of those early days? First, that field work (particularly the kind that required home visits) added an essential dimension that was largely missing in my classroom work—a view of the actual conditions in which poor people live their lives. In the classroom, I learned about the structure of welfare agencies in this country but the first-hand experience of the system through the eyes of clients was powerful and informative. Once I got over the shock of entering a very different world and the sense of helplessness that these conditions inspired, I was relieved to discover that if I could find a way to bring myself into the interview and connect with a client, we could get some "therapeutic" work done. I was being taught that building relationships with clients was central, and I was discovering, beginning with the girls' club members, that this was true.

In my first job as a social worker on the home care team at Montefiore Hospital in Pittsburgh, my objective was to help patients and families manage the impact of illness and mediate difficult aspects of their lives. Under the tutelage of a very talented social work supervisor named Sarah Bergholz, I learned not to think of myself as a therapist but as a social worker, using psychoanalytic theory when I could find ways to apply it, but also drawing heavily on common sense and practical, problem-solving approaches.

ON-THE-JOB-TRAINING

In 1962, after working for a year in Pittsburgh, I took the advice of friends from Boston and moved there, taking a job at Beth Israel Hospital. In my first weeks on the job, I was struck with the extent to which the Social Work Department was respected by the doctors for its high level of professionalism, but I was even more drawn to the Psychiatry Clinic located adjacent to Social Service.

I arrived during the final years of Grete Bibring's tenure as director—a golden age of psychiatry at Beth Israel. The senior members of the psychiatry department were Europeans, like Bibring, who had trained with Freud and his disciples. The department was renowned as a training center and for pioneering a form of psychiatric consultation to the medical and surgical units. Psychoanalytic concepts were taught to the house staff to help them understand the issues involved in the care of medical and surgical patients. I quickly joined my social work colleagues, attending psychiatric grand rounds, ward consults, and teaching conferences run by the psychiatrists, and absorbed as much as I could. Thus, my earliest exposure to psychoanalytic therapies in vivo occurred in this pragmatic and intellectually stimulating atmosphere.

Classical theory was taught in both pure and modified

form in a fairly formal and hierarchical manner—very much in the European tradition. At Grand Rounds, Dr. Bibring would be the first to comment after a speaker had finished. Then various members of her department, in order of their seniority, would stand and offer ideas. Psychiatric residents were mostly seen and not heard at these conferences and social workers were even more invisible, although their roles treating parents in the Child Psychiatry Department were firmly established.

My assignment was in the Medical Outpatient Department. As I assimilated lessons about the interplay of psychic factors, somatic symptoms, and personality, I developed a conceptual base for my work that was rooted in classical drive theory and ego psychology. These paradigms were consistent with my social work training and I adapted them readily to my work on the medical units. It was useful to think about ego strengths, defenses, and character structure as I tried to help patients and families manage medical crises and return to pre-illness levels of functioning. Although I enjoyed the collaboration and high levels of activity on the medical floors and the opportunities to see the immediate effects of a helpful interpretation or supportive comment, my growing interest in psychoanalytic theory led me to look for ways to learn more about psychotherapy.

SHIFTING FOCUS

My opportunity came when one of my patients, an African-American woman with asthma, high levels of anxiety, and occasional panic reactions, was referred to the psychiatry clinic by her medical doctor. Because she and I had an existing relationship, I was asked to do the psychiatric evaluation, and then, at an Intake Conference, to proceed with the recommended long-term treatment. I agreed on the condition that I would be assigned a psychiatric supervisor who could teach me more about psychotherapy. At that point in time, there were no supervisors in the social work department who would have claimed this expertise, which was held exclusively by psychiatrists and a small number of psychologists in the psychiatry department. My social work supervisor was encouraging of my growth and cross-departmental training as long as it did not interfere with covering my regular assignments.

This shift in my focus paralleled shifts in the profession of social work as many social workers, like myself, sought training in psychotherapy. The early leaders in social work such as Jane Adams and Mary Richmond, known for their efforts on behalf of social change and oppressed populations, were replaced by social workers such as Gordan Hamilton and Florence Hollis whose focus was on individual, psychological change—largely through "long-term treatment." This was the emphasis during my graduate training and, despite the appeal of my work with poor clients as a student and with medical patients at the hospital, I set my sights on becoming a psychotherapist.

By then, Grete Bibring had retired and Jack Vorenberg was acting chief of Psychiatry. He was most gracious about assigning a supervisor and I acquired a few more psychiatric cases (at my request) so that I could get the maximum benefit from the supervision. I began to do evaluations of people referred to the psychiatry clinic and to attend intake conferences. I was delighted to have maneuvered this shift in my work and supervision by taking advantage of an employment environment that was flexible. This was the late 1960s and early 1970s, the era of the Vietnam War and the Great Society.

Many of us protested the war by doing psychiatric evaluations of men who believed that their emotional conditions made them ineligible for the draft. We found ways, whenever possible, to endorse their deferments. At the same time, the clinic benefited from Lyndon's Johnson's Great Society policies that made mental health services available to people who could not afford private treatment. We paid much less attention to financial accountability in those days and provided treatment to each client for as long as seemed necessary at costs that clients could manage. The outpatient psychiatric clinic, with its flexible fee scale, attracted people with low incomes from neighborhoods adjacent to the hospital along with the many college and graduate students who populated Boston. Some of my clients paid as little as a dollar a session.

The flexible and permissive atmosphere that made treatment available to many clients, and in-service training open to all mental health professionals, also allowed for opportunities to expand one's job possibilities. After five years of seeing clients at Beth Israel and learning about the therapeutic process, I made another important shift in my career—I began to teach. I wanted to talk about the ideas I was learning and found a ready audience in the case aides in the Social Service Department. They were college graduates who often had some understanding of psychology and human behavior and were hired to handle the more straightforward social service referrals involving the provision of concrete services or discharge planning. While no one expected case aides to be psychotherapists, I thought their work could benefit from some understanding of psychoanalytic concepts as applied in a medical setting. I was imitating the early teaching conferences I had attended.

EARLY EXPERIENCES AS A PSYCHOTHERAPIST

In this heady atmosphere, I was receiving intensive on-the-job training in psychotherapy and teaching, along with ongoing experiences of collaboration, consultation, and short-term work on the medical units. The paradigms that prevailed continued to be classical psychoanalytic drive theory and ego psychology. With my "therapy patients," I was largely inactive, asking questions and offering occasional interpretations or clarifications of behavior patterns. I assessed their ego functioning, noted central conflicts and defensive structure, and thought in terms of oedipal and pre-oedipal issues. I would encourage patients to free associate and try to understand the symbolic meanings and transference implications of their remarks. I operated under the belief that if I could help clients understand their patterns, and fully appreciate the futility in their neurotic ways, they would change. In those pre-Kohutian days, one's stance could be a little harsh and even shaming. "It isn't surprising that you feel frustrated, given your tendency to get involved with unavailable men," one might say to a female patient whose relationships always ended unhappily.

A New Paradigm

My psychiatric supervisor, Len Freedman, brought about a welcome expansion of my understanding of human behavior and ways of doing therapy by introducing me to object relations theory, a paradigm that was becoming more influential throughout the psychiatric community. I inhaled the work of Winnicott (1965), Klein (1964), Fairbairn (1952), and Guntrip (1971, 1975) and their ideas became the base of theoretical beliefs that continue to inform my work. These writings took hold because they allowed a broader conceptualization of clinical work that was especially helpful with clients who struggled with issues related to early attachment difficulties. Winnicott's contributions had the most appeal for me and Len helped me apply ideas about the true and false self, the holding environment, the capacity to be alone, the capacity for concern, and the need to see one's important objects survive one's fantasized destruction of them.

One clinical vignette stands out from this period and demonstrates the shift in clinical stance that I was beginning to make under the influence of object relations theory.

> A young, Jewish woman who was working on her doctorate in English at a local university came for therapy because of a long-standing depression, which she thought was interfering with her school achievement and her relationships. She was the only child of concentration camp survivors and had been born in a displaced persons camp after the war. She grew up in an unhappy, depressed home with an ever-present sense of the horror of her parents' war experience. At the beginning of one of our weekly meetings she described a time in her childhood when, on a shopping trip with her mother, she saw a doll in a store window that she wanted desperately. She wept as she told how she never even mentioned her desire to her mother because in her family, it seemed so frivolous. Her mother wouldn't possibly have understood the importance to my patient of having this beautiful doll. Seeing what I knew to be a familiar pattern in her life, I commented on how accustomed she was to accom-

modating her parents' needs and being the good, quiet, unde-
manding daughter—characteristics that continued to permeate
her current relationships to her detriment.

Then toward the end of the session she mentioned that she
would like to start coming twice a week and wondered if this
were possible. Taken aback, having never seen a patient twice
weekly, I equivocated, saying that I would like to think about it
and talk more the following week. What I really wanted was to
consult my supervisor about the possibility of doing more
intensive work with her. When I raised the question with Len,
he pointed out that my client was letting her "true self"
emerge in the therapy. This was her way of asking me for the
doll. He indicated that it would have been better if I had said
"yes" immediately but he thought she and I could recover from
that error if I said "yes" the following week.

In this way I was being taught to not just interpret, clarify
themes, and provide insight, but, in keeping with an object relations perspective, to let the work occur within the evolving therapeutic relationship. This advice resonated with my own inclinations. In contrast to my stiff pronouncements and efforts at neutrality, I was now being encouraged to respond in ways that were
more direct and emotionally authentic and to use the therapy not
just to establish intellectual insights but also to create an experience of a responsive, connected relationship.

THE LESSONS OF MY OWN PSYCHOTHERAPY

Both approaches to treatment were reflected in my own
psychotherapy. My therapist, a senior member of the Boston psychiatric community, tended to be relatively inactive and traditional in his approach. Using the frameworks of drive theory and ego
psychology, he enabled me to gain insight into my self-defeating
ways and experience the frustration associated with this behavior.
Sometimes I experienced a lot of shame associated with these sessions, but I accepted that as necessary to the change process and

incorporated it at times in my work with clients. For example, on one occasion when I complained bitterly about a reassignment at work, I said of my boss, "She has no right to treat me this way." My therapist pointed out quickly that, as my boss, she indeed had the "right" to change my assignment. Knowing that what he said was true, I felt chagrined at the inappropriateness of my expectations. After I studied self-psychology, I realized that this lesson might have been less shaming if it had been offered along with some empathy for having an assignment changed without consultation.

But my therapist could also be direct, honest, and emotionally responsive and work in a manner more grounded in object relations theory. There were a few times when he gave advice or shared stories from his own life that he thought would be helpful. Two examples stand out and both are related to my marriage. After getting engaged at age 39 to a divorced man whose young teenage children were living with him, I became afraid of going forward with the marriage. I explained to my therapist that I was sure I would ruin my fiancé's family. We understood the childhood roots of this belief—I had often been told that I was "ruining things for the family" when I made a fuss about decisions my parents made. But this awareness did not help me let go of my fears and I came close to breaking my engagement. In a way that was quite uncharacteristic of him, my therapist offered some very direct advice. He said that there was no guarantee that the marriage would work out, but, he thought, if I broke my engagement I would always regret not taking the risk to find out. That statement was enormously helpful and allowed me to move ahead.

Later, when I came in and talked about the difficult time I was having with my step-children, he would listen and then explain their perspective. He pointed out that they were only children and wondered why I saw them as so powerful. These questions were helpful and allowed me to analyze my reactions but I was bothered by his consistent tendency to empathize with their position and not mine. Finally I came in one hour and begged him to please hear my story just once from my perspective and recognize how painful it was for me. He was quiet for a while and then provided some information about himself that helped us get the therapy back on track. He explained that his parents had divorced when he was young and his father remarried a woman he didn't like. He told of an incident when his stepmother read his diary including a description of how much he disliked her and then informed his father who made him recant and apologize to her. He said he could see how his experiences had gotten in the way of his hearing about my family life from my perspective, and he let me know that he regretted what had happened between us. My relief at understanding his empathic failure was profound, and I was most grateful for his honesty.

I believe that those times of human connection were what carried the therapy. They were the moments that stayed with me long after it ended. While they could be seen as lapses in my therapist's fairly traditional, neutral approach, in my mind they were essential. Gradually, I came to be less afraid of letting my true self enter my clinical work when it felt appropriate.

The experiences in my treatment and supervision that I have just described might seem commonplace in today's therapeutic milieu with the current focus on intersubjectivity and interest in the uses of self-disclosure. In the late 1960s and 1970s they were more unusual—certainly different from the way psychotherapy was taught and written about, if not from the way it was practiced. Early social work training and supervision with its pragmatic lessons, my psychiatric supervisor's emphasis on object relations theory, and my therapist's direct responsiveness were to expand my understanding of ways of using the therapeutic relationship and making it the centerpiece of the treatment. I directed my attention to my relationship with a client. Instead of focusing on more intellectual interpretations of transference manifestations (although, I did this sometimes), I mainly tried to understand the client by feeling my way into what was happening between us and then providing, through my responsiveness, what I thought was emotionally needed.

HISTORIC TRENDS AND CAREER DEVELOPMENTS

The writings of Heinz Kohut began to be known in Boston in the 1970s, causing considerable controversy in the psychoanalytic community. I attended a conference in Boston at which Kohut spoke, not long before his death. One of the more conservative members of the Beth Israel psychiatry clinic sat beside me and muttered intermittently throughout his speech. Her responses to Kohut were similar to the views of a substantial number of the psychiatric community in Boston. She asserted that Kohut's ideas were *not* new and she resented that they were being presented and greeted as if they were. Furthermore, she was angry that he was not giving credit to the object relations theorists who provided the foundation for his writings and work. I listened but tried to keep an open mind.

Kohut concluded the conference with a plea to the psychiatric community to live with the tensions created because his ideas did not fit into a classic conflict and drive theory conceptualization. He argued that there might be a continuum along which both theories could be placed, with self-psychology applying to patients with pre-oedipal problems whereas drive theory was more useful for patients with Oedipal issues. He wanted psychiatrists to entertain different ideas, even if contradictory, and see which made more sense over time.

I was not very caught up in the nuances of these debates, but I read the revolutionary paper of Kohut, "The Two Analyses of Mr. Z" (1979), and then, *The Restoration of the Self* (1977) with great interest. I discussed his work with colleagues, and many of us liked the emphasis on empathy. As I considered some of the more humiliating lessons of my own treatment, it seemed worthwhile to find more empathic and less shaming ways of helping patients.

Another historic development that had an impact on my work was the introduction of brief forms of psychoanalytic treatment—particularly the models developed by Mann (1973) and Sifneos (1979). When John Nemiah became director of the Beth Israel Psychiatry Clinic in 1968, he brought Peter Sifneos to the

Beth Israel with him. Sifneos set up a training program in STAPP, short-term anxiety-provoking psychotherapy, and many of us attended seminars to learn this model. Patients had to pass a set of rigorous standards to be accepted into STAPP and the standing joke at the clinic during that time was that most of the therapists wouldn't have qualified. While I came to prefer James Mann's brief treatment model, also demonstrated at conferences at Beth Israel and elsewhere, there were important lessons to be learned from both approaches. The fundamental idea that I garnered from this exposure was that you could do a piece of intensive, focused work with a patient in a short period of time and that if successful, the change in one sector of personality could help the patient resolve other issues.

I applied these concepts in my work with students at the Brandeis University Counseling Center where I held a part-time job for several years as a supervisor and clinician. These experiences became the foundation of my understanding of brief treatment—a subject I was eventually to teach.

CAREER CONSOLIDATION AND A SHIFT TO ACADEMIA

At this point in my professional life, my conceptual framework was an amalgam of different kinds of learning—theoretical and experiential. I had added object relations theory and later self-psychology to my earlier theoretical base in drive theory and ego psychology. It was not so much that I embraced multiple perspectives within a meta-theory that suggested each was a different version (or vision) of reality. That would come later with the study of constructivism. At that point, adding a new theory was still grounded in the objectivist belief that it provided a closer approximation of the truth. However, the first paper I published, "The Use of Empathy in Supervision" (Dean, 1984), focused on different ways of knowing the client and the different stories of a client that exist in supervision, prefiguring my later interest in constructivism and narrative.

Experientially, I was becoming more sure of myself as a therapist. I had a busy private practice and worked half-time at

Beth Israel, seeing clients in brief and long-term treatment. I was supervising social work students and psychiatric residents, running the MSW student training unit at Beth Israel, and the teaching conferences for students and case aides. I was providing group supervision for social workers in the department on their psychotherapy cases. There were enough cases to go around and many opportunities for social work training in long-term, open-ended treatment. In contrast to my early days at Beth Israel, social workers, psychologists, and psychiatrists could be experts at psychotherapy and we supervised, taught, and learned from one another. No one was very territorial and a comfortable, interdisciplinary, collegial atmosphere existed for a brief time. Then, in the late 1970s, a growing emphasis on financial accountability in the hospital led to increased competitiveness, an emphasis on the biological nature of mental illness, and a closing of ranks by the psychiatry department.

At that time my work with social work students brought me in contact with the directors of field work at Simmons College School of Social Work—first Diana Waldfogel and later Jim McCracken. I spoke with them both about my interest in teaching at Simmons. By then, having decided that I wanted a teaching career, I used every opportunity to teach, hoping that these experiences would eventually lead to a full or part-time faculty position. In 1978, I was offered and accepted a part-time job as a field advisor at Simmons which eventually led to a full-time, tenure-track position as assistant professor at Simmons, teaching clinical practice.

HEIGHTENED AWARENESS

At first, teaching Advanced Clinical Practice to second year master's level social work students at Simmons was a continuation of my interest in psychotherapy. Most of my students were interested in psychoanalytic principles and many wanted to be therapists in clinic or private practice settings. But gradually, under the influence of Carol Swenson, a new chairperson in the clinical practice sequence, the emphasis at Simmons shifted to one more consistent with the practice curriculum of other schools of social work—an ecological model that focused on transactions between the outer world and people's inner lives. There was an emphasis on sensitivity to ethnic, racial, and cultural diversity and a concern with social justice and the oppressive forces with which people struggle. While there was still room for teaching about intrapsychic factors and psychoanalytic theory, this content was now being placed within a much broader perspective. With an appreciation for the ways in which I was reconnecting with social work values and earlier interests, I tried to be responsive to the new curriculum and integrate it with the psychoanalytic principles that continued to inform my own work.

Being part of a social work setting raised my consciousness in many areas. As my colleagues articulated feminist issues, I came to more fully understand this perspective and adopt it. The psychoanalytic feminist critiques of the phallocentrism of Freudian theory by Benjamin (1988) and others led me to jettison some aspects while retaining others. African-American colleagues and students brought to my awareness a closer view of the impact of racism as it operated in the school as well as in society. The challenges in regard to racism and feminism echoed the changing awareness of these issues in society. These were concerns with which I had always identified, although now I was better informed and more fully conscious of the issues. But the consciousness raising that occurred in the school in relation to gay and lesbian issues had a more dramatic effect as it totally changed my understanding of homosexuality and attitude toward it.

I had been raised with the conventional stereotypes and prevailing professional prejudices toward homosexuals, and had been taught to see homosexuality as a form of at least limited development, if not pathology. While I had worked with a few gay and lesbian clients, my understanding of their lives was very limited, and although I was well intentioned, I was ill-informed and uneasy. Gay and lesbian students at Simmons lobbied the faculty to include more content on their issues in the curriculum in general and to have one week during the academic year in which sexual diversity would be the focus of teaching across the curriculum.

At first, I approached that week with trepidation. But, my gay and lesbian students helped out and their coming out stories, told at presentations in connection with Sexual Diversity Week, allowed me to see them as individuals struggling not with a choice but an orientation that for many was basic. I learned first hand of their experiences with prejudice and stigmatization, and became better informed about what it is like to be gay or lesbian. This exposure gradually began to dispel my earlier misunderstandings and homophobia. It is hard to convey the profound impact of this new awareness to those who take an enlightened view of homosexuality for granted. I count it as one of the most important changes in my adult life with many ramifications for my teaching and practice. My coming of age in regards to these matters paralleled changes in the mental health field.

MORE EDUCATION AND ANOTHER PARADIGM SHIFT

Stimulated by my heightened consciousness and the intellectual tensions created by it, and recognizing the need for a doctorate if I wanted an academic career, I enrolled in the doctoral program in social work at Boston College in 1984. The most important influences from this education occurred in a course entitled The Philosophy of Practice, taught by Richard Bolan, an urban planner with an interest in philosophy and an ability to use it to inform professional practice (Bolan, 1980). We read contemporary philosophical writings concerning the shift from empirical theory to critical theory along with various critiques of positivism and the movement to a post-positivist orientation. In the postmodern accounts of the nature of professional practice, there was an emphasis on reflexivity, intuitive processes and the kind of "knowing-in-action" that is at the heart of clinical work (Schon, 1983).

This was my first exposure to constructivism and to critiques of objectivist views of knowledge and it became the foundation of a new belief system. These were the main constructs in my understanding:

- constructionist and constructivist orientations to knowledge assert that we cannot objectively know the structures that exist beyond ourselves;

• our knowledge of these structures occurs through inter-personal, social, and psychological processes and is always partial, situated in language, and offering a perspective on reality;

• constructivists emphasize the role of cognitive structures in influencing the ways that meaning is formulated while social constructionists emphasize the role of cultural, social, historical, and political influences;

• language is not a mirror of nature but, instead, "language and reflection actually shape experience" (Stern, 1997, p. 26);

• terms such as postmodernism, post-structuralism and constructionism refer to different strands of the philosophical movement that began in the 1960s and challenged the objec-tivist roots of science and the post-enlightenment belief in a stable, knowable world.

What was the meaning of assimilating these ideas at this point in my career? They had a major impact. Until then I had held theories as sacred truths and seen supervisors and mentors as experts. Now, as I became aware that theories were meta-narra-tives, each representing a different view, I recognized that all views, including those of "experts," were partial and not to be privileged. The postmodern emphasis on personal knowledge, reflexivity, and multiple perspectives gave me permission to trust my own knowledge. Because the doctoral studies came at the mid-point of my professional life, there was a coming together of the educational process and personal development such that the learning reinforced the self-confidence I was gaining professional-ly. I was eager to explore the implications of these ideas for clinical practice.

NEW SETTINGS FOR PRACTICE

In 1989, as an extension of my interest in constructivism and social constructionism, I spent a sabbatical year studying fam-ily treatment and narrative therapies. I visited the Centro Milanese di Terapia della Famiglia in Milan to gain a better understanding of the Milan school which occupied a critical place in the evolution of systemic and constructivist family treatment. Returning to Boston, I took a course in narrative and systemic approaches at Cambridge Family Institute where, under the excellent tutelage of Sally Ann Roth and Kathy Weingarten, I learned more about working with client's narratives and crystallized my own thinking. I began to write about epistemology and the application of narrative approaches to social work practice and teaching (Dean, 1989; Dean & Fenby, 1992).

My way of thinking about and doing clinical work had changed. While I did not give up my interest in psychoanalytic theory, I added a constructionist orientation. Having once seen Freudian theory as a "truth," I now recognized the usefulness of holding multiple theoretical perspectives and seeing each as a possible interpretation of behavior or model for practice. Having given up the notion of neutrality and recognizing the extent to which the observer inevitably influences that which is observed, I was more willing to put my own ideas forward in a clinical interview—labeled clearly as my ideas. I saw the social and political aspects of diagnostic categories and the fallacy of translating the client's story into the therapist's diagnostic language. I became interested in creating a collaborative process in the clinical relationship through which meaning is co-constructed by client and clinician together. From the family therapists, I learned the value of using different kinds of questions that helped clients create new meanings and stories that led to the changes they desired. Two clinical experiences that I began during my sabbatical year gave further momentum to these explorations—volunteer work with the Social Service Department of Chelsea Memorial Health Center and volunteering as a group leader at AIDS Action Committee, a grass roots organization that raised money and provided services to people with AIDS.

I volunteered in Chelsea to gain first-hand knowledge of the experiences my students were having in their field work settings. In this poor, racially and ethnically diverse community, I worked with families, couples, and individual adults and children for the next five years. I saw once again the impact of poverty and various forms of oppression on people's lives. While my psychodynamic perspective helped in some ways, it was not enough. I had to pay attention to the contexts in which clients lived, and find ways to talk with them that bridged the differences between their worlds and mine. It helped to be open, active, curious, and flexible and to appreciate both the circumstances of their lives and the ways they made sense of these circumstances.

I learned, for example, that when a four-year-old boy became very hungry at certain intervals during our work and devoured the snacks I provided, it was not because he was emotionally needy. His hunger occurred at the time in the month before his mother's next welfare check was due when she characteristically ran out of money and food. While her therapist tried to help her become a better manager of her meager welfare check, I had to help him manage his hunger. I also learned first hand about the roots of racism from this boy as he talked about the "bad Cambodians" in his neighborhood whose "badness" as far as I could determine had to do with having more toys than he did and not sharing them.

In another situation, I came to understand the challenge of helping a depressed and impoverished young Irish mother maintain sobriety as she explained, "It's not sobriety that I'm afraid of, it's reality." Her reality was indeed grim, and her comment gave new meaning to my understanding of the recovery process. The approaches associated with the narrative therapies often helped with these clients, but their situations taught me something of the limits of both narrative and psychodynamic approaches. While it was sometimes possible to help people change, at other times the intersecting oppressions in their lives made change impossible. It was not a question of motivation but rather one of being overwhelmed by life circumstances.

Horrified by the devastating impact of the AIDS epidemic on the gay community, and more comfortable in my work with gay students and clients, I volunteered at AIDS Action Committee and co-led a support group for gay men with AIDS from 1989 to 1996. This powerful experience expanded my awareness of what it was like to be a gay man living with AIDS in Boston in the 1990s. It also provided many insights into group process (Dean, 1995, 1998). Although I had been trained in a psychodynamic model of group work at Beth Israel, I now incorporated the lessons of the narrative therapies in my group work and was alert to the importance of stories. While I saw the constraints of oppression and illness on the members' lives, I also saw them use stories to create new meaning, change their lives, and, through political action, bring about social change. My co-leader and I experimented with formats that encouraged storytelling.

For example, we began meetings with a "check-in" period in which we would go around the group and give each person time to tell briefly of the important events of the week and highlight any subjects they wanted to talk about in more depth later in the meeting. It was important to the group members that the leaders also checked in. While we would talk about personal events, we were careful to choose those that would not be burdensome to the group. But there were times when we told of painful and important happenings in our lives such as the death of my co-leader's mother who lived with her during the final stages of her illness, or the death of my nephew from AIDS. The men in the group were responsive and helpful, and showed us that support moved in both directions.

At times, a story told during "check-in" would serve as the focus for the entire group meeting.

> One night Greg told about how he was fired from his job because of what he was made to think was ineptitude. He had been under pressure at work, and, while feeling ill, made several mistakes which were the stated reasons for the firing. When we questioned his assumption, another story emerged. He had been fired shortly after he disclosed his HIV status to one of his supervisors. Group members wondered if Greg had been discriminated against because he had AIDS. Their questions led

*Greg to seek legal counsel, sue his employer, and ultimately
receive a small but very meaningful settlement. Throughout
the process he reported back to the group. The men continued
to support his efforts when he became discouraged and ultimately helped him decide to accept the settlement offered by his
employer. Through this action, he and the group became part of
a larger political movement protesting discriminatory employment practices and claiming the rights of people living with
AIDS.*

This period of experimentation with narrative approaches
in different practice settings has been accompanied by my immersion in reading and writing (Dean, 1993a; 1993b; Dean & Fleck-
Henderson, 1992) about social constructionism and narrative therapies. It has led to a refocusing of my approach to practice and
teaching.

MAKING THE PERSONAL PROFESSIONAL

From the time I began working at Beth Israel in the early
1960s, I worked hard to assimilate and then articulate psychoanalytic theory as a supervisor and teacher, but it was never a totally
comfortable fit. With the discovery of postmodernism, I felt as if I
had found my theoretical and clinical home. The constructivist orientation to multiple perspectives resonated with my social work
training and clinical experience because it left more room for an
appreciation of the circumstances of people's lives and the diversity of their experiences. Whereas at a time of professional insecuri-
ty, I clung tightly to being expert and "professional," now I was
ready to give up this hierarchical format and think of treatment as
a collaboration in which the "expert" knowledge that clients
brought was respected. This was particularly obvious in Chelsea
and in the AIDS group where I did indeed have much to learn
from clients and group members. There was a coming together of
new learning and a growing security as a clinician that allowed me
to experiment.

The constructionist focus on ideas as well as feelings with

the therapist able to offer ideas—not as answers but as possibilities—reminded me of the most helpful aspects of my own therapy.
It also made sense to use questions not so much for purposes of
obtaining information but to open up new meanings. Sometimes
questions could help clients find stories at the margins of awareness that revealed preferred aspects of themselves. If these stories
could be brought into focus and elaborated, they could replace the
problem-saturated stories that dominated people's lives (White &
Epston, 1990).

The following example shows my use of a narrative
approach along with more traditional psychoanalytic understanding.

> I was working with a young man who came to a session
> expressing considerable shame at his tendencies to keep to him-
> self. He had just come back from a work conference in San
> Francisco and had been severely criticized by a co-worker for
> going off on his own and not sticking with the group from
> work. He was puzzled by this reaction. It had not occurred to
> him to hang out with the people from his workplace—he was
> more interested in exploring San Francisco.

> At first I tried linking his behavior to his past according to the
> understanding of his early relationships that we had acquired
> in the treatment thus far. But helping him understand some of
> the sources of his tendency to do things on his own, made him
> feel more shame. With this approach not working I turned to a
> narrative strategy, and tried to see if there might be another
> story about his aloneness that carried a different meaning. I
> asked if he might describe himself as a person who "covets
> aloneness." When he agreed but said he thought this was bad, I
> asked if he could imagine any ways that "coveting aloneness"
> could tell him something good about himself. Returning to the
> subject of his experience at the conference, he explained that he
> enjoyed his independence and had an agenda of sights he want-
> ed to see in San Francisco. I suggested that he seemed to be a
> person who valued independence and had his own agenda. He

agreed and together we elaborated on these qualities and their effects on his life. Feeling better about these new descriptions of himself, he could then talk of conflicting wishes—sometimes he sought aloneness and sometimes he wanted to be with people. We discussed how at times it was hard to sort out which he wanted.

At the end of the meeting, he told me, "You said something that really helped me tonight." When I asked what that had been, he became playful, in contrast to his earlier, depressed mood, and said "I'm not going to tell you." Then he relented and explained, "It had never before occurred to me that coveting aloneness could have its good side." He seemed quite genuinely pleased when he left and told me later that this conversation marked a turning point in the treatment and in his beginning to feel better about himself.

In constructivist terms, we had co-created a new story. It wasn't that he necessarily become less desirous of being alone but his relationship to that aspect of himself changed. I asked questions that allowed him to unearth a different story about being a person who chose to be alone. I named the attributes we were discussing in ways that allowed him to appreciate them more. He then was able to elaborate on the new story and incorporate it into a more positive view of himself. I was active and I was not neutral. This is in keeping with the post-positivist belief that there are always values implicit in the questions therapists ask and the ones they don't ask, in the ways they name some things and call attention to them and ignore others. I moved from an initial psychodynamic approach to a narrative one and then, when this led the client to tell of his conflict about being with people, back to a psychodynamic way of thinking. And finally, I was interested in the client's idea of what was and wasn't helpful in the treatment and sought to discuss this and integrate it into our work.

This brief example illustrates how I might incorporate some of the newer, narrative approaches within my usual way of working with clients. I have not replaced psychodynamic theories with narrative/constructivist perspectives but instead use these ideas in combination and enjoy a greater flexibility. Remembering Kohut's suggestion of tolerating the tension inherent in trying to combine perspectives that are not totally consistent, I endeavor to do so. Most recently I have been exploring the limits of a narrative/constructivist orientation and the relativism that accompanies it in relation to social justice and ethical norms (Dean & Rhodes, 1998).

REFLECTIONS ON PERSONAL AND PROFESSIONAL TRENDS

Looking back on my career, at the beginning of my seventh decade, I feel that I have come full circle. With my second sabbatical in 1999, I have begun to explore the impact of narrative approaches on cross-cultural practice. A grant for travel and study allowed me to pursue these interests at a conference in Australia on narrative approaches and at the School of Social Work at Curtin University in Perth as a visiting scholar and teacher. Upon returning I began work as a volunteer at the Solomon Carter Fuller Mental Health Center in the South End where I see Hispanic and African American families and children. At this point in my professional life, my roots in social work seem better represented in my current practice. I have embraced new clinical approaches that I see as having considerable merit with a range of client population groups, while still valuing the rich psychoanalytic training and background that serves as a foundation for my work. Although I am enjoying a sense that my current practice and teaching are aligned with my personal values, it is inevitable that the work in the South End will shake up these assumptions and show me the limits of my understanding. If I can learn from my South End clients more about the problems in their lives and find ways to be helpful, this will enrich my ongoing teaching and writing. I know no other way to step outside my prejudices and expand my knowledge except to connect with new communities and populations and experiment with new practice approaches.

As a teacher, I often think about the future of social work and psychotherapy as I consider what are the important lessons to pass on to my students. In this age of managed care, their contacts with clients in their field-work placements can be very brief. Yet, it still seems important for them to have knowledge of a range of therapy models while appreciating their limits so they will bring some depth of understanding to the agency-based practice for which they are trained and not be solely governed by solution-focused approaches. In the future, managed care may well limit the possibilities of working in open-ended formats with some clients and it will become imperative for all practitioners to find ways of flexibly providing service while managing these limits—by doing time-limited work and serial work with clients who return as problems indicate and insurance permits. At the same time, we must continue to advocate for longer treatment formats in those situations when it is important and keep clients informed of the options they may lose by accepting insurance restrictions and coming to believe that very brief treatment is appropriate for all conditions.

However, I do not think that managed care poses the only danger to contemporary clinical practice. I have also been struck by the parochialism of some of my social work and psychiatric colleagues and the tendency for each of the mental health professions (social work, psychology, psychiatry, and nursing) to become more insular. In addition to this professional isolationism, there is also an unwillingness to move beyond the "tried and true" theoretical frameworks, to experiment with new models, and do clinical work with a range of patient populations. Too often my psychoanalytic friends are unwilling to see the merit in other theoretical approaches while my fellow social workers—especially those in academic circles—are uncomfortable with psychoanalytic frameworks. My experience has taught that there is much to be gleaned from drawing on a range of theories while recognizing that each is partial and limited, derived in a particular context, and not representative of "truth" about the human condition and the ways that people change.

Exposure to different client groups can also be a powerful mechanism for growth as a clinician if one does not begin by assuming that one's ways of working are necessarily appropriate for all client situations. We need to learn how to help different clients by paying careful attention to what they tell us works for them. The best moments in my career have come from trying out new theories, experimenting with new models of practice, and seeking experiences with different groups of clients. This has enabled me to find my professional self in the places and practices that are most compatible with the person I believe myself to be. I wish no less for those therapists who will represent the field in the next millennium.

REFERENCES

Benjamin, J. (1988). *The bonds of love*. New York: Pantheon Books.

Bolan, R. S. (1980). The practitioner as theorist. *Journal of the American Planning Association, 46*, 261-274.

Bruner, E. (1986). Ethnography as narrative. In V. W. Turner and E. M. Bruner (Eds.), *The anthropology of experience* (pp. 139-155). Urbana and Chicago: University of Illinois Press.

Dean, R. G. (1984). The role of empathy in supervision, *Clinical Social Work Journal, 12*, 129-139.

Dean, R. G. (1989). Ways of knowing in clinical practice, *Clinical Social Work Journal, 17*, 116-127

Dean, R. G. (1993a). Constructivism: An approach to clinical practice. *Smith College Studies in Social Work. 63*, 127-146.

Dean, R. G. (1993b). Teaching a constructivist approach to clinical practice. *Journal of Teaching in Social Work*, (Special Edition), *8*, 55-76. Also in J. Laird (Ed.), *Revisioning social work education: A social constructionist approach* (pp. 55-75). New York: Haworth Press.

Dean, R. G. (1995). Stories of AIDS: The use of narrative as an approach to understanding in an AIDS support group. *Clinical Social Work Journal, 23*, 287-304.

Dean, R. G. (1998). A narrative approach to groups. *Clinical Social Work Journal, 26*, 23-37.

Dean, R. G., & Fenby, B. L. (1992). Exploring epistemologies:

Social work action as a reflection of philosophical assumptions, *Journal of Social Work Education, 25,* 46-54.

Dean, R. G., & Fleck-Henderson, A. (1992). Teaching clinical theory and practice through a constructivist lens. *Journal of Teaching in Social Work, 6,* 3-20.

Dean, R. G. & Rhodes, M. (1998). Social constructionism and ethics: What makes a "better" story? *Families in Society, 79,* 245-261.

Erikson, E. (1963). *Childhood and society.* New York: Norton.

Fairbairn, W. R. D. (1952). *An object relations theory of the personality.* New York: Basic Books.

Guntrip, H. (1971). *Psychoanalytic theory, therapy, and the self.* New York: Basic Books.

Guntrip, H. (1975). My experience of analysis with Fairbairn and Winnicott. *International Review of Psychoanalysis, 2,* 145-156.

Klein, M. (1964). *Contributions to psychoanalysis.* New York: McGraw-Hill.

Kohut, H. (1977). *The restoration of the self.* Madison, CT: International Universities Press.

Kohut, H. (1979). The two analyses of Mr. Z. *International Journal of Psychoanalysis, 60,* 3-27.

Mann, J. (1973). *Time-limited psychotherapy.* Cambridge, MA: Harvard University Press.

Schon, D. A. (1983). *The reflective practitioner.* New York: Basic Books.

Sifneos, P. E. (1979). *Short-term dynamic psychotherapy.* New York: Plenum.

Spence, D. P. (1982). *Narrative truth and historical truth.* New York: W. W. Norton & Company.

Stern, D. B. (1997). *Unformulated experience.* Hillsdale, NJ: The Analytic Press.

White, M., & Epston, D. (1990). *Narrative means to therapeutic ends.* New York: Norton.

Winnicott, D. W. (1965). *The maturational process and the facilitating environment.* New York: International Universities Press.

CHAPTER 5

ONCE UPON A TIME
SOPHIE FREUD, LICSW, PH.D.

A t this later stage of my life, the phase that the literature calls Young/Old, I try to evaluate what has gone right, and what has gone wrong. Forever a teacher, I give myself grades for my different main roles, grades that relate both to the satisfaction that I have experienced, as well as to my sense of how well I have performed these roles. Although I ask myself whether I would make similar choices "the next time around," I try to remember Kundera's (1984) saying that "the first rehearsal for life is life itself" (p. 8) and I try to accept the mistakes I have made. Still, I wonder whether I could manage better at a second rehearsal.

BORN WITH A THERAPEUTIC SILVER SPOON IN MY MOUTH

My role as psychotherapist or as clinical social worker, a title that I prefer, was never primary to my identity. It always intersected with at least one other role that was more important to me, first the more absorbing role of mother, and later, the more compelling role of educator (Freud, 1988b; Loewenstein, 1980). In this latter role, I would spend a whole lifetime first learning and then teaching theoretical thought systems and clinical methods. An apt inscription for my tombstone might be: "Here lie buried 60 years of one thousand psychology books—may they rest in peace." Yet, curiously enough, these three central roles of my life demanded of me quite similar attitudes, such as dedication to the interest of individuals who were counting on me to further their development, attentiveness to their uniqueness, some form of genuine affection, and a combination of acceptance and challenge. I have come to feel that the essence of a good enough clinical encounter, its very secret, lies not in theory or methods, but in the above demeanor. It sounds simple enough, yet, for some reason, it is only at this moment in life, when personal pressures for achievement and family obligations are receding that I have attained both this clarity of vision and sufficient peace of mind to carry it out to some extent. Clients have become people, not totally unlike friends, and friends have become people not totally unlike clients, and I try to show interest and respect once I have agreed, not without caution, to some form of encounter.

Others would suppose that I, as the granddaughter of Sigmund Freud, was born with a therapeutic silver spoon in my mouth. Not so, not so at all. It took an inordinately long time for me to reach this measure of understanding. Why did it take so long? Why did nobody ever come forth and make it clear?

My first therapeutic endeavor was involuntary and a dismal failure. My mother had recruited me as early as I can remember to be not only her most significant other, but also her personal psychotherapist. I was her intimate confidante, the recipient of her sorrows, disappointments, and anxieties. This role lasted until her death, almost twenty years ago, in 1980. I used to ask my social work students who among them were parentified children, and the majority always raised their hands, including, of course, myself. I am in firm agreement with the theory that many mental health professionals become therapists to make up for not having been able to heal their own parents.

My youth was disrupted by World War II and the Holocaust, but thanks to magic, capricious happenings and not least to my grandfather's fame, our family survived both events. I thus owe my grandfather, or at least his fame, a great deal, perhaps my life. He was, moreover, a kind and generous grandfather, albeit distant and suffering. Throughout my childhood we met weekly for a few minutes in his office, he gave me pocket money and appeared to assure himself of my well-being. I loved him very deeply. It pains and angers me greatly that his most faithful followers continue his unfortunate tendency of labeling differences of opinions with his theory as personal attacks—Freud bashing—even 60 years after his death.

The series of events that led me from Vienna to Paris, to Nice, to Casablanca, and to Lisbon, in the middle of the war, until I arrived safely at the age of 18 at Radcliffe College in Cambridge, Massachusetts, left me with the firm conviction that life hangs by a silken thread and that 90 percent of all that happens is accidental, due to large uncontrollable forces. Still, 10 percent of fate can be attributed to personal control and I was never one to neglect that 10 percent.

I view my life as having been punctuated by effort, self-discipline, and hard work and I expected the same of my children and students. They all got used to me, especially in retrospect. Besides, I feel that I have been fair, predictable, and not unmerciful. I have mellowed with age, but not all that much. I think of these characteristics with pride, but I know that our strengths are also our weaknesses and that people love us for the same traits that they dislike us for. Naturally I cannot quite exempt my clients from these same expectations, and to this day, in spite of the above lofty words regarding therapeutic dedication and compassion, I still get impatient with clients who do not expend sufficient effort on their own behalf.

Before reading my one thousand psychology books, I managed to find time in my peregrinations through Europe and North Africa to read an almost equal number of literary books in German and French. But in college, my inadequate English was insufficient to sustain my literary interests and I majored in psychology as the easiest, yet almost equally interesting choice. My entrance into social work school had some of the same elements of drifting and compromise. After all, people's "real" stories were almost as interesting as the stories read in books.

Let this be my answer to the repeated question whether my grandfather influenced my career choice. I certainly had no sense of direction at the age of 22. Never would I have predicted, in those young days, that I would become an ambitious academic. My life took its own directions, and now and then I stopped and tried to catch up to where it was leading me.

RESISTANCE TO THE TRUTHS OF THE DAY

It was not in childhood or adolescence, but at the Simmons College School of Social Work, in the late 1940s, that my thorough indoctrination into psychoanalytic theory began. Several of my instructors were psychoanalysts and not a few, such as Felix Deutsch or Grete Bibring, were also immigrants, albeit a few years earlier than I, from my home-town of Vienna. They had brought with them Freud's holy scriptures to the new world. I was then an eager, obedient, and receptive student who loved and respected my teachers if they gave me the slightest reason to do so. Yet, as I look back to that time in my early twenties, I am most proud not of being an honor student but in having resisted being brain-washed into some of the truths of the day.

My second year student placement was at the James Jackson Putnam Children's Center, a child guidance center for preschool children, with a therapeutic nursery school. The Putnam Center was then the training ground for the psychoanalysts who would soon take over the leading positions of the Boston mental health community as well as becoming the theoretical leaders in the field. The Center was led by two directors with totally con-trasting styles. One was Dr. Molly Putnam, niece of James Jackson Putnam after whom the Center was named, who epitomized the virtues of a perfect New England Lady. The other was the elegant, eccentric Beata Rank, divorced widow of Otto Rank. The latter was also queen of the Boston psychoanalytic community—if London had Anna Freud and Melanie Klein, we had our Tolla Rank. Due to her former association with my family, she took me under her personal wing and I am glad that I remained faithful to her in her difficult old age. She would later die isolated and mentally confused in a nursing home but her grand funeral was attended by the entire Boston mental health community. Personally I would prefer to hear all my eulogies while still alive, while nobody need attend my cremation. But forgive me, I am alive and healthy and do not mean to dwell on my death.

The Putnam Children's Center treated autistic children and had developed the usual odious theories about them so eloquently outlined in Bettelheim's lamentable books (see, for example, Bettelheim, 1967). The parents of these children, although of apparently normal demeanor, were thought to project dark, destructive, unconscious feelings upon their poor young children and thus were held responsible for this strange condition. I worked to a large extent with these parents and could never be convinced of this theory. For my masters social work thesis, I chose to study the siblings of autistic children and showed that, by and large, *they* fell into a normal developmental range, so perhaps the fault did not lie with the parents. My rebellious attitude was interpreted as resistance (what else?) but I was a mere student who would grow up some day. "Don't you understand that this mother is invested in having her child smear feces all over the house?" said my supervisor. "This father has a need to put a camera between himself and his child," said a leading child psychiatrist while showing the father's home movies about his autistic son. Yes, it is true, I am still angry, after all this time. I have forgotten many things in my life, but not judgments like this, made about desperate parents.

I need to jump many years ahead, to a similar and second victory over an almost identical brainwashing attempt since these two events now give me almost the most satisfaction as I review my long and colorful career. While the Putnam Center experience took place in the mid-1940s, the second experience was about thirty-five years later, when I trained as a family therapist in Philadelphia, in London, and in Italy. This time I resisted the "truth" that parents drove their children schizophrenic (more about this later). Intimate acquaintance with families who had the misfortune of having a schizophrenic young adult child had convinced me otherwise.

While ready to be indoctrinated into psychoanalytic theory, I was thus not a totally submissive believer. The Holocaust had left all of us with events to be explained by our theories—an ongoing lifelong quest. How can people have an internalized superego and murder, torture, and burn alive whole populations? I asked myself and asked my teachers. Morality, I reasoned, must be located in the social environment in which people lived, not inside people's psyche.

There were also other difficulties. Why would a criterion of female emotional maturity be the capacity for a vaginal orgasm, I asked my teachers—not entirely sure about the nature of my own orgasms. And was sex really all that central when people around me were competing and stabbing each other in the back for offices with windows, titles, positions, and money to send their children to private schools? Naturally, they were also having illicit love affairs, but true passion was in their fights for power, control, and deference from others. And what about penis envy which I did not remember having experienced since my brother envied my status as my mother's favored child, rather than the other way around? My teachers never knew the answers to my many questions and took flight in banalities. Many years later I would return to these same early questions and write about them, in an attempt to find at least some tentative answers (Loewenstein, 1974b, 1978a, 1979a, 1985b; Freud, 1988b).

APPRENTICESHIP YEARS

I also hoped to learn from my instructors and supervisors what made for effective psychotherapy, what made for a healing relationship. I felt, in those early days, that they were withholding some secret information from me, which I needed to be an effective social work therapist.

My first job was in a family service agency located in a

cold water flat in Jamaica Plain, Boston. I was given 10 very thick case records of Irish-American families in which the wives, for years, had dropped by for financial help whenever their husbands had drunk up the small weekly paycheck. It was a time when family agencies were still sustained by generous private endowments which they disbursed to "the worthy poor." But 1948 was the very moment in history when the agency policy had determined that financial gifts could only be given as part of a casework plan. This was very awkward since people understood very quickly that they had to invent emotional issues to qualify for financial help—which was not very hard, after all. My youthful contempt for this ambiguous picture was unjustified. The agency was an informal store-front type setting, a free drop-in center for people in crisis which could well serve as a first level community mental health model. Forty years later, returning for my sabbatical to Vienna, I would have the opportunity to work in an adult education center (*Volkshochschule*) which provided a somewhat similar drop-in office for people in need of consultation to solve some important emotional problem. People would come alone, with partners, even with whole families, for one, two, or more sessions, although it tended to be a time-limited service. The informal semi-educational setting maximized my spontaneity and creativity and I had the astonishing experience of being able to help people in a very short time.

Although I am jumping 40 years ahead, I shall give a short example of this experience.

> *A woman in her late forties, of apparent middle-class status, presented me with an "impossible situation." Her former husband had chosen to live next door to her with his new wife. Every time she stepped out of doors she had to watch the wife work in their garden, or sip lemonade on the porch. It was a constant source of chronic irritation for her. After some discussion, I said I knew exactly how she felt. Indeed, I had once lived in a situation where my ex-husband with his new partner occupied the flat adjoining mine. While taking my daily bath, I*

could almost hear them making love on the other side of the wall. We both started to laugh, totally and heartily, about the absurdity of life, about our common destinies as women, about shrugging one's shoulders at the inevitable and going on with life. My client stood up, clasped my hand in gratitude and said she could manage from now on.

(I should add that I would never venture into this kind of self-disclosure with a more long-term client.)

After a few years out for early child-rearing, it was with relief and enthusiasm that I found a job in the field of child welfare, dealing with pregnant mothers who had to make a decision about their future child's fate, with foster parents, and with adoptive parents. I do not want to claim the world has become an easier place. Soon, a dozen corporations will own all of us and we will dance to their profit tune. But there are some things that have radically changed in my own infinitely short lifetime. The term "illegitimate child" has disappeared from our vocabulary as has the surrounding shame, at least in this culture.

In these earlier days, adoption workers sought a physical and sociocultural match between babies and adoptive parents, not to mention the rules about religious match. Not believing in these rules, I once offered a thriving baby of Italian background to an Anglo-Saxon couple, who not only refused the baby, due to its olive skin coloring and dark hair, but assured me that my misguided practice would become the talk of the Boston community. Adopting children across racial and international lines would not happen for at least another 15 years.

I now view my self-confidence regarding making life-determining decisions in the adoption field when less than 30 years old with some disquietude, but those were not my thoughts at the time. Besides, I was carefully supervised and my new mentor would become a lifelong friend. For a time, the concrete nature of the adoption and child welfare tasks suited my need for action and for making a difference much better than the illusive uncertainty of psychotherapy. As a rule, the process of connecting a baby who needed a family with a family who needed a child was truly exhilarating.

The Riddle of the Sphinx

Eventually, however, after about five years, I was drawn back to the field of child guidance and psychotherapy. I suspect, not without embarrassment, that the higher prestige at that time of "psychiatric social work" as compared to "mere child welfare" may have been a factor in redirecting me. Or perhaps it was my unfulfilled hope of solving the riddle of the Sphinx, in this case penetrating the secret of psychotherapy, which drove me back. I first returned to the Putnam Center to work under Sylvia Perry, reputed to be among the foremost social work clinicians in Boston.

Some of my clients of that time will forever remain part of my internal world. Foremost among them is Mrs. M., almost a caricature of an overprotective anxious Jewish mother who spent her three years with me complaining about her life, her children, her husband, the family health, and their lack of money. But she was not my mother, and did not even remind me of my mother, so I could bear her complaints and even find some measure of communality with her—I too was raising my own difficult children at that time. Mrs. M. certainly taught me patience and forbearance.

I was glad to participate in the Putnam Center's study of bereavement in young children and my favorite client was a working-class man whose little girl had reacted badly to the death of her mother. It was this father's first opportunity to reflect about his own life and he engaged in the process with surprise and interest. But my uncertainty about the nature of change and how it came about continued, although it was contained, since I outwardly succeeded in the tasks of a clinical social worker. After acquiring more experience in other settings, I was eventually offered my first academic job as field-work instructor for the Simmons School of Social Work in charge of supervising five students in the Department of Child Psychiatry at the Beth Israel Hospital.

THE DYSFUNCTIONAL CHILD GUIDANCE MODEL

The department had been led by Dr. Grete Bibring and had become an elite clinic in Boston, a major training center for residents in child psychiatry, most of them men too young to be parents. The department was also steeped in orthodox psychoanalytic theory which was taught endlessly in weekly seminars and put into practice in the clinical assessments of our weekly case conferences. I needed no change in outlook or perspective since the child guidance clinic culture of the Beth Israel Clinic was identical to that of the Putnam Center. Part of that culture was a strict hierarchy, with social workers clearly subordinate to doctors. Social workers were not allowed to treat children but relegated to the presumed less important task of seeing parents, mostly mothers, although it was a time of discovery that fathers too could be important in the lives of children. Fathers were often assigned to the psychiatric residents, perhaps because they were held in higher esteem than mothers. It was left open whether parents too were patients, informants, or merely to be forcefully instructed on how to treat their children. "Get this child out of the mother's bed," a psychiatric resident would angrily demand from his team-member social worker. I can hardly remember an occasion when a whole family met with both team members, but family conflicts were not infrequently reproduced within the team. The child guidance culture also demanded an elaborate intake process in which all possible developmental data about the child, as well as other family data had to be gathered. I remember an angry reprimand by a senior psychiatrist in an intake presentation of a delinquent adolescent in which the student had forgotten to ask information about the nature of his bowel movements as a baby. Now that we have learned more about the unreliable nature of memory, this compulsive gathering of many years' old data seems even more absurd. The process cured me forever from seeking a detailed early history.

No attempt was made to start a helping process during the intake procedure, and once again, when I irreverently explained to a mother how to treat the waking-at-night problem of a toddler, and the problem was almost instantly solved, I was severely censured. I had neglected the "underlying pathology" in the situation. Once a child was accepted for treatment, a one, two, or three year long program of treatment was started, with new residents and new social work students taking over at the turn of each academic year. When the quota was filled, new applicants were put on a waiting list, which might last a whole year. The most basic premise of this child guidance culture was the conscious or unconscious culpability of parents. I had learned and incorporated this basic philosophical stance during my student internship at the Putnam Center and it had properly haunted me during the raising of my own children (Freud, 1988b).

AN EXCURSION INTO MY OWN PSYCHOTHERAPY

Naturally, the question of a personal psychoanalysis had come up many times, since I was living in a culture where this was considered an essential part of one's personal development and education as a mental health professional. Supervisors had urged me in that direction, friends in analysis or friends who were psychoanalysts had tried to persuade me, teachers had recommended it, and I am still amazed that I held out against so much pressure. No doubt the observation that the mental health of my friends and colleagues had not improved after psychoanalysis helped me in this decision. To my somewhat puritan spirit, a psychoanalysis has always seemed an incredible narcissistic self-indulgence.

It was during the time at the Beth Israel that I engaged in my only personal psychotherapy experience, propelled by my worry over one of my children. It lasted two years at which time my therapist had to leave town. He wanted to refer me to a colleague, but I resisted. It was not that the experience had been a negative one. On the contrary, I had chosen a gentle, low-keyed, and courteous male psychoanalyst, respectful of my defenses, apparently interested in my thoughts and feelings, and sufficiently interactive for my needs. Too bad my husband suffered in comparison. In fact, I resisted because the therapy, or perhaps the therapist, had become too important to me. The relationship threatened my counter-dependent style which had served me well enough, so far, and which I was not willing to surrender, neither for a psychoanalysis, nor for psychotherapy. Naturally such reasons for our decisions are no more than constructions that are coherent with the sense we make of our life story. This personal therapy did not help me with the riddle of the Sphinx. I did not experience any change in my behavior or relationships even with the child in question and I did not learn anything new about my life. It was for me simply a chance to have an experience of delightful attentiveness, for one hour a week.

MY CONVERSION EXPERIENCE

Next, in my mid-forties, I started to feel increasingly confined and impatient with the constraints of psychoanalytic theory, which began to seem irrelevant to the problems of our families. Neither did I welcome the realization that I would remain forever a low figure on the hospital's totem pole. In 1967, at the age of 43, I was able to break out of this stagnant prison and enrolled in the Heller School for Social Welfare at Brandeis University.

It is rumored that the Heller School accepted me with the hope of converting the granddaughter of Freud from a psychoanalytic to a social science perspective. They succeeded—up to a point—since I have always found it possible to integrate old perspectives into new ones, without needing to reject them in their entirety (see, for example, my recent paper on my grandfather as a postmodernist, Freud, 1998a). Besides, I am deeply irreverent and will never be totally faithful to any one perspective.

My conversion experience at Brandeis was neither with my teachers, nor with social policy or political analysis, nor even with the magic of quantitative research, but instead around my encounter, during an elective course, with the writings of the micro-sociology and symbolic interactionism of Erving Goffman (1961, 1963, 1971, 1974). The scales fell from my eyes and the perspective that I had taken for granted my entire adult life suddenly shifted. Life was about striving for interpersonal respect, not about the expression or repression of sexual and aggressive instincts. I also loved the metaphor of life as theater. Outer space, which had always been more dominant in my thinking than inner space, had finally been given its proper due (Loewenstein, 1979a).

I deliberately called the change in my meaning-making outlook a conversion since it alienated me from family tradition, at least to some extent. Family loyalty is an important value for all of us, but becoming my own woman, the wish to seek my own understandings, however flawed and tentative, has outweighed most other values in my life course.

It was a short path from Goffman to embracing system theory and the illuminating writings of Gregory Bateson (1972). We create our own world, Bateson teaches us, by drawing differences mostly through the means of language, upon an uncertain amorphous world. Bradford Keeney (1983) has expressed this most vividly: "Language is an epistemological knife. It slices the world into bits and pieces, provides names, names of names, and names of names of names" (p.110). Dear Gregory Bateson, due to my admiration for most of your thinking, I forgive you your double bind theory which applies to many situations, but is unfair to parents of schizophrenic children. In my view the irrational thinking found in many such families is due to the contagious nature of insanity or, for that matter, any other strong emotion and belief system. And I believe that children can infect their parents as easily as the other way around.

FINDING MY TRUE CALLING

I now come to the part of my life in which my identity shifted to that of an educator of clinical social workers. I became chairperson of the Human Behavior Sequence at the Simmons School of Social Work, which meant that I was in charge of the theoretical aspects of clinical training. My first task, I concluded, was to broaden the psychoanalytic perspective of the school, admittedly over the dead body of several colleagues. But I succeeded since, as it happened, I was swimming with, rather than against, the tides. I introduced first-year masters students to as many theoretical perspectives as could be crammed into their first year of study. While I continued to see a limited number of clients, I did so mostly to stay abreast of my students. My writing and book reviewing also arose as a natural part of my new academic obligations.

Actually, I had started to teach while still at the Beth Israel, with my first successful attempt a course that was to help teachers of young children deal with their pupils' parents. I had realized how difficult this parent-teacher encounter had been for me as a parent, and was correct in supposing that it was equally uncomfortable and anxiety-provoking for teachers. The first time I entered a classroom as a teacher, I knew I had finally come home, found my true calling, and found an opportunity to realize my talents, my interests, my pleasure in show(wo)manship (Loewenstein, 1980). Moreover, I was pleased to find that my clinical training had constituted a perfect preparation for teaching. As I stated at the beginning of this essay, similar attitudes of respect, interest, and encouragement are demanded from an attentive teacher and an attentive therapist. I would further maintain that such interest, rather than defensiveness when angry, accusing, and critical voices are raised in the classroom, is another important common denominator. Moreover, an atmosphere of drama and strong emotions seemed to deepen learning both in the classroom and in the clinician's office. My two identities of teacher and therapist felt so compatible that they led me to see the strong teaching component in therapeutic encounters and the therapeutic component in the learning process. Social workers, I thought at that time, should think of themselves as community educators rather than psychotherapists (Freud, 1987).

IN SEARCH OF PROFESSIONAL DEVELOPMENT

Group psychotherapy seemed to be an especially apt setting in which new learning, and even simply new information, could have a healing effect. Through the years, I acquired training and then conducted, with considerable pleasure, many diverse types of groups, with a greater sense of certainty than I had felt in individual work, that the experience helped people cope more adequately with their difficult lives (Loewenstein, 1985a; Loewenstein & Morrison, 1979). Dr. Robert Weiss (1975) gave me the opportunity to be an assistant in his groups for recently separated men and women, and the theory and methods of life-transition, or psycho-educational groups in general, greatly appealed to me. I felt that social workers, at the interface of inner and outer space, were ideally suited to conduct such groups and introduced them into our curriculum (Loewenstein, 1978b, 1979b).

My initiative in obtaining training in many types of group work is one good example of my seeking professional development in order to become a more rounded social work educator. A similar example was my pursuing of training in the field of family therapy, an activity to which I devoted my first sabbatical (Freud, 1988b).

I welcomed family therapy with open arms. Its method of treating the family together seemed to be the answer to the dysfunctional aspects of the traditional child guidance model, and its systemic theoretical frame also seemed liberating. It took me some time to understand that one basic premise had not changed: the parents were still the alien forces, to be subdued or tricked by clever strategies. This was forcefully brought home to me through a videotape I saw during my training as family therapist which might be familiar to some of you. I am referring to Dr. Salvador Minuchin's (in)famous tape of his work with parents and their anorectic daughter. At the end of the tape the parents are so provoked by Dr. Minuchin that the father forcefully stuffs food into his daughter's mouth. It is a painful tape to watch even if the treatment led to the girl's improvement. I have come to think that never in life, in politics or in psychotherapy, in education or in child rearing, should the end justify the means. The notion that at least some parents might as easily be viewed as well-meaning collaborators is a recent one, perhaps started by the psycho-educational model for parents who had a schizophrenic young adult child living at home, and then continued by White and Epston (1990) and their Australian colleagues (1990). The mental health community has welcomed this more benign view of family functioning, and this changing perspective seems to have contributed to some of the declining enthusiasm for structural and strategic family therapy.

In 1979, I spent one month at the Philadelphia Children's Hospital to be trained in structural family therapy under Dr. Minuchin's leadership, and it is my unconventional view that this small kernel of malevolence against parents also entered into the training of family therapists. Supervisors routinely watched their student interns struggle with a family for a few minutes from behind a mirror, then entered the consulting room, performed a series of magic interventions which made all the difference, and departed, or else stayed and cured the family in one fell swoop.

Once, we were shown a tape in which the therapist tried to empower a young woman to assert herself as mother toward her baby, rather than allowing the baby's grandmother to take over. In the middle of this process the supervisor, an older woman, entered the room, took over, and told the young female therapist how to carry on. I wondered aloud just what message the young mother was receiving from this interaction. This proved to be a very unpopular question. I also asked about the accepted custom of viewing the father as head of the household and treating him with much more deference than the mother, apparently because he had to be seduced into treatment, while the more motivated mother had brought them all to the clinic. Even a father's violent behavior tended to be side-stepped and minimized. And then there was my difficulty around the schizophrenogenic family.

At the end of the month I asked the members of our small team-group why nobody had ever asked me to have lunch with them. They responded: After the questions you asked, we did not want to be seen with you. This is a true story of micro-tyranny in a training center, which does not diminish my respect for Dr. Minuchin's innovative creativity and my agreement with many of his ideas.

I survived the month of lonely lunches and went on to the family therapy program at the Tavistock Clinic in London where I was allowed to raise difficult questions. My critical article on their quaint method of supervision—through an earbug connecting the trainee-therapist with a supervisor—was even accepted in their book on training family therapists (Loewenstein, Reder, & Clark, 1982). Some years later, women family therapists, including some from that same Philadelphia clinic, protested against the patriarchal spirit of the family therapy movement (Luepnitz, 1988) and my feminist writings (Loewenstein, 1983) were quoted in that context.

I had approached feminism not so much as a new set of values, but as a belief system in which I felt quite at home, and recognized values that I had always taken for granted. Feminism was proposing new perspectives on psychotherapy, some of them challenging traditional psychodynamic thinking. I particularly resonated with its non-pathologizing strength perspective and its tendency to normalize many dysfunctional behaviors as quite understandable and even rational within the context in which they had developed and perhaps even holding some useful function in the woman's current context. I also valued its attempt to minimize the power differential between client and therapist, although this had never struck me as quite as great as claimed by the literature, given that one needs clients to be a therapist. I feel some pride and have been given recognition for having introduced a feminist perspective not only to my own students, but into the field of social work where it thrived because of its compatible values (Freud, 1992, 1994; Loewenstein, 1974a, 1983).

A POSTMODERN STANCE

This not quite linear journey of reminiscences has now brought me to my current perspectives. Perhaps you have guessed, dear reader, that I had started to move toward, and now come to embrace postmodern thinking. I am intrigued by every aspect of postmodern thinking, including cybernetics, cognitive constructivism, structure determinism, social constructionism, and narrative theory, and feel such enthusiasm regarding its applications to psychotherapy that I have given workshops on its theories all over the United States and Europe (Freud, 1988a).

Having been critical of the iatrogenic addiction to psychotherapy for a long time, I am naturally seduced by the possibilities of brief treatments that these new theories offer. For example, listening to Insoo Kim Berg's audiotape on treatment of a violent man captivates my therapeutic imagination and, at a younger age, I might have actively sought training in such a method. There are a few elements of these new approaches that are orthogonal to psychodynamic thinking and that I have embraced: the emphasis on strengths and exceptions to the problem; the emphasis on the present and the future, rather than the past; lack of interest in seeking causes and making elegant interpretations—although linking different events that follow a similar pattern continues to strike me as useful. On the other hand, many of the new ideas, such as the goal, in narrative theory, of constructing a more positive hopeful life story, or reframing a difficult situation by viewing it through a new perspective, are all well within an updated psychodynamic framework, enriching and clarifying, rather than substituting for that model. Having rejected the either/or word for the either/and principle, I have no difficulty in introducing these elements to students who are being trained within a psychodynamic framework. This is especially true in the question of focus on past versus present, which would demand adaptation to a particular client's needs.

Ironically, my fate, or my choice, has placed me in a setting without managed care constraints, where many very troubled clients tend to expect long-term treatment, students expect to learn it, and long-term treatment is still gladly offered. I volunteer as a social work therapist at the Community Legal Services and Counseling Center in Cambridge, Massachusetts. With the exception of the two directors, the entire staff is recruited from volunteer mental health professionals who wish to work there, either because of the availability of volunteer senior social work supervisors, or simply for the chance of helping people. The Center accepts low-income clients, for whom other mental health services are not available, for a sliding fee. I see individual clients or sometimes couples, and supervise a group of social work and psychology student interns. Solution-focused methods would not be suitable in such a setting because at least as many clients come to seek support and accompaniment (complainants, in solution-focused language) as clients who seek change (customers) (Berg & Miller, 1992).

I saw a woman at the Center for three years, who, although employed as a salesperson, had nobody in her life to whom she could talk freely. Sometimes she wanted my help in solving a problem, but mostly she knew what she needed or wanted to do. What she needed from me was an attentive ear one hour a week to listen to the stressful events of that week. I have often used time, even therapeutic time, in much less fruitful enterprises. There are fewer and fewer places and people in our society that simply accompany and sustain emotionally isolated individuals.

I believe, in any case, that the solution-focused therapists' limited tolerance of complaining—problem saturated talk—and their almost instant shift to exceptions to the problem is oppressive and a weakness of that school (Berg & Miller, 1992). Psychotherapy, and even brief psychotherapy, deserves to be a place where sadness, anger, grief, disappointment, and grievances may be expressed.

The Center is a very compatible setting for both my own work and my style of supervision. After a lifetime of studying theories, I am, at this point, if not Beyond Good and Evil, at least beyond one specific theory or method. We are learning that our brain responds before we have had time to consider our own reaction and that is exactly what my brain does while counseling. All the old and new theories and methods that I have embraced, taught, discarded, and reconsidered have built such a strong neuronal network that a very compelling sense of things drives my interactions with clients and my thinking about them in supervision. I sense what is called for in a particular situation and any explanations are mere afterthoughts.

But my students do not have a lifetime of experiences from which to draw. I need to understand the elements of my automatic brain network to pass them on. Perhaps it will be easiest to explain my current therapeutic world view by drawing on what I try to convey to my students at the above described counseling center. They may be getting other, contradictory messages from other supervisors and instructors but with time they will find their own style.

Be yourself, I tell them. Act as if this relationship were a friendship, without the usual reciprocity of attending to each other's needs that one expects of friendship. Reciprocity lies instead in the privilege of making a difference to another person. Be humble about wanting to make a difference, a measure of difference being preferable to too much difference (Freud, 1988b). This last warning is especially important to social workers such as child welfare workers who sometimes wield awesome power over other people's lives.

See if you can find some compassion and caring for that person, perhaps based on some communality. Lacking that, therapy can become very arduous. Find out early what clients want from you and how they will know that things are going better. If they may have come to you out of sheer loneliness you may choose to see them for a while and then to connect them with an activity group or a therapy group if that is possible, or you could provide that service and not be disappointed when your client is not interested in change. It does not mean that you are not making a great deal of difference in their lives.

Leaning on both the feminist and the constructivist perspective, I definitely encourage my students to take a strength perspective. Be curious about your clients' lives and what competencies have helped them to survive. As their story unfolds, highlight strengths they have manifested along the way, even modest strengths. See if their story lends itself to a new and more positive bent. Some schools of psychotherapy feel therapy should be an arduous and painful process. I do not agree. Find ways to express affirmation, respect, hope, and admiration if it can be genuine. Celebrate their achievements with them. Some people have friends who may be supportive in bad times, but are not inclined to listen to victories. Modesty may be a virtue in the world at large, but you are one person who encourages boasting. Give your clients the certainty that you are rooting for them, care about their successes, and feel disappointed with them when something goes wrong, albeit naturally not too disappointed. I indicated at the beginning of this chapter that I had a very difficult mother (see also, Freud, 1988b), but I know she wished me well, with all her heart and soul. It is life enhancing to know that at least one or two people are deeply invested in one's well-being.

Psychodynamic therapy is regulated by strict rules regarding the therapist's behavior. Many of these rules have proven their usefulness and need to be taken very seriously because they protect the client, the therapist, and the process. Many of them are spelled out in our professional codes of ethics, others grow out of theoretical considerations. Indeed, the rules that forbid therapists to misuse their clients for emotional, sexual, financial, or other exploitative purposes are the bedrock of psychotherapy. Rules are also useful because of the dramatic impact when they are broken in small ways. I once did some informal research about the most significant therapy experiences of a group of doctoral social work students. Many of them remembered incidents in which the therapist had broken their usual rules, given them a cup of tea on a rainy afternoon, a visit to the hospital during illness, a hand on the shoulder in moments of great grief, some straightforward practical advice from a therapist whose rule it was never to give advice.

My students worry about giving advice. Will it create dependency? Will it interfere with the client's autonomy and own sense of competence? Since I personally seek as many opinions as possible whenever I make a decision, which helps me to come to my own conclusion, I feel less cautious in this area. Naturally, the pros and cons of different options must be investigated but I know I err in voicing opinions, giving too much advice, although I surround that practice with tentativeness. But I am very pragmatic when it comes to the basics of living.

> *A client is uncertain whether she should stay with her partner who has a chaotic lifestyle and often gets on her nerves. She has multiple sclerosis and is easily tired and irritated and sometimes he aggravates her condition. On the other hand, he is also extremely caring and devoted to her. I say cautious things about having MS and living all alone. I ask whether ways could be found for her to have a more protected space in her own home, a refuge for her when she becomes irritable. Their apartment gets rearranged, the relationship improves.*

Giving advice is closely related to another major controversial theme, that of self-disclosure. I make the distinction, here, among three areas: answering demographic questions; mentioning similar experiences to those the client brings, either at one's own initiative, or when questioned; and disclosing the impact of a client's behavior on oneself. In terms of the last category, I think there needs to be a strong alliance before one can give clients feedback on how their difficult behavior affects one.

Now and then I am moved to share how I manage my own life. I might talk about "my opportunity theory" which deals with seizing opportunities that present themselves in every life, albeit often in the disguise of frightening risks. Or I might talk to a lonely person about the cherished companions that audio-books have become for me.

> *A client has made plans to teach in a foreign country. She looks forward to this, but feels an absolute need to meet a man who will accompany her on this venture. "I have often taught in foreign countries," I might say, "and have found it liberating to be alone because it makes it easier to make new friends. A companion can become a burden." She looks astonished. "Perhaps you have a point," she says.*

Answer questions about yourself you are comfortable answering, and rather than probing the question, see whether your answer makes a difference to them. If you have had the same problem as your client, think of the effect, the benefits, and complications that your self-disclosure may create. The danger of burdening a client with one's own issues is very great, given that many clients (as well!) are parentified children. On the other hand, admitting that one has also struggled with similar problems can relieve a client of enormous shame. It is best for therapists to disclose only problems that happened in the past and no longer cause pain or anguish. But there may be other ways to normalize your clients' behaviors, often a useful move. Be sure not to establish one-upmanship on your client in terms of having experienced pain. If you have not had the same experiences, or if your client is socioculturally very different, let them know your readiness to learn from him or her. It is in any case always useful and fair to let the clients know that you are learning from them perhaps as much as they are hopefully learning from you. I hope that my children, my students, and my clients have come to realize that they were and continue to be my most important teachers.

Try to be as honest and direct as possible, which includes voicing different perspectives from your clients or warning them about the likely consequences of certain behaviors. You may have to set very firm limits in terms of destructive behaviors toward self or others. Clients are not always friendly and may even become very angry and very critical, perhaps accusatory. Criticism may have at least a kernel of truth and should not be instantly dismissed as projections. Some of the most relationship-enhancing moments can take place when criticisms are taken seriously, closely examined, and one's own fallibility admitted and apologized for. Getting thoughtful and honest feedback to their criticism is not an opportunity that most people have in their everyday lives. Yet, therapists also need a measure of self-protection and I see no therapeutic function to endless unjustified accusations.

Sometimes the best we can do for people is to help them to accept themselves with their particular strengths and vulnerabilities.

> I had a client who worried about having frequent anxiety
> attacks in response to relationship problems. For years he

sought one therapeutic experience after another, wanting
answers, wanting change. I highlighted his accomplishments
as a competent business man—he was a shoe repairman—and
encouraged him to accept himself as he saw himself—a man
capable of devotion with a "super-caring" style—as having
advantages (being a good and feelingful person) as well as
costs (suffering pain and anxiety).

Some people need to learn to take more responsibility for their actions, I tell my students. But for many others, it is the exact opposite. Do not believe the Freudian [sic] dictum that everything we do is either deliberate or dictated by our unconscious needs and wishes. So much in life is haphazard or a result of few other options, or a perception of few options, conditioned by the circumstances of a particular moment or life situation.

"I only had good sex a few times, outside my two marriages,"
a sophisticated client told me. "Something must be very wrong
with my sexual impulses." It emerged that, at age 18, the age
of her first marriage, both she and her husband had been inex-
perienced youngsters. Her second marriage was a marriage of
convenience, at a time when she needed a mate with whom she
could have a child. She had never been very attracted to this
husband. "Do not believe all the theories they feed you," I said
to her. "They will give you indigestion. It is excellent that you
have had a chance to develop your sexuality in these other spe-
cial relationships."

I also encourage my students to bring drama into the therapy hour, role play given the opportunity, rehearse difficult upcoming situations, raise their voices if indicated, use humor whenever possible, in short, to be playful and spontaneous given any space for such feelings.

I must end this section about students with an explanation that as a supervisor and instructor, students become my clients and I follow many of the same rules for them, albeit more loosely than I do with clients. I am especially sensitive to the modeling process through which the supervisor-student relationship is apt to become reflected in the student-client relationship. Most students need a great deal of encouragement, reassurance, and affirmation. A small vignette might render the climate of our small student group which I supervise.

> *David, a sensitive young man still acquiring more self-confidence confessed to the group how he had "messed up" once again. He had been working with a client around his problems of domestic violence. It was raining and the client had an umbrella . David had said "I like that type of umbrella, I must buy one like that," whereupon the client handed him his umbrella, insisted that he had several of that kind at home, and left David with the umbrella. "How could I have done that?" he asked himself with semi-mocking self-blame. I joined the laughter and reassuring reactions in the group. "This difficult violent man might really care about you much more than you realize," I said, "and this is his way of showing it. He is probably not in the habit of dropping umbrellas all over the place." We all agreed that this unfortunate umbrella nevertheless needed to be returned. He was to make much of the client's spontaneous generosity, call the gift a welcome loan and, if necessary, explain that the rules did not allow him to accept gifts. I then invited David to role-play the return of the umbrella which he did with good humor.*

THERAPY AS OPIUM FOR THE MASSES

It must have become obvious to you, my readers, that I have had a love-hate relationship with psychotherapy all my life. I chose it as a profession, escaped into academia for 30 years, avoided private practice, yet have returned to it in my retirement years. But my ambivalence regarding the profession continues.

On the one hand, I was glad for my colleagues when social workers gained the right to be reimbursed by third-party insurers, although managed care with its regulations regarding number of allowed sessions has made private practice a less satisfactory enterprise. But apart from that, I have always been uneasy that an enterprise in which maximum effectiveness means loss of customers should be under private auspices. The privatization of hospitals, mental health centers, and even prisons (!) fills me with dismay. I would wish fervently that the (excessive) profit motive could be eliminated from physical and mental health practices whether by private organizations or even private practitioners (Freud, 1991).

I have had the privilege of being part of an Ethics Hotline for NASW (the National Association of Social Workers) (Freud, 1998b). The calls we receive have become, in my eyes, a microcosm of the daily stresses, anxieties, and indignities that mental health professionals are subjected to through arbitrary, callous adminis- tration or bureaucratic rules. When an organization, such as a mental health agency, is privatized, many of its social workers are fired, but asked the next day whether they want to continue their work as fee for service workers on an ad hoc basis and without benefits. Whistle blowers regarding an organization's unethical practices are summarily dismissed, given two hours to clear their desks and accompanied by a security guard out of the building. They call the Ethics Hotline to ask how they can terminate with their clients under such conditions. They can not. I am in great fear that the disrespectful treatment of mental health professionals may eventually be passed on to their clients, especially if the latter are even more powerless than social workers are starting to feel.

But I have other concerns as well. Institutions such as counseling centers in universities or Employee Assistance Programs are laudable endeavors, but if they are used merely as dumping grounds for people who don't quite fit the mold, rather than used as canaries in mines, signaling malignant conditions, they have a limited function. The same can be said of the whole institution of psychotherapy and society in general. Our society produces more and more people who, for one reason or another, are overwhelmed by its multiple demands, responding with dys- function for which we have created an ever increasing number of diagnoses. It behooves us to be extremely attentive to the social cir- cumstances connected to different disorders and to follow an optimal public health model.

In public health, diseases are combated through sanitation, clean water, and cleaner air, rather than through a case by case diagnosis and treatment, as we tend to do in psychotherapy. Now and then we meet important voices who make this very connection, such as James Gilligan (1996) in his admirable book on the epidemic of violence and Matthew Dumont in his book, *Treating the Poor* (1992), which deplores with bitterness the dismantling of our all too brief community mental health approach. Both authors emphasize the disastrous effects of poverty and lack of dignity on mental health. In this context I should also mention Philip Cushman's book, *Constructing the Self, Constructing America* (1995), which demonstrates to what extent psychological theories and treatments, far from being based on independent scientific knowledge, have always mirrored the culture and political climate of their historical moment. But for every 50 books on new technical approaches to psychotherapy, whether favoring biology or psychotherapy, there may be one such book that adopts this holistic approach. An ever increasing number of children are receiving Ritalin for hyperactivity, with little interest in examining the suitability of typical classroom expectations for many young children. There is little question that psychotherapy, including psychotropic medication and the talking cure, has replaced religion as "the opium of the masses."

I shall be reconciled with the profession if it starts to view "injustice collection" as one of its primary tasks, a process that is then to be funneled into the political arena. It would be best, for this activity, if professionals did not practice on a full-time basis isolated from the world at large in their offices, but engaged in psychotherapy as a part-time occupation, intermingled with other enterprises. Such a division of labor would make private practitioners less dependent on individual clients and allow therapists to observe and experience society first hand.

Psychotherapy is a moral, value laden, and political enterprise. We must never forget that. And now, my readers, I seek a last piece of advice: Should I choose psychotherapy as a profession in the twenty-first century, if I have another chance?

REFERENCES

Bateson, G. (1972). *Steps to an ecology of mind.* New York: Chandler.

Berg, I. K. (Speaker). It's not my fault. (Cassette Recording). Milwaukee: Brief Family Therapy Center.

Berg, I. K. & Miller, S.D. (1992). *Working with the problem drinker: A solution-focused approach.* New York: Norton.

Bettelheim, B. (1967). *The empty fortress: Infantile autism and the birth of the self.* Glencoe, IL: Free Press.

Cushman, P. (1995). *Constructing the self, constructing America.* Reading, MA: Addison-Wesley.

Dumont, M. (1992). *Treating the poor.* Belmont, MA: Dymphna Press.

Freud, S. (1987). Social workers as community educators: A new identity for the profession. *Journal of Teaching in Social Work, 1,* 111-126.

Freud, S. (1988a). Cybernetic epistemology. In R. Dorfman (Ed.), *Paradigms of clinical social work* (pp. 356-387). New York: Brunner/Mazel.

Freud, S. (1988b). *My three mothers and other passions.* New York: NYU Press.

Freud, S. (1991). Guest Editorial: Psychotherapy for better or for worse. *Smith College Studies in Social Work. 61,* 123-132.

Freud, S. (1992). Dropping out: A feminist approach. In C. W. LeCroy (Ed.), *Case studies in social work practice* (pp. 228-234). Belmont, California: Wadsworth Publishing Co.

Freud, S. (1994) . The social construction of gender. *Journal of Adult Development, 1,* 37-45.

Freud, S. (1998a). The baby and the bathwater: Freud as a post-modernist. *Families in Society. 79,* 55-463.

Freud, S. (1998b.) Starting an ethics hotline. *Focus.* December.

Gilligan, J. (1996). *Violence.* New York: Random House.

Goffman, E. (1961). *Asylums.* Garden City, NY: Anchor Books, Doubleday.

Goffman, E. (1963) *Stigma.* Englewood Cliff, NJ: Prentice-Hall.

Goffman, E. (1971). *Relations in public.* New York: Basic Books.

Goffman, E. (1974). *Frame analysis.* New York: Harper & Row.

Keeney, B. (1983). *Aesthetics of change*. New York: Guilford.

Kundera, M. (1984). *The unbearable lightness of being*. New York: Harper & Row.

Loewenstein, S. F. (1974a). Integrating content on feminism and racism into the social work curriculum. *Journal of Education for Social Work, 12,* 91-96.

Loewenstein, S. F. (1974b). An overview of the concept of narcissism. *Social Casework, 58,* 136-142 .

Loewenstein, S. F. (1978a). An overview of some aspects of female sexuality. *Social Casework, 59,* 106-115.

Loewenstein, S. F. (1978b). Preparing social work students for Life Transition Counseling within the Human Behavior Sequence. *Journal of Education for Social Work, 14,* 66-73.

Loewenstein, S. F. (1979a). Inner and outer space in social casework. *Social Casework, 60,* 19-29.

Loewenstein, S. F. (1979b). Helping family members cope with divorce. In S. Eisenberg & L. E. Patterson (Eds.), *Helping clients with special concerns* (pp. 193-217). New York: Houghton Mifflin.

Loewenstein, S. F. (1980). The Passion and challenge of teaching. *Harvard Educational Review, 50,* 1-12.

Loewenstein, S. F. (1983). A feminist perspective. In A. Rosenblatt & D. Waldfogel (Eds.), *Handbook of clinical social work* (pp. 518-548). San Francisco: Jossey Bass.

Loewenstein, S. F. (1985a). Group theory in an experiential group. *Social Work with Groups, 8,* 29-40.

Loewenstein, S. F. (1985b). Freud's metapsychology revisited. *Social Casework, 66,* 139-151.

Loewenstein, S. F. & Morrison, A. (1979). The Newsletter: A catalyst for learning in psychotherapy. *American Journal of Psychotherapy, 33,* 128-38.

Loewenstein, S. F., Reder, P. & Clark, A. (1982). The consumers' response: Trainees' discussion of the experience of live supervision. In R. Whiffen & J. Byng-Hall (Eds.), *Family therapy supervision* (pp. 115-129). New York: Grune & Stratton.

Luepnitz, D. A. (1988). *The family interpreted: Feminist theory in clinical practice.* New York: Basic Books.

Weiss, S. R. (1975). *Marital separation.* New York: Basic Books.

White, M., & Epston, D. (1990). *Narrative means to therapeutic ends.* New York: Norton.

CHAPTER 6

SWIMMING UPSTREAM: VOYAGE OF A LESBIAN PSYCHIATRIST

NANETTE K. GARTRELL, M.D.

My career as a psychotherapist has been focused on social change. I am a lesbian-feminist psychiatrist, teacher, researcher, and organizer. At the University of California, San Francisco, I am an associate clinical professor of psychiatry; I teach ethics and feminist psychotherapy theory. In the private sector, I have had a psychotherapy practice since 1979; in the public sector, I volunteer my professional services to chronically mentally-ill homeless people in San Francisco.

As a psychotherapist, I consider myself a pragmatic, insight-facilitating, cognitive-behavioral problem solver. I have been strongly influenced by theorists who emphasize the significance of diversity—in gender, race, ethnicity, religion, sexual orientation, physical disability, gender identity, appearance, weight, class, age, immigrant status, relationship status, and political affiliation. I have been a long-term advocate of clearly-defined professional boundaries within the practice of psychotherapy. Being out as a lesbian psychotherapist—to all clients regardless of their sexual orientation—has been important to me ever since I opened my private practice.

My beliefs about psychotherapy have evolved considerably since I was a psychiatric resident at Massachusetts Mental Health Center, Harvard Medical School (MMHC), from 1976 to 1979. I had gone to medical school with a goal of being able to provide nonhomophobic health services to lesbians. When I decided to specialize in psychiatry, I chose MMHC because it was one of the top training programs in the country. However, the program was strongly psychoanalytically-oriented, with no full-time women on the faculty. My supervisors were white, male, heterosexual psychoanalysts.

During college and medical school, I had combed through the fine print of Freud's narratives, and those of his many revisionist followers, hoping to find a nonjudgmental place for my lesbianism within psychodynamic theory. Instead, I found that homophobia pervaded the psychoanalytic literature. My search broadened to incorporate feminist political and sociological discourse, and I became fascinated with the social construction of knowledge. I resonated with the lesbian-feminist argument that all theory was susceptible to temporal, cultural, political, and personal bias, and that all schools of psychology were vulnerable to the subjectivity of their creators. Unfortunately, there was no support for that kind of thinking at MMHC in the late 1970s. Consequently, I found myself without a mentor, without a theoretical framework, and without a relevant training program.

Lesbian Activism, 1967—1976

Before I describe the evolution of my current psychotherapeutic style, let me share some relevant highlights from my personal development. I came out as a lesbian during my freshman year at Stanford in 1967. For the next three years, I thought that my partner and I were the only lesbians on campus. Although I never considered my lesbianism to be inherently pathological, at the same time I knew that homosexuality was considered a mental illness according to the Diagnostic and Statistical Manual of Mental Disorders (DSM) (American Psychiatric Association, 1968).

My first foray into lesbian activism consisted of writing a series of term papers advocating increased social tolerance of lesbianism. The positive feedback I received from several professors bolstered my confidence in my decision to come out to close friends and family. During my junior year, I sought counseling at Stanford's student health center because of uncertainty about my career path. The evaluating woman psychiatrist told me that I needed long-term psychotherapy because I was unwilling to explore my resistance to heterosexuality.

Fortunately, this homophobic recommendation came at a time when I had a number of lesbian friends and supporters, so its impact was not as destructive as it might have been. The first social gathering of lesbians at Stanford had recently been held in my apartment, and I had begun to network with San Francisco lesbian activists. After hearing of my visit to the health center psychiatrist, these activists suggested that I see a lesbian therapist instead. They gave me the name of a lesbian analyst in San Francisco, and later that year, I began my analysis.

I processed my hopes, fears, and goals in analysis. I had planned on a career in medicine when I was still in high school. My family had suffered financial hardships for many years, and I was determined to situate myself in an economically secure profession. After I came out, I envisioned myself as a lesbian physician activist. My analyst seemed very supportive of my career plans; yet, she was extremely closeted. Her training had been steeped in homophobia. When I asked her the best way to come out to people, she responded: "You'll have a far more successful life if you conceal your lesbianism. Whenever anyone asks you a personal question—fishing for information about your private life—just say that you've had a terrible experience and that you prefer not to talk about it. After all, that's not really lying, because we all have terrible experiences all the time. You could be referring to anything terrible that has ever happened to you." Saddened and dismayed, I realized that my analyst was far too closeted to be an ally in my struggle to be open and honest about my lifestyle. Nevertheless, I continued working with her on other issues, where I benefited from her guidance.

Through my literature reviews, I knew how dangerous the lesbianism-as-illness concept could be. Untold numbers of lesbians had been imprisoned or involuntarily psychiatrically hospitalized because of their lesbianism. Many had been forced to undergo treatments—including electroconvulsive therapy—in futile attempts to change their sexual orientation (Katz, 1976). It was clear to me that nonhomophobic studies on lesbians were sorely needed. In 1971, I surveyed members of the Northern California Psychiatric Association and found that most considered lesbianism a normal variation of sexual expression (Gartrell, Brodie, & Kraemer, 1974). This finding led me to encourage my senior research advisor, Keith Brodie, the American Psychiatric Association (APA) Program Committee Chair who later was elected president of the APA, to include nonbiased presentations on homosexuality at APA annual meetings. These presentations helped educate the membership about the importance of eliminating homosexuality from the DSM.

My next study was undertaken in response to a report by Kolodny, Masters, Hendryx, and Toro (1971) which suggested that gay men had lower testosterone levels than heterosexual men. Utilizing the same research design and analysis as the Kolodny study, we found that gay men had higher testosterone levels than their heterosexual counterparts (Brodie, Gartrell, Rhue, & Doering, 1974). Several years later, as an extern at the National Institutes of Health, I conducted the same study on lesbians, and found that lesbians had comparable testosterone levels to heterosexual women (Gartrell, Chase, & Loriaux, 1977). Both of these studies helped to dispel the notion that homosexuality could be "cured" by an alteration in testosterone levels. It was exciting to generate data that could counter the homophobic stereotypes I so often experienced.

During medical school at the University of California, I won a scholarship to a conference entitled "Human Dimensions in Medical Education." I spent four days in a small group led by Carl Rogers. Rogers (1951) modeled his client-centered approach in our group process. I was attracted to the notion that individual potential could be realized when therapists offered accurate empathic understanding and unconditional positive regard to clients. Rogers distanced himself from theoretical schools that relied on the "expertise" of the therapist. Instead, his belief in the healing potential of compassionate therapeutic relationships was intriguing to me. Rogers' nonjudgmental approach to human interaction was a refreshing change from the homophobic oppressiveness I had experienced in other theoretical frameworks.

PSYCHIATRIC TRAINING, 1976—1979

By the time I finished medical school in 1976, I had already published several articles, and my prospects for admission to a top psychiatric residency program were good. I had been wooed by Columbia and essentially assured of a position there by the psychiatry chair during my interview with him. My final interviewer was none other than the architect of the DSM himself. After reviewing my list of publications, he asked if I was a lesbian. When I replied affirmatively, he asked if I played the "masculine" or the "feminine" role in my relationships. I replied that I did not see the relevance of these questions to my application for residency. He then changed the focus to a discussion of recent changes in the DSM—removing the diagnosis "homosexuality" and introducing the diagnosis "ego-dystonic homosexuality." I questioned the usefulness of ego-dystonic homosexuality without a parallel ego-dystonic heterosexuality. When he objected to the parallel diagnosis, I said that I had met a number of radical feminists who, dissatisfied with their relationships with men, would have been delighted to convert to lesbianism. Even though he seemed interested in our dialogue, I was not admitted to the program.

Keith Brodie, who had recently become the psychiatry chair at Duke, contacted the Columbia chair to inquire about my rejection. Columbia, he was told, had a psychoanalytically-oriented department with very "traditional" ideas about lesbianism. The admissions committee had decided that my comfort with my lesbianism (i.e., I did not consider it a "problem to be eradicated") rendered me incompatible with Columbia's training program. Consequently, I ended up at MMHC, where, at least during the admission process, my lesbianism was no obstacle.

I terminated with my San Francisco analyst as I prepared to move to Boston. She recommended that I continue my analysis in Boston. After four years under her care, she informed me that I had had "a good, basic introduction to psychoanalysis." Although four years seemed a bit lengthy for an "introduction," when I arrived in Boston, I began shopping for a nonhomophobic female therapist. After careful screening, I set up an appointment with an older, highly-respected, Harvard-affiliated analyst. During the initial consultation, I gave her a rundown of my previous therapy, as well as a report on my life circumstances at that time. She asked if I was feeling particularly troubled by any unresolved issues. I answered matter-of-factly that I was not, but that I had assumed I would continue my analysis for years—to work out whatever conflicts or crises presented themselves. After all, I said, I was just starting my residency, and I considered personal psychotherapy an unofficial requirement for trainees. She replied that I seemed to have had a jump-start on self-understanding by entering analysis during college. She pointed out that I seemed very happy with my life. I had recently started a new relationship with the woman who has now been my life partner for 25 years. I had come out to family members who were very supportive of me. I had a wonderful network of friends, and I had an exciting career ahead of me. She recommended that I defer resuming my analysis either until I encountered an insurmountable psychological obstacle or I decided to enroll in the analytic institute. I walked out of her office feeling as though I had just been given a clean bill of mental health!

At that moment, neither she nor I knew that no analytic institute in the United States had yet admitted an openly lesbian or gay candidate. My previous analyst had been completely closeted when she had started her training. When I learned that I would have to conceal my lesbianism during the admission process, and possibly agree to analyze my "resistance to heterosexuality" while there, I decided to forego analytic training.

During residency, I failed to encounter any "insurmountable obstacle" that warranted a return to treatment. Meanwhile, I covered for classmates whenever they left the hospital for their analytic sessions. As a senior resident, I discovered a new form of therapy—tap dancing—that challenged and delighted me. My tap teacher, Leon Collins, was an African American hoofer who was the greatest living embodiment of unconditional positive regard in my educational experience. He praised and encouraged me, even though I secretly suspected that I had two left feet. Just before graduation, I arranged for payback coverage by my peers for one-hour-per-week tap therapy—much to everyone's amusement. The contrast between my enthusiasm when I returned from tap therapy and their moroseness when they returned from analytic sessions was always quite striking.

Meanwhile, I was drawn to Jean Baker Miller's (1976) self-in-relation theory of women's development. I sought her out, and over time, developed a lovely collegial relationship with her. It seemed more logical, given the great disparity in our knowledge and experience, that I would have become one of Jean's many protegees; however, Jean has always approached relationships with students and trainees very nonhierarchically. I admired Jean's ability to teach and empower other women, while encouraging critique and refinement of her views.

In subsequent years, Jean's model was expanded upon by the Stone Center group (Jordan, Kaplan, Miller, Stiver, & Surrey, 1991). Although I was enthusiastic about their efforts to construct feminist psychological theory from women's experiences, I was disappointed that their observations seemed most relevant to economically-privileged, white, *heterosexual* women. It seemed apparent to me that lesbian relationships came closest to the egalitarian ideal that the group advocated; yet, in the late 1970s and early 1980s, the group's primary focus was the dominant/subordinate heterosexual paradigm. During my first presentation in the Stone Center's Work-in-Progress series (Gartrell, 1984), I suggested that lesbian relationships be studied as model egalitarian relationships. I also discussed potential homophobic pitfalls that might be encountered by therapists treating lesbian clients. I surprised the audience—mostly mental health professionals—by proposing that lesbians be treated only by out lesbian therapists. I discussed the risk of heterosexual or closeted therapists imposing unresolved homophobia on clients, and the importance of positive role models for lesbian clients.

By that time, in addition to my academic appointment at Harvard, I had opened a private practice (Gartrell, 1997) and had already garnered substantial experience treating lesbians. As my reputation grew, I began to treat very closeted professional lesbians—ranging from government officials to academicians and scientists, many of whom commuted from other states to see me. Most had suffered enormously from the rigors of maintaining a secret life. Already, I had witnessed the benefits of encouraging these clients to come out, as, one by one, they overcame their fears and developed more honest relationships with their families, friends, and colleagues. From this experience emerged an early therapeutic stance of advocacy, woven out of my own successes from having been "out," and my observations of the tragic consequences of leading a secret life. None of these clients regretted coming out, especially since being out enabled them to respond to homophobia with externally-directed anger rather than internally-directed self-hatred.

Advocacy Within the APA, 1977–1987

At this juncture, I would like to focus on another important thread in my professional development, the first stitches of which were sewn during residency. I had received an honorary leadership fellowship to serve on an APA task force. This task force had been constituted to develop a curriculum on the psychology of women for psychiatric residency training programs. When we submitted our detailed 200-page proposal in 1980, APA officials refused publication because of a single sentence written by me: "Homosexuality is a normal variation in sexual expression."

Given that homosexuality had been eliminated from the DSM six years previously and, by then, the APA had an official policy of nondiscrimination against lesbians and gays, I refused to delete the sentence. Instead, I resigned from the task force, withdrew my contributions from the curriculum, and removed my name from authorship. Many of my co-authors—including Judith Herman, Jean Baker Miller, and Joe Pleck—followed suit. As a result the curriculum was never published. Thus began my disillusionment about the possibility of eradicating homophobia within organized psychiatry.

I presented a paper at the 133rd Annual Meeting of the APA (in 1980) on my clinical work with lesbians (Gartrell, 1981a). When I submitted the paper to the American Journal of Psychotherapy, the editor told me that it would be published, as long as I consented to a rebuttal by Charles Socarides, well known for his view that homosexuality was inherently and always pathological. Because I advocated nonhomophobic treatment for lesbian clients, it appears that the AJP considered my article too radical to print without input by Socarides. I allowed the rebuttal, on the condition that I was given the last word. In his commentary, Socarides called lesbianism an "emotional disorder," stated that lesbians engaged in "perverse acts" that could result in "death of the species," and claimed that lesbians were "severely handicapped in...interpersonal relations" (Socarides, 1981). I countered that he did not cite a single study on lesbians to support his claims, while referencing the numerous investigations that had found lesbians and heterosexual women to be indistinguishable in psychological adjustment (Gartrell, 1981b). Although I assumed that any intelligent reader would consider scientific data more valid than Socarides' opinions, I could not help but contemplate the destructive effects of psychotherapeutic treatments developed from such an approach.

In the midst of this dialogue with Socarides, my only sister was diagnosed with a very aggressive rhabdomyosarcoma. She was 27 years old, and she died nine months later. We had always assumed that we would grow old together and be there for each other—regardless of how many others came and went in our lives. Her untimely death changed my perspective on living day-to-day—forever. I promised myself that—as much as possible—I would live my life as though I too could discover that I had only one year left to live. That meant asking myself frequently whether I would have any regrets, if my life were suddenly cut short—and then making the necessary changes, if I had any. This day-to-day living empowered me to confront homophobic obstacles more vigorously; it also motivated me to help clients learn to live in the present.

Having grown up in the academic environments of Stanford and Harvard, I was familiar with the concept of delayed gratification. In a world where publications were valued more than vacations, I had assumed the requisite posture of working hard so that I could enjoy life (i.e., read, relax, travel, sleep) 40 years hence when I retired. Most of my clients entered treatment with the same belief system, and they were unhappy. When my sister died, so did my belief in delayed gratification. After recovering from the tragedy of her death, I began to read for pleasure, to use every moment of my allowed vacation, and to take weekends off. I still published enough to be promoted, but no longer devoted all my "leisure time" to work.

I began asking elderly folks to tell me about their regrets concerning missed or lost opportunities in their earlier years. None of them ever wished they had put more effort into their work. Instead, they regretted not having had more time with their children, not having taken vacations alone with their partners, not having focused enough on their own growth (educational, spiritual, or personal), and not having paused "to smell the roses." Most of these individuals felt that it was too late to make amends. A study by Metha, Kinnier, and McWhirter (1989) reported similar findings. I have told many clients of these surveys, and encouraged them to be mindful of regrets that can accumulate over a lifetime.

Meanwhile, I had become more visible within the APA. In 1982, I was appointed national chair of the APA's Women's Committee. Our mandate was to advocate women's mental health issues within the U.S. Although psychologists had documented ethical violations within their discipline, no efforts had yet been made to deal with sexual exploitation of patients by psychiatrists. I knew that the APA would never support educational programs on psychiatric abuse unless its prevalence had been substantiated. I called for an APA-sponsored investigation into the problem. I developed and pilot-tested a questionnaire to be completed anonymously by all U.S. psychiatrists. No surprises this time: the resistance was palpable. Documenting psychiatric sexual abuse was considered tantamount to destroying the credibility of the psychiatric profession (Gartrell, Herman, Olarte, Feldstein, & Localio, 1986).

When it became clear that the APA intended to stall my investigation indefinitely, I conducted a series of studies independently (Gartrell, Herman, Olarte, Feldstein, & Localio, 1987, 1988; Gartrell, Herman, Olarte, Localio, & Feldstein, 1988; Herman, Gartrell, Olarte, Feldstein, & Localio, 1987). Several years later, I surveyed internists, obstetricians, gynecologists, surgeons, and family practitioners (Gartrell, Milliken, Goodson, Thiemann, & Lo, 1992). Sexual abuse by these physicians turned out to be as prevalent and as harmful as abuse by mental health professionals.

Data from these studies have been used to promote criminal statutes prohibiting sexual abuse by health professionals, to support malpractice claims by victims, to educate consumers about nonabusive care, and to develop preventative-educational programs in medical and mental health training. In addition, despite considerable opposition, the American Medical Association and the APA have amended their ethics codes to specify that sexual contact with current or former patients is unacceptable.

As the public became more informed about appropriate professional boundaries, victims of sexual exploitation by health professionals began to speak out about their abuses. Prominent psychiatrists within the APA were accused of sexual misconduct, and many of the accused acknowledged their violations. The resistance to my cleanup campaign within the APA seemed to parallel the prevalence of power abuses by leaders in the field.

My research on professional boundary violations led to many years of clinical work with victims of violence. I collaborated with colleagues in developing parameters for establishing clear boundaries in clinical practice (Gartrell, 1992, 1994). I also served as an advocate in guiding clients through the complaint process. Understanding that exploitative therapists foster unnecessary dependence on themselves as a prelude to the abuse, I encouraged clients to pursue multiple avenues of support—from survivor groups to self-defense classes. I tried to illuminate paths to healing within a context of caring and respectful relationships. Helping clients recover from post-traumatic stress disorder involved various combinations of listening, empathy, understanding, guidance, and support.

My schooling in feminist political theory was far more relevant than my training in psychodynamic theory while working with victims of violence. Witnessing the aftermath of violence perpetrated by dominants (typically males) over subordinates (typically females), I developed a strong affinity for feminist analyses which advocated fighting back against oppression. For example, I was powerfully influenced by the work of sociologist Pauline Bart, whose studies demonstrated that women who resisted assault were less likely to be raped, and even if they were raped, suffered fewer psychological sequelae than nonresisters (Bart, 1975, 1979, 1981; Bart & O'Brien, 1985). Data from my work with victims paralleled her findings. Clients who filed grievances, took self-defense courses, or studied patriarchal oppression fared far better than those who were reluctant to do so. I became an advocate of recovery strategies that empowered my clients—with the treatment goal of helping them direct their anger externally rather than internally.

PSYCHOPHARMACOLOGIC AUGMENTATION, 1982—

Although currently we take it for granted that psychopharmacologic agents are part of the treatment regimen for a wide variety of outpatients, that was not the case during my training. In the early to mid-1980s, I began to use psychopharmacologic agents to treat so-called healthy outpatients. In my practice were some clients who, despite years of psychotherapy, maintained a "half-empty-glass" attitude toward life. I characterized them as the folks who, upon winning the lottery, would more likely complain about the tax implications than celebrate their good fortune. Successful professionals who were not clinically depressed, they had come to me after years of unhelpful treatment by other providers, who had used other modalities. When these clients also failed to improve after many months in my care, I began to experiment with antidepressant usage. This experimentation occurred when psychopharmacologists were finding that antidepressants had a broader range of usefulness than had previously been understood. I was fascinated to observe that, by taking antidepressants, my "half-empty-glass" clients became happier, more optimistic, and more enthusiastic about their lives. It saddened me to realize that they had spent so much time and money in psychotherapy, when antidepressants were far more efficacious. My threshold for offering pharmacologic agents changed dramatically in that era, and as a result, I began to do more short-term treatment.

LESBIAN FAMILY WORK, 1986–

At about the same time, a major sociological phenomenon had begun within the lesbian community that captured my attention. With increased access to donor insemination (DI), lesbians were electing to become mothers in record numbers. Since the early 1970s, researchers had been investigating children raised by lesbian mothers in response to the prevailing judicial opinion that lesbians were unfit parents. By the mid-1980s, numerous controlled studies had established the psychological well-being of children growing up in lesbian families (Patterson, 1994). Most of those studies concerned children who had been conceived in heterosexual unions whose mothers later identified as lesbian. Very little was known about children born to women who already considered themselves lesbian. In 1986, I began the National Longitudinal Lesbian Family Study (Gartrell, Banks, Hamilton, Reed, Bishop, & Rodas, 1999; Gartrell, Hamilton, Banks, Mosbacher, Reed, Sparks, & Bishop, 1996). This 30-year study was designed to provide longitudinal data on a population of lesbian families in which the children had been conceived by DI. Its findings are expected to shed light on the everyday realities of child rearing in a homophobic world.

The demographics of my clinical practice changed in response to this transformation in the lesbian community. Lesbian mothers and prospective mothers began consulting me about motherhood concerns. Fortunately, my study gave me a head start on anticipating various age-related homophobic challenges they might encounter (such as knowing which pediatricians and preschools were lesbian-family friendly). I now consider myself a national resource as well as a therapist in my work with this population.

Psychotherapy at the Millennium

So how would I describe the tapestry that has evolved out of the various changes in my belief system about psychotherapy? In pentimento-style, I began with psychodynamics, and added layers of lesbian feminist theory, political activism, Rogerian humanism, tap therapy, clinical work, and personal experience. At this stage of my life, I find that most "new" clients are psychotherapy veterans. Typically, they have seen one or more therapists previously, and have a reasonable understanding of their own dynamics. Long ago, I learned that insight alone could not guarantee an improved quality of life. I found that behavior change—leading to healthier, more fulfilling relationships—was the far greater challenge.

When consulting with a prospective client, I assess the client's needs in relation to my areas of expertise. If I determine that I may be of assistance, I require the client to establish a list of treatment goals. We review these goals together to ascertain that they are reasonable within the agreed-upon time frame. If the client's financial resources allow more flexibility, I explain that we will periodically review the goals and the progress.

I utilize a combination of insight-oriented (Hall, 1985; Kaschak, 1992) and cognitive-behavioral (Padesky & Greenberger, 1995) treatment modalities. I aim to provide the most effective and efficient treatment possible. Augmenting with pharmacologic agents if warranted, I establish clear boundaries early in treatment and discourage dependence on me in lieu of reciprocal, "real world" relationships. Most of my clinical work is goal-oriented and time-limited.

In recent years, I have kept a log of the feedback clients have given me during their "exit interviews" or annual reviews. As I perused this log in preparation for this chapter, I found that their assessments largely matched my own. To enhance my own description of my current therapeutic style, I would like to quote from some of these clients. I have selected from a diverse cross-section of recent clients, and have disguised identifying information.

> *A middle-aged lesbian mother consulted me because she was overwhelmed by the responsibilities of motherhood and work. She had been treated by several different psychodynamic therapists for a total of 15 years. Her treatment goal with me was to find a way to have some time to herself without feeling guilty. We met weekly for a year, and focused our work on time management. "I see you as an 'Efficiency Expert'—as in the old Hollywood film 'Cheaper by the Dozen,'" she said. "I present you with a complex tangle of needs, and then you tease out the most important threads and figure out ways I can take action to bring about concrete outcomes. I felt powerless to cope with motherhood when I started seeing you. You showed me that scheduling—something I hated—could be a powerful tool to save some time for myself."*

A lesbian caterer who had seen me on and off for many years was working with me on a career change. Since she had a history of paralyzing indecisiveness, our recent work consisted of constructing lists of obstacles she needed to tackle each week, along with strategies for handling them. Reflecting on her treatment with me, she commented: "Obviously, my needs have changed over time. Lately, I've used you as a sounding board for work-related problems. You have more of a problem-solving direct approach than, you know, when did your mother drop you and what did your father bring home to you after your first day of school."

A gay physician entered treatment because he was depressed and unhappy with his work. He had previously spent six years in psychoanalysis. In addition to treating him psychopharmacologically, I helped him reorganize his life priorities. We also worked on strategies for improving his self-esteem. "You helped me take care of myself while I was working in a system which depleted my will to do so," he said. "You taught me to change the way I see my environment, even if I couldn't change my environment. Simple strategies you taught me had such a profoundly positive impact on my life—like placing a personal ad, changing the way I eat, learning to love my body. I've made so much progress in changing ingrained negative scripts of self-hating and self-criticism."

"You've been very process-oriented and dynamic," said a lesbian mental health professional who consulted me to address her internalized homophobia, among other issues. Finding lesbian professional role models had been important to her. "I've really appreciated your critical interventions at critical times. I've especially liked that you're normal acting—not weird, as a person."

An elderly lesbian publisher had left treatment with another therapist because she had failed to see any improvement in her overall sense of well-being. We met with her weekly for two years during which most of our work was devoted to her struggle with chronic illness and chronic pain. Forced to make liberal use of pain medications, she was frustrated that her thinking was sometimes fuzzy. The therapy with me served as an organizing tool for her. "I valued your ability to take my cryptic thought process and assemble it into a cogent summary," she said. "Your retrospective overviews and interpretations were always helpful. Your comfort in discussing physical health problems separate from emotional, and the ease with which you brought the two together were especially important."

A perimenopausal heterosexual female administrator consulted me about her frustration over being unable to find a man who met her standards for a relationship. Friends had encouraged her to lower her expectations. I questioned the usefulness of committing herself to a man she did not respect. We met weekly for three years. At the end of treatment, she said: "The feedback you gave me was always practical, which I liked—I think because I kind of lacked any direction from my mother. You have been sort of a positive female role model for me."

"What matters most to me is your consistency of positive reinforcement that is just continual in terms of building self-esteem—especially in areas that I didn't even think I lacked it," said a young, heterosexual artist who often felt slighted by friends. In weekly psychotherapy with me, she struggled to establish friendships and relationships that were more reciprocal. Continuing her assessment of our work together, she commented: "You combine actual proactive strategies of things to do to make my life more effective that have been so amazing. Like—here is a concrete thing you told me to do—to scrub the bathtub rather than call X (referring to my suggestion that she refrain from calling an inattentive male friend by doing something more constructive, such as scrubbing her bathtub; if he hadn't called by the time she was done, at least she had a clean

tub). Your helpfulness extends to every area—like when I need a doctor—you suggest a good one. It's really all encompassing."

CONCLUSION

It is clear from this client feedback that my therapeutic style in some respects reflects the needs of particular clients. With some, I function as a pragmatic problem solver. With others, I do more dynamic work. As clients' needs change in the course of treatment, so does my therapeutic style. My goal is to provide the most effective and efficient treatment possible for each client.

Overall, I believe that my psychotherapeutic style has been influenced more by political than psychological theory. Lessons learned from my own struggle against the homophobia and sexism within organized psychiatry made it impossible for me to treat individuals without addressing the oppressive social structure in which we live. My commitment to living in the present has fueled my passion for correcting injustices within the mental health system. I am optimistic that exploitation by health providers will eventually be curtailed as women gain greater power to set and enforce standards of professional conduct. I am also hopeful that this millennium will bring a reduction in patriarchal oppression and a greater appreciation of diversity—so that the psychotherapy practices of the 21st century can be more value-free and less culturally-biased.

REFERENCES

American Psychiatric Association. (1968). *Diagnostic and statistical manual of mental disorders* (2nd ed.). Washington, DC: Author.

Bart, P. (1975). Rape doesn't end with a kiss. *Viva, 11*, 39-41, cont. 100-101.

Bart, P. (1979). Rape as a paradigm of sexism in society. *Women's Studies International Quarterly, 2*, 347-357.

Bart, P. (1981). A study of women who both were raped and avoided rape. *Journal of Social Issues, 37*, 123-137.

Bart, P., & O'Brien, P. (1985). *Stopping rape*. Oxford: Pergamon Press.

Brodie, H.K.H., Gartrell, N., Rhue, T., & Doering, C. (1974). Plasma testosterone levels in heterosexual and homosexual men. *American Journal of Psychiatry, 131*, 82-83.

Gartrell, N. (1981a). The lesbian as "single" woman. *American Journal of Psychotherapy, 35*, 502-509.

Gartrell, N. (1981b). Reply by Nanette Gartrell, M.D. *American Journal of Psychotherapy, 35*, 515-516.

Gartrell, N. (1984). Issues in psychotherapy with lesbian women. *Work-in-progress, No.10*. Wellesley, MA: Stone Center Working Paper Series. [Also published as Gartrell, N. (1984). Combating homophobia in the psychotherapy of lesbians. *Women & Therapy, 3*, 13-29]

Gartrell, N. (1992). Boundaries in lesbian therapy relationships. *Women & Therapy, 12*, 29-50.

Gartrell, N. (1994). Sexual abuse of women by women in counseling, therapy, and advocacy. *Women & Therapy, 15*, 39-54.

Gartrell, N. (1997). Out in academic psychiatry: Degrees of freedom. In B. Mintz & E. Rothblum (Eds.), *Lesbians in academia* (pp. 63-68). New York: Routledge.

Gartrell, N., Banks, A., Hamilton, J., Reed, N., Bishop, H., & Rodas, C. (1999). *The national lesbian family study: 2. Interviews with mothers of toddlers*. Manuscript submitted for publication.

Gartrell, N., Brodie, H.K.H., & Kraemer, H. (1974). Psychiatrists' attitudes toward female homosexuality. *Journal of Nervous and Mental Disorders, 159*, 141-144.

Gartrell, N., Chase, T., & Loriaux, L. (1977). Plasma levels in heterosexual and homosexual women. *American Journal of Psychiatry, 134*, 1117-1119.

Gartrell, N., Hamilton, J., Banks, A., Mosbacher, D., Reed, N., Sparks, C., & Bishop, H. (1996). The national lesbian family study: 1. Interviews with prospective mothers. *American Journal of Orthopsychiatry, 66*, 272-281.

Gartrell, N., Herman, J., Olarte, S., Feldstein, M., & Localio, R.

(1986). Psychiatrist-patient sexual contact: Results of a national survey. I. Prevalence. *American Journal of Psychiatry, 143*, 1126-1131.

Gartrell, N., Herman, J., Olarte, S. Feldstein, M., & Localio, R. (1987). Reporting practices of psychiatrists who knew of sexual misconduct by colleagues. *American Journal of Orthopsychiatry, 57*, 287-295.

Gartrell, N., Herman, J., Olarte, S., Feldstein, M., & Localio, R. (1988). Management and rehabilitation of sexually exploitive therapists. *Hospital and Community Psychiatry, 39*, 1070-1074.

Gartrell, N., Herman, J., Olarte, S., Localio, R., & Feldstein, M. (1988). Sexual contact between psychiatric residents and educators: Results of a national survey. *American Journal of Psychiatry, 145*, 690-694.

Gartrell, N., Milliken, N., Goodson, W., Thiemann, S. & Lo, B. (1992). Physician-patient sexual contact: Prevalence and problems. *Western Journal of Medicine, 157*, 139-143.

Hall, M. (1985). *The lavender couch*. Boston, MA: Alyson.

Herman, J., Gartrell, N., Olarte, S., Feldstein M., & Localio, R. (1987). Psychiatrist-patient sexual contact: Results of a national survey. II. Attitudes. *American Journal of Psychiatry, 144*, 164-169.

Jordan, J., Kaplan, A., Miller, J.B., Stiver, I., & Surrey, J. (1991). *Women's growth in connection*. New York: Guilford.

Kaschak, E. (1992). *Engendered lives: A new psychology of women's experience*. New York: Basic Books.

Katz, J. (1976). *Gay American history: Lesbians and gay men in the U.S.A.* New York: Thomas Y. Crowell Company.

Kolodny, R., Masters, W., Hendryx, J., & Toro, G. (1971). Plasma testosterone and semen analysis in male homosexuals. *New England Journal of Medicine, 285*, 1170-1174.

Metha, A., Kinnier, T., & McWhirter, E. (1989). A pilot study on the regrets and priorities of women. *Psychology of Women Quarterly, 13*, 167-174.

Miller, Jean Baker (1976). *Toward a new psychology of women.*

Boston, MA: Beacon Press.

Padesky, C. & Greenberger, D. (1995). *Clinician's guide to mind over mood*. New York: The Guilford Press.

Patterson, C. J. (1994). Children of the lesbian baby boom: Behavioral adjustment, self-concepts and sex role identity. In B. Greene & G. M. Herek (Eds.), *Lesbian and gay psychology: Theory, research & clinical applications* (pp. 156-175). Thousand Oaks, CA: Sage.

Rogers, C. (1951). *Client-centered therapy*. Boston, MA: Houghton Mifflin.

Socarides, C. (1981). Psychoanalytical perspectives on female homosexuality: A discussion of "The lesbian as a 'single' woman" by Nanette Gartrell, M.D. *American Journal of Psychotherapy, 35*, 510-515.

The author would like to acknowledge the assistance of Dr. Esther Rothblum, Dr. Dee Mosbacher, Dr. Marny Hall, Jasna Stefanovic, Jane Futcher, Amalia Deck, and Joan Biren, in the preparation of this chapter.

CHAPTER 7

A MODEL OF CONNECTION FOR A DISCONNECTED WORLD

JUDITH V. JORDAN, PH.D.

T herapy is a deeply personal, alive, moving relationship of healing and change in which the connection between therapist and client serves as both the incentive for change and the vehicle for change. Mutual empathy is at the core of change; and responsiveness on the part of the therapist lies at the heart of mutual empathy. This movement of caring, empathy, deepening understanding of self, other, and relationship is nurtured in an environment of profound respect and openness to uncertainty.

TRAINING AND EARLY WORK: THEORY AND TERROR

My early therapeutic work, however, was driven by theory and terror. Let me address theory first. In my actual clinical work, I was trained in object relations and ego psychology theories with a strong emphasis on more classical psychoanalytic tenets. My academic graduate program espoused healthy skepticism and empiricism (B.F. Skinner's office was on one floor of William James Hall, my department building, and Henry Murray's and Erik Erikson's offices were on another). Professors supported the questioning of many classical theories before they were ever even read. My internship and subsequent postdoctoral training for the first 10 years of my professional development, however, were heavily psychoanalytic in orientation. This training was buttressed by my own four-year psychoanalysis. I trained in a highly renowned psychiatric hospital that boasted a cadre of the leading analysts in the Boston area. In this medical model setting we treated both inpatients and outpatients. The psychiatry of that time was only beginning to envision a world of chemical interventions and the training was in psychodynamic psychotherapy. One lone behavioral therapist practiced in this setting; he was assigned the treatment of eating disorders and phobias. Although marginalized 25 years ago, he now heads the psychology department, and the formerly psychodynamic internship is cognitive behavioral in orientation.

At that time, in the late 1960s and early 1970s, in that setting, therapy was seen as alleviating pain through the development of insight; unconscious conflicts were brought into consciousness through the judicious use of interpretation. The transference was explored, if not analyzed, and insight created the motivation for change. With the help of once to twice weekly therapy, it was thought that most neurotic problems could be solved. Psychoses were seen as requiring more rigorous treatment, sometimes five times weekly sessions as well as careful use of medication. Supportive therapy was available for those people whose ego structures were thought to be too vulnerable for the more "worthy" work of uncovering and working through. But it was seen as "second best" or settling for something less than real structural change. There was an emphasis on intrapsychic change and growth, on internalizing functions, on helping people become less conflicted and more autonomous.

I tried hard to read and understand this traditional, psychoanalytically oriented theory as put forth by many intelligent analysts and therapists. Despite a commendation from the

Harvard Department of Clinical Psychology for outstanding achievement in my graduate program, in trying to learn this theory and practice I constantly felt stupid and inadequate. Supervision did nothing to lessen my sense of inadequacy, although many superiors were quite admiring of my work. There was a built in sense of not "getting it," of trying to internalize that which my supervisors knew and I didn't. I tried to understand their theories and suggestions without really feeling invited to ask them questions. I learned not to expect open sharing of uncertainty or struggle by my supervisors. I felt there was a reluctance on their part even to examine what really contributes to change in therapy (a question that was eternally arising for me!). Years later, as director of the internship training program at McLean Hospital in Belmont, Massachusetts, I was to ask almost every applicant I interviewed and every student I supervised, what do you think makes for change in therapy? And I loved the discussions that we had on this topic!

The terror for me in my early years came from many of these supervisors whom I carried about on my shoulder, in my head. There were several rather fierce, analytically trained men who served as my primary supervisors in my early years. They struck me as brilliant, incisive, sometimes seeming to exercise x-ray vision to see through me and my patients. They made astoundingly clear pronouncements about my patients, me, theory, papers by colleagues. I felt sure they could see my every flaw. In difficult, excruciatingly unclear therapy sessions I often longed for their wise presence at the same time that I feared my own inadequacies would be exposed. For years I secretly kept hoping someone would tell me what a real interpretation was (I didn't want to expose my ignorance by asking). I wished I hadn't had to read Kernberg five times to get the meaning. I wished Kohut and Freud and Fenichel and others could have found a more direct and simple language to communicate their wisdom. Each time I picked up one of the psychoanalytic tomes, I encountered my own stupidity. And I was intimidated. When I had questions about these approaches, I was sure that they ensued from my own inadequacy, not from some lack of clarity or wrong thinking in the theory.

In the practice of therapy, I was taught to be neutral, opaque, silent, and not too supportive, encouraging, or "nice." In fact, I was criticized for being "too nice." I was taught to be analytic and objective, to see any problem as being about the patient and to pursue the genetic material, i.e., the difficulties in early child-rearing that led to the current pain. Families were the context: parents, more specifically mothers, were targeted as pathogenic. Old problems were seen as being repeated in the therapy relationship as well as in the patient's current relationships. Difficulties arose from faulty intrapsychic structures. Social issues were rarely addressed. The larger context was omitted. There was no mention of cultural or political factors in the development of psychopathology. There was no acknowledgment of diverse cultural experiences, no awareness of the destructive impact on people of sexism, racism, classism, heterosexism.

Although able to muster some critical thinking about this system, I, along with many of my peers, was eager to belong to this erudite group of analysts and therapists. We wanted desperately to be seen as competent, to be able to practice in the way of our supervisors, to help patients. We overlooked the often dismissive attitude or subtle "blaming the victim" that went on in the field although often I winced when I heard patients portrayed as "bottomless pits" or "flaming borderlines" or "needy, masochistic women." I winced and I thought I was not properly schooled or learned or wise. I felt it was my problem, my "softness" or "too niceness" that made me uncomfortable with the pathologizing discussions about patients.

Moving Out of the Old Models

But slowly the pain of this system, for me, for my colleagues, for my patients began to erode my belief in it. I began to see, in particular, that women were often judged harshly by what felt like male standards. I began to hear the voices of trauma survivors long before the field as a whole was listening and respecting their stories. And I was troubled by the response of distancing, judging, and one-sided understanding. I was troubled by a kind of pathological certainty in the field. The professionals had the answers. The patients were often not trusted and not invited into a place of respect. I began to feel that too many of the practitioners I saw around me were playing games with their patients' lives, invoking pat "interpretations" that were dismissive and not honest to the patients' experience. I was troubled by the pathologizing and what seemed like the arrogance of some practitioners who felt they did not have much to learn about women, about people of color, about trauma survivors, about people from different classes. The intrapsychic explanation reigned. And that meant that mental health practitioners didn't have to be concerned about larger social issues. When feminist therapists pointed to political issues contributing to pathology, they were ridiculed and seen as "Johnny (Jenny?) one-notes." Interest in the sociopolitical context was seen as shallow, unlike psychodynamic theory which dealt with the deep and real: the intrapsychic. Often, individuals espousing sociopolitical understandings of personal suffering were pathologized (angry women, too political, strident, oppositional, lacking objectivity).

In 1978 I joined a support group of women, three psychologists and a psychiatrist (Jordan, Kaplan, Miller, Stiver, & Surrey, 1991). And as I listened to my colleagues, I began to rethink some of my own pain as a psychologist. Rather than seeing myself and my discomfort with existing systems as "the problem," I began to see the system as needing some rethinking. First, I wanted to understand better the pathologizing of women by the dominant models (characterizations such as hysterical, dependent, masochistic, borderline, too needy, too emotional, not analytic enough). Second, I felt that relationships were at the core of all psychological growth and I felt the power of connection had been overlooked. Third, I was beginning to question the reigning paradigm of the separate self. Emulating the model of Newtonian physics (molecular, about separate objects secondarily coming into relationship), traditional Western psychology had posited "separateness" as primary and relatedness as secondary. Increasingly, my understanding of human beings was leading me to see relatedness as primary and separation as secondary and probably defensive. Fourth, I felt that movement toward mutuality rather than separation was the main thrust of human development. I saw mutuality as being achieved through the development of empathic attunement. And finally I felt that context (social, natural, economic, psychological) is crucial to understanding people and shifting their patterns.

Slowly, I began to disidentify with the analytic model in which I was trained, although I acknowledge that many threads of the core beliefs of that model are still embedded in my thinking (e.g., in working with relational images one can see the echoes of working with transference; and the notion of growth in connection and moving out of isolation is similar to many of the early insights of "the talking cure"). But I no longer felt I could describe myself as an analytically oriented therapist. I began thinking of myself as a relational theorist and therapist. This was back in 1978 when such relational ideas of how to practice therapy were viewed quite skeptically and at times with alarm and worry by the more classical theorists. The language of connection and disconnection, mutuality, relatedness, therapists' engagement in responsive interactions was at that time seen as worrisome at best. Now we see emphasis on connection and on a relational, two-person psychology in many approaches.

The Relational Model

The relational model suggests that everyone yearns for connection but that because of early as well as later injuries, violations, and chronic disconnections in relationships people learn to keep aspects of themselves out of connection in order to feel safe. Thus, strategies of disconnection are developed (Miller & Stiver, 1997) to keep certain aspects of ourselves alive but out of connection: we become inauthentic in order to stay in the only relationship that may be available to us, usually with someone who is older and has more power. The less powerful person must sacrifice his/her needs and authentic expression of her/himself in order to stay in the relationship if the more powerful person is rejecting, humiliating, or nonresponsive. Since our primary yearning as human beings is to connect with others, to be in a state of related- ness (with other people, with oneself, with nature, with one's con- text), those aspects of experience which lead us to fear connection (e.g., a rejecting or abusing parent, a racist society) or tell us that we will not be accepted as we are, lead us into isolation. In isola- tion, we feel cut off from ourselves and from others; further, we feel immobilized, self-blaming, and unable to imagine an empath- ic response from others. This experience is often characterized by shame. In shame, we yearn for connection and feel unworthy of it (Jordan, 1989). We feel that our whole being is unworthy of love, unworthy of empathy, and we feel that we have no control over this. So in an effort to hide and protect ourselves we move into fur- ther isolation. And isolation in the relational model is seen as the primary source of psychological suffering.

While my original training in therapy taught me to be neutral, opaque, and nonresponsive, my practice has evolved in the direction of mutuality in the therapy relationship. Mutuality in therapy involves an attitude of mutual respect and mutual respon- siveness and growth; as used here, it does not imply sameness of role or equality. Clearly, patient and therapist occupy different roles and carry different responsibilities. They are joined in the common purpose of trying to alleviate suffering and promote the growth of the patient. The relational model of development and clinical practice suggests that growth toward mutuality is the pri- mary developmental trajectory for human beings. This growth occurs importantly through mutual empathy and mutual empow- erment. In therapy, mutual empathy involves letting the patient see how he/she has moved the therapist. That is, in order for empathy to lead to growth and change, the patient must be able to see and feel that he/she has had an impact on the therapist and the relationship, i.e., she must be empathic with the therapist being empathic with her. She must see, feel, know that the therapist has been affected and moved. Chronic disconnection results from the experience of not finding a response from another person, e.g., a less powerful person is hurt or violated by a more powerful one and the less powerful one is not encouraged to bring her feelings into the relationship; her response is invalidated or unwelcome. She must then suppress her real response and as Jean Baker Miller notes, "twist herself" to fit into the only relationship available to her (Miller, 1988). In this process, she begins to disconnect from her real experience and becomes less authentic. She also learns that she is not relationally effective, that she is not worth being responded to; this leads to isolation. The person feels isolated, immobilized, and blames herself for this state of affairs; she feels she is unworthy of connection.

The way back into the healing connection is through empathic joining and finding an empathic response in the other person that heals the original empathic failure and disconnections. This movement gives the patient an experience of relational competence, of being able to move the other person and affect the relationship. Self-empathy and empathy is fostered in this movement. Thus, although early analytic therapeutic approaches suggest nonresponsiveness is healing, where the transference can be fostered, played out and reworked (at the extreme in the notion of the blank screen necessary to foster a transference neurosis), I would suggest that healing occurs when the patient learns what impact she can have on the therapist. In order for this to happen, the therapist must be genuine, engaged, and responsive. Authenticity is informed by the guiding intention to help the patient. This does not open the way for reactivity or knee-jerk responses on the part of the therapist. Careful, considered clinical judgement guides the responsiveness of the therapist. But in this real engagement between patient and therapist, there is new learning and real healing of chronic disconnection.

HEALING THE DISCONNECTIONS

Chronic disconnection and isolation, as elaborated by Miller and Stiver (1997), are the source of most human suffering. Acute disconnections (empathic failures, poor attention, failure to respond) are ubiquitous and happen all the time in all relationships. They do not ordinarily become the source of chronic disconnections or "condemned isolation"(Miller, 1988). When someone empathically fails, misunderstands, or hurts another person and that person can represent the experience in the relationship, be heard, be responded to and be made to feel that her feelings and experience matter to the other person, the disconnection is moved back toward stronger connection. In fact it is in the healing of these acute disconnections that we gain a sense of trustworthy connection and of being effective in relationships. We gain a sense that we matter, that we mean something to the other person. If, however, the other person, often someone with more power, is not responsive to the representation of our feelings, we learn that we cannot have an impact on the other person or the relationship and we develop strategies of disconnection. Strategies of disconnection are in fact strategies of safety or survival. In order to keep unacceptable, unrepresentable, and vulnerable aspects of ourselves from being exposed to an uncaring other, we begin to disconnect from our internal experience, and we begin to disconnect from authentic connection with this rejecting other. We call these strategies of survival because in extreme cases, such as early violation, abuse, and abandonment, the injured person believes that these strategies are necessary to stay alive (and in the original, traumatizing environment, that may be true). At less extreme levels, we believe that in order to keep these aspects of ourselves alive or safe and to stay in some semblance of connection, we must keep them out of sight, hidden, unknown by others. In disconnection we are split off, out of touch with our own energy, and disconnected from the energy of relationship.

Therapy involves healing these disconnections and bringing people back into connection. Relational resilience, the capacity to move back into connection following an acute disconnection, is fostered (Jordan, 1992). Since we believe that connection creates growth and change, this has to be the first step of healing and movement. In therapy, we are looking for movement back into connection. This is not a simple, linear process, however. Because the strategies of disconnection are actually often felt to be strategies for survival, it can be extremely threatening to patients to think of relinquishing these strategies of disconnection. In fact, many people entering therapy experience a deep ambivalence about letting go of these protective strategies. The vulnerability necessary to move from strategies of disconnection back into the original yearning for connection is simply not possible for many people, particularly in their place of pain. Thus, the entry into therapy can lead to an escalation of a person's needs for strategies of disconnection. The therapist's task, then, is not simply to deconstruct the strategies of disconnection and push the patient back toward connection. The therapist must be empathic with both the need for disconnection, the strategies of disconnection, and with the yearning for connection.(Miller & Stiver, 1997). I believe the experience of empathic attunement and mutual empathy provides a primary place of healing, as the patient begins to move out of isolation back into connection. Thus I do not feel that empathy is only useful as a means to understanding. The joining, the experience of being with is in and of itself healing. But this also occurs in the context of meaning making and feeling understood. It is not an either-or situation. As people feel connected, they also increase their understanding of themselves, others, and relationships.

As a therapist, I feel I "hold" the larger sense of a movement toward connection while I honor the smaller movements into disconnection. This may sound simple. Sometimes it is. But often it is deeply challenging for the therapist. I will illustrate with the issue of working with trauma. Abuse of children (sexual or physical) represents an extreme, severe case of chronic disconnection. A powerful person, in a position of trust, violates the needs of the child (to be protected and respected) in order to gratify his or her own needs. The child learns that her vulnerability is dangerous, that her own yearnings for connection make her vulnerable to the manipulations and violations by more powerful others. She learns that her own needs for protection and care do not matter, that her feelings will not be heard or respected. She develops strategies of disconnection in an effort to stay safe, ultimately to stay alive. She learns that she has no impact on relationships, that she has no relational competence and that she is better off if she disconnects not only from others but from her own feelings and memories.

Someone with this kind of trauma history coming into therapy often feels extremely endangered. Therapy invites her into a situation that in many ways resembles the original abuse situation: a powerful person who has a position of authority and is supposed to be trustworthy, invites her to be vulnerable behind closed doors. For many trauma survivors, the therapy situation itself triggers a trauma response. As therapy moves on, strategies for disconnection are constantly being triggered. When the therapist fails the patient in some empathic way, the patient often experiences this as a signal of imminent danger (what Dan Goleman [1995] calls the amygdala hijack) and moves into extreme measures of disconnection, what we might call traumatic disconnection. In those moments, the therapist is experienced as a possible perpetrator and the patient often abruptly withdraws, becomes angry, or begins self-destructive activity. The therapist often feels puzzled, upset, misunderstood, and goes into her/his own disconnection. Often therapeutic impasses ensue at these times of mutual disconnection.

Paradoxically, these abrupt movements into disconnection also occur for trauma survivors following times when they begin to relinquish strategies of disconnection. When therapy is moving along in the direction of more connection, more trust, more authenticity and vulnerability, the patient may suddenly go into a major disconnection, as the terror of being more vulnerable and connected begins to surface. For the therapist, this can produce frustration, consternation, and disconnection, as the therapist feels that things were "going well" when suddenly the patient moved into an abrupt and severe disconnect (very angry, scared, self-destructive, withdrawn, symptomatic). At these times it is crucial that the therapist understand the nature of these whiplash, traumatic disconnections and that the therapist "hold" the larger picture of movement toward connection. The patient is terrified of letting go of her strategies of disconnection with the ensuing increase in vulnerability.

Over time, it is clearly the work of the therapy to help the patient figure out when relationships are safe and when they're not, how to protect herself in situations where there is nonmutuality and where the other person is potentially destructive. Movement toward mutuality does not imply a naive opening to all relationships. On the contrary, a major part of the work, particularly with individuals who have been badly hurt or traumatized, is to help them develop the capacity to differentiate growth-fostering, mutual relationships from destructive or non-growthful relationships. Within generally "safe enough" relationships it is also important to develop the capacity to discern when there is sufficient responsiveness to ensure the protection of one's vulnerability.

SOME CLINICAL VIGNETTES

A brilliant, therapy-wise patient, who had seen several other therapists before she began working with me, taught me a great deal about the importance of this discernment. She was someone who could pick up my mood in the short walk from the waiting area to my office. And she was usually accurately attuned to my level of fatigue, irritation, occasional buoyant hope, and so on. The problem was that she would then immediately assume that my mood was reactive to her. And if she picked up that I was annoyed or tired, she would feel that I was angry or upset about having to see her or about something she had said or done in the previous session. This often led to a protective disconnection on her part, where she would become silent, sometimes crying or glaring at me. I would then work very hard to understand where her feelings were coming from and often we would wind up very disconnected, in an impasse.

Over time, I actually found that when I was experiencing negative affect in particular, on the mornings when I was seeing her, it helped both of us if I could let her know that this was one of those days when she might pick up that I was slightly tired or irritated. I further explained that the quality of my presence might be less good than at other times and that I wanted her to know that I actually brought that with me from my life. I rarely gave details about where specifically this was being generated; she did not need that level of disclosure. But I wanted her to be clear in these cases that my mood was not responsive to her or my feelings about her.

While old models would have had me explore her fantasies about what my grumpiness was about, and would have encouraged her anger or disappointment, I found that sharing what I knew of my mood was most helpful to her. It validated something she was picking up, it acknowledged that she was not the source of my affect, it let her know that I was in touch with my affect and taking responsibility for it, and it helped her differentiate those times when I was available in a more attuned way and when I was a little "off," something about which she developed a kind of hypervigilance in her childhood with her abusive parents. She was still angry and disappointed with me for my less good attunement. My explanation did not derail her anger on this issue; it simply gave her a clearer picture of what was going on and helped her develop more accurate and effective expression of her anger. But she did not go into a traumatic disconnection with all the elaboration about her own unworthiness or my dangerousness. I also provided her with authentic feedback, when it felt clinically indicated, about her real impact on me and the relationship.

The practice of mutual empathy, with appropriate engagement and working with the disconnections, led to dramatic shifts in this young woman's relational images which had been dominated by images of perpetration and victimization. She began to experience herself as someone who was respected, effective, able to accurately assess others' feelings and motivations, and she developed expectations of being effective in relationships.

Rather than a more traditional path of therapist neutrality and interpretation of transference distortions, our model addresses the reworking of relational images which are conceptualized as images and expectations or relational patterns (e.g., a relational image might be "When I need something from someone I love, they get angry and abandon me"). These images are more effectively understood and transformed when the therapist is engaged and responsive. This involves working with old images and expectations of relationships, altering them gradually through understanding where they came from and providing a different relational experience, e.g., an accepting or caring response where previously a rejecting or abusive disconnection had occurred. This might be called a *corrective relational experience* although it is in no way purposely constructed or contrived; it simply occurs when the therapist's authentic, clinically informed responsiveness to the patient disconfirms the certainty of the dysfunctional relational images/expectations of the patient. This opens the way for new growth in connection.

Since mutual empathy is at the core of this movement, let me give another short vignette illustrating this.

> *Sue was a young woman who began treatment because she was feeling mildly depressed and alienated from herself and others. She was a very bright and capable young woman who grew up in a wealthy family where she rarely saw either parent. As she described her family, there was a marked sense of distance, coldness, and social striving. In her presentation to the world, Sue seemed crisp, efficient, and friendly, although slightly aloof. In our work together, she often kept a safe distance, and strong affect was rare. As she began to recover memories of sexual and physical abuse by an older brother, her veneer began to crack. She began to recall the terror of trying to find a safe place to hide in the large, empty house through which her brother stalked her. On one occasion when she was reporting this, tears came to my eyes, I got goose bumps and I said, "This is so like those terrifying dreams you've had of being in a concentration camp, trying to find a safe place." I made no*

*effort to hide my feelings. She looked closely at me and said
"You're crying." I acknowledged my tears and said "I'm so
moved by the vulnerability and fear of that little girl," (and I
was, indeed, deeply touched). She then teared up also, something new for her. And she continued, "I really matter to you,
don't I? You really care. This touches you!" She was amazed in
a quiet way, both moved and appreciative. Later she referred to
this exchange as the moment she rejoined the human community, not alone in her vulnerability and terror. This was a
moment of mutual empathy: I was moved by her, showing her
the impact she had on me, staying with her in this moment of
open vulnerability and she in turn was moved by my response.
She also found solace in my understanding of how terrified and
isolated she was and how profoundly that had affected her.*

HEALING CONNECTIONS: THE PERSONAL AND THE SOCIAL

Psychodynamic therapy seems to be moving in the direction of recognizing the power of relationship and connection in
people's lives. Although when my colleagues and I began developing the relational model 20 years ago, there was widespread
anxiety and scorn ("this is dangerous and unwise"), we are now
often greeted by these same practitioners with "we knew this all
along." While the originality of our contribution tends to get
erased in this latter reaction, it does speak to the widespread
acceptance of "two person" models, of the importance of intersubjectivity, of the centrality of relationship, of the healing power of
the therapeutic relationship. Technique, rigid adherence to theory,
whether analytic or otherwise, seems to be giving way to the richer appreciation of the transformative power of growth-fostering
relationships. I feel hopeful about this movement in therapy.

Unfortunately, it occurs at a time when there are increasing pressures on therapists to undertake short-term, technically
driven interventions. These pressures come from an economic
rather than a clinical base. The HMO/insurance driven treatment
programs tend to be anti-relational. And in that climate there is a

tendency to see relationship-centered therapy as regressive and destructive. The focus on "quick fix" solutions obscures the centrality of connection in people's lives and tends to put behavioral outcomes at the core. I worry about this trend. I worry less about the biological emphasis in psychiatric treatment although it, like any approach, can be misused and over-applied. But, in many ways I believe there is actually a biology of connection and disconnection; we are just beginning to understand the impact of connection on serotonin production for instance. I think, in the next decade, brain studies will reveal enormous biological sequelae of connection and disconnection. I have no doubt that brain functioning and structure changes as a function of connection. While an initial treatment with psychopharmacology may be essential to heal extreme disconnection (for instance in addressing trauma where medication can alter the severe symptoms that keep people locked out of connection), empathic connection in therapy can also serve to heal the psyche and the disrupted psychobiology created by faulty or absent connections.

But psychotherapy as commonly practiced continues to focus too narrowly on the treatment of the individual or on individual "dysfunctional" systems, like couples or families. I believe the importance of the larger context, for instance, in the form of sexism or racism, needs to be much more present in the consulting room and in psychological developmental/clinical theories. And therapists need to take more significant action in the world to alter the conditions of disconnection (violence, oppression, abuse, addictions) that impact far too many people. Thus, the disconnections that concern me are not only the internal disconnections an individual suffers with, or the disconnections between family members or people at work.

I am also concerned about the societal sources of disconnections, the discrimination and power imbalances based on race, ethnicity, sexual orientation, and class. These disconnections create enormous pain for many people. They will not be healed by individual or group therapy. Further, the dominant "separate self," individualistic frame of reference limits the scope of psychology and reinforces patterns of individualistic striving in the culture. These patterns interfere with the building of community. We need to aim at the larger target: socio-political change.

Let's for a moment consider the "problem of shame." Many people come to therapy suffering with feelings of shame which lead to disconnection and isolation. Some of these feelings arise within individuals as a result of concerns in their families. But many people are actively shamed in the culture. Shame is a powerful sociopolitical force that isolates and silences people. All marginalized people (people of color, lesbians and gays, women, poor people) know the force of shaming. Shaming is actively done by any dominant group to ensure that its reality becomes the reality. Shame isolates and silences. Both of these forces reinforce oppression. Connection and community provide the keys to movement out of isolation and oppression. Communal health, not just individual health, must be the goal.

THE CULTURE OF PSYCHOTHERAPY

Psychotherapy exists within a particular culture of professional practice. The traditional culture of therapy supports the following myths: therapists are the experts; change is unilateral; intrapsychic change is at the heart of the work; aggression and selfishness rather than yearning for connection and compassion are at the core of people's psyches; the person with power, the therapist, should be invulnerable or should not be too emotionally responsive. All of these myths arise from a system that overvalues separation and the separate self. Not only do we subject patients to unreachable goals of mature human functioning (self-sufficiency, certainty) but unrealistic expectations about ourselves as human beings are epidemic among therapists. Pressure to be the expert, the well-adjusted authority dispensing wisdom from on high, is widespread. The resulting shame of therapists unable to match their own standards of "mental health" leads to significant pain and disconnection. Therapists need to develop a sense of being participants in change. Therapists and patients take on different roles, with different expectations and these constraints are important and need to be respected. The patient is there to be helped, to change. The therapist is there to help. Change in the therapist, which is inevitable if therapy is really creating change in the patient, is important but not the focus of the therapy. But "everyone is much more simply human than otherwise" (Sullivan, 1953, p. 32) and we need to take responsibility for our human limitations. The therapist's humility and respect for the wisdom and the struggles of the patient are essential for the development of mutual empathy and change. A major disconnection can be created by heavy reliance on theory or dogma or holding impossible images of personal perfection for ourselves or others.

RESPECT, HUMILITY, AND COMPASSION

In addition to my belief in the value and importance of relationship, of mutual empathy, and of attention to context in the work of psychotherapy, I also believe that the particular path of healing is as unique as the relationship in which it occurs. There are a few caveats, a few attitudinal suggestions we can make to those learning the work of psychotherapy: respect for the patient is essential; the patient's vulnerability must be protected; an attitude of mutual growth and learning, with the well-being of the patient held at the core, fosters the work; an appreciation of the power of connection and the pain of isolation and disconnection helps the therapist find the place of possible growth in the patient; and humility and tolerance for uncertainty on the part of the therapist is crucial. When I am struggling with uncertainty or the particularity of healing in each therapeutic relationship, I often think of a line written by John Keats to his brother. He wrote, it is important to develop "the capacity to be in uncertainty, Mysteries (sic), and doubt without irritable reaching after fact or reason" (Keats, 1818/1987). It takes a certain amount of humility and self-empathy on the part of the therapist to stay in that place of uncertainty and mystery.

Little has been written about humility and compassion in the therapeutic literature. A lot has been written about narcissism, rage, aggression, the ego. I believe that humility and compassion are essential to real connection and to real healing, in both the therapist and patient. We need to accept our limits, not as strictures, faults, and places of shame but as aspects of who we are, of how we function in the world. We need to relate to others from a place of acceptance of who we are, who they are, of self-empathy and empathy for others. People tend to strive for specialness or become encapsulated in egocentricity when connections fail. Isolation breeds striving for superiority. When we have to assume a position of "better than," we move out of mutual connection. When we do not have compassion (being with, empathy, accepting in a loving way our and other's shortcomings), we move into judgement. Judgements, like exercising power over others or objectifying others, erode connection and mutuality. In a culture that reveres stardom, being special, better than, the lone star at the top, humility is sometimes seen as the lot of the loser. But in humility we assume our real place with other people, in nature. Therapists, too, must work from a place of caring and humility. We have few, if any, absolute answers: we bring caring; we share fluid expertise, a back and forth of learning and growing; we invoke certain relational skills and qualities of attention and awareness; we bring a commitment to the well-being of the patient. Our own lives sometimes do not reflect the best of our understandings and hopes. And yet we commit ourselves to the growth of understanding and healing and growth. More and more, I see the uniqueness of each therapy, the ways in which decisions are particular to each individual relationship. That only makes sense working from a relational, contextual model. Students and other therapists often search for universal techniques or answers. The best I can provide is a philosophy, an attitude of respect and mutuality, guidelines, a set of beliefs and values about what helps people grow. And I do that always with an openness to learning differently, from patients, from students, from colleagues. Trying to be as aware as I can of relational dynamics, trying to maintain an attitude of learning, and contributing to an expanding sense of relatedness serves as my core path. I believe that the primary human condition is one of connection and mutuality. I believe that the work of therapy is to bring people back into this condition of connection and relatedness, out of the painful illusion of separation and isolation. And I believe that the humble work of building relationships characterized by mutual empathy is at the heart of this path.

REFERENCES

Goleman, D. (1995). *Emotional intelligence*. New York: Bantam Books

Jordan, J. (1989). Relational development: Therapeutic implications of empathy and shame. *Work in Progress, No. 39*. Wellesley, MA: Stone Center Working Paper Series.

Jordan, J. (1992). Relational resilience. *Work in Progress, No. 57*. Wellesley, MA: Stone Center Working Paper Series.

Jordan, J., Kaplan, A., Miller, J.B., Stiver, I, & Surrey, J. (1991). *Women's growth in connection*. New York: Guilford.

Keats, J. (1987). Letter to "My dear brothers" In R. Gittings (Ed.), *The letters of John Keats*. Oxford: Oxford University Press. (Original letter dated 1818)

Miller, J.B. (1988). Connections, disconnections, and violations. *Work in Progress, No. 33*. Wellesley, MA: Stone Center Working Paper Series.

Miller, J.B., & Stiver, I. (1997). *The healing connection*. Boston: Beacon Press.

Sullivan, H.S. (1953). *The interpersonal theory of psychiatry*. New York: W.W. Norton.

CHAPTER 8

MY PROFESSIONAL JOURNEY: THE DEVELOPMENT OF MULTIMODAL THERAPY

ARNOLD A. LAZARUS, PH.D.

EVENTS THAT MOLDED MY THINKING

P urists are still very much among us, but I will venture to predict that many of the contributors to this book will reveal how they had started out by adhering rigidly to one discipline and subsequently saw the error of their ways.

In this connection, I was heavily influenced by Standal and Corsini's (1959) book in which 23 *critical incidents* were described wherein therapists deviated from their standard methods and orientations. Thus, a psychoanalyst became uncharacteristically authoritarian and forbade a woman who was having indiscriminate and unprotected sex from continuing to do so; another therapist began pounding his desk and admonished his patient to quit his verbal diarrhea; a committed nondirective therapist, instead of remaining reflective, took an uncharacteristically active stance. Twenty-eight experts of the day offered their comments. To their dismay, several therapists reported that by deviating from their ingrained training, the results were positive rather than detrimental.

The Standal and Corsini book was most liberating and stood in stark contrast to the exhortations of my professors, instructors, supervisors, and even the graduate assistants who played a role in my undergraduate and graduate education between 1952 and 1960 at the University of the Witwatersrand in Johannesburg, South Africa. Faculty and adjunct faculty members included militant Freudians, two self-proclaimed followers of Harry Stack Sullivan, and a Rogerian who promoted nondirectiveness with religious zeal. There were also several experimental psychologists on the faculty who were staunch behaviorists. In 1956, one of them had made arrangements for Joseph Wolpe to present his theories and methods of "conditioning therapy," which comprised a series of lectures and clinical demonstrations. I clearly recall how my fellow students and I, all thoroughly imbued with Freudian viewpoints, regarded Wolpe's reasoning and treatment methods as ludicrous and naive.

At this juncture, an epiphanous event opened new vistas for me. My wife (at that time, my girlfriend) had an acquaintance who suffered from extreme agoraphobia and pervasive anxiety. She had been treated by the top-rated clinicians in Johannesburg to no avail, and a prefrontal lobotomy had been recommended. I prevailed upon her to consult Wolpe, hoping that his unorthodox methods might succeed where the traditional ones had failed. I stressed that she had nothing to lose, because once they had cut into her brain, there was no turning back. With the patient's permission, I observed the therapy behind a one-way mirror, and Wolpe engaged me as a paraprofessional wherein I served as the patient's escort during several in vivo excursions. My establishmentarian professors and teachers had categorized Wolpe as a member of "the lunatic fringe," and as I sat watching him applying deep muscle relaxation, systematic desensitization, role playing, thought stopping, and other standard behavioral techniques, my skepticism, as the saying goes, went through the roof. However, his client or patient began showing unmistakable signs of progress. For example, during our in vivo desensitization sessions, the client was able and willing to extend the range of the distances traversed both while walking and by car, and she reported feeling much less anxious in general. At the end of three or four months, significant gains had accrued and any recommendations for a prefrontal lobotomy were dropped.

In discussing this remarkable turnaround with my orthodox professors and teachers, their pejorative consensus was that the young woman had undergone a "transference cure," and that her "flight into health" would soon be offset by symptom substitution or a relapse into an even more profound state of agitation and anxiety. After all, according to them, the deep unconscious roots of her problems had merely been glossed over (ignoring the fact that she had undergone years of psychoanalytic treatment before Wolpe's entry onto the scene). When months passed by, and no relapse was evident, I inquired when their dire predictions would eventuate. I received no satisfactory answer, and one of my trainers seemed to capitulate when he said that, in rare instances, defenses can be bolstered to such an extent that the underlying conflicts remain permanently submerged.

Nevertheless, this n =1 event did not win me around to Wolpe's viewpoint, but subsequently, when I took the risk of applying relaxation, desensitization, assertiveness training, and so forth with my own clients (a fact I had to conceal from my supervisors), I came to regard these methods as far more robust than the purely interpretative methods I was expected to employ. By the time I received my Ph.D. in 1960, I had come to a realization that, by today's standards, is very pedestrian—*there is no singular right way for everyone.* But back then, when psychoanalysis was widely regarded as a general cure-all for social and personal problems, this was an eye-opening and liberating notion.

Circa 1956, I joined a coterie of Wolpe's followers, who met regularly at his home in Johannesburg, to compare technical strategies, to discuss the learning theory bases of clinical problems and their resolution, and to review the lacunae and non sequiturs in psychoanalytic theory and practice. I was a graduate student at the time and found it incredibly exciting to be a part of this cabal. Wolpe was appointed to chair my doctoral dissertation, which compared group therapy using systematic desensitization to more traditional group methods with phobic subjects (Lazarus, 1961). Toward the end of 1960, when Wolpe emigrated to the United States where he accepted an offer to join the faculty at the University of Virginia in Charlottesville, I inherited his private practice and headed up the meetings with the contingent of unorthodox theoreticians and clinicians in Johannesburg. My zeal for what I had christened "behavior therapy" (Lazarus, 1958) culminated in the book I co-authored with Wolpe (Wolpe & Lazarus, 1966).

DEVELOPMENT OF A TECHNICALLY ECLECTIC AND BROAD-SPECTRUM VIEWPOINT

In 1963, my wife and I traveled half way across the world with our four-year-old daughter and two-year-old son to California where I was offered a Visiting Assistant Professorship at Stanford University. By that time, I was already adding to Wolpe's techniques (e.g., Lazarus & Abramovitz, 1962). In 1967 when I was offered a full professorship and joined Wolpe at Temple University Medical School in Philadelphia, it soon became evident that our paths had diverged. I regarded Wolpe's approach as too rigid and narrow. There seemed to be several useful techniques that non-behavioral clinicians were employing that readily lent themselves to a learning theory explanation (e.g., Gestalt therapists, transactional analysts, Adlerians, and especially rational-emotive therapists). I published a brief note to the effect that it is important to adopt promising techniques from diverse sources without necessarily subscribing to the theories or tenets that gave rise to them. To differentiate this approach from run-of-the-mill eclecticism, and to separate it from theoretical integration, I called it *technical eclecticism* (Lazarus, 1967). Wolpe viewed this as heresy and it led to a severe disaffection which grew into enmity.

Central to my current beliefs about psychotherapy is the assumption that *breadth* (helping clients attain a wide range of coping responses) is more important than depth. Gardner Murphy (1969) stressed that "Psychologists who will be extant in the year 2000 will have to be...enormously more *broadly* trained than the subspecialized people turned out today" (italics in original). "Psychoarcheological" explorations into the past do very little to remedy the cognitive and social skill deficits that lead many people to seek therapy. Although, as I have already emphasized, I became disenchanted with psychodynamic theorizing early in my career and gravitated to the methods I termed "behavior therapy" (Lazarus, 1958), the importance of *breadth* only became distinctly apparent to me several years later. It may help to understand the changes in my thinking and practice if I discuss a pivotal case I treated in 1966. Interestingly, as mentioned above, Wolpe's treatment of an agoraphobic woman in 1956 had provided me with a whole new perspective, and in 1966, another agoraphobic woman served to open my eyes to additional vantage points.

> *The severely agoraphobic and fearful woman to whom I am referring was aged 35. I found her to be a responsive and highly motivated client. She responded well to a standard range of behavioral techniques consisting of imaginal and in vivo desensitization, behavior rehearsal, assertiveness training, and couples counseling. After five months of therapy she was able to enjoy taking long walks alone, shopping, visiting, and traveling without distress. Important changes had accrued above and beyond the client's capacity to venture out of her home—her marriage relationship and sexual experiences were more gratifying; she was no longer socially submissive and enjoyed a wider range of social outlets. Nevertheless, although the client was delighted by her newfound ability to remain anxiety-free while traveling and engaging in the niceties of social interaction, she continued to view herself as a worthless person. She referred to herself as being like a 12-year-old who was now able to cross the street alone, but was contributing nothing to society. At this juncture, what is now called "cognitive therapy"*

was clearly indicated, and we launched into an assessment of her more fundamental attitudes and beliefs. She concluded: "If you want to feel useful, you have to be useful." Consequently, she founded an organization that distributed basic essentials such as food and clothing to impoverished people. This behavior, *based upon her* attitudes *and* self-concept *led her to view herself as "eminently worthwhile." In a follow-up interview she stated: "Thanks to the fact that I exist and care, thousands of people now derive benefit," and she proclaimed herself "eminently worthwhile."*

This case is described in greater detail in my book *Behavior Therapy and Beyond* (Lazarus, 1971a; 1996), arguably one of the first books on "cognitive-behavior therapy."

It was the aforementioned agoraphobic woman who first led me to realize that "behavior therapy" alone might be insufficient to take people—to use a football analogy—into the end zone. It soon became quite apparent to me that it was often necessary to venture beyond the customary parameters of behavioral interventions into such territory as values, attitudes, and beliefs. Although the early books on behavior therapy discussed the need to "correct misconceptions" (Wolpe, 1958; Wolpe & Lazarus, 1966), the focus was solely on erroneous ideas and did not address the realm of the client's self-talk, his or her basic values, or other cognitive processes. Indeed, when I emphasized the need to explore and modify such concerns, and when I drew a distinction between what I termed "broad-spectrum behavior therapy" and "narrow band behavior therapy," the reactions from Wolpe and many of my fellow behavior therapists were less than positive. I was subjected to scathing criticism and was accused of bringing "mentalism" back into the fold and of being a closet analyst.

This was an extremely stressful period. I had grown accustomed to living with criticisms from psychoanalytic circles, but when many behavioral researchers and clinicians also became rancorous, I felt completely disenfranchised. What prevented me from giving up the ship at this point? Friends and colleagues assured me that I had many supporters and urged me to test the waters by running for president of the Association for Advancement of Behavior Therapy (AABT). Wolpe was completing his term of office as president at the time, and he launched an aggressive letter-writing campaign strongly exhorting the members of the AABT to vote for Leonard Ullmann—not for me. To my amazement and delight, I won the election and served as President of the AABT from 1968 to 1969. In my outgoing address, I spoke about "arch-behaviorism giving way to a basically neobehavioral view which stresses the fundamental importance of cognitive mediation. . ." (see Lazarus 1971b). I knew full well that, in many quarters, this view would not be well received, but I refused to stifle my convictions.

But times have changed. Goldfried and Davison (1994) in their updated edition of *Clinical Behavior Therapy* (first published in 1976) state: "One no longer needs to argue for the admissibility of cognitive variables into the clinical practice of behavior therapy. Indeed, more than two-thirds of the membership of the Association for Advancement of Behavior Therapy now view themselves as 'cognitive-behavior therapists' " (p. 282).

THE STOCK-TAKING MENTALITY AND FOLLOW-UP INQUIRIES

Most of my conclusions about the conduct of therapy were derived from careful outcome and follow-up inquiries. I come from a family of small retail businessmen—my father, brother, uncles, and older cousins were all shopkeepers. As a child, I would hear a good deal about *stock taking*. In essence, every six months, each retailer would determine which goods and products were selling well, what could be done to ensure the continuance of this trend, what merchandise was not selling, and what steps could be taken to remedy this situation. I applied this stock-taking mentality to my professional endeavors. Twice a year I would study the clients I had treated, and would ask, in essence, "Which clients have derived benefit? Why did they apparently profit from my ministrations? Which clients did not derive benefit? Why did this occur and what could be done to rectify matters?"

Follow-up investigations were especially pertinent. They led to the development of my broad-spectrum outlook because, to my chagrin, I found that about one-third of my clients who had achieved their therapeutic goals after receiving traditional behavior therapy tended to back slide or relapse. Further examination led to the obvious conclusion that *the more people learn in therapy, the less likely they are to relapse.* There is obviously a point of diminishing returns. In principle, one can never learn enough; there is always more knowledge and skills to acquire, but for practical purposes, an end point is imperative. So what are people best advised to learn so as to augment the likelihood of having a full and fulfilling life?

Clearly there are essential behaviors to be acquired—acts and actions that are necessary for coping with life's demands. The control and expression of one's emotions are also a *sine qua non* for adaptive living—it is important to correct inappropriate affective responses that undermine success in many spheres. Untoward sensations (e.g., the ravages of tension), intrusive images (e.g., pictures of personal failure and ridicule from others), and faulty cognitions (e.g., toxic ideas and irrational beliefs) also play a significant role in diminishing the quality of life. Each of the foregoing areas must be addressed in an endeavor to remedy significant excesses and deficits. Moreover, the quality of one's interpersonal relationships is a key ingredient of happiness and success, and without the requisite social skills, one is likely to be cast aside, or even ostracized.

THE DEVELOPMENT OF MULTIMODAL THERAPY

The aforementioned considerations led to the development of what I initially termed *multimodal behavior therapy* (Lazarus, 1973, 1976a) which was soon changed to *multimodal therapy* (Lazarus, 1976b, 1981; Lazarus, Kreitzberg, & Sasserath, 1981). Emphasis was placed on the fact that, at base, we are *biological* organisms (neurophysiological/biochemical entities) who *behave* (act and react), *emote* (experience affective responses), *sense* (respond to tactile, olfactory, gustatory, visual, and auditory stimuli), *imagine* (conjure up sights, sounds and other events in our mind's eye), *think* (entertain beliefs, opinions, values and attitudes), and *interact* with one another (enjoy, tolerate, or suffer various interpersonal relationships). By referring to these seven discrete but interactive dimensions or modalities as Behavior, Affect, Sensation, Imagery, Cognition, Interpersonal, Drugs/Biologicals, the convenient acronym BASIC I.D. emerges from the first letter of each one.

The BASIC I.D. or multimodal framework rests on a broad social and cognitive learning theory (Bandura, 1977, 1986; Rotter, 1954) because its tenets are open to verification or disproof. Instead of postulating putative complexes and unconscious forces, social learning theory rests upon testable developmental factors (e.g., modeling, observational and enactive learning, the acquisition of expectancies, operant and respondent conditioning, and various self-regulatory mechanisms). It must be emphasized again that while drawing on effective methods from any discipline, the multimodal therapist does not embrace divergent theories but remains consistently within social-cognitive learning theory. The virtues of *technical eclecticism* (Lazarus, 1967, 1992; Lazarus, Beutler & Norcross, 1992) over the dangers of *theoretical integration* have been emphasized in several publications (e.g., Lazarus, 1989b, 1995; Lazarus & Beutler, 1993). The major criticism of theoretical integration is that it inevitably tries to blend incompatible notions and only breeds confusion.

THE MAIN ELEMENTS OF THE MULTIMODAL ORIENTATION

The polar opposite of the multimodal approach is the Rogerian or Person-Centered orientation which is entirely conversational and virtually unimodal (Bozarth, 1991). While, in general, the relationship between therapist and client is highly significant and sometimes "necessary and sufficient," in most instances, the doctor-patient relationship is but the soil that enables the techniques to take root. A good relationship, adequate rapport, a constructive working alliance are "usually necessary but often insufficient" (Fay & Lazarus, 1993; Lazarus & Lazarus, 1991a).

Many psychotherapeutic approaches are trimodal, addressing affect, behavior, and cognition—ABC. The multimodal approach provides clinicians with a comprehensive template. By separating sensations from emotions, distinguishing between images and cognitions, emphasizing both intraindividual and interpersonal behaviors, and underscoring the biological substrate, the multimodal orientation is most far-reaching. By assessing a client's BASIC I.D. one endeavors to "leave no stone unturned."

The elements of a thorough assessment involve the following range of questions:

B: What is this individual doing that is getting in the way of his or her happiness or personal fulfillment (self-defeating actions, maladaptive behaviors)? What does the client need to increase and decrease? What should he or she stop doing and start doing?

A: What emotions (affective reactions) are predominant? Are we dealing with anger, anxiety, depression, combinations thereof, and to what extent (e.g., irritation versus rage; sadness versus profound melancholy)? What appears to generate these negative affects—certain cognitions, images, interpersonal conflicts? And how does the person respond (behave) when feeling a certain way? It is important to look for interactive processes—what impact do various behaviors have on the person's affect and vice versa? How does this influence each of the other modalities?

S: Are there specific sensory complaints (e.g., tension, chronic pain, tremors)? What feelings, thoughts, and behaviors are connected to these negative sensations? What positive sensations (e.g., visual, auditory, tactile, olfactory, and gustatory delights) does the person report? This includes the individual as a sensual and sexual being. When called for, the enhancement or cultivation of erotic pleasure is a viable therapeutic goal (Rosen & Leiblum, 1995). (The importance of the specific senses, often glossed over or even by-passed by many clinical approaches, is spelled out by Ackerman, 1995).

I: What fantasies and images are predominant? What is the person's "self-image?" Are there specific success or failure images? Are there negative or intrusive images (e.g., flashbacks to unhappy or traumatic experiences)? And how are these images connected to ongoing cognitions, behaviors, affective reactions, and the like.?

C: Can we determine the individual's main attitudes, values, beliefs, and opinions? What are this person's predominant shoulds, oughts, and musts? Are there any definite dysfunctional beliefs or irrational ideas? Can we detect any untoward automatic thoughts that undermine his or her functioning?

I: Interpersonally, who are the significant others in this individual's life? What does he or she want, desire, expect, and receive from them, and what does he or she, in turn, give to and do for them? What relationships give him or her particular pleasures and pains?

D: Is this person biologically healthy and health conscious? Does he or she have any medical complaints or concerns? What relevant details pertain to diet, weight, sleep, exercise, alcohol, and drug use?

The foregoing are some of the main issues that multimodal clinicians traverse while assessing the client's BASIC I.D. A more comprehensive problem identification sequence is derived from asking most clients to complete a Multimodal Life History Inventory (Lazarus & Lazarus, 1991b). This 15-page questionnaire facilitates treatment when conscientiously filled in by clients as a homework assignment, usually after the initial session. Seriously disturbed (e.g., deluded, deeply depressed, highly agitated) clients will obviously not be expected to comply, but most psychiatric outpatients who are reasonably literate, will find the exercise useful for speeding up routine history taking and readily provide the therapist with a BASIC I.D. analysis.

In multimodal assessment, the BASIC I.D. serves as a template to remind therapists to examine each of the seven modalities and their interactive effects. It implies that we are social beings who move, feel, sense, imagine, and think, and that at base we are biochemical-neurophysiological entities. Students and colleagues frequently inquire whether any particular areas are more significant, more heavily weighted, than the others. For thoroughness, all seven require careful attention, but perhaps the biological and interpersonal modalities are especially significant.

The Biological Modality wields a profound influence on all the other modalities. Unpleasant sensory reactions can signal a host of medical illnesses; excessive emotional reactions (anxiety, depression, and rage) may all have biological determinants; faulty thinking, and images of gloom, doom, and terror may derive entirely from chemical imbalances; and untoward personal and interpersonal behaviors may stem from many somatic reactions ranging from toxins (e.g., drugs or alcohol) to intracranial lesions. Hence, when any doubts arise about the probable involvement of biological factors, it is imperative to have them fully investigated. A person who has no untoward medical/physical problems and enjoys warm, meaningful, and loving relationships, is apt to find life personally and interpersonally fulfilling. Hence the biological modality serves as the base and the interpersonal modality is perhaps the apex. The seven modalities are by no means static or linear but exist in a state of reciprocal transaction.

A patient requesting therapy may point to any of the seven modalities as his or her entry point. Behavior: "My skin-picking habit and nail biting are getting to me." Affect: "I suffer from anxiety and depression." Sensory: "I have these tension headaches and pains in my shoulders." Imagery: "I can't get the picture of my mother's funeral out of my mind, and I often have disturbing dreams." Cognitive: "I know I set unrealistic goals for myself and expect too much from others, but I can't seem to help it." Interpersonal: "My husband and I are not getting along." Biological: "I need to remember to take my medication, and I should start exercising and eating less junk."

It is more usual, however, for people to enter therapy with explicit problems in two or more modalities—"I have headaches that my doctor tells me are due to tension. I also worry too much, and I feel frustrated a lot of the time. And I'm very angry with my brother." Initially, it is usually advisable to engage the patient by focusing on the issues, modalities, or areas of concern that he or she presents. To deflect the emphasis too soon onto other matters that may seem more important, is only inclined to make the patient feel discounted. Once rapport has been established, however, it is usually easy to shift to more significant problems.

Thus, any good clinician will first address and investigate the presenting issues. "Please tell me more about the aches and pains you are experiencing." "Do you feel tense in any specific areas of your body?" "You mentioned worries and feelings of frustration. Can you please elaborate on them for me?" "What are some of the specific clash points between you and your brother?" Any competent therapist would flesh out the details. However, a multimodal therapist goes farther. She or he will carefully note the specific modalities across the BASIC I.D. that are being discussed, and which ones are omitted or glossed over. The latter (i.e., the areas that are overlooked or neglected) often yield important data when specific elaborations are requested. And when examining a particular issue, the BASIC I.D. will be rapidly but carefully traversed.

There is a lot more to the multimodal methods of inquiry and treatment and the interested reader is referred to some of my other publications that spell out the details (e.g., Lazarus, 1989a, 1995, 1997). In general, it seems to me that narrow school adherents are receding into the minority and that competent clinicians are all broadening their base of operations.

HOW HAS THE MULTIMODAL MODEL CHANGED OVER THE PAST 20 YEARS?

The BASIC I.D. spectrum has continued to serve as a most expedient template or compass. A question often raised is whether a "spiritual" dimension should be added. In the interests of parsimony, I point out that when someone refers to having had a "spiritual" or a "transcendental" experience, typically their reactions point to, and can be captured by, the interplay among powerful cognitions, images, sensations, and affective responses.

Several useful questionnaires have been developed. For example, apart from refinements to the Multimodal Life History Questionnaire that have resulted from field testing, a *Structural Profile Inventory* (SPI) has been developed and tested. This 35-item survey provides a quantitative rating of the extent to which clients favor specific BASIC I.D. areas. The instrument measures the extent to which people are action-oriented (Behavior), their degree of emotionality (Affect), the value they attach to various sensory experiences (Sensation), how much time they occupy with fantasy, day dreaming, and "thinking in pictures" (Imagery), how analytical they tend to be (Cognition), how important other people are to them (Interpersonal), and the extent to which they are healthy and health-conscious (Drugs/Biology). The reliability and validity of this instrument has been borne out by research (Herman, 1992; Landes, 1991). Herman (1991, 1994, 1998) showed that when clients and therapists have wide differences on the SPI, therapeutic outcomes tend to be adversely affected.

Multimodal therapy is so broad, so flexible, so personalistic and adaptable that tightly controlled outcome research is exceedingly difficult to conduct. Nevertheless, a Dutch psychologist, Kwee (1984), organized a treatment outcome study on 84 hospitalized patients suffering from obsessive-compulsive disorders and extensive phobias, 90 percent of whom had received prior treatment without success. Over 70 percent of these patients had suffered from their disorders for more than 4 years. Multimodal treatment regimens resulted in substantial recoveries and durable nine-month follow-ups. This was confirmed and amplified by Kwee and Kwee-Taams (1994).

In Scotland, Williams (1988), in a carefully controlled outcome study, compared multimodal assessment and treatment with less integrative approaches in helping children with learning disabilities. Clear data emerged in support of the multimodal procedures. Although the multimodal approach *per se* has not become a household term, recently, the vast literature on treatment regimens, be they journal articles or entire books, has borrowed liberally from multimodal therapy, with authors referring to multidimensional, multi-method, or multifactorial procedures.

THE CURRENT WORLD OF PSYCHOTHERAPY AND WHERE WE MAY BE HEADING

Many changes have taken place in the psychotherapy arena since I emerged with my doctorate in clinical psychology in 1960. At that time, clinical psychology was a new and unfamiliar discipline, and the idea of having non-medical personnel performing "treatment" was controversial. In South Africa, the Medical and Dental Council created an auxiliary register for psychologists who had obtained at least an approved master's degree and had satisfactorily completed a year's internship. Thus, clinical psychologists were seen as ancillary personnel who were permitted to practice under the aegis and supervision of licensed physicians.

In the 1960s, the practice of psychotherapy was the predominant domain of psychiatrists. In the media, whenever any form of mental or emotional interventions were mentioned, the services of a *psychiatrist* were secured. Only recently has the expression "You need to see a psychiatrist," almost been matched by "You ought to see a psychologist." In the 1960s, most psychologists were attached to academic departments of psychology where they performed animal experiments and ran studies (not treatments) on human subjects. Those who worked in applied settings were predominantly *psychometricians* who administered intelligence and personality tests. Psychologists battled to be seen as legitimate *therapists*, to receive third-party payments for their services, and to be independent practitioners. This was soon eclipsed by the influx of therapists who were neither psychiatrists nor psychologists. For example, originally, *social workers* had focused their primary energies on assisting economically underprivileged and socially maladjusted people for whom they would endeavor to arrange material aid. Today, most graduates with a Masters of Social Work degree (MSW) have ventured far away from the agencies and hospitals that had been their primary employment settings. Although the majority are peripherally familiar with psychology, they now hang up shingles and practice psychotherapy and provide counseling services in private practice settings. In many states, social workers have lobbied quite successfully to obtain third-party payments. They have been joined by a bewildering array of *counselors* who also offer guidance and emotional assistance. In today's marketplace, most clients are being seen by social workers and sundry counselors. Many psychiatrists have become administrators; others confine their practices to biological psychiatry. Instead of treating private clients, many psychologists have sought gainful employment in school and industrial settings, or have turned to their presumed expertise in testing—for example, neuropsychological assessments for use in forensic situations.

Peterson (1997) has written eloquently and profoundly about professional psychologists and their education. He contends that anyone "who cannot write a thoroughly informed statement about clinical vs. actuarial prediction, construct validity, and the other issues in clinical psychology that Meehl has so brilliantly elucidated, (is) psychologically illiterate and undeserving of the Doctor of Psychology degree" (p. 247). But does advanced training and credentialing make for better therapists? Not according to Robyn Dawes (1994) whose book *House of Cards* provides trenchant data that point to the fact that greater training, more experience, and higher degrees do not make for better therapists. (Expertise and experience are not synonymous.) Add to this the impact of postmodern theory within psychotherapy—a view that the knower constructs rather than perceives or discovers reality—and virtually all the canons of science go by the wayside. (Held, 1995, has written a penetrating critique of postmodernism.) The proliferation of New Age therapists who adhere to mystical and transpersonal philosophies simply adds chaos to confusion.

The saving grace, in my opinion, is that a fair number of clinical researchers and clinicians are *au fait* with the principles of scientific investigation. They fully recognize the differences between anecdotes and evidence; they understand the nuances of the scientific method; they are able to detect experimental artifacts and separate specious and spurious contaminants from actual data; many have identified experimentally supported methods that point the way to selecting appropriate treatments for specific problems; and they have developed sophisticated sequences of manualized treatments that lend precision to the remediation of diverse clinical problems.

The advent of manuals over the past 20 years has improved the quality of treatment research. Manuals permit one to know what was done in a step-by-step fashion and thus it becomes possible to replicate specific treatments. Much controversy, however, has arisen in this regard. Clinicians question whether manuals used in laboratory studies are applicable in clinical settings. What is the role of clinical judgment? The reader is referred to a lead article by Wilson (1998) and to seven commentaries in the fall 1998 issue of *Clinical Psychology: Science and Practice*.

For the foreseeable future, it would appear that third-party insurance payers will arrive at more and more restrictive criteria for reimbursement, and greater demands will be imposed to show that specific treatments have empirical evidence to support their efficacy and effectiveness (Seligman, 1995).

Some concluding words: Gravitate to broad-based methods of assessment and therapy; learn about science and the scientific method; master specific treatments of choice for particular conditions and disorders; strive mightily to find out *what* is being used in clinical practice, *why* particular methods have been discounted whereas others are viewed with favor; and learn *how* to administer experimentally validated treatments of choice. And remember that if any method or procedure sounds too good to be true, it probably is!

REFERENCES

Ackerman, D. (1995). *A natural history of the senses*. New York: Vintage Books.

Bandura, A. (1977). *Social learning theory*. Englewood Cliffs, NJ: Prentice Hall.

Bandura, A. (1986). *Social foundations of thought and action: A social cognitive theory*. Englewood Cliffs, NJ: Prentice Hall.

Bozarth, J. D. (1991). Person-centered assessment. *Journal of*

Counseling & Development, 69, 458-461.

Dawes, R. M. (1994). *House of cards: Psychology and psychotherapy built on myth.* New York: The Free Press.

Fay, A., & Lazarus, A. A. (1993). On necessity and sufficiency in psychotherapy. *Psychotherapy in Private Practice, 12,* 33-39.

Goldfried, M. R., & Davison, G. C. (1994). *Clinical behavior therapy.* New York: Wiley.

Held, B. S. (1995). *Back to reality: A critique of postmodern theory in psychotherapy.* New York: Norton.

Herman, S. M. (1991). Client-therapist similarity on the Multimodal Structural Profile Inventory as predictive of psychotherapy outcome. *Psychotherapy Bulletin, 26,* 26-27.

Herman, S. M. (1992). A demonstration of the validity of the Multimodal Structural Profile Inventory through a correlation with the Vocational Preference Inventory. *Psychotherapy in Private Practice, 11,* 71-80.

Herman, S. M. (1994). The diagnostic utility of the Multimodal Structural Profile. *Psychotherapy in Private Practice, 13,* 55-62.

Herman, S. M. (1998). The relationship between therapist-client modality similarity and psychotherapy outcome. *Journal of Psychotherapy Practice and Research, 7,* 56-64.

Kwee, M. G. T. (1984). *Klinische multimodale gedragstherapie.* Lisse, Holland: Swets & Zeitlinger.

Kwee, M. G. T., & Kwee-Taams, M. K. (1994). *Klinishegedragstherapie in Nederland & vlaanderen.* Delft, Holland: Eubron

Landes, A. (1991). Development of the structural profile inventory. *Psychotherapy in Private Practice, 9,* 123-141.

Lazarus, A. A. (1958). New methods in psychotherapy: A case study. *South African Medical Journal, 32,* 660-664.

Lazarus, A. A. (1961). Group therapy of phobic disorders by systematic desensitization. *Journal of Abnormal and Social Psychology, 63,* 505-510.

Lazarus, A. A. (1967). In support of technical eclecticism. *Psychological Reports, 21,* 415-416.

Lazarus, A. A. (1971a). *Behavior therapy and beyond*. New York: McGraw-Hill.

Lazarus, A. A. (1971b). Foreword. In R. D. Rubin, H. Fensterheim, A. A. Lazarus, & C. M. Franks (Eds.), *Advances in behavior therapy*. New York: Academic Press.

Lazarus, A. A. (1973). Multimodal behavior therapy: Treating the BASIC ID. *Journal of Nervous and Mental Disease, 156*, 404-411.

Lazarus, A. A. (1976a). *Multimodal behavior therapy*. New York: Springer.

Lazarus, A. A. (1976b). Multimodal therapy. *Contemporary Issues in Mental Health, 1*, 44-51.

Lazarus, A. A. (1981). *The practice of multimodal therapy: Systematic comprehensive and effective psychotherapy*. New York: McGraw-Hill.

Lazarus, A. A. (1989a). *The practice of multimodal therapy: Systematic, comprehensive and effective psychotherapy*. (Updated ed.). Baltimore: The Johns Hopkins University Press.

Lazarus, A. A. (1989b). Why I am an eclectic (not an integra-tionist). *British Journal of Guidance & Counseling, 17*, 248-258.

Lazarus, A. A. (1992). Multimodal therapy. In J. C. Norcross & M. R. Goldfried (Eds.), *Handbook of psychotherapy integration* (pp. 231-263). New York: Basic Books.

Lazarus, A. A. (1995). Multimodal therapy. In R. J. Corsini and D. Wedding (Eds.), *Current psychotherapies* (5th ed.) (pp. 322-355). Itasca, IL: Peacock Publishers.

Lazarus, A. A. (1996) *Behavior therapy and beyond*. Northvale, NJ: Jason Aronson.

Lazarus, A. A. (1997). *Brief but comprehensive psychotherapy: The multimodal way*. New York: Springer Publishing.

Lazarus, A. A. & Abramovitz, A. (1962). The use of "Emotive Imagery" in the treatment of children's phobias. *Journal of Mental Science, 108*, 191-195.

Lazarus, A. A. & Beutler, L. E. (1993). On technical eclecticism.

Journal of Counseling and Development. 71, 381-385.

Lazarus, A. A., Beutler, L. E., & Norcross, J. C. (1992). The future of technical eclecticism. *Psychotherapy, 29*, 11-20.

Lazarus, A. A., Kreitzberg, C. B., & Sasserath, V. J. (1981). Multimodal therapy. In R. J. Corsini (Ed.), *Handbook of innovative psychotherapies* (pp. 502-514). New York: Wiley.

Lazarus, A. A. & Lazarus, C. N. (1991a). Let us not forsake the individual nor ignore the data: A response to Bozarth. *Journal of Counseling & Development, 69*, 463-465.

Lazarus, A. A. & Lazarus, C. N. (1991b). *Multimodal Life History Inventory*. Champaign, IL: Research Press.

Murphy, G. (1969). Psychology in the year 2000. *American Psychologist, 24*, 523-530.

Peterson, D. R. (1997). *Educating professional psychologists: History and guiding conception*. Washington, DC: American Psychological Association.

Rotter, J. B. (1954). *Social learning theory and clinical psychology*. Englewood Cliffs, NJ: Prentice-Hall.

Rosen, R. C. & Leiblum, S. R. (Eds.). (1995). *Case studies in sex therapy*. New York: Guilford.

Seligman, M. E. P. (1995). The effectiveness of psychotherapy. *American Psychologist, 50*, 965-974.

Standal, S. W., & Corsini, R. C. (Eds.), (1959). *Critical incidents in psychotherapy*. Englewood Cliffs, NJ: Prentice-Hall.

Williams, T. A. (1988). A multimodal approach to assessment and intervention with children with learning disabilities. Unpublished Ph.D. dissertation, Department of Psychology, University of Glasgow.

Wilson, G. T. (1998). Manual-based treatment and clinical practice. *Clinical Psychology: Science and Practice, 5*, 363-375.

Wolpe, J. (1958). *Psychotherapy by reciprocal inhibition*. Stanford: Stanford University Press.

Wolpe,. J. & Lazarus, A. A. (1966). *Behavior therapy techniques*. Oxford: Pergamon Press.

CHAPTER 9

A QUARTER CENTURY OF PSYCHOTHERAPY

RONALD F. LEVANT, ED.D.

I am delighted to have the opportunity to reflect on psychotherapy for this timely new volume because it has been so central to my life both personally and professionally. It is well known that many of us drawn to the mental health field have participated in psychotherapy, and that is certainly true of me. It is also the case that psychotherapy has been a central focus of my professional career beginning in graduate school and continuing through the present.

WHO I AM

Since earning my doctorate in Clinical Psychology and Public Practice from Harvard in 1973, I have been a clinician in solo independent practice, clinical supervisor in hospital settings, clinical and academic administrator, and academic faculty member. I have served on the faculties of Boston, Rutgers, and Harvard Universities and am currently dean and professor at the Center for

Psychological Studies at Nova Southeastern University. Although psychotherapy has been a central part of my career, I also have interests in family and gender psychology and in advancing professional psychology. I maintained a research program on the effects of preventive psychoeducational programs for families from 1975 to 1988 and have been investigating masculinity ideology in multicultural perspective from 1989 to the present. In addition, I have been involved in advocacy for professional psychology since 1978 through elective and appointive offices that I have held in my state and regional psychological associations, several divisions of the American Psychological Association (APA), and APA itself, where I now serve as recording secretary.

THE CONTEXT CHANGES: 1970s TO 1990s

It is interesting to reflect on the larger contextual changes of the last quarter century since I earned my doctorate. At that time (the early 1970s) the legislative foundation for the independent practice of psychotherapy by non-M.D.s was being laid in the form of licensure, and freedom of choice and vendorship laws were being passed in many states. Deinstitutionalization of the state mental hospitals was underway and recently constructed community mental health facilities were taking over their care. Public attitudes toward mental health services were starting to shift so that people with milder diagnoses were able to shrug off the stigma and view psychotherapy as potentially helpful to them. These developments and others led to a boom in the practice of psychotherapy from the late 1970s to the early 1990s that encompassed not only psychologists and psychiatrists but also masters-level practitioners of every stripe.

Meanwhile in the profession, we were still arguing with Hans Eysenck (1952) about whether psychotherapy worked. Allen Bergin (1971) observed in the first edition of Bergin and Garfield's *Handbook of Psychotherapy and Behavior Change*: "It is slightly amazing to find that 18 years after his original critique of therapeutic effects, Professor Hans Eysenck is still agreed and disagreed with more than any single critic on the psychotherapy scene..." (p. 217).

We were also enamored of "schools" of psychotherapy, which on the one hand were proliferating to ridiculous levels, but on the other hand afforded the best research window available at the time to identify school-specific, "active ingredients" of psychotherapy, and thereby improve outcomes. Alas, the search for theory-specific effects was even then disappointing, as Luborsky, Singer, and Luborsky (1975) concluded after reviewing 100 controlled studies of therapy outcome. Echoing the verdict of the dodo bird in *Alice in Wonderland*, they found that "everybody has won and all must have prizes" (p. 1003).

Now, of course, it has been generally accepted, since the Smith and Glass (1977) meta-analysis of the effects of psychotherapy, that therapy works. Moreover, after large scale comparative studies such as the National Collaborative Study of Depression, it has also been generally accepted that the effects of therapy are more nonspecific than specific, and have more in common with the placebo effect than with any "active ingredients." On the therapist's side these nonspecific effects include the provision of warmth, empathy, and caring, the instillation of hope, and the teaching of psychological skills such as managing emotions, handling relationships, and coping with adversity. On the client's side these effects include the expectation of benefit, the motivation to change, and internal strengths.

Mirroring the times, I began my career identified with a theoretical perspective—the client-centered school—and now find myself being much more comprehensive in my approach, incorporating theories and techniques from the systems, psychodynamic, and cognitive-behavioral approaches, and tailoring my approach to the needs of the client. Let's take a look at how this evolved.

Personal Development

I grew up in a working-class semi-Jewish family (both parents were ethnically Jewish but my father was not religious, and in fact termed himself an atheist), with a breadwinner immigrant father who worked as a printer, a homemaker-mother (daughter of an immigrant), and a younger brother. My parents were together until my father's death in 1994. This nuclear family was embedded in a larger extended family: My father had two brothers and several close cousins and my mother had four siblings and numerous cousins, and most of these folks had families. Most of this clan lived in Southern California. Growing up, some of my best memories are of large family get-togethers with lots of aunts, uncles, cousins, and grandparents (who were alive during my childhood and early adolescence).

One additional feature of my family of origin is noteworthy. It was a "father knows best" model. Disagreements were handled by power assertion. The balancing of multiple perspectives was unheard of. As a child I often felt misunderstood and that things were unfair or "arbitrary" (a word I often used). These experiences no doubt provided the basis for my professional interests in empathy, perspective-taking, and negotiation.

In the early 1970s, as a graduate student, I brashly tried to be my family's self-appointed therapist. Needless to say, this approach failed miserably. Later, as a family psychologist I tried for years to do differentiation work on my relationships with members of my family of origin as prescribed by Murray Bowen (1978). As I worked on defusing my emotional reactions in order to detriangulate from family dynamics, I was gradually able to extend, from hours to several days, the period of time from crossing the threshold into my family's home to regressing to the surly adolescent I once was. This was very difficult work, which was very slow going and facilitated by individual psychotherapy.

I was amazed when I later experienced the truth of Donald Williamson's (1981) insights about how parents themselves must feel they can relinquish their parental roles in order to complete the termination of the intergenerational hierarchical boundary, and how this is sometimes facilitated by *rite de passage*. In my family, this did not occur when I left home, nor when I married, nor when I became a father, nor when I completed my graduate education. It finally occurred at my daughter's wedding, when my parents, in their 70s, came to feel that I had established sufficient adulthood for them to become my "former parents." At the wedding events, they began treating me more like a peer. That this was due to a genuine change in our relationship rather than a more general mellowing on their part was apparent when my father got into a huge argument with my brother (who normally avoided such things), of the type in which I would have been involved in the past.

PROFESSIONAL TRAINING

I was a graduate student at Harvard in the early 1970s in a clinical-community psychology program. The intellectual context in which my professional socialization took place was one that emphasized, at the macrosystems level, social change and egalitarianism. At the level of psychological practice, this translated into George Miller's (1969) call to give psychology away to the public, work with neglected inner-city ethnic minorities, create alternative treatments and settings more appropriate for these populations than traditional approaches, and develop prevention programs.

My graduate school professors embodied this ethos in their work. This group included Ira Goldenberg, David McClelland, William Rogers, Chester Pierce, Charles Hersch, Gerald Klerman, and Richard Rowe. My principle mentor was John Shlien, with whom I began a collaboration the summer before the program started that led to the creation of an innovative therapeutic day-school setting (the Robert W. White School) for the treatment of lower socioeconomic, ethnic minority adolescents who were adjudicated as delinquents. During this era the state was deinstutionalizing the reformatories and funding community-based placements for these kids, some of whom had been institutionalized for many years (Levant, 1974; Shlien & Levant, 1974). I found John to be a remarkable man who listened in ways that I had never before observed nor experienced. His effect on hardened delinquent kids was phenomenal. And I, as well, felt truly understood for the first time when talking with him. John had been a student of Carl Rogers at the University of Chicago and he later succeeded Rogers as chair of the Clinical Psychology Program and as director of the Counseling Center. He came to Harvard in the late 1960s. John and I have maintained a friendship and colleagueship, and co-edited a book on client-centered therapy and the person-centered approach (Levant & Shlien, 1984).

As a graduate student in clinical psychology, I also did practica and an internship, all in the Boston area, where most of my supervisors were, in some fashion, psychodynamic. This group included John Arsenian, Aaron Lazare, Lee Macht, Lee Reich, and Stanley Wayne. I absorbed quite a bit of psychodynamic thinking during my training. However, because of my sense of loyalty to the client-centered perspective, I experienced a degree of conflict with the nomothetic and directive aspects of psychodynamic thinking, which were at odds with the Rogerian perspective. Hence, I did not make explicit use of psychodynamic thinking at that time nor for many years thereafter. It was not until my own personal analysis in the 1980s that I grew sufficiently comfortable with psychodynamic perspectives to begin to weave them into my work.

The final thread of my training occurred after I had completed my doctorate, during a year I spent working on a private psychiatric inpatient facility. There I completed a crash course in the family therapy literature (provided by one of my graduate school classmates, Kathy Colman), and began conducting family therapy with consultation and supervision of Bernard Levy, Bernard Gray, and Fr. Philotheus Faros.

BELIEFS ABOUT PSYCHOTHERAPY AT THE BEGINNING

I began my a career as a family psychologist with a Rogerian orientation. That was an odd combination. Much of the work of the early pioneers of family therapy (Nathan Ackerman, Don Jackson, Jay Haley, Murray Bowen, Carl Whitaker, Salvador Minuchin, and Virginia Satir, the only female in the group) was about as far from a client-centered approach as one could get. But one has to remember that these folks began their work as a subversive activity in a climate in which it was considered anathema to see the members of the patient's family (a job delegated to the social worker in traditional settings). To accomplish this, they had to work with "hopeless" cases that the traditional therapeutic community viewed as untreatable: schizophrenics, delinquents, psychosomatic patients, drug abusers, and the like. Unfortunately, they also bought into the notion that these cases were hopeless, and so approached their task with the idea that they needed the therapeutic equivalent of a sledge hammer to counter the family's resistance to change.

Being a client-centered family therapist was thus somewhat incongruous. Despite the fact that Rogers was rated the third most influential theorist, ranking ahead of such influential family therapy pioneers in a survey of clinical members of the American Association of Marital and Family Therapy (Sprenkle, Keeney, & Sutton, 1982), many people viewed Rogerian therapy as far too gentle for the difficult families they were working with using structural or strategic techniques. I wondered to what extent the therapists' biases and assumptions constructed these "difficult" families.

During the earlier part of my career, my work took three major paths. First, I developed a model of family therapy based on client-centered principles. I found only a handful of people who had attempted this. Building on their work, my approach to client-centered family therapy viewed the family system as a subjective and lived phenomenon, and the family as an emergent intersubjective entity capable of both change and stability (Levant, 1978, 1982, 1984b). Therapy in this approach requires of the therapist the basic Rogerian attitudes of empathy, unconditional positive regard, and genuineness, as well as the ability to balance multiple perspectives, a process similar to what Boszormenyi-Nagy and Spark (1973) have described as multidirectional partiality. In keeping with trends that began to emerge in the family therapy field in the 1980s, concepts such as resistance and homeostasis were eschewed. The focus was on the individuals in the family and how they construct their realities and co-construct their relationships. Although I never performed empirical research on this approach,

I did use it in my clinical practice for many years, during which I tried a number of variations. What I found was a process of change similar to that described by Bowen (1978), wherein the focus tended to be more on one person for a period of time, during which the other family member(s) become to varying degrees empathic observers. As the first person became more self-aware and developed a more solid sense of self, defensiveness fell away and this person was more able to listen empathically to other members of the family, to whom the focus turned, with the first person then acting as an empathic observer. Thus, therapy in this approach focuses on self-development (or what Rogers termed congruence) and the development of the ability to take other person's perspectives (or empathy) as the basis for systemic change.

The second path was directly teaching family members these skills of empathy and emotional congruence, using the methods of psychoeducation. Originally termed "deliberate psychological education" by Mosher and Sprinthall (1971), this approach is based on the constructivist principles that people are self-evolving entities, that dysfunction represents not "illness" but rather problems in living, that people can solve such problems with their own resources if they have sufficient skills, and that psychological skills (such as empathic ability, congruence, assertiveness, communication, problem solving and negotiation) can be taught. I also learned from the Guerneys (1977) who pioneered psychoeducational work with families. My psychoeducational model (the Personal Developmental Program) was developed during the period 1975 to 1988. Programs for foster parents, working-class parents, single parents, stepparents, and fathers were developed and evaluated (Levant, 1986).

The third path was to try to get to the bottom of this notion of "schools of therapy" and make some sense of it. Focusing on the more manageable task of schools of family therapy (of which there were 22 at the time), I began a process of systematically learning as much as I could about each of the schools through teaching a year-long doctoral course in family psychology. I was able to read and lecture on the major theoretical writings, show and discuss videotapes of the major figures in the field, invite guest lecturers representing different schools, and attend weekend workshops conducted by leading family therapists. I found that terms and concepts from different schools overlapped to a large degree, especially the mid-level operational concepts, such as triangles, fusion, homeostasis, and the like. Furthermore, I found that the 22 schools fell into three general models—historical, structure/process, and experiential—based on such matters as temporal perspective, the focus of change, the role of the therapist, the underlying meta-theory, and the duration of therapy (Levant, 1984a). This tripartite model was subsequently validated by researchers at Purdue University (Mohammed & Piercy, 1983; Piercy, Laird & Mohammed, 1983).

Formative Events

Looking back on the last 25 years, I can see two major formative processes or events, both of which occurred fairly early in my career. The first, more of a process, was my personal therapy that lead to an analysis in the early 1980s. This helped me to grow more comfortable with myself and feel less ashamed of my self-perceived inadequacies, which in turn allowed me to make some critical connections between what I was experiencing on a personal level and what I was involved in professionally, as I shall shortly discuss.

The second formative event was the founding of the Boston University Fatherhood Project in the early 1980s, which was a research, service, and training program focusing on enhancing fathers' involvement in the care of their children.

As mentioned earlier, I had been developing and evaluating prevention-oriented programs for parents since 1975. During this time I was also struggling on a personal level with the role of the divorced but involved father. For the longest time I kept these domains separate, largely because of the shame I felt about my role as a father—shame that was particularly acute because of my unresolved feelings about my own father. Not yet having had the experience of exonerating him for the ways that I felt he failed me, I was unremittingly hard on myself for the ways that I felt that I was failing my daughter.

In the late 1970s, after some therapy, I began to put the two things together, and instead of continuing to think I was the dumbest father there ever was, I asked the question of what resources existed for fathers like myself who wanted to be fully involved, effective parents of their children. The answer was: Nothing. A review of the major literature reviews on parent education available at the time (Loiselle, 1980) revealed that none of the studies indicated whether the parent groups included fathers. Echoing Michael Lamb (1979), I concluded that the father was the forgotten parent and that parent education was synonymous with mother education. In response, I (with the help of doctoral students Greg Doyle, Wendy Nelson, Joe Rabinovitz, and Liz Tarshis) turned to the task of designing psycho-educational parenting programs for men (Levant & Kelly, 1989). That, of course, was the proverbial fork in the road that opened up my subsequent career involvement in fathering and ultimately in the new psychology of men and the new psychotherapy for men.

CURRENT POSITION

From the early 1980s to the present my professional work with men and my own development as a man have been increasingly intertwined. While working on overcoming my own sense of shame for perceived personal failings, I became increasingly aware of the role that shame plays in most men's lives, locked into their hearts by the harsh injunctions of the male code. In the groups that I lead, men's hidden shame emerges with great force when I ask them to do Yalom's (1985) "Top Secret" task. After sufficient trust has developed in the group, cards are passed around and the men are instructed to write down their top secret, the one thing they have never told anyone and never would tell anyone. After they have finished writing, I collect the cards and announce that I am going to read them aloud. After the groans and protests stop, I make a big deal of shuffling the cards to achieve anonymity, and then read them. What I have found is that many of the things men are so deeply ashamed of are utterly banal and clearly reflective of acceptable human imperfection. Men who for years felt that they were the only ones to have shown such a lack of courage, strength, or other manly quality find that, in fact, they are not the only ones ever to have done that when they hear that some men have very similar—sometimes identical—secrets. Although many sources of shame are contemporary (such as failing in a job, a marriage, or succumbing to substance abuse), it is surprising how many of these shameful secrets go back decades in the man's life: "Chickening out" of a fight in the 7th grade; lusting after another male; feeling weaker on the inside than one dared show on the outside, being afraid, being sad, being needy—in short having human emotions.

The degree to which men feel ashamed of their own human emotions came into focus for me while leading fathers' groups, where I discovered that many men lack the ability to put their own emotions into words, a phenomenon that I have termed "normative male alexithymia" (Levant, 1997; Levant & Kopecky, 1995). I recall asking a divorced father whose son had stood him up for a father-son hockey game how he felt about it. His response: "He shouldn't have done it!" "No," I said, "I didn't ask you what you thought he should have done. I asked you what you felt." The father's response: "Oh. Let me think... I guess I felt, I think I felt, I must have felt ... upset." In contrast, ask a woman what she felt when her daughter stood her up for an afternoon of shopping at the mall, and listen as she peels off layer after layer of her feelings: "At first I was angry. Then I got worried, because I didn't know what happened to her. Then I was really disappointed, because I was really looking forward to spending this time with her before she left for college."

This widespread inability among men to identify emotions and put them into words has enormous consequences. It blocks men who suffer from it from utilizing the most effective means known for dealing with life's stresses and traumas—namely, identifying, thinking about, and discussing one's emotional responses to a stressor or trauma with a friend, family member, or therapist. Consequently it predisposes such men to deal with stress in ways that make certain forms of pathology more likely, such as substance abuse, violent behavior, sexual compulsions, stress-related illnesses, and early death. It also makes it less likely that such men will be able to benefit from psychotherapy as traditionally practiced.

I have developed an analysis of the male emotion socialization process, methods to assess men for their ability to give voice to their own emotional experience, and techniques to teach those men who are normatively alexithymic the skills of emotional self-awareness and self expression. Since that work has been well documented I will not repeat it here but rather refer the reader to the relevant publications on theory and technique (Levant, 1990; Levant & Brooks, 1997; Levant & Kopecky, 1995; Levant & Pollack, 1995; Pollack & Levant, 1998). There are also several published case studies (Levant, 1998; Levant & Silverstein, in press), including a videotaped full-length treatment case (Levant, 1997).

CLINICAL VIGNETTE

Craig, a 40-year-old successful stockbroker, called for an appointment because he "felt nothing" about the fact that he and his wife of 18 years were expecting their first child. The first born son of a rural family, responsibility was his middle name. His sister had a disabled child whom he financially supported. Apart from the fact that his wife was pregnant and he thought he "should" feel something about that, Craig did not find it particularly odd that he "felt nothing." He usually felt nothing. The last time he cried was when his dog was hit by a car. That was 10 years ago.

I worked with Craig for several weeks using the five-step psychoeducational program that I have developed to help men increase their emotional self-awareness and overcome normative alexithymia (Levant, 1997, 1998; Levant & Kopecky, 1995). Craig worked hard during this period and became more able to identify his emotions and put them into words.

Craig said at the outset that he thought that a lot of his problems had to do with his father. His father was 11 years older than his mother, was 38 when Craig was born, and died of a heart attack 13 years ago. Craig believed that his father had a great life as an Air Force officer during World War II—a life that he had to leave behind when he married and started a family, and one that he seemed to miss greatly throughout Craig's childhood. Because of his father's self-absorption and detachment, Craig was always unsure of his father's feelings about him. And yet he yearned to get closer. For example, Craig's lifelong hobby was participating in Scottish rites and learning about his Scottish ancestry, an activity in which he had earlier hoped he could involve his father. The first time I saw Craig display emotions openly was when he spoke of how he had always wanted to see his Dad in a kilt, carrying a set of pipes.

As therapy progressed, Craig's initial detachment about his father turned to curiosity. Craig discovered he had many questions he wanted to ask his father, so we constructed a therapeutic ritual in which he would write down the questions that he had for his father on 3" x 5" cards. I also suggested digging out old family photos to stimulate his memories. His initial response to these tasks was to get very angry that his father "just wasn't there." He later talked of how, when his father needed him after his first heart attack, he decided he was too busy to visit. In describing this event, he said "It's a family curse. I come from a long line of uncaring fathers."

The therapy deepened on a trip to see his mother, during which he visited his father's grave. He described the experience as "raw emotion." His sadness poured out of him as he stood alone at his father's headstone, reading through his cards filled with unanswered questions.

He was later able to locate an old friend of his father, Henry, who remembered the day Craig was born. Henry said that that was the only time he saw Craig's father cry. We can never *know how accurate Henry's recollection is, but that is not the point. Craig was able to use this information to be able to feel for the first time in his life that maybe his father really did care about him after all. With this shift Craig then was able to begin to address a lifelong sense of shame, which stemmed in no small measure from his relationship with his father.*

Having made progress in addressing his sense of shame and recapturing his ability to tune into and verbalize his emotional life, Craig began to experience some strong feelings about his expectant fatherhood—fear, worry and anxiety. He began to worry about whether the baby was going to be all right, given his wife's age (40 also). He also investigated some obscure genetic diseases that ran in families of Scottish descent. I encouraged him to address his worries directly, by attending one of his wife's visits to the obstetrician. He did so, and was reassured about the baby's health, and also heard the baby's heartbeat. His fear then turned to joy and excitement. We ter-minated one month before the baby was due. I got a postcard two months later:

Ron, the baby was two weeks late. But he's a big guy, 8 lbs. 13 oz. And he definitely looks Scottish!

Craig

WHERE ARE WE HEADING?

This is a particularly interesting juncture for me to be reflecting on psychotherapy, because I have had a hiatus of a year and a half during which I have done no clinical work or clinical supervision, and minimal teaching and writing on clinical issues. I closed my practice in the Boston area and left my position as a clin-ical supervisor at Cambridge Hospital in June 1997 to take a job as dean of a professional school of psychology in South Florida. Because of circumstances (not having had a Florida license and the demands of the new job), it has not been possible to undertake any clinical work. However, I recently earned my Florida license, and one of the first things that entered my mind was "now I can start seeing clients again."

This hiatus allowed me to step back from the demands and exigencies of day-to-day practice and take a broader look at the field. Like most psychotherapists, I was bedeviled by managed care. As an established practitioner working in a niche area (difficult-to-treat men), I did have a reasonably full practice, only about one third of which was managed care, but I experienced the drip drip drip of managed care torture, including ever-shorter review periods, ever-longer and more intrusive outpatient treatment reports, and ever-lower fees. Plus the loss of the sense of being a professional when your work is reviewed so closely by such inexperienced reviewers. My maternal grandfather was a tailor who did "piece-work" making uniforms for military academies. Piecework was what I felt I was doing in my work for some managed care companies.

It might be helpful to put this into the larger context of the industrialization of heath care. In the past decade we have witnessed the transformation of health care from a cottage industry to something approaching an oligopoly. This increasing concentration of the industry has resulted in ever-larger health care corporations competing for greater market share by aggressively driving down costs using techniques such as standardization and automation. In this process psychological services are being redefined as commodities that can be provided by increasingly less-well-trained caregivers, providing crisis intervention-type services based on treatment manuals, perhaps even monitored by computer programs and supervised over the Internet. In this context, some leading psychologists (Cummings, 1995) and managed mental health care executives have asserted that there is an oversupply of mental health providers, and that as many as 50 percent of us will be forced to leave the field. If medical necessity is narrowly defined—psychotherapeutic treatment aimed at the restoration of functioning and treatment episodes limited to a handful of sessions—then there may be too many providers, particularly the more highly trained psychologists.

But this view violates what is known about psychotherapy, which I have discussed above, and which was recently confirmed in the Consumer's Union survey of 4,000 readers' experiences with emotional problems, reported in *Consumer Reports* (1995). The study found that respondents benefited greatly from psychotherapy and that longer-term treatment provided better results than short-term treatment. Interestingly, patients whose length of therapy or choice of therapist was limited by managed care did worse. The study has certain limitations, including a nonrandom, self-selected sample, and reliance on self-report, but as I have argued elsewhere (Levant, 1995; Seligman & Levant, 1998), the standard psychotherapy outcome research methodology (known as efficacy research) trades off fidelity to the actual treatment situation for rigor. The *Consumer Reports* study (a good example of what is known as effectiveness research) does just the opposite: It is a large scale study of psychotherapy as it is actually experienced by consumers, with some limitations in rigor. Since both types of studies have their limitations, we stand to learn more about the actual effects of psychotherapy when we combine the results of randomized controlled treatment trials with studies of consumer experience and satisfaction; and when we do that, psychotherapy receives particularly strong empirical support and it becomes quite clear that psychotherapy is being drastically downgraded in the current marketplace. Our professional associations are actively fighting this move to downgrade psychotherapy. How successful they will ultimately be is not clear.

When I was offered the job of dean of a professional school, concerns about managed care and the future of professional practice—particularly of psychotherapy—were uppermost in my thoughts. It was clear to me that professional schools could not continue to produce large numbers of psychologists who were seeking careers as traditional outpatient psychotherapists. They wouldn't survive, nor would we. Instead I began thinking about the question of redefining psychology as a primary care profession (Levant, 1996). As a specialty profession, we deal only with the people who self-identify as having psychological problems and who have access to a mental health specialist, which is just the tip of the iceberg, in terms of those who need psychological services. As a primary health care profession, we would be able to tap the much larger group of people who do not have access to mental health care or who do not identify their problem as psychological. We would continue to practice assessment and psychotherapy, with some modifications tailored to this new and in some ways more challenging (because less psychologically-minded) population.

To grasp the potential for psychology of being a primary care profession, reflect on a few facts about health care: (1) Seven out of the nine leading causes of death have significant behavioral components (McGinnis & Foege, 1993); (2) At least 50 percent (and maybe as much as 75 percent) of all visits to primary care medical personnel are for problems with a psychological origin (including individuals who present with frank mental health problems and those who somatize) or psychological component (including those with unhealthy lifestyle habits such as smoking, those with chronic illnesses, and those with medical compliance issues) (Frank & Ross, 1995; Johnstone, Frank, Belar, & Berk 1995); and (3) The vast majority of people receiving mental health treatment are cared for by medical professionals with minimal specific training in mental health (Frank & Ross, 1995). The Cartesian world view, which separates mental health from physical health, is breaking down, and as a result psychology has a tremendous opportunity to evolve into a premier primary health care profession. At the very least this would put psychologists on the front lines of health care, working collaboratively with physicians and nurses. The more visionary—if improbable—perspective is that health care should be reorganized so that psychologists serve as primary caregivers at the gateway to the health care system, functioning to diagnose and treat the more prevalent psychological problems, and referring to medical physicians when indicated.

CONCLUSION

The art of practicing psychotherapy depends to a great extent on the person of the psychotherapist, his or her personal maturity and emotional health, as well as warmth, empathy, and genuineness. However, psychotherapy clients or patients also bring a lot of resources to the table in the psychotherapeutic enterprise, and many of psychotherapy's most dramatic results have come about by the therapist-client relationship helping the client tap his or her own resources and strengths. Psychotherapists are not equally effective with everyone—there are better and worse therapist-client matches—and the wise psychotherapist recognizes his or her strengths and limitations. My work as a practicing psychotherapist and as a teacher and clinical supervisor for 25 years has refined and confirmed these views.

In closing, I have to say that I remain optimistic about the future for psychotherapy. I know from both my personal and professional experience that the benefits that good psychotherapy provides in helping people resolve problems, improve relationships, and enhance their lives are without equal in our society. The future will bring change, perhaps along the lines discussed above, perhaps in other ways, but the core of psychotherapy will continue to be a vital endeavor, no matter the form in which it is practiced.

The advice I would give a person newly entering our profession is: Be flexible, learn to become an entrepreneur, and recognize that the development of your professional career requires skills that you probably didn't learn in graduate school, such as an ability to figure out how to respond to pressing social needs by imaginatively creating roles for yourself, and an ability to market yourself in these roles. Remember that in the 100-plus years of its existence, psychology has grown and diversified beyond the wildest dreams of its early pioneers, and has produced research-based applications for nearly every aspect of human behavior.

REFERENCES

Bergin, A. E. (1971). The evaluation of therapeutic outcomes. In A. E. Bergin & S. L. Garfield (Eds.), *Handbook of psychotherapy and behavior change* (pp. 217-270). New York: John Wiley.

Boszormenyi-Nagy, I. & Spark, G. M. (1973). *Invisible loyalties.* Hagerstown, MD: Harper and Row.

Bowen, M. (1978). *Family therapy in clinical practice.* New York: Jason Aronson.

Consumer Reports. (1995, November). Mental health: Does therapy help? pp. 734-739.

Cummings, N., (1995). Impact of managed care on employment and training: A primer for survival. *Professional Psychology, 26,* 10-15.

Eysenck, H. J. (1952). The effects of psychotherapy: An evaluation. *Journal of Consulting Psychology, 16,* 319-324.

Frank, R., & Ross, M. (1995). The changing workforce. The role of health psychology. *Health Psychology, 14,* 519-525.250.

Guerney, B. G., Jr. (1977). *Relationship enhancement.* San Francisco: Jossey Bass.

Johnstone, B., Frank, R., Belar, C., & Berk, S. (1995). Psychology in health care: Future directions. *Professional Psychology: Research and Practice, 26,* 341-365.

Lamb, M. E. (1979). Paternal influences and the father's role: A personal perspective. *American Psychologist, 43,* 938-943.

Levant, R. F. (1974). The planning, development and administration of a therapeutic school for adolescents (The Robert W. White School). *Dissertation Abstracts International,* 34:5684-B (University Microfilms No. 74-11, 324).

Levant, R. F. (1978). Family therapy: A client-centered perspective. *Journal of Marriage and Family Counseling, 4,* 35-42.

Levant, R. F. (1982). Client-centered family therapy. *American Journal of Family Therapy, 10,* 72-75.

Levant, R. F. (1984a). *Family therapy: A comprehensive overview.* Englewood Cliffs, NJ: Prentice-Hall.

Levant, R. F. (1984b). From person to system: Two perspectives. In: R. Levant & J. Shlien (Eds.), *Client-centered therapy and the person-centered approach: New directions in theory, research and practice* (pp. 243-260). New York: Praeger.

Levant, R. F. (Ed.). (1986). *Psychoeducational approaches to family therapy and counseling.* New York: Springer.

Levant, R. F. (1990). Psychological services designed for men: a psychoeducational approach. *Psychotherapy, 27,* 309-315.

Levant, R. F. (1995, Fall). Outcomes measurement and empirically validated treatments: What's all the fuss about? *Psychotherapy Bulletin, 30,* 20-22.

Levant, R. F. (1996). The psychological physician: Onward to the future. *Journal of Clinical Psychology in Medical Settings, 3,* 167-172.

Levant, R. F. (1997). *Men and emotions: A psychoeducational Approach.* The Assessment and Treatment of Psychological Disorders Video Series. Hicksville, NY: Newbridge Communications, Inc.

Levant, R. F. (1998). Desperately seeking language: Understanding, assessing and treating normative male alexithymia. In W. Pollack, & R. F. Levant (Eds.), *New psychotherapy for men* (pp. 35-56). New York: John Wiley & Sons.

Levant, R. F., & Brooks, G. R. (Eds.). (1997). *Men and sex: New psychological perspectives.* New York: John Wiley and Sons.

Levant, R. F., & Kelly, J. (1989). *Between father and child.* New York: Viking.

Levant, R. F., & Kopecky, G. (1995). *Masculinity, reconstructed.* New York: Dutton.

Levant, R.F., & Pollack, W. S. (Eds.). (1995). *A new psychology of men.* New York: Basic Books.

Levant, R. F., & Shlien, J., (Eds.). (1984). *Client-centered therapy and the person-centered approach: new directions in theory, research and practice.* New York: Praeger.

Levant, R. F., & Silverstein, L. (In Press). Integrating gender and family systems theories: The "both/and" approach to treating a postmodern couple. In D. Lusterman, S. McDaniel, & C. Philpot (Eds.), *Casebook for integrating family therapy.* Washington, DC: American Psychological Association.

Loiselle, J. (1980). *A review of the role of fathers in parent training programs.* Unpublished manuscript, Boston University.

Luborsky, L., Singer, B., & Luborsky, L. (1975). Comparative studies of psychotherapies. *Archives of General Psychiatry, 29,* 719-729.

McGinnis, J. M., & Foege, W. H. (1993). Actual causes of death in the United States. *Journal of the American Medical Association, 270,* 2207-2212.

Miller, G. A. (1969). Psychology as a means of promoting human welfare. *American Psychologist, 24,* 1063-1071.

Mohammed, Z., & Piercy, F. (1983). The effects of two methods of training and sequencing on structuring and relationship skills of family therapists. *America Journal of Family Therapy, 11(4),* 64-71.

Mosher, R. L., & Sprinthall, N. A. (1971). Deliberate psychological education. *Counseling Psychologist, 2(4),* 2-82.

Piercy, F. P., Laird, R. A., & Mohammed, Z. (1983). A family therapist rating scale. *Journal of Marital and Family Therapy, 9,* 49-59.

Pollack, W. S., & Levant, R. F. (1998). Eds.). *New psychotherapy for men.* New York: John Wiley & Sons.

Seligman, M. E. P., & Levant, R. F. (1998). Managed care policies rely on inadequate science. *Professional Psychology: Research and Practice, 29,* 211-212.

Shlien, J., & Levant, R. (1974). The Robert W. White School. *Harvard Graduate School of Education Association Bulletin, 19,* 12-18.

Smith, M. L., & Glass, G. V. (1977). Meta-analysis of psychotherapy outcome studies. *American Psychologist, 32,* 752-760.

Sprenkle, D. H., Keeney, B. P., & Sutton, P. M. (1982). Theorists who influence clinical members of AAMFT: A research note. *Journal of Marital and Family Therapy, 8,* 367-369.

Williamson, D. S. (1981). Personal authority via termination of the
     intergenerational hierarchical boundary: A "new" stage
     in the family life cycle. *Journal of Marital and Family
     Therapy, 7*, 441-452.

Yalom, I. (1985). *The theory and practice of group psychotherapy.* New
     York: Basic Books

CHAPTER 10

EMBRACING UNCERTAINTY AND COMPLEXITY IN PSYCHOTHERAPY

CAROLYNN P. MALTAS, PH.D.

Melinda came to see me 25 years ago, just as I was beginning my career as a clinical psychologist. A 32-year-old graduate student, she came to an outpatient training clinic because of serious depression in the context of severe marital conflict and possible divorce. She had been in a brief therapy during her freshman year in college when she had experienced suicidal impulses after breaking up with a boyfriend from home. She had found that therapy of little help and requested a therapist who would "go deeper and get to the roots of things." As part of her evaluation, I requested psychological testing to assess the depth of her depression and the current risk of suicide. Her responses suggested pervasive "primitive oral longings," a potential for "regression in the face of loss" with a risk of suicidal gestures, and a "mixture of intellectualizing defenses along with hysterical personality traits." The diagnosis was mixed

character disorder with obsessional, hysterical, and borderline features. We began a twice weekly psychoanalytically oriented individual therapy. When she asked about bringing her husband in, I suggested that focusing on the marital problems at this point might serve as a resistance to full involvement in the therapeutic relationship with me.

How would I see Melinda today? The assessment questions I would frame and the therapeutic interventions I might recommend would be quite different. Accounting for the changes in my personal belief system about psychological problems and my treatment model calls for an examination of influences on me that are generally at the periphery of my conscious experience. In fact, in my day-to-day clinical work, I experience my formulations and choice of a focus for a patient as stemming directly from the clinical needs of those requesting help, not from factors internal to me. I know that this is partly an illusion, but it seems a necessary one to keep me from becoming immobilized by self-scrutiny. This chapter allows me the opportunity to turn the questions back on the questioner, to examine the different lenses through which I have viewed clinical situations over my career as a clinical psychologist.

SETTING THE STAGE

Twenty-five years ago, I assessed and treated individuals from an exclusively intrapsychic perspective and gradually shifted to one that is more interpersonal, contextual, and systemic. Where once I gave primacy to conflicts between ego, id, and superego, I now more often focus on interpersonal conflicts in the close relationships of patients, including, but no longer privileging, the therapeutic relationship. In the last five years, my interests have broadened to include conflicts within larger networks of relationships. In particular, I have been interested in conflicts in multi-therapist treatment situations and conflicts during divorce that bring in extended family, therapists, and lawyers.

My career as a clinical psychologist began with graduate school in 1970 at Boston University, which was, at the time, identified with Freudian psychoanalytic theory and psychoanalytic ego psychology. Concurrently I was in psychoanalysis with a "classical" psychoanalyst and did two internships, the first at McLean Hospital in Belmont, Massachusetts, and the second at Children's Hospital Medical Center in Boston, both heavily psychoanalytic in that era. I spent the next 22 years on the staff of McLean in the Psychology Department doing psychodiagnostic testing, treating outpatients and inpatients, supervising psychology interns, and consulting to treatment programs. For 12 of those years I also worked on the Adolescent and Family Treatment Unit at McLean, treating couples, families, and adolescents, and carried out research on family interaction. For the next 10 years, I co-directed the McLean Institute for Couples and Families and taught assessment and therapy to psychology interns, social work fellows, and psychiatry residents. Since leaving McLean in 1995, I have been in private practice, trained and worked as a divorce counselor and mediator, and been involved in several professional groups with other psychoanalytically-oriented couple and family therapists.

I Define Myself as a Freudian

My earliest professional belief system was Freudian psychoanalytic theory. I had been dazzled by a college course in which we read Freud's complete works in chronological order. Since Freudian psychoanalysis was disparaged by my psychotherapist parents, whose professional commitment was to community psychiatry, child guidance, and primary prevention, this was the only psychology course I permitted myself to take as an undergraduate. As a result I passed up the opportunity to take courses with Jerome Bruner, Erik Erikson, B.F. Skinner, and Robert Coles, which I now deeply regret. Psychoanalytic theory provided me with intellectual excitement and the sense of differentiating from my parents. It also led me to my own psychoanalysis and a clinical psychology doctoral program known for its psychoanalytic orientation.

My formal training was primarily in the psychoanalytically-informed assessment, diagnosis, and treatment of individual patients—children, adolescents, and adults. During more than 15 years at McLean, I carried out and supervised almost one thousand batteries of psychodiagnostic testing. I became a highly skilled diagnostician who both recommended and carried out treatments I thought matched the mental illnesses that were contained within individual patients. As a therapist, I was trained to listen for and interpret resistance, defenses, and unconscious conflicts, largely through analyzing the transference. However, despite my formal allegiance to Freud, my analyst, and my analytic supervisors, I periodically felt dissatisfied with the exclusively intrapsychic focus, feeling that too much about human pain and motivation was left out. I felt strongly that, for myself as well as for my patients, current real relationships outside of therapy were important vehicles for change and growth.

I did not initially think much about my patients' families beyond their historical interest, since I believed that what was important about those early relationships would become manifest in the transference. In situations where the present-day families did become a focus, I often saw them as interfering, undermining the treatment, or flatly toxic to the patient. In this, I mirrored Freud's own view of the families of his patients (Freud, 1917). During my training on inpatient units, I absorbed the widespread view that most patients were so damaged by their families that it was our duty to protect the patients from further injury and offer ourselves as a new kind of family. Only gradually did it become clear that, despite our views, most patients eventually went home to the families who constituted their primary attachments.

I BECOME AN OBJECT RELATIONS FAMILY THERAPIST

My only exposure to family therapy during training was in graduate school where I was, for a short while, co-therapist in an observed family therapy seminar. I found it exhilarating to be working with actual family relationships! After a few years at McLean, I sought out the opportunity to become part of the Adolescent and Family Treatment Unit (AFTU) under the leadership of Edward Shapiro (Shapiro & Carr, 1991). Twelve years there, working with hospitalized adolescents and their families in family and couple therapy, shaped my career and had a powerful impact on my thinking about psychological problems and their treatment.

The AFTU treatment model originated with a group of young psychiatrists under the leadership of Roger Shapiro at the NIMH in the early 1970s (Shapiro, 1982). This group attempted to use psychoanalytic theory to elucidate the family dynamics of hospitalized adolescents but found classical Freudian theory lacking in concepts that bridge the intrapsychic and the interpersonal realms. British object relations theory, and particularly the concept of projective identification, seemed more useful in addressing directly the impact on current relationships of the internal residues of early relationships.

Projective identification, originally described by Klein as an intrapsychic defense, came to be understood by this group as a way of linking unconscious dynamic factors within individual family members, in this case primarily the parents, with the family interactions that produced symptomatic adolescents (Berkowitz, 1984; Shapiro, 1979; Zinner, 1970; Zinner & Shapiro, 1974). In this mechanism, internalized images of self and of relationships are projected onto external others and actualized interpersonally through unconscious verbal and nonverbal pressures. Compared to the concept of transference, this view of projective identification emphasizes behavioral enactment and the mutual involvement of both parties in the interaction. Framed like this, conflictual family interactions, expressing unconscious conflicts within individuals, now seemed a legitimate focus for a psychoanalytic psychotherapist.

Once I began to look at interactions through the lens of projective identification, I saw this process everywhere in close relationships; but it did not always appear to be as primitive or pathological as often described (Kernberg, 1975; Meissner, 1978). For example, I noted how, angry and frustrated at the end of a day at home with young children, I could infect my husband with my irritation and incite his angry outburst at a child. I would then deal with his behavior and negative emotions, feeling little connection to them myself anymore. Muir (1982) points out that there are "two basic kinds of psychic functioning—an individual mode and a transpersonal mode." He quotes Laing's statement that "in actual families and in real life, generally, persons attempt to act on the experience of other persons" and "regulate the inner worlds of others in order to preserve their own" (Laing, as quoted in Muir, 1982, p. 323). Transpersonal defenses can be relatively benign efforts to understand or be understood experientially by intimate others. But when projective identifications continually cut people off from awareness of their own internal states and repeatedly distort realistic appraisal of the other person's characteristics, the results are impoverishment of relationships, psychological rigidity, and the inhibition of growth. An important goal then of interpersonal therapies is to help patients recognize and reclaim what has been externalized and enacted with others so that internal conflicts can be acknowledged and worked through.

In the AFTU families, parents were thought to be unconsciously using the adolescents to enact aspects of their own conflicts, a process in which the adolescents colluded, out of a need to preserve their family ties. Frequently, the adolescent represented for the whole family group the gratification of impulses, while the father might represent inhibition and control, and the mother warmth and vulnerability. Thus internal conflicts within various family members over closeness versus autonomy, or impulse gratification versus restraint would be transformed into interpersonal conflicts over curfews, sexuality, and drugs.

This was a very different way to think about "the problem" I was assessing and treating from the one I had learned from classical psychoanalytic theory. If the components of a conflict were not internalized in one person but rather were, through transpersonal defenses, parceled out among various family members, who should be in treatment? The AFTU model invariably included all the members of the nuclear family and offered but one treatment structure. One therapist treated the adolescent, another the parental couple, and those two therapists together saw the family, who also participated in a multiple family group therapy. I was troubled by this uniform answer to a very complicated question.

Skynner's (1976) concept of the "minimum sufficient network" (MSN) provided a helpful way to think about who needs to be included in a particular treatment. He defines the MSN as the "psychological or social structure containing enough of the three sub-systems—superego, ego, and id—for autonomous function to be possible" (1976, p. 168). These psychological functions, which he also describes as conscience, self-control, and desires, can be contained within the boundaries of an individual, dispersed throughout a nuclear or extended family, or involve other figures within a community. Skynner's response to questions about how to delimit the MSN is to ask further questions: Who is disturbed? Who is disturbing? Who has the motivation to alter the situation? Who has the capacity to alter it? I still return to these questions as I explore ways to "diagnose" or assess problems in interpersonal systems and to formulate treatments that are as multifaceted and individualized as the patients themselves.

> *I think about Melinda and how I might have seen her had she come for treatment while I was deeply involved with the AFTU treatment model. I might have hypothesized that a fear of abandonment linked together the depressions upon leaving home, losing her first boyfriend, and now potentially separating from her husband and child. I also wonder what would have happened if Melinda's first major depression and suicide attempt had led to her hospitalization on the AFTU. What would I have seen about her interactions within the family that might clarify her difficulties separating and managing her emotional equilibrium? Other clinicians at McLean commonly argued against our treating adolescents together with their families*

*when the issues involved separation and individuation. In con-
trast, we believed that helping the whole family with separation
often protected the adolescent from feeling disloyal and fearing
abandonment. Perhaps Melinda and her family could have
worked through the fear that to separate and individuate was
to attack the sanctity of the family and that she must be evil to
have such desires.*

*Family therapy might have helped the adolescent Melinda
modify her negative image of herself and given the parents a
chance to rework object relational conflicts stemming from
their families of origin. If she and her family had been able to
understand and work through these shared family conflicts and
undo the collusive defenses, perhaps Melinda's current marital
situation and depression might never have occurred.*

I Focus on Treating Couples

After years of considering formal psychoanalytic training,
I made a final decision not to pursue it. Given my belief in the centrality of relationship problems in most of my patients, I no longer
found compelling this model of intensifying and interpreting the
relationship between therapist and individual patient as the way
to bring about therapeutic change. Rather, I preferred to use therapeutically the patients' naturally occurring close relationships,
which would remain central to them long after their relationships
with me had ended.

Working with couples, I can link my psychoanalytic
understanding of the individual partners with systemic understanding of the couple as a unit greater than the sum of its parts. I
find fascinating the creation of a new family system that results
from the interweaving of two individuals' dynamics, personalities,
histories, and beliefs. I like Berger and Kellner's (1964) description
of marriage as one long, intimate conversation in which the partners define and redefine themselves and the outside world. Many
views, originally quite different, are modified and merged, as the
partners' identities depend increasingly on how they are seen by

the other. This merged entity develops stable patterns and rules of engagement that, over time, may defensively rigidify. When sitting with a couple, I can hold onto this dual vision of the two individuals and their interactive system, while such a dual vision is much harder to sustain when flooded by the complex data of larger family interactions.

As I started seeing more couples, I began teaching an object relations approach to couple and family therapy at McLean and in the community. I also began writing about couple issues, such as the interpersonal management of narcissism (Maltas, 1991), midlife marital crises (Maltas, 1992), and the impact on intimate relationships of a history of sexual abuse (Maltas, 1996; Maltas & Shay, 1995; Shay, 1992). My couple therapy bible has been *Marital Tensions* (Dicks, 1967), an application of Fairbairn's theories of psychological development to the married couple, developed at the Marital Unit of the Tavistock Clinic. Dicks describes the mutual acceptance of each other's projections as a kind of unconscious contract between spouses, to help each other maintain certain self-images and unconscious ties to early objects. The willingness and capacity to do this for each other is viewed as central in the choice of a marital partner, allowing for both defensive and reparative functions of marriage.

> By 1980, if Melinda had appeared in my office, I would likely have recommended both individual and conjoint assessments for both partners. Since Melinda had sought treatment for depression prior to marrying James, we would have needed to explore individual characteristics like her biological vulnerability, early family history, dynamics around separation, loss, unconscious guilt, and so on. But I would also have needed to understand the meaning and function of this symptom in the marital relationship. As Melinda described both her husband James and her mother as critical and controlling, I would have wondered about the roles of repetition and projective identification in the marriage. Was she compelled to experience dissatisfaction in her intimate relationship as a way of holding onto internalized parental figures? Might she unconsciously elicit

this behavior in James, who she knew had a critical side to him?

It would have been equally important to understand the contribution of the husband's unconscious dynamics to the presenting problems. I would have wanted to meet individually with James, and would have predicted that he would have appeared to me rather different than the man portrayed by Melinda. He might have presented a story of devotion and caretaking of a "sick" wife, and I would have hoped to understand what psychological issues she might have been expressing for him through her depression. Perhaps a depressed mother was his prototype for a love relationship, or perhaps it was his own depression or another vulnerable emotional state that he kept at bay by evoking it interactionally in his wife.

Assessing them conjointly would have allowed me to discern the unconscious "fit" between the partners' dynamics and their shared contribution to the marital unhappiness. If they were on an irrevocable course toward separation, that might well be the source of her depression, but the depression might also be having a powerful negative impact on the marriage. I would have wanted to know if their relationship had the potential to meet their deepest needs to be affirmed as loveable. What were they seeking in each other, what hurts and past disappointments did they hope to heal, and what has interfered with their getting what they longed for from each other? What was the unconscious contract, and if fulfilled, would it facilitate healthy development? Or was it an agreement to fight old battles in a new setting?

A Reflective Interlude

Mid-point in my professional career, I participated in a year-long seminar with David Kantor, Ph.D., a brilliant and charismatic couple and family therapist. His fascinating model seems to me to integrate object relations and family systems theories, though Kantor would not identify his ideas as psychoanalytic. The centerpiece of his model is the "critical identity image," a condensation of needs, fantasies, and disappointments, which is seen as the key to unlocking unfinished developmental processes (Kantor & Lehr, 1975). Kantor's seminar, comprising 12 other experienced family and couple therapists, was eye-opening, less because of his particular model, than because he forced me to articulate my own. He challenged each of us to discover and elaborate the implicit theories and beliefs which shape our own work. Taping and playing for each other couple therapy sessions, as well as studying detailed process notes, I became more aware of my implicit, only partially conscious, model. I tried to infer from my behavior in the sessions my deeply held beliefs about normality and pathology in intimate relationships, about how people change, and about the role of the therapist in promoting change. My views about the sources of interpersonal problems and their treatment, as described in the following paragraphs, have not fundamentally altered since that time. Later developments, which will be explored in subsequent sections, are more accretions than alterations.

I begin with a belief in the centrality of unconscious conflict to human unhappiness and impairment. Since people live simultaneously in an internal and external world, there is always a tension in one's closest relationships between the real relationship with the other and the internal images and unconscious wishes, fears, and needs that shape the perception of that relationship. Couple and family relationships are the prime arena for interpersonal enactments of many unconscious conflicts in the individuals and for repetition of both longed-for and feared aspects of early relationships.

I seek to understand how an intimate relationship serves both conscious and unconscious needs to reinforce certain valued self-images and keep externalized aspects of self that are unacceptable and disavowed. I seek the link between what was initially cherished in the intimate partner and what later becomes despised, a traceable trajectory from mutual idealization to disappointment and conflict. The shadow side of the initial attraction is often the potential to find and manage in the other conflictual parts of the self and one's inner objects. I deeply believe that individual and relational growth can resume, and an entire range of affective experiences can emerge, when couples become more accepting, in each other, of what has been seen as unacceptable, and therefore suppressed, in themselves.

I have seen a variety of relationship structures that can work for different couples and families. But there are certain overarching relationship qualities that I look for and promote: flexibility in roles, a tolerance for differences, awareness of painful emotions, the ability to talk about difficult topics, skills to negotiate and compromise when needs or preferences clash, and, above all, generosity in interpreting each other's behavior and a sense of humor about day-to-day conflicts. I identify and reinforce relationship strengths much more than I did in my earliest years, while continuing to probe for unrecognized inner forces undermining conscious desires for intimacy. I also remain aware of social and cultural pressures that predispose couples to experience mutual disappointment and frustration. Factors that contribute to the high levels of marital dissatisfactions include: the cultural ideal of romantic love as the basis for long-term committed relationships, expectations for undiminished sexual passion throughout marriage, continuing gender inequality, lack of societal supports for working parents, and diminishing expectations that couples stay together and resolve problems rather than divorce.

In working with couples and families, I first want to create a safe environment where the various family members can feel understood and accepted by me, even though they may be unable initially to understand or accept each other. This is in itself a curative element, for it demonstrates that multiple perspectives that were seen as mutually exclusive, and therefore mutually invalidating, can be contained and validated by the therapist. I challenge defensively polarized delineations of each other, such as seeing a self-deprecating wife as if she had no ambitions herself, or a "macho" father as if he felt no identification with his fearful son. I want them to see each other, like themselves, like all human beings, as full of complexity, contradiction, and conflicts. I help them see that each one's ways of perceiving and behaving is understandable, and probably was even adaptive, in their childhood albeit not useful, even destructive, now. I thus attribute self-protective motives to behaviors understood by the partners only as destructive. All of these therapeutic elements contribute to the development of mutual empathy, a primary goal of conjoint therapy.

I search for the links between real, current interpersonal behaviors in couple relationships and internalized self and object images from the partners' early lives. Because strong emotional ties already exist between partners, we do not have to await the development of a transference relationship with the therapist to deeply engage in the therapy process. The couple's or family's subjective experiences of one another form the focus of the therapy rather than the transference to the therapist. However, at certain points, my relationship with them both as a unit and as individuals can also reveal a great deal about their inner relational world and may be helpful to address (Scharff & Scharff, 1991). For example, my upset over a husband's dismissal of all my observations may help me understand his wife's sense of being contemptible in his eyes. Conjoint treatments also provide the chance work with triadic transferences, such as the parallel between my perceived alliance with the wife and the husband's childhood feeling of being outside the circle of his parents' intense involvement with each other.

I Discover that I am also a Systemic Therapist

The above description is a reasonably accurate picture of my conscious belief system about conjoint therapy as I formulated it during the Kantor seminar. However, what I actually did in sessions, and what that revealed about what I believe, was not always the same as what I stated or wanted to believe. The biggest discovery of that year of introspection and scrutiny of my clinical work was how much I had incorporated from other schools of family therapy and theory, even while I was framing most of what I did in psychoanalytic terms. Listening to taped sessions, I was surprised to find that I no longer relied predominantly on verbal interpretations, but often made active interventions aimed at changing behaviors.

When reading and teaching about other schools of couple and family therapy, I sometimes thought of direct efforts to change behaviors as manipulative, controlling, or superficial. These attitudes could not be squared with my interventions as revealed on my treatment tapes. Like my patients, I was denying or minimizing aspects of myself that would create conflict for me. Rather than challenge the views of esteemed colleagues, and my own conscious allegiance to a psychoanalytic object relations approach that is largely interpretive, I simply thought one way and acted another.

Extensive experiences working with couples and families, and learning about and teaching family systems theories, had led me to incorporate many systems concepts and techniques without ever formally acknowledging it. Historically, family systems therapists have focused less on what originally causes a symptom than on what sustains it in the here and now (Steinglass, 1978). They look at symptoms in one person in the context of the organization of the family system as a whole, and attempt to change structures and disrupt problematic interactions. Because family systems theories underscore homeostatic features of systems, in particular feedback loops, interventions are often quite active, and sometimes quite dramatic, in order to overcome the family system's alleged propensity to maintain stability over time. Systems therapists focus quite concretely on how to effect change in the presenting problems, and, as a result, their therapies are in practice quite eclectic, and also include behavioral and psychoeducational interventions.

The manner and interventions of some of the more charismatic leaders of family systems schools, like Jay Haley, Salvador Minuchin, and Mara Selvini-Palazzoli, are geared toward taking control of the situation, on the assumption that a family system inevitably resists change. I could, however, adopt some of their techniques without necessarily adopting an adversarial stance. For example, when delivered with humor rather than as a command, "prescribing the symptom" or suggesting "restraint from change," can bring into awareness a patient's ambivalent feelings, without provoking oppositional behavior. Positive reframes are a way of helping family members consider that symptomatic behavior may actually help stabilize a system in distress. Devising a task that completely reverses an attempted, but ineffective, solution to a problem can help break a self-perpetuating cycle.

In practice, I was confronting my patients with how they actually behave together, not just their explanations, justifications, or theories about how they behave. And I was challenging them to "do something different," implying that understanding can follow from behavioral change as readily as it precedes it. The following non-exhaustive list comprises my imports from the world of systemic family therapy: focusing on interactional cycles; pointing out circularity, i.e., that each person's behaviors are both cause and effect in an interaction; shifting structural aspects of families like roles, boundaries, and hierarchies when they are dysfunctional (Minuchin & Fishman, 1981); using strategies like restraint from change, positively connoting symptoms, and reframing family member's motives to break impasses; circular questioning (Selvini-Palazzoli, 1980); giving tasks inside and outside of the session (Haley, 1976; Hoffman, 1990); working directly on improving skills for communicating clearly, being better listeners, and being less certain about their ability to know, without asking, the other's thoughts and feelings (Gottman, 1990; Gottman & Krokoff, 1989); educating the couple about such things as sexual functioning, family life cycles, and parenting skills; and addressing the impact on the couple of their social and cultural context, especially cultural assumptions about gender roles (Goldner, 1985; Goldner, Penn, Sheinberg, &Walker, 1990; Hare-Mustin, 1986).

I try to teach the couple to be better observers of their own interactional patterns: Who does or says what to whom and when? What follows? How does it escalate? How does it end? What is likely to trigger another negative cycle? Once they identify patterns, I try in various ways to get at least one of them to alter the predictable sequence or I structure new kinds of interactions in the session and direct them to carry out assignments at home that will reinforce the change. Even when dealing with transpersonal defenses like projective identification, I do not work exclusively in an interpretive mode. Like Catherall (1992), I may focus on various pieces of these complex, multileveled interactions, perhaps trying to change one key behavior, or challenging a fixed perception. For example, in preventing one family member from derailing a painful conversation, or challenging one person's certainty about what another feels, I effectively block a projective identification. I work directly on communication skills because the less communication is ambiguous or vague, the less it permits defensive distortion. Directing one person to take on a task that contradicts the way they have been defensively delineated in the relationship is another kind of action-oriented intervention I employ to address an unconscious dynamic.

I also work actively with sexual problems, including assigning sensual and sexual tasks between sessions and then analyzing the couple's experiences. As Kaplan (1979) and others note, the most interesting material about sexual problems often emerges in the context of patients trying a new sexual behavior and/or struggling with their resistances against doing it. I talk very openly about sexual behaviors, body parts, and dysfunctions, trying both to model and give permission for less-constricted and embarrassed attitudes about sexuality. I give the couple books to read and send them to movies, both to educate them and to prompt interesting discussions with each other about their reactions and views.

Lastly, like many clinicians from all orientations, I now more readily consider medication. The number of my patients whose lives and relationships have changed for the better because of the judicious use of antidepressants is amazing. The meaning to the family system of one or more persons taking medication is another major area I would like to study.

While initially I thought of these various active interventions as "unpsychoanalytic," I have come to see this as too simplistic an assessment. In line with more recent views of the role of the therapist (Aron, 1991; Mitchell, 1993; Renik, 1993), I believe that any action or absence of action on the part of the therapist reveals something about the therapist's subjectivity. Interventions directed at behavior change are no different from other interventions in terms of being open to a range of reactions and interpretations by patients. As long as I remain self-reflective and attuned to the responses of my patients, I see these active interventions as not only compatible with an analytic framework, but essential to one that is truly interpersonal rather than exclusively intrapsychic. In the end, it was the families and couples themselves who taught me pragmatically that interpretations, however correct, are not always effective. Confusing communication and behavioral patterns, like chronic fighting, pursuit and withdrawal, or threats to leave, serve as defensive barriers against painful affects. Such interactional features are the couple-level equivalent of "character armor" in the individual and must be addressed before interpretations can be effective. I now find I oscillate between identifying and disrupting rigid behavioral patterns in the present, mining them for the ore of unconscious images and fantasies from the past, and eliciting hopes and needs for the future.

In recent years, I have more consciously looked for other writings that value both psychoanalytic and systemic approaches (Framo, 1970; Gerson, 1996; Goldner, 1985; Stechler, 1988). I have also sought out analytic writers who support, within a psychoanalytic framework, a more active stance that does not so heavily favor verbal communication as the medium of cure (Aron, 1996; Frank, 1992; Wachtel, 1977; Wachtel & Wachtel, 1986). The increasing interest shown to interactional phenomena among diverse psychoanalytic schools, what Gabbard (1995) calls the "emerging common ground," makes me feel less outside the mainstream.

Had Melinda come to me in the last ten years with her depressive symptoms, marital unhappiness, and fears of divorce, a host of questions would have come to mind that earlier might have been given short shrift. In addition to unconscious dynamic meanings, and the function of her symptoms within the family system, I would think a great deal about how biological vulnerability affects relationships. Because of the systemic imbalance inherent in suggesting medication to one partner, I would probably suggest they go together to talk with a psychopharmacologist. I would request that the psychopharmacologist underscore the circular interactions among biology, negative cognitions, and interpersonal stress in the development of depression.

If we could identify patterns in the marriage that may be precipitants to depression, or a dysfunctional response to it, I would try to work out strategies for behavior change. I no longer think that couple therapy is likely to be a sufficient treatment for a major depression, regardless of the precipitant, but I would indicate to the couple that strengthening the marital bond has been shown to contribute to relapse prevention (Foley, Rounsaville, Weissman, Sholomaskas, & Chevron, 1989).

What about suicidality and the serious characterological features that so worried me when I first met Melinda? I would no longer have the same confidence that those issues were purely internal to her rather than at least, in part, contextually determined. People often function in a far more regressed fashion in their closest relationships than anywhere else in their lives. Melinda, in fact, proved to be a highly effective and mature woman in her academic and maternal roles. Rather than look for some decontextualized indicator of ego strength, I would assess the capacity and the motivation of both partners to integrate into the marriage repudiated parts of self, kept externalized by projective identifications. I would assume that there was a healthy impulse behind their choice of each other and explore whether removing certain protective barriers could liberate that potential.

My Interest Turns to Larger Systems

The idea that others can be induced to interpersonally enact aspects of one person's psychic functioning continues to be a rich source of questions and observations for me. Recently, my thoughts about transpersonal defenses and the minimum sufficient network (MSN) for treatment have turned to larger interpersonal networks. I have been examining conflicts in multi-therapist systems and in the multileveled systems of lawyers, therapists, friends, and extended families who provide a support network for couples dissolving a marriage.

At AFTU, we paid close attention to the complexities of multiple therapists treating the same patients (Zinner, 1989). Though disputes among treaters were legion, it was an article of faith that conflicts, for example, between an adolescent's individual therapist and the nursing coordinator, represented a splitting and projection of the adolescent's disavowed self and object images. When the treatment staff could arrive at a shared understanding that their disparate views represented different aspects of the patient, the staff could then help the patient to integrate these split-off parts.

Even with this background, I was unprepared for the difficulties in collaborating with other therapists on an outpatient basis, especially when the therapists have radically divergent views of and formulations about patients (Winer, 1989). Therapists treating different components of a family system frequently get drawn into complex family dramas, often unwittingly reinforcing one particular version of a very complicated picture, sometimes to the detriment of the patient or the patient's external relationships. Very sensitive and difficult work is demanded of the differing therapists to reintegrate into each therapy what has been split-off. It requires listening to the other therapist's differing views as, at least in part, a reflection of their patient's multi-layered subjective experiences, not as a sign of the therapist's incompetence. When I have been unable to collaborate constructively with other therapists, I help patients themselves recognize when their own inner conflicts are being enacted by the therapist system and take responsibility for their contribution to the systemic conflict. I also help them to understand the inevitability of the different therapists' perceptions and formulations, both as a function of the therapists' models and tasks, as well as the different data available to them.

As a divorce therapist and mediator, I have also observed parallel situations, where conflicts at one level of a system are enacted at another level. When a marriage breaks down, the family system in crisis brings in other people to replace the disintegrating structures. Paradoxically, some of the impasses that can occur during the divorce process result from well-meaning interventions of people in the network of extended kin, new partners, friends, and the legal and mental health systems' efforts to support the partners (Johnston & Campbell, 1988).

Escalating conflict is fueled when the supporters of each embattled partner participate in a kind of "tribal warfare," demonizing one partner to support the self-esteem of the other. With the best of intentions, these supporters and advocates, including therapists and lawyers, sometimes encourage uncompromising stances, characterize the other partner as purely self-serving, and support tactics that may undermine the couple's ability to work together. Unfortunately, respectful collaboration among the various professionals involved in the separation and divorce process is no easier than it is within the mental health field. The same kinds of splits often occur, with various professionals destructively enacting pieces of the couple's conflict. Polarizations and defensive reactions to perceived threats quickly lead to an escalation of conflict similar to that which brought the couple to divorce in the first place. The polarized views of the couple, voiced by friends and professional supporters alike, as comprising a victim and a victimizer, may provide short-lived comfort at the cost of long-lived conflict.

I DISCOVER I AM POSTMODERN

In recent years, I have become aware of another change in perspective that affects how I view virtually every aspect of my clinical work. While on the AFTU, I had participated in a research project to codify affective interactions during family therapy. The researchers, who shared a basic psychoanalytic object relations orientation, were never able to agree on what was occurring in the family interactions we studied. We might agree on the language, less on the tone of voice, little on the affect, and rarely on meanings or motives. As a researcher, I expected to feel more like the "scientific observer" I had started out wanting to be. Instead, I began to feel that it was impossible to factor out our individual subjectivities as we tried to agree on what was happening.

In a similar vein, in my work with couples and families, I have been continually amazed by the discrepancy between the reports of two or more apparently sane people describing a shared interaction. It appears that every patient believes that if I had witnessed the event, I would have seen what they saw and would validate their claim to truth. After years of trying to figure out what "really happened," I now wonder whether certain aspects of interpersonal events have an "objective reality" that can be distinguished from how they are perceived and interpreted. Without realizing it, I, like many in our culture, was becoming postmodern.

Postmodernism represents a general shift, in many fields, away from a search for universal truths and essential meanings to beliefs that individuals construct mental images of reality based on their idiosyncratic perceptions and assumptions (constructivism) and/or interpersonally negotiate the meaning of events (social constructionism). Both constructivism and social constructionism contribute to the current view that there can be multiple realities, viewed from different perspectives. Interpretations of "reality" depend on contextual elements such as history and culture, and on individual factors such as gender and power. In the 1980s and 1990s, in the field of psychology, a critique was developing of the "scientific expert" who constructs concepts of normality and deviance while unaware of the construction process. Other psychologists were reaching the same conclusion as I that what had, in the past, seemed "obviously true" could now be seen to vary depending on who the observer is, where she or he stands, and through what theoretical lens psychological events are viewed

(Anderson & Goolishian, 1986; Hoffman, 1990; Gergen & Gergen, 1984; Schafer, 1992).

My postmodern stance reveals itself in therapy when I express my belief that people are always in the process of constructing meanings, and actively interpreting what they perceive, rather than passively registering reality. When I ask patients to tell their stories or share their perspectives, I am anticipating the accusations by incredulous listeners that the speaker is lying, distorting, or at best having a lapse of memory. I try to explain the inevitability of different perspectives and different interpretations and indicate that the potential to reinterpret events or rewrite stories can be liberating. But the postmodern view of multiple realities is counterintuitive for a patient who is outraged that his or her perspective is not being validated as correct. I understand that reaction, for I must admit that the postmodern idea of multiple realities contradicts my own moment-to-moment subjective experience of registering what is "really out there."

As I review my evolution from Freud to object relations, to family systems, to postmodernism, I still picture myself getting closer and closer to the truth, and in the end finally getting it right. And I still long for, and sorely miss, that sense of certainty that classical psychoanalytic theory once provided me. But I now view that search for scientific certainty as a comforting fantasy; I no longer really expect to find the one true model to which I can swear allegiance. Perhaps the gift of postmodernism is to legitimize the use of multiple perspectives rather than unitary models. The field of psychotherapy has long been fragmented into subgroups, with each group convinced that its approach is the most effective and that they possess a truth not seen by the others. I have come to believe that each model does have a piece of truth, if not a corner on it. I embrace the idea that shifting from one perspective to another can illuminate for me some previously confusing aspect of human psychology that I might have missed had I held onto theoretical purity. People are very complicated, and interpersonal systems increase that complexity exponentially. Why choose only to look at them through the lens of drive theory, or self psychology, or object relations theory, or family systems theory? When these partial views are brought together, we begin to grasp how they all fit together into a whole that no one theory fully illuminates.

Postmodern skepticism also raises for me a host of questions about the role of my own biases, blind spots, and unconscious beliefs. How much are my clinical views shaped by my own family of origin, my marriage, my parenting? How much do I unconsciously filter what I see to maintain harmony with my friends, my mentors, and colleagues? These questions obviously do not have answers that are verifiably true either; but as I ask them, I begin to see links between who I am and what I do that, in the past, eluded me, and which enrich my thinking about clinical issues.

These reflections leave me in a pensive state. How do any of us arrive at a shared perspective, given the numbers of personal experiences and proclivities that seem to have shaped mine? Perhaps no one else perceives experiences exactly as I do, which creates a dread of isolation. But perhaps my own sense of individuality is equally deceptive, as I am shaped by my interpersonal context much more than I seem to recognize on a moment-to-moment basis. Even what I have thought to be private, individualistic perceptions and cognitions must be far more a product of social discourse than I know. How else to explain the shifts in my own thinking from psychodynamic to relational to systemic to postmodern and narrative models, paralleling broad changes in the larger culture of psychotherapy? I am, inevitably, a product of my time and place and social context. My psychological belief system and psychotherapy model is a unique and highly personal selection and arrangement of elements that are in themselves unoriginal, but in my hands, filtered through my experiences, they have been most fruitful.

REFERENCES

Anderson, H., & Goolishian, H. A. (1986). Human systems as linguistic systems: Preliminary and evolving ideas about the implications for clinical theory. *Family Process, 27,* 371-393.

Aron, L. (1991).The patient's experience of the analyst's subjectivity. *Psychoanalytic Dialogues, 1,* 25-51.

Aron, L. (1996). *A meeting of minds.* Hillsdale, NJ: Hillside Press.

Berger, P., & Kellner, H. (1964). Marriage and the construction of reality: An exercise in the microsociology of knowledge. *Diogenes, 46,* 1-24.

Berkowitz, D. A. (1984). An overview of the psychodynamics of couples: Bridging concepts. In C. C. Nadelson & D. C. Polonsky (Eds.), *Marriage and divorce: Contemporary perspectives* (pp. 117-126). New York: Guilford Press.

Catherall, D. R. (1992). Working with projective identification in couples. *Family Process 31,* 355-367.

Dicks, H. V. (1967). *Marital tensions.* New York: Basic Books.

Ehrlich, F. M., Zilbach, J. Z., & Solomon, L. (1997). The transference field and communication among therapists. *Journal of the Academy of Psychoanalysis, 24,* 675-690.

Fairbairn, W. D. (1952). *An object-relations theory of the personality.* New York: Basic Books.

Foley, G. M., Rounsaville, B. J., Weissman, M. M., Sholomaskas, P., & Chevron, G. (1989). Individual vs. conjoint interpersonal therapy for depressed patients with marital disputes. *International Journal of Family Psychiatry, 10,* 29-42.

Framo, J. L. (1970). Symptoms from a family transactional viewpoint. *The International Psychiatry Clinics, 7,* 25-171.

Frank, K. A. (1992). Combining action techniques with psychoanalytic therapy. *International Review of Psycho-Analysis, 19,* 57-79.

Freud, S. (1917). Introductory lectures on psychoanalysis. *Standard Edition 16,* (pp. 448-463).

Gabbard, G. O. (1995). Countertransference: The emerging common ground. *The International Journal of Psychoanalysis, 76,* 475-85.

Gergen, M. M., & Gergen, K. J. (1984). The social construction of narrative accounts. In K. J. Gergen & M. M. Gergen (Eds.), *Historical social psychology* (pp. 173-189). Hillsdale, NJ: Lawrence Erlbaum.

Gerson, M. J. (1996). The embedded self: A psychoanalytic guide to family therapy. New York: Analytic Press.

Goldner, V. (1985). Feminism and family therapy. *Family Process, 24*, 31-47.

Goldner, V., Penn, P., Sheinberg, M., & Walker, G. (1990). Love and violence: Gender paradoxes in volatile attachments. *Family Process, 29*, 43-364.

Gottman, J. M. (1990). *Why marriages succeed or fail*. New York: Fireside Press.

Gottman, J. M., & Krokoff, L. F. (1989). Marital interaction and satisfaction: A longitudinal view. *Journal of Consulting and Clinical Psychology, 57*, 47-52.

Haley, J. (1976). *Problem-solving therapy*. San Francisco: Jossey-Bass.

Hare-Mustin, R. T. (1986). The problem of gender in family therapy theory. *Family Process, 26*, 15-27.

Hoffman, L. (1990). Constructing realities: An art of lenses. *Family Process, 29*, 1-12.

Johnston, J. R., & Campbell, L. E. G. (1988). *Impasses of divorce: The dynamics and resolution of family conflict*. New York: Free Press.

Kantor, D., & Lehr, W. (1975). *Inside the family*. San Francisco: Jossey-Bass.

Kaplan, H. S. (1979). Disorders of desire and other new concepts and techniques in sex therapy. New York: Brunner/Mazel.

Kernberg, O. F. (1975). Borderline conditions and pathologic narcissism. New York: Aronson.

Maltas, C. P. (1991). The dynamics of narcissism in marriage. *Psychoanalytic Review, 76*, 568-571.

Maltas, C. P. (1992). Trouble in paradise: Marital crises of midlife. *Psychiatry, 55*, 122-131.

Maltas, C. P. (1996). Reenactment and repair: Couple therapy with survivors of childhood sexual abuse. *Harvard Review of Psychiatry*, 3, 351-356.

Maltas, C. P., & Shay, J. J. (1995). Trauma contagion in partners of survivors of childhood sexual abuse. *American Journal of Orthopsychiatry*, 65, 529-539.

Meissner, W. W, (1978). The conceptualization of marriage and family dynamics from a psychoanalytic perspective. In T. Paolino & B. McCrady (Eds.), *Marriage and marriage therapy* (pp. 25-88). New York: Brunner /Mazel.

Minuchin, S., & Fishman, H. (1981). *Family therapy techniques*. Cambridge, MA: Harvard University Press.

Mitchell, S. A. (1993). *Hope and dread in psychoanalysis*. New York: Basic Books.

Muir, R. C. (1982). The family, the group, transpersonal processes and the individual. *International Review of Psychoanalysis*, 9, 317-326.

Renik, O. (1993) Countertransference enactment and the psychoanalytic process. In M.J. Horowitz, O.F. Kernberg, & E.M. Weinshel (Eds.), *Psychic structure and psychic change. Essays in honor of Robert S. Wallerstein, M.D.* (pp. 137-160). Madison, CT: International Universities Press.

Schafer, R. (1992). *Retelling a life*. New York: Basic Books.

Scharff, D. E., & Scharff, J. S. (1991). *Object relations couple therapy*. Jason Aronson, 1991.

Selvini Palazzoli, M., Boscolo, L., Cecchin. G., & Prata, G., (1978). *Paradox and counterparadox*. New York: Jason Aronson.

Shapiro, E. R. (1982). The holding environment and family therapy with acting out adolescents. *International Journal of Family Psychiatry*, 3, 69-89.

Shapiro, E. R., & Carr, A. W. (1991). Lost in familiar places: Creating new connections between the individual and society. New Haven & London: Yale University Press.

Shapiro, R. L. (1979). Family dynamics and object-relations theory: An analytic, group-interpretive approach to family therapy. In S. C. Feinstein & P. L. Giovacchini (Eds.), *Adolescent psychiatry* (pp. 18-135). Chicago: University of

Chicago Press.

Shay, J. J. (1992). Countertransference in the family therapy of survivors of sexual abuse. *Child Abuse & Neglect, 16*, 585-593.

Skynner, A. C. R. (1976). *Systems of family and marital psychotherapy.* New York: Brunner/Mazel.

Stechler, G. (1988). The integration of psychoanalysis and family systems. In M. Meisels & E. Shapiro (Eds.), *Tradition and innovation in psychoanalytic education* (pp. 217-228). Analytic Press.

Steinglass, P. (1978). The conceptualization of marriage from a systems theory perspective. In T. Paolino & B. McCrady (Eds.), *Marriage and marriage therapy.* New York: Brunner/Mazel.

Wachtel, E. F., & Wachtel, P. L. (1986). *Family dynamics in individual psychotherapy.* New York: Guilford Press.

Wachtel, P. L. (1977). *Psychoanalysis and behavior therapy.* New York: Guilford Press.

Winer, R. (1989). The re-creation of the family in the mind of the individual therapist and the re-creation of the individual in the mind of the family therapist. In J. S. Scharff (Ed.), *Foundations of object relations family therapy* (pp. 335-356). New York: Aronson.

Zinner, J. (1976). The implications of projective identification for marital interaction. In H. Grunebaum & J. Christ (Eds.), *Contemporary marriage: Structure, dynamics and therapy* (pp. 293-308). Boston: Little Brown.

Zinner, J., & Shapiro, R. L. (1974). The family as a single psychic entity: implications for acting out in adolescence. *International Review of Psychoanalysis, 1*, 179-186.

Zinner, J. (1989). The use of concurrent therapies: Therapeutic strategy or reenactment? In J. S. Scharff (Ed.), *Foundations of object relations family therapy* (pp. 321-334). New York: Jason Aronson.

I would like to thank Susan Abelson and Jessica Hamman for their comments on an earlier draft of this chapter.

CHAPTER 11

WHAT I HAVE LEARNED: GROWTH THROUGH DISILLUSION

JOHN T. MALTSBERGER, M.D.

I began my medical studies in 1955, arriving in Boston that summer at the height of one of the last great poliomyelitis epidemics. I remember the thrill of my first days at the Harvard Medical School, when the students were volunteering to help nurse the many critically ill patients in "iron lung" respirators. It was a dramatic and intoxicating introduction to the struggle against disease and death. My medical education was from the first day on Avenue Louis Pasteur not only personally formative, but for the most part, exhilarating.

I had come to medical school planning to specialize in psychiatry, but narrowly escaped the temptations of neurology and surgery. In my senior year, I regained my original course, principally because of the powerful influence of two very great teachers and mentors, Ives Hendrick and Elvin Semrad, both of the Massachusetts Mental Health Center, where I was ultimately to complete five years of residency training in adult and child psychiatry.

I began my psychiatric training in 1959, four years after chlorpromazine had come into general use. The first North American clinical trials of imipramine were carried out in 1958 (Healy, 1997). Thus it was that the "major tranquilizers" had just been introduced, and there were no good generally available antidepressant drugs. Insulin shock as a treatment for schizophrenic patients was still being carried out at my hospital, although lobotomy had been abandoned except for a rare patient with severe and intractable obsessive compulsive disorder. Between 1943 and 1950 more than 500 lobotomies had been performed at the Massachusetts Mental Health Center. Electroconvulsive treatment was given to our more severely depressed patients in 1959, having been introduced in the United States in 1940 (Valenstein, 1986). The state hospitals around the country were still crowded, and the fearful "insane asylum" era was still very much alive in the popular mind. I saw Olivia De Havilland's film, *The Snake Pit*, when I was 15 years old. I shall never forget its portrayal of suffering and abandonment.

I mention these details to emphasize that at the time I began my training there was very little available for the treatment of serious mental illness, and to paint for you the background against which psychotherapy of severely disturbed patients was held out as the best hope. Harry Stack Sullivan had died in 1949, and Frieda Fromm-Reichmann in 1957. In Boston, in 1959, McLean Hospital's Alfred Stanton (a protégé of Sullivan and Fromm-Reichmann) and the Massachusetts Mental Health Center's Elvin Semrad were Boston's master teachers of psychotherapy of severely disturbed patients. Stanton had little influence on my professional development. Semrad's influence (he was my teacher between 1959 and 1969) was enormous, and to him I owe not only a deep professional debt, but also a profound personal debt.

Though I was not aware of it at the time, powerful unconscious influences were at work in my mind, which invited identification with seriously mentally ill patients. As a ten-month-old child I suffered from a severe infantile diarrhea that required a hospitalization of some weeks. In 1934, this spelled total separation from my mother, restraints in tightly wrapped sheets, and naso-gastric drips. My mother recalled the pediatrician's ordering the nurses to "get her out of here." My younger brother was born when I was just under three years old, and this resulted in another separation of about six weeks when I was sent to stay with my grandmother. Shortly thereafter I developed asthma, an ailment that persisted through my latency years. I still recall the terror of breathlessness (I was afraid I would die) and the remarkable relief that the quiet visits of the family doctor would bring. Just by sitting by my bed, Dr. John Lightsey (that was his name) could sometimes interrupt an asthma attack. If that did not suffice, he would prescribe (I still remember his pink capsules) ephedrine sulfate, 1/8 grain. That always did the trick. I profoundly identified with Dr. Lightsey as a small boy, and it was he who set me on the path to medical school, consolidating my closeness to him by presenting me with his microscope when he retired from practice when I was in high school.

Abandonment anxiety was my basic ailment and remained my deepest though largely unconscious fear for years. I had enough anxiety and mild depressive symptoms through university years to have some appreciation of mental suffering. I had an early and important personal experience of how fear and a sense of choking to death from asthma could be quieted by the presence of a doctor. My experiences of observing Elvin Semrad's kindly, profoundly intuitive interviews with psychotic patients (they often would give up their craziness as he helped them articulate what they could not endure emotionally) was like watching Dr. Lightsey at the bedside. Dr. Semrad would often say that in psychiatry the doctor had only one tool at his disposal—*himself.*

A large proportion of my medical school class moved forward into psychiatric residencies after graduation. Most of us were fairly uncritical of the received wisdom that psychotherapy was the best treatment for most mental disorders, the origins of which lay, we believed, in developmental difficulties and complications.

Genetic and neurochemical considerations received little attention, although "constitutional" factors were understood to increase vulnerability to harmful developmental injuries. Some of my fellow residents were skeptical of psychoanalytic theorizing of this kind and tended to move in the direction of psychopharmacology, an area of psychiatry that expanded explosively in the 1960s. Others of us, however, were passionate true believers. In retrospect it strikes me as strange that we few were prepared to believe so earnestly in the therapeutic power of psychotherapy and psychoanalysis. Of course, for reasons of our own, we needed to believe. Further, the gold-standard of double-blind empirical trials was just beginning to assert its supremacy. The professional journals still had room for case reports and for treatment studies without controls.

The truth of the matter is that I began residency training with an unconscious conviction that words had something close to magical powers to heal the mentally ill, and I was sure that if they were uttered empathically and in the correct order the patients would get better. It was a kind of incantatory theory of therapy. In retrospect it seems the kind of healing I had in mind was not unlike that practiced by the priests of Asklepios at Epidaurus. There, the patients, suitably purified and prepared, were visited by the priests in the night who interpreted their dreams and advised them, effecting "cures."

Of course it did not take me long to recognize that my therapeutic efforts by way of empathic understanding and interpretation seemed to have little effect on my very sick patients. I assured myself that in time my skills would become more perfected, and that after all, psychotherapy took a long time.

My first year of training was on an inpatient unit, and Dr. Semrad's policy was to encourage his residents to spend several hours each week listening to and trying to understand each patient. I took full and voluminous histories and recorded many pages of notes of what the patients said to me, and what I said to them. I discussed these with my supervisors. Some of my patients seemed to get somewhat better and were discharged, but it

seemed to have little to do with me. I began to doubt my therapeutic powers. By February 1960, I was sufficiently discouraged by
my results to experience some depressive symptoms myself. The
angry, self-injuring borderline patients threatened me, and the
truly suicidal patients (there were many) were very frightening
indeed. I was greatly relieved to begin a personal psychoanalysis.

A critical moment in my psychotherapeutic disillusionment occurred that winter when I found myself sitting for yet
another barren, silent hour with a young woman with a schizoaf-
fective disorder. She was secretive, suspicious, and, worst of all,
she cut herself, sometimes severely, on her arms. The frequency of
her cutting was increasing, and one morning at staff "report" (all
the patients were reviewed daily in a gathering of nurses, residents, and other workers) someone suggested that maybe the reason the patient was getting worse was because of some fault in the
psychotherapy. I shall never forget the quiet in the room as everyone looked at me. It seemed at the time that the chief resident
looked at me with particular bleakness. I felt utterly helpless and
very guilty.

I sat with her yet again that afternoon in my small office,
converted from what had been a locked seclusion room in past
years. By now she had been my patient for several months, and,
because none of my interpretations or clarifications, based on what
I could puzzle out from the history I had so sedulously collected,
appeared to make the slightest difference, I had also tended to
lapse into silence. As I sat gazing unhappily at the tattered old rug
that I had brought into my "office" in order to make it seem a little less institutional, I had a horrible fantasy. The pattern of the rug
had a series of oval shapes in it which suddenly seemed to resem-
ble cross-sections of blood vessels. I imagined fountains of blood
spurting up from those ovals in my rug. Suddenly I knew that I
wanted to cut the patient's carotid arteries.

Now I know that I was experiencing what has since
become known as "projective identification" (Ogden, 1979). Then
I only knew that I had felt something absolutely dreadful and
strictly against what I took for the professional rules. I felt that I

was in serious trouble. I had not yet reached that level of psycho-logical maturity so that I had a full grasp of the difference between wishing and doing, and to wish to murder a patient made me seri-ously doubt that I should be working in psychiatry. Somehow I made it to the end of the session (strictly timed by my watch for fifty minutes) and walked downstairs where I found Dr. Semrad with his office door ajar, seated at his cluttered desk. I asked if I might have a word with him.

The countertransference irruption I had experienced seemed too terrible to confess to anybody but my analyst, but I needed some help. In my best medical school manner I began to present the patient's case to him, but as I did so, I became more and more upset. The more upset I became the more disorganized my recital grew. Finally I stammered out that the patient was cut-ting herself more and more often, that she seemed to respond to nothing I could think of to say, and that I felt absolutely helpless and even guilty. At that point I began to weep, which seemed to me to make matters even worse. I thought I myself must appear quite sick to Dr. Semrad, and that my lack of self-control would show him I certainly should not be attempting to carry out psy-chotherapy with very sick patients. I was afraid I would be fired from the residency.

He waited patiently and kindly until I recovered some-what, and then said: "It is very evident to me how much you care about your patient, and how her suffering is making you suffer. I think if you show her what you have just shown me, she will stop the cutting. Sometimes we should show our deeper selves to our patients and give them the full benefit of our egos."

Returning to the ward I found my patient sitting quietly and silently in the lounge. I asked her to come back to my office, and without holding back any of my sadness or guilt told her how terrible I felt about her cutting, and that I did not seem to be of any use to her at all. I had come out of hiding, as it were, and offered myself to her as a much fuller, feeling person, rather than as a reserved, self-protective young purveyor of interpretations. She did in fact stop cutting herself, we were able to develop a relationship in which my reserve was set aside and I became less guarded and more honest. Some real psychotherapy took place, and the patient was able to be discharged a few weeks later, continuing as an outpatient.

Dr. Semrad's remarkable intervention with me led to some very helpful psychoanalytic work. As I learned more and more about my own proclivity to turn anger against myself, I became more tolerant of a wide variety of countertransference experiences. The warmth and kindly manner of my analyst helped me to develop a warmer, kinder attitude toward myself. The analytic work helped me see how much I had feared punishment and disapproval from supervisors, most of whom (not all) were in fact on the side of my growth and who were not hostile or judgmental.

I began to get over my notions that correctly recited incantations (interpretations) were particularly helpful, and I became less an automaton as I became more comfortable with my feelings. Dr. Semrad taught me many things, but among others were these lessons: 1) You don't have to *do* anything to help patients get better. Just stick with them and try not to get in their way. 2) Your task as a therapist is to help the patient to acknowledge what he finds intolerable, to help him bear it, and then to help him get it into perspective. 3) You have to love your patients and really want to understand them. That is all you have to do; trying hard to understand somebody who has never been understood before is very therapeutic.

In the spring of my first psychiatric year, a patient assigned to another resident, my friend, somehow smuggled a bottle of chloroform into the hospital, secluded herself in a disused room, wrapped a sweater about her face, and anesthetized herself to death. Most of my fellow residents were profoundly distressed by this experience, not only her doctor, who was of course very upset, but the rest of us as well. The loss of this patient brought it home to me that there was no omnipotence in psychotherapy. One can only try; love and understanding are sometimes not enough to get a patient over the hurdles if the forces of hate are too great. (This patient was a particularly angry woman whose diaries, discovered posthumously, revealed her delusional conviction that her therapist wanted her to commit suicide.)

Out of these experiences rose my career-long interest in suicide, that ultimate abandonment, when the patient throws his doctor away because he has failed sufficiently to relieve the suffering, and has been unable to show the patient any satisfactory reason to carry on. My fellow resident Dan Buie and I resolved after the chloroform catastrophe that the only possible response to such a loss was to learn as much as we could about suicide, by studying our suicidal patients as closely as we could, comparing notes, and studying what we could find in the literature.

We were both disappointed in what was available in the literature, which mostly seemed to consist of statistical recitals of details about patients far from the actual interior experience of near-suicide. We were sufficiently warm friends to acknowledge to each other that sometimes we found our patients hateful. When one of us tentatively broached this subject to a supervisor, he was rebuked. "You have no right to hate a patient," the supervisor said.

Our response to this was quietly to ask around among our fellow residents about such feelings, and we soon learned that countertransference anger, fear, hate, and the like were fairly universal. We were also learning quite a bit about our darker selves as we explored some of the more disagreeable recesses of our minds in the course of psychoanalysis. From this resulted our first of several publications together on the subject of suicide. The initial paper addressed hate in the countertransference (Maltsberger & Buie, 1973).

Suicidal patients are as close as one can come in psychiatry to patients who are dying, drowning, if you will, gasping for breath before they sink down into deep water and are gone forever. They have never ceased to stay at the center of my professional interest. Over many years I have seen countless such patients, and have become involved with those whom the lost patients have abandoned and left behind—family, friends, and others. This interest has brought me into the work of the American Foundation of Suicide Prevention, in which I have had the honor to serve as a board member, and for which I worked to establish a regional branch in New England. I have served as president of the American Association of Suicidology, which complimented me with the Louis I. Dublin Award in 1994 for my work in suicide.

I had been taught that suicide represented anger turned around against the self, arising from the internalization of someone at once hated, loved, and lost. This was, of course, Freud's (1957) formulation in *Mourning and Melancholia*. Dutifully, I studied my suicidal patients, and, when I could, offered interpretations about unconscious anger. I was disappointed that this seemed largely to get me nowhere. I continue to feel that Freud was correct in his formulation, but experience showed me that suicidal patients suffer from such ego constrictions and deficiencies, and that their defenses against murderous rage are so intense, that such interpretations often get nowhere. Indeed, I sometimes observed that this kind of deep interpretation made the patients feel I was accusing them of some deep badness, and this weakened the therapeutic alliance.

Time taught me that it was better to concentrate on the *defense* of anger turned against the self, and to repeatedly point it out to the patients, inviting them to join me in understanding why they felt so compelled to be so cruel to themselves.

I think that of all the things I have learned about what drives patients to suicide, two things stand out. The first is that most patients who end their lives kill themselves in order to escape intolerable subjective agony or anguish—Shneidman (1993) has called this suffering "psychache." It is at the heart of the matter. Patients do not kill themselves because of anger turned against themselves, or because they are depressed, or because they are psychotic, or because they are socially isolated, or old, or sick, or alcoholic. These things are important and may contribute to the mental suffering. But it is the suffering itself that is most usually suicide's ultimate cause. Many suicides can be understood, therefore, as a kind of auto-euthanasia. Many such patients who die could be saved with aggressive psychopharmacological intervention if not electroconvulsive therapy. Unless clinicians are empathically together with what their patients suffer, unless they grasp that the suffering is becoming intolerable, these interventions may come too timidly or too late.

Therapists need, in particular, continuously to assess patients for the deadly triad of intense mental suffering (anguish) coupled with strong self-hate and despair of recovery. It is pain that drives most patients to suicide. The perception, true or illusory, that one has been hopelessly abandoned by others, is likely to flood the mind with such feelings (Maltsberger, 1986).

The second thing that I have learned is that central to many suicides is the incapacity of patients to experience their bodies as inseparably integrated with the sense of themselves. Many who do away with themselves feel their bodies are on the fringe of the self, or even quite separate from the self. This illusion underlies the false conviction that psychic survival is possible even if one destroys one's body (Maltsberger, 1993, 1999).

To recapitulate: my first disillusionment followed the comparatively early discovery that there is nothing magical in earnest, well-meant interpretations intellectually sifted out of histories and immediate interview material. I had to learn that any interpretation from whatever source must be aimed at the patient's heart and not his head—this requires empathy, understanding, kindness, timing, and luck.

A second disillusionment followed my discovery that in spite of the very best empathic efforts of therapists who genuinely care for their patients, suicide will sometimes occur. Dr. Semrad once said that if the patient understands he is deeply cared for by somebody (including the therapist) he will not commit suicide. Unfortunately, while I believe this is true, the statement has two prongs, one the therapist, the other, the patient. Even if the therapist cares deeply, the patient may not be able to grasp it or use it. Some patients, by virtue of their mental illness, or perhaps sometimes because of a hate-filled character, are *unable* to understand that anybody cares about them in a genuine way, or, if they do, it simply does not matter enough to interrupt the suicidal process.

A third correction, if not disillusionment, of my youthful ideas about psychotherapy with deeply disturbed patients is this:

so called "supportive" psychotherapy is not inferior to so called "insight-oriented" psychotherapy. Again, my early ideas about the therapeutic powers of interpretation and making what is unconscious conscious have required a good deal of modification.

I now want to move forward and try to say something about what I think I have learned in working with disturbed patients that I only faintly grasped at the beginning of my training. I think I know some things that truly do help.

Sicker patients, especially suicidal ones, are so deficient in their capacities for self-regulation that their egos can only make limited use of the classic psychoanalytic method, or even of the usual methods of psychoanalytic psychotherapy as applied to patients with comparatively intact narcissistic capacity. The therapist must do his best to provide to these more crippled patients those self-regulatory functions that the patients cannot provide for themselves, hoping that in time the patients, through slow internalization of the therapist's help, will grow in capacity to regulate themselves.

What follows here applies to the psychotherapy of suicidal patients in particular, but to a very considerable extent, also to that of patients with severe character disorders. I continue to feel that psychoanalysis is the treatment of choice for patients with sufficiently sturdy ego capacities, but it is obviously not suited for many others. Psychoanalytic theory casts a helpful light for our understanding of our more troubled patients, however. The great majority of the suicidal patients who become significantly involved in psychotherapy that lasts more than a few weeks suffer from narcissistic character disturbances of a borderline nature.

I am particularly indebted to Dr. Dan Buie (personal communication) who has clearly summarized what these narcissistic deficiencies are. He specifically notices how these patients experience great difficulty in distinguishing between the therapist's real qualities and their transference to him. For these patients, to feel that the therapist is filled with hate is to know that he is so. They have very limited capacity to distinguish between what they think and feel about others, and the reality of others. In this respect the patients are very close to psychotic cases; they are vulnerable to transference psychoses, and, indeed to other psychotic phenomena, albeit of a brief nature. In short, their capacity for reality testing is deficient.

These patients often cannot contain affect without going into action. They cannot form and work through a reasonably coherent transference. Their sense of self is unstable and fragile, susceptible to disorganization by narcissistic shocks. They may hate themselves with great passion, and feel they have no worth to others.

First of all, the treatment must be carried out with full emphasis on the real relationship, not so much on the transference relationship. The therapist must give the patient the full benefit of his own ego as a model for identification. He must become for the patient that which the patient needs to become in order to carry forward as a reasonably autonomous adult. One of the principal characteristics of the real relationship must be that the therapist will love the patient, and not conceal this fact.

I hasten to add that I do not mean the therapist should love the patient erotically. Sometimes, of course, therapists do feel erotic responses to their patients, but such responses belong to the countertransference and must be inhibited. The love which is essential is the kind of disinterested love and respect a good teacher feels for a student: an unselfish, disinterested, loyal and benevolent concern for the good of the other person. Every intervention that the therapist makes with these patients needs to be informed with this feeling. The greatest deficiency of all in suicidal patients is their incapacity to feel any loving concern for themselves. They need to take this in and learn it from the therapist.

It is this attitude that makes it possible for the therapist to experience his own countertransference responses to the patient and not to act on them. Indeed, sometimes the responses may be erotic, but more often, the patient's relentless hostile barrage will generate intense feelings of countertransference hate. The therapist who has the capacity to know himself deeply will be aware at times that he would like to make the patient suffer: he will feel anger, and, beyond anger, sadistic impulses to retaliate on the patient and torment him in return. If the therapist is not able to contain his sadistic excitement in reasonable comfort, he will begin to experience impulses to get rid of the patient. The two components of countertransference hate are malice (sadism) and aversion. Neither should be acted out, but aversive or rejecting actions by the therapist are particularly likely to generate suicide attempts.

The therapist must be prepared to help the patient contain anxiety, anguish, and rage against the self and to assist him in quieting them down and modulating them without going into destructive action. This is the soothing function of psychotherapy; the patient requires emotional "holding," not in the physical sense, but in the relational.

The patient requires validation, also. These individuals in the course of development have received little by way of encouragement, or of positive reactions from important others. How is a child to know that he has any valuable qualities if the parents or their surrogates do not acknowledge them, name them, or praise them? By naming and acknowledging good qualities, the therapist validates the patient's worth and slowly helps him build up self-respect. If a patient is generous, intelligent, musically talented, or possesses any other admirable qualities or traits, the therapist should point them out and express admiration directly.

The patient requires education from his therapist. This therapeutic intervention can be a very broad one, but few of these patients are skilled in social relationships. When the therapist can notice more adaptive ways the patient might respond in common situations of stress, the therapist should teach the patient the new adaptation. These patients commonly need to learn, as Benjamin Franklin said, that "a teaspoon of honey will catch more flies than a cup of vinegar." This is not an easy lesson for these patients who so commonly have been raised on vinegar instead of loving mother's honey. Another important educative function of the therapist is to teach patients that there are better ways to obtain emotional help from others than by making suicidal threats or by self-injury. They must learn to put their feelings into words and to speak to others in such a way that others grasp what they suffer and will be disposed to respond constructively.

Reality testing is an important therapeutic intervention. The patient's hateful projections, which distort the good will and intentions of the therapist into something cruel and ugly, need careful, respectful examination as the therapist helps the patient compare what he feels to what he knows has been the constructive history of the therapeutic relationship. When the therapist is told, for example, that the patient is sure the doctor wants to get rid of him, the patient must be asked what he has observed in their interaction, recent or past, that would support such a view. When a distortion is presented in support of the hateful projection, the distortion should be discussed and the patient shown the real perspective. I would call this clarification in the service of defense analysis, viz., the defense of distortion. If the patient discerns that the therapist has made a mistake, or has slipped into some small angry acting out, the therapist must be prepared to acknowledge the mistake and to apologize for it.

Limit-setting is difficult but essential in the treatment of these patients. When the therapist sees that the patient is on the edge of some self-destructive activity, he needs to help the patient see where his behavior will lead. If the patient is in such passionate excitement that discussion and anticipatory investigation is not enough, the therapist must be prepared to intervene, firmly but kindly, in such a way that the patient is prevented, in a loving way, from harming himself or others. This kind of activity may sometimes involve involuntary hospitalization of a patient bent on suicide, or a gentle but firm insistence that the patient surrender a cache of pills which are being saved up in preparation for an overdose. Interfering in this way almost always invites a rage reaction from the patient, who will respond with the accusation that the therapist is being punitive. Loving education and persuasion are called into play here, as the patient is shown that not every frustration is motivated by hate, and that frustrations can be imposed out of caring concern.

These perspectives have arisen out of my years of training, from work with my own patients, and from many discussions with my colleagues, especially Dr. Dan Buie. He and Dr. Gerald Adler have set forth many of these ideas in greater detail elsewhere (Adler & Buie, 1979; Buie & Adler, 1982). I greatly regret that Elvin Semrad wrote so little about psychotherapy. He did not put pen to paper comfortably, and what he did write showed a powerful predilection for the passive voice. I suspect that he felt what he had to teach could not well be conveyed by the written word, so that he concentrated all his energies on his teaching and his students. Sometimes he remarked that he relied on his students to write down, in time, what he had taught them, after it had been purified in the crucibles of their own experience. There is one book (Semrad, 1969) which he published with the help of a number of his students which I wish were better known.

Time and experience have taught me that words are not all-powerful, and that interpretations often fall blunted on the floor. Even the deepest understanding of the psychodynamic organization of a patient is no guarantee that a well-planned treatment will be effective. I have also learned that no matter how deeply one may care about helping a patient recover, love is not always enough.

I nevertheless continue to believe, just as I did 40 years ago, that many patients, even profoundly disturbed ones, can make great strides toward autonomy and health if they are consistently and lovingly offered an opportunity to be understood. The therapist must be prepared to listen with devoted attention, and to put his own experience, and such ego resources as he can summon, at the patient's disposal. Usually he must be prepared to do this for a very long time. He must understand his own countertransference responses in a deep way and use them in the service of helping the patient grow. Everything that transpires in the treatment should be in the service of the patient's growth, and there is no room in it for the therapist's narcissistic gratification. This is a hard recipe to follow, and it takes a long time to develop therapeutic skill. But I passionately believe that psychotherapy of this kind—it is a passionate enterprise—helps most patients get better. I have seen it happen time and time again, and that I have no double-blind statistical study to prove it does not disturb me very much.

I continue to feel that personal psychoanalysis is an essential experience in the formation and development of psychotherapists. I know of no other means whereby therapists' difficulties with their own aggression and narcissistic vulnerabilities can be uncovered, understood, and helped. Without my own extensive experience as a patient on the couch I do not think I could ever have been an effective therapist. As I grow older, I can look back over almost 40 years of psychotherapeutic work and understand how much my own extensive experience as a patient opened the way for me to help others in their turn.

There is a story by Henry James in which a dying author looks back over his artistic career and regrets his late development, the imperfections in what he has been able to achieve. Yet he is able to acknowledge that he has accomplished something worthwhile.

"We've done something or other," he says. To this his doctor replies, "Something or other is everything. It's the feasible. It's *you.*"

What the writer says about his work has always seemed to me true of my work as a psychotherapist and a psychoanalyst, as it is perhaps for all kinds of artists. I believe effective psychotherapy is an art, and if there is no passion in it, it is an ineffectual and feeble thing. Henry James makes his fading protagonist say, "We work in the dark—we do what we can—we give what we have. Our doubt is our passion, and our passion is our task. The rest is the madness of art." (James, 1893, pp. 354-355).

REFERENCES

Adler, G., and Buie, D. H. (1979). Aloneness and borderline psychopathology: The possible relevance of child developmental issues. *International Journal of Psychoanalysis, 60,* 83-96.

Buie, D. H., and Adler, G. (1982). Definitive treatment of the bor-
    derline patient. *International Journal of Psychoanalytic
    Psychotherapy, 9*, 51-87

Freud, S. (1957). Mourning and melancholia. In J. Strachey, (Ed.
    and Trans.), *The standard edition of the complete psychologi-
    cal works of Sigmund Freud* (Vol. 14, pp. 237-258), London:
    The Hogarth Press. (Original work published 1917)

Healy, D. (1997). *The antidepressant era*. Cambridge,
    Massachusetts: Harvard University Press.

James, H. (1893). The middle years. Reprinted in *Henry James:
    Complete stories, 1892—1898*. New York: The Library of
    America, 1996.

Maltsberger, J. T. (1986). *Suicide risk: The formulation of clinical
    judgment*. New York: NYU Press.

Maltsberger, J. T. (1993). Confusions of the body, the self, and oth-
    ers in suicidal states. In A. Leenaars, (Ed.), *Suicidology:
    Essays in honor of Edwin Shneidman* (pp. 148-171).
    Northvale, N. J.: Jason Aronson.

Maltsberger, J. T. (1999). The psychodynamic understanding of
    suicide. In D. Jacobs (Ed.), *The Harvard Medical School
    guide to suicide assessment and prevention* (pp. 72-82). San
    Francisco: Jossey-Bass Publishers.

Maltsberger, J. T., & Buie, D. H. (1973). Countertransference hate
    in the treatment of suicidal patients. *Archives of General
    Psychiatry, 30*, 625-633.

Ogden, T. H. (1979). On projective identification. *International
    Journal of Psycho-analysis, 60*, 357-373.

Semrad, E. V. (1969). *Teaching psychotherapy of psychotic patients:
    Supervision of beginning residents in the "Clinical Approach."*
    New York: Grune and Stratton.

Shneidman, E. (1993). *Suicide as psychache*. Northvale, N J: Jason
    Aronson.

Valenstein, E. S. (1986). *Great and desperate cures*. New York: Basic
    Books.

CHAPTER 12

PSYCHODYNAMIC THERAPY: HEADING IN NEW DIRECTIONS

ELIZABETH LLOYD MAYER, PH.D.

I began graduate school as an economist. The world of economics at Harvard during the late 1960s was a heady one. The Union for Radical Political Economy was forming. There were problems to be solved and controversies to be engaged. Human happiness was at stake. Poverty was waiting to be tackled, along with all the mixed blessings of the welfare state. So we spent our time specifying how education increased worker productivity and how investment in human capital served both Gross National Product and the general good. We were out to make the world a better place for people.

But as graduate school progressed, I started feeling further and further from those beginnings. The lovely precision of econometric models seemed increasingly irrelevant to anything in the real world. One morning over breakfast, I was dipping into Martin Buber's *I and Thou* when I suddenly woke up. I realized why the work I'd been doing felt wrong-headed. It was. It had all been based on three simple axioms. They were about as far from Buber's I-Thou universe as it was possible to get. They were:

(1) Human preferences are always rational.

(2) Human preferences are always consistent.

(3) Human preferences are always transitive (i.e., if A is preferred to B and B is preferred to C, A is always preferred to C).

The absurdity of predicting how human beings behave based on those assumptions hit me. In short order, I left graduate school. I spent the next few years trying to figure out how people's preferences *really* influence the way they behave. And one way or another, that led to my becoming a psychoanalyst. But I did take a long way round. I immersed myself first in gestalt psychology, then family systems work, then various existential approaches to psychotherapy. I ran the Esalen Summer School and learned about the Human Potential Movement. Finally I recognized that, impatient as I'd been with econometric model-building, I was still looking for a systematic way to think about people that could help predict why they did what they did. And short of psychoanalysis, I wasn't finding it.

So I set about becoming a psychoanalyst. I encountered some great teachers and some highly gifted clinicians. I recall one particular conference led by Harold Sampson, Ph.D., director of research at Mt. Zion Hospital's Psychiatry Department in San Francisco. I was a first-year post-doctoral fellow. Someone had asked a question about clinical intuition, and Sampson had remarked that intuition results from a correct set of paradigms about people. Now that, I thought, makes sense. And suddenly it put that elusive thing called intuition in the sphere of something subject to systematic thinking. On top of that, Sampson was starting from precisely the place that had given me trouble in economics. Instead of assuming that human preferences were always rational, consistent, and transitive, he was suggesting we need basic assumptions about people which describe how they actually operate. Given such assumptions, he was asserting that the thing I'd so admired in the great therapists I'd observed—that remarkable, ineffable thing called intuition—might remain remarkable, but didn't have to be quite so ineffable.

With that began my serious engagement with psycho-analysis. And I would say that the ongoing effort to define a genuinely correct set of basic assumptions about people remains the heart of the psychoanalytic endeavor for me. Out of that effort comes the possibility of helping people live differently and feel differently. The fire that enlivens clinical work derives from the fundamental optimism I find in the basic set of assumptions about people to which psychoanalytic work has brought me.

The first of those assumptions is that human motivation is rooted in people's desires to be loved and to love. In being loved, people want to be loved not just by others but also by themselves. And in loving, they want to love not just themselves but others as well. The distortions of human existence are at bottom distortions of the ways that basic desire for love gets expressed and lived out.

The other essential assumption is that the desire for love is embedded in a mind that doesn't know itself, a mind that operates according to beliefs, memories, and wishes which are out of awareness and not subject to conscious regulation—in brief, unconscious. It's that fact which helps make sense out of the patently irrational and self-destructive things people do in their efforts to love and be loved.

Taking those assumptions as basic locates people's problems not in the nature of their desires, but in the misguided ways they go about achieving them. That's why it's optimistic. That's also why I find psychoanalytic thinking to have immense pragmatic import. Psychotherapy becomes the project of helping people recognize their misguidedness such that they can go about living better. A patient in psychotherapy can recognize, say, how a brother's illness following childhood squabbling between the two of them might have seemed like it resulted from their squabbles, especially if the patient always triumphed and wanted to see his brother laid low. From a memory like that, it's no great leap for a patient to recognize how his continued phobic avoidance of anything smacking of squabbles might be based in a deeply-held conviction that squabbles lead to catastrophic suffering and illness. From there, new sense can be made of the present as a function of the past. New choices about how to live, based on a re-assessment of current reality, become possible.

Those are fairly simple and ordinary ideas. Nonetheless, these days I find they're the essential assumptions which orient me in the psychoanalytic enterprise. They bring certain corollaries with them which have distinct practical consequences for how I work with people. For example, they set the stage for the phenomenon of transference as a marvelous aid to observation. When, moment-to-moment, I grasp how a patient goes about feeling loved and loving in our work together, I gain a vivid sense of precisely how the influences which mold that patient's interactions operate in profoundly unconscious ways—often to the serious detriment of the patient's getting what he or she wants in life.

But I should add that the psychoanalysis I grew up with didn't sound nearly so simple or ordinary. Nor was it based in logic as simple and ordinary as the logic I'd admired in Sampson's remark about clinical intuition. Instead there were plenty of code words and formulaic statements about how it was all supposed to work. Much of what I found myself reading in order to get educated required a psychoanalytic education to understand. Mystification was rampant. I vividly recall one teacher's response when I asked him to explain how he so accurately predicted what patients were likely to do, based on astonishingly little information about them. He looked at me with kindly but august authority and said, "Just wait 40 years. Eventually you'll know what you need to know."

What saved things was that every once in a while, I'd return to reading the early progenitors—Freud, or maybe Ferenczi or Horney. And then I'd be reminded that the psychoanalytic project had initially been rooted in ordinary observations about ordinary people having ordinary conversations. True, they were conversations dedicated to the not-so-ordinary goal of maximizing one person's self-knowledge. But the *form* of the original psychoanalytic situation—as Sigfried Bernfeld (1941/1985) brilliantly described—was nothing more than the simple form of ordinary conversation. One person was merely following certain everyday conversational principles about how you get another person to tell you whatever's on his or her mind. Those were principles that could be explicated and spelled out in ordinary, everyday language.

The psychoanalysis I grew up with is currently straining at the seams. I believe a good deal of that strain results from how very far from simple and ordinary the psychoanalytic conversation has moved. The mystification that troubled me in my training represents an ongoing problem for analysts as well as patients. In what follows, I'll talk first about how returning to something simpler and more ordinary might galvanize a newly lively, helpful psychoanalysis and psychotherapy. But I'll go on to talk about a familiar paradox: genuine simplicity invokes complexity of an extraordinarily profound nature. It's a complexity different from the complexity of obfuscation. It's closer to the complexity Blake was after when he identified the world existing in a grain of sand.

Once we start pursuing the world of complexity inside a simpler, more ordinary psychoanalytic conversation, I see us entering some radically uncharted territory. I think we'll find ourselves grappling with organizing assumptions and conceptual implications significantly unfamiliar to most of us raised in traditions of Western science and philosophy. And, therapeutically galvanizing as the impact of greater psychoanalytic simplicity may turn out to be, I believe it's those unfamiliar implications which will be truly critical in leading us to a richer, more energetic vision of psychology. Part of what I think we'll find is that the hundred years since Freud have had us looking at the tip of the iceberg in our assessments of how the two basic psychoanalytic assumptions I outlined earlier—the centrality of love and our pervasive unconsciousness—operate to determine not only how we live, but also how we might manage to find ways of living better.

However, before exploring how that may lie ahead, I'll address the issue I believe needs to come first: how we might set about returning the psychoanalytic project to something simpler and more ordinary. There are three ingredients I see as critical to accomplishing that. The first involves simply acknowledging the fact that the purpose of the psychoanalytic conversation is to help people. The second involves being willing, as therapists, to discuss with our patients exactly what we're doing and why: spelling out how we envision their participation in the psychoanalytic conversation as something which is indeed likely to help them. The third involves clarifying within ourselves the job we see psychotherapy accomplishing: what we personally believe it really can accomplish versus what it can't.

So back, first, to the idea that we're out to help people. That sounds irrefutably basic, but it's a premise that, over the course of my psychoanalytic education, sometimes felt peculiarly distant from clinical discussion. It got particularly distant when something called analytic gain took on a life of its own, distinct from therapeutic gain (Bader, 1994). There were lots of ways people defined analytic gain. Since there was plenty of controversy over what constituted an analytic process, there was plenty of controversy over what the gain from that process should entail. Mostly, definitions of analytic gain started diverging from something recognizable as therapeutic gain when the gain called analytic functioned to justify some particular theory of the analytic process. If, say, an analyst was convinced that the central mutative factor in psychoanalysis was recovery of repressed memories, then recovering repressed memories became a dominant analytic goal. And when recovering memories helped a patient get better, tensions between analytic and therapeutic goals remained quiescent, sometimes even nonexistent. But that kind of coalescence didn't always occur. Patients might recover memories or develop transference neuroses or achieve any number of purported analytic goals without much effect on their overall unhappiness. Then the idea that we're quintessentially out to help people stopped functioning as quite so basic.

I remember hearing a case presentation some years ago in which lack of therapeutic gain seemed glaringly, destructively evident. The analyst was doggedly pursuing what he viewed as a patient's resistance to acknowledging his homosexual transference to the analyst. The patient was getting steadily more depressed. The analyst was humble enough to acknowledge the problem might be his—but by that, he meant maybe he hadn't yet found the right way to get the patient to recognize his disavowed erotized feelings for the analyst. In the analyst's mind, that recognition was critical. He viewed transference as the crucible within which meaningful analytic work—hence meaningful analytic gain—had to take place. The patient, on the other hand, wanted to spend his hours talking about how unfulfilled he felt after sex with his girlfriend. He wanted to talk about his girlfriend, not the analyst. They were at an impasse.

There were many ways of viewing that impasse, but as I listened to the analyst describe the situation, I found myself recalling an episode from my childhood. My family had been spending a month in the country with a large clan of cousins. Cousinly friendships among same-aged pairings were at a premium. Certain couplings worked brilliantly. Others challenged the considerable negotiating skills of the entire gathering. Among the toughest was the relationship between my nine-year-old sister and a cousin six months younger. It was hard to imagine two more temperamentally different children. One afternoon, they decided (looking back on it, some elder relative had probably decided) that a baking project might be suited to nourishing the collaborative spirit. Miraculously, it had seemed to work. My sister managed one set of ingredients while the cousin managed another. They measured, sifted, and stirred. But progress towards the oven seemed curiously blocked. Both girls were on the verge of tears and several explosive remarks had been exchanged by the time a well-meaning aunt finally intervened. Bit by bit, she got to the bottom of things. My sister had been following a recipe on the left-hand side of an open cookbook, while our cousin had been following one on the right. They'd *almost* managed a collaboration: they'd agreed that baking together would be fun; they'd agreed which cookbook they liked—they'd even agreed on chocolate cake. All they hadn't done was have a conversation about *which* chocolate cake.

The patient who got depressed after sex with his girlfriend was in much the same situation with his analyst. He and the analyst had agreed he needed help; they'd agreed analysis might be a good way for him to get that help. They'd even agreed that the patient's discomfort with his sexual desires was critically contributing to the fact that he was depressed. They just hadn't agreed on *which* of the patient's uncomfortable sexual feelings should be addressed as a recipe for getting better. For the analyst, promise of change lay in understanding the transference. For the patient, transference felt irrelevant. The patient's recipe for change involved focusing on feelings about his girlfriend, not the analyst. Like my sister and cousin, each was doggedly pursuing a different recipe for getting where they'd together agreed they wanted to go. The impasse wasn't about whether there was merit in either recipe. The impasse arose because they simply hadn't had the conversation which might have identified the fact that they were following recipes which, regardless of merit, were just plain different recipes.

I think that's one version of the simple, ordinary conversation that often doesn't happen between therapists and patients. Are they agreed on the recipe they're following? On the steps they'll follow to get there? On how the means are related to the ends they're after? Are they, in other words, on the same page?

If our central effort with patients is to help them, I think we need a clear and explicit agreement with them about exactly what form of help we're offering, in relation to the form of help they're wanting (Grossman, 1994). That brings me to the second necessary ingredient for returning the psychoanalytic project to something simpler, more ordinary and ultimately more useful. We need to have actual conversations with our patients about whether we're after the same thing: about how we're collaborating to get there and about the recipe we're following in hopes of producing what we're after. If a therapist thinks understanding transference is the best way to help a patient, that therapist needs to be sure he or she has helped the patient grasp why working to understand transference is useful. Equally, if the therapist senses that a patient is operating with a recipe for cure different from the therapist's, that recipe needs to be made explicit so the therapist can manage to collaborate with it—or decide not to. For either party to know whether genuine collaboration is possible, both need to feel comfortable laying whatever recipe they're following thoroughly on the table.

Making those things explicit entails conversation. It's pretty direct, simple, and ordinary conversation. In fact, the ordinariness itself is part of what strikes me as critical. It goes a long way towards undercutting the mystification that's clouded our efforts to be clear about the nature of the collaboration psychotherapy involves (Renik, 1996, 1999).

And now we're at the third issue I consider critical if we're to regain the power of a psychoanalytic method that resides in returning it to something simpler and more ordinary. We need to clarify for ourselves as therapists the precise nature of the job we think therapy is out to accomplish. Doing that means confronting the mystification that's plagued us and also asking ourselves why it's hung on.

My own guess is that it's hung on because *mystification provides a potentially relieving and reassuring context for the state of not knowing*. Mystification invites patients to feel they're not supposed to know while it invites therapists to feel at peace hiding from the fact that they don't. That reassurance is appealing because, no matter how vigorously we pursue systematic elucidation of the therapeutic process, certain aspects of the psychotherapeutic endeavor are profoundly characterized by the need to tolerate uncertainty (Bernstein, 1999; Eisold, 1999). There remains extraordinary mystery in the fact that a relationship between two people can function to heal and transform lifelong pain. On the one hand, there's an inordinate amount we just plain don't know about how and why that happens. On the other, it may be there's something in the fact of mystery itself which is requisite to the process. If that's the case, it suggests questions about the nature of what we've labeled certainty and its place in particular forms of knowing—especially, perhaps, its place in the knowing which characterizes how we

understand effects of relatedness. The fact is that psychotherapeutic work as we currently grasp it requires an ability to acknowledge and live with mystery.

Discomfort with the mystery we need to tolerate may be
the biggest thing fueling our temptation to mystify. It takes humility to accept mystery. It's a humility that develops out of genuine
confidence about what we do know, given how much we don't.
Nagging concerns that we should know more or that we
shouldn't be trying to help people with all the problems we still
have ourselves, don't make for humility. They make for defensiveness and anxiety. They make the state of not knowing dangerous
and aversive. They don't make it easy to admit to a patient how
much one doesn't know. They make it even harder to welcome
hearing from a patient how much the patient thinks one doesn't
know.

At bottom, I don't believe we can make ourselves available for doing our best therapeutic work unless we scrupulously
sort out what we actually know about how therapy works from
what we don't. We're challenged—each of us—to perpetual and
ongoing honesty about how everything we know remains embedded in what we don't. That honesty is precisely what leads to confidence about what we really do know. In the face of that confidence we can—on a good day—tolerate admitting what we don't.

It's far from easy to retain steadfast investment in systematic knowing while staying honest about what circumscribes its
limits. Fuzzy thinking—the inevitable corollary of mystification—
is a tempting alternative. For example, systematic development of
clinical method is a natural consequence of premises like the one
Sampson articulated for me early on about the nature of clinical
intuition. His suggestion that clinical intuition derives from a correct set of paradigms about people provides the foundation for
building a systematic model of clinical method. But, however
much we're able to specify about that foundation, we also need to
recognize how much we still don't know about how intuition
works, not to mention what its actual therapeutic effects ultimately are. In fact—as I'll spell out later—it's my belief that what we

eventually find out about all we don't know now, may turn what we currently know—say, about intuition—thoroughly on its head. It's arduous and humbling work to keep allowing for that possibility while shouldering the task of rigorously spelling out the models we are in fact able to reach for.

Mystification offers an alluring retreat. In the anxiety of feeling we don't know enough, mystification can feel seductively easier and more comfortable. But, because mystification sanctions uncertainty about what people actually know, the comforts of mystification backfire and backfire badly. They lock therapists into guilty feelings that they should know more than they do, while locking patients into guilty worry that maybe they're wrong to believe they actually know all they do. In the long run, nobody ends up more comfortable.

I'm reminded again of my sister, cousin, and the failed chocolate cake. The explosive remarks between the two girls were focused on how each had evidence that the other wasn't cooperating. But it didn't take much in the way of subsequent inquiry to discover how each was secretly afraid the problem was her own. The more each worried about being the one who hadn't gotten it right, the further they got from being able to have a conversation which might have illuminated the fact that they simply weren't working from the same page.

That, I think, is where mystification really hurts a therapy. It takes us away from being able to have simple, ordinary conversations with our patients about what we're doing and why. Having such conversations depends on our having confidence that we actually do have something to offer. But our ability to welcome and engage those conversations depends even more on our confidence that we actually *know* what we're offering so we can talk about it comfortably and with conviction. In the face of that confidence, simple, ordinary conversations about what we're doing and why follow as a matter of course.

The agenda I've described requires that we be perpetually willing to assess our work in relation to certain questions. Are we in fact helping our patients live better? Is our moment-to-moment psychotherapy leading patients to live the lives they've actually got with maximum engagement and fulfillment? Is a patient's psychotherapy facilitating a patient's life or starting subtly to substitute for it? Is exploration of unconscious conflict truly furthering how patients work at accepting life or is it distracting patients from looking honestly at the lives they have?

As we ask ourselves those questions, I think we'll find we're inevitably extricating our psychotherapeutic work from the mystification that has troubled our field. I think we'll find that we are in fact returning the psychoanalytic conversation to something simpler and more ordinary for ourselves as well as our patients. In the process, I believe we'll find our work profoundly vitalized by a sense that we're re-discovering the power of psychoanalytic insight to change people so they can construct better lives.

What Lies Ahead?

I've been describing how we might arrive at a kind of stripped-down psychoanalytic theory, a theory frankly clinical in nature and focused on how we can best help our patients, day-to-day and one-on-one. That's been my focus because, after the mountains of chaff have been lifted from what's accumulated as the body of psychoanalytic knowledge, I find that what remains is a remarkably effective set of clinical tools. For me, the psychoanalytic theory which matters is the theory built to make sense out of how those tools work.

But when I look to psychoanalysis as a system of thought which describes human psychology at its broadest, most contemporary, and most complete, I see a theory in need of some radical enrichment. The biggest question I see for the future is how our understanding of the two basic assumptions I earlier described as essential to psychoanalytic thought—the centrality of love and our pervasive unconsciousness—will grow and develop. As our understanding of those two things expands, it's my guess we'll be joining colleagues in other branches of science by recognizing a vastly more connected universe than our psychoanalytic worldview has previously incorporated. The implications of recognizing that connectedness will, I believe, be enormous. The challenge will be to see how those implications penetrate our understanding of the human mind as well as the nature of the therapy we practice.

I think we'll be best able to meet the challenge by looking in two directions. One will involve confronting recent developments in psychoanalytic thinking and considering what the far reaches of those developments are likely to entail: how, especially, those far reaches may prove useful in altering some of our habitual assumptions about the human mind and its interface with the world.

The other direction that I think we'll find worth pursuing will take us outside analysis and have us examining a set of observations from other fields that bear closely on the nature of mind and its relation to the world outside. They're observations which are distinguished by the fact that they appear, at least for the moment, frankly anomalous in terms of our usual theories of mind.

But let's look first to analysis as it's recently been undergoing both clinical and theoretical ferment. Perhaps the most striking development in psychoanalytic thinking over the past decade has been the ubiquitous questioning of what's been called one-person psychology. While there have been a perpetual few ever since Freud who have insisted on the importance of the interpersonal and the relational in constituting both psychological development and clinical process (Horney, Ferenczi, Fromm, and Sullivan among others), that emphasis and those analysts were for generations marginalized by mainstream psychoanalytic thinking.

In recent years, that has changed. These days, it's impossible to pick up a major psychoanalytic journal without finding articles centrally focused on the crucial impact of a relational field or emphasizing concepts like intersubjectivity as the heart of the analytic process. Connection and relationship have assumed center stage. We've moved increasingly away from Freud's focus on individual exploration of the boundaried mind as our way into knowing the unconscious or understanding human motivation. No longer does the analyst help the patient look inside while the analyst remains outside.

That's represented a huge shift in actual practice as well as in general psychoanalytic world-view. But it's a shift very much in keeping with shifts taking place in other fields. And those fields run the gamut, from realms of psychology that have traditionally been those most opposed to psychoanalysis to the hardest of the so-called hard sciences. The ubiquity of the shift deserves our interest.

On the one hand, it deserves our interest because it may put us in the fortunate position of looking to other fields to help illuminate where we ourselves may be heading. On the other, it suggests we may be participating in a wider cultural transition regarding contemporary understanding of mind, consciousness, and the nature of what we call reality. If that's true, psychoanalysis stands to make—I believe—a highly distinctive and important contribution to the way that transition develops.

And that's an exciting possibility. It's exciting because it may provide a fresh venue for the application of psychoanalytic ideas, which will invigorate not only our own work but also work in a wide range of other fields. The relevant point here is that *the psychoanalytic method is not simply a method of cure; it's also a method of observation.* As such, it has unique observational properties. It's a method designed to make vicissitudes of love and unconscious processes visible in ways they ordinarily are not. It is vicissitudes of precisely these two things that are starting to appear as newly relevant to investigators whose work has previously been firmly lodged in the familiar structures of objective thinking—but who increasingly recognize the need to account for subjectivity and intersubjectivity as critical variables in their considerations. Their recognition appears to be inevitably emerging from what I earlier described as perceptions of the universe characterized by a quality of connectedness greater than our scientific world-view has previously suggested.

For example, from the world of academic psychology, the *American Psychologist* (1998) recently published "The Greening of Relationship Science," originally presented as part of a

Distinguished Scientific Contribution address by Ellen Berscheid to the American Psychological Association. Berscheid heralds what she terms "a new science of relationality," which is multidisciplinary in scope and has dramatic implications for helping us understand how every sphere of human endeavor is characterized by qualities of interconnectedness we haven't previously identified.

In the world of business and corporate leadership, *The Connective Edge: Leading in an Interdependent World* (Lipman-Blumen, 1996) was recently nominated for a Pulitzer Prize. The author, Jean Lipman-Blumen, suggests that we're entering what she calls "The Connective Era," in which we're achieving new understandings of how a pervasive connectedness radically alters our sense of the world in which business needs to function. Along the same lines, Margaret Wheatley's (1994) text, *Leadership and the New Science*, has become a classic for management consultants. Her central point is that the corporate world is increasingly recognizing what she describes as "unseen *connections* between what were previously thought to be separate entities...revealing the primacy of relationships. Is it any wonder," Wheatley asks, "that we are beginning to reconfigure our ideas about management in relational terms?" (1994, pp. 10, 12).

The physicist John Wheeler (1974) began to address the impact of recognizing new qualities of connectedness for physics in a discourse published by *The American Scientist*:

> We are inescapably involved in bringing about that which appears to be happening. We are not only observers. We are participators. In some strange sense this is a participatory universe (1974, p. 689).

The philosopher Henryk Skolimowski (1994) has developed Wheeler's work to suggest that the concept of a participatory universe makes major demands on scientific methodology as we've known it. The notion of a participatory universe requires, he says, that we initiate strategies for investigative methodologies which are themselves participatory, methodologies in which self-awareness on the part of the investigator and a capacity for empathy with that being investigated represent crucial variables in considering the effect of the observer on whatever is constituted as observation.

Skolimowski is not alone. Harman (1998) calls for a contemporary approach toward scientific inquiry in which our usual objective and analytical modes of knowing are enhanced by a greater emphasis on "identifying with the observed, and experiencing it subjectively. This implies...recognition of the inescapable role of *the personal characteristics of the observer*, including the processes and contents of the unconscious mind" (p. 114). Bertoft (1996) suggests that modern science requires analytical investigation be more fully complemented by observation based in "a way of seeing...beyond the intellectual mind into the realm of experience. This means that we experience the way of seeing from within instead of trying to approach it from the outside—which is the way of the abstract intellect. We become participants in the way of seeing instead of being onlookers" (p. 328). Individuals like Jonas Salk of the Salk vaccine, Nobel prize-winning geneticist Barbara McClintock, and a number of others, have written extensive personal accounts of how they found the process of scientific discovery-making to be distinguished by this empathic, participatory knowing. They vividly describe experiences of literally *becoming* the objects they were investigating. Salk wrote about how, when designing experiments, he would actually imagine himself as an immune system, engaging with a virus or cancer cell (Salk, 1983). McClintock described the extent to which what she called "a feeling for the organism" enabled her to know each corn plant well enough to make her discoveries, enabling her to experience each plant as absolutely unique and different from any other (Keller, 1983). One of McClintock's contemporaries, June Goodfield, put it succinctly. "If you want to really understand about a tumor, you've got to *be* a tumor" (Keller, 1983, p. 207).

At the same time, we're starting to see a proliferation of scholarly literature regarding the place of consciousness in literally establishing (not just *interpreting* but actually *establishing*) physical reality (Abram, 1996; Bertoft, 1996; Harman, 1998; Harman & Clark, 1994; Lorimer, Clarke, Cosh, Payne, & Mayne, 1999). Sir James Jeans (1943), mathematician, physicist, and astronomer, was one of the first to articulate the radical nature of this shift for science:

> Today there is wide agreement...that the stream of knowledge is heading towards a non-mechanical reality; the universe begins to look more like a great thought than a great machine... Mind no longer appears to be an accidental intruder into the realm of matter; we are beginning to suspect that we ought rather to hail it as the creator and governor of the realm of matter (1943, p. 137).

Nobel prize-winning neuroscientist Roger Sperry (1981) suggests:

> Current concepts of the mind-brain relation involve a direct break with the long-established materialist and behaviorist doctrine that has dominated neuroscience for many decades. Instead of renouncing or ignoring consciousness, the new interpretation gives full recognition to the primacy of inner conscious awareness as a causal reality (1981, p. 1).

Larry Dossey (1995), whose work on the interface between traditional and complementary medicine has placed him in the forefront of contemporary medicine, declares:

> ...something has to be added to the laws of physics and chemistry before certain biological phenomena can be understood completely. This "something" is related to the mysteries of consciousness, which in orthodox medicine has not yet found a home (1995, p. 83).

And Robert Jahn, professor of Aerospace Sciences and dean emeritus of the Princeton University School of Engineering and Applied Science, states with his associate, Brenda Dunne (Jahn

& Dunne, 1987):

> The physical and psychological relationships between
> consciousness and its physical world entail subtle effects
> and processes that in some cases appear to violate the
> most fundamental scientific premises of space, time, and
> causality...various subjective and aesthetic factors not
> normally accommodated by traditional scientific
> methodology seem crucially relevant (1987, p. *x*).

We're seeing the occasional scientist from every branch of
science start to entertain previously unprecedented questions
about whether and how a science of the subjective might represent
a conceivable undertaking, eventually taking its place alongside
objective science as legitimate scientific terrain.

The general import of these considerations is twofold. On
the one hand, the universe is being characterized by qualities of
connectedness far more extensive than our Western scientific
world-view has tended to acknowledge. On the other, we're starting to put consciousness and the human mind squarely in the center of what science calls reality and the scientific study of that reality.

Strikingly, the issues raised by both those shifts in perspective turn out to be ones long familiar to psychoanalysts. As far
back as 1941, Sigfried Bernfeld spoke about the psychoanalytic
method as an observational instrument uniquely suited to scientific investigation not only of *mind*, but also of subjectively and
intersubjectively influenced—i.e., *participatory*—facts of observation:

> From seeking to gain insight into Nature, we have shift-
> ed the emphasis to agreeing with our fellow scientists on
> an intersubjective body of knowledge... The psychoana-
> lyst gets his basic facts from the psychoanalytic treat-
> ment, a process of actively influencing the object
> observed... *In using the technique....the psychoanalyst gets
> knowledge of facts which are not at all available to observation*

without that technique... Thus this technique is equivalent to
the use of a new observation instrument. What we see through
the microscope we cannot check by eyeglasses (1941, pp. 343,
350, italics mine).

Frederick Turner (1991), in addressing the requirement
created by quantum theory to register what he calls the partnership between events and their observers in ways still new to science and in ways that take human consciousness into account,
develops Bernfeld's point that the subtlety of what we observe
depends on the nature of the instrument through which we look.
(Or, in Bernfeld's words, we need to take account of the fact that
we can't see through eyeglasses what the microscope makes visible.) Says Turner:

> Many events and objects can be registered by very crude
> "observers," that need only be made of matter to do their
> job. Others, though—and here things get interesting—do
> need rather sophisticated observers; and there are many
> whose more complex aspects only come into existence at
> the call of such sophistication and sensitivity. Or let us
> put it this way—the observer is enfolded, in whatever
> way the observer is capable, in the being of the prior
> event that is observed. If the observer is crude, its report
> will form part of the brute consensus of matter; but if the
> observer is very sensitive, new properties will appear,
> and will really begin retroactively to exist, within the
> past event that is observed (1991, p. 145-146).

The process that Turner calls the "enfolding" of the
observer is, I believe, exactly what the psychoanalytic observational instrument, especially as enhanced by recent explorations in
relational theory, may help other branches of science take more
fully into account. Certainly self-awareness and empathy—the elements Bertoft, Harman, Jahn, Skolimowski, and others have identified as relevant to contemporary scientific methodology—have
been explicit and critical variables in gathering psychoanalytic
facts of observation from the beginning.

Thus far, I've been describing how, as we look to the future, psychoanalytic principles of observation may enrich the ways other fields develop. But it's my guess that applying those principles in other fields will have prompt and profoundly enriching feedback to us as psychoanalysts and psychotherapists. That potential is already brewing. We see it, for example, in the burgeoning findings from mind-body medicine and psychoneuroimmunology. As we're discovering how pain diminishes endocrine and immune function, or how fear slows post-operative recovery, or how stress delays wound healing, or how mental visualization can speed all varieties of physical cure, we're learning more and more about the startling immediacy with which unconscious perceptions and beliefs are connected to physiological response (Pert, 1997). In addition to mind-body connectedness, we're increasingly recognizing the degree to which the literal experience of connectedness to other human beings operates as a significant factor in healing (Dossey, 1999).

At the moment, studies demonstrating those factors are largely correlational in nature. But as investigators look more deeply into how such factors actually operate, the kinds of observational tools developed by psychoanalysis will, I believe, prove critically useful. Meantime, our own appreciation of the radically healing dimensions of what we do as psychotherapists stands to be vastly increased. As we grasp what psychoneuroimmunology is showing us about how people heal, I think we'll gain new insight into the healing import of precisely what psychotherapy is about: exploring unconscious ideas and increasing people's capacities for loving and being loved.

I believe we're also starting to see opportunities for the application of psychoanalytic investigative methodology in studies of the ways mental intention can alter biological fields outside our own bodies and even affect the functioning of machines. And this is where we come to considering the smattering of observations that are hardest to fit into our usual world-view, those observations that remain strikingly anomalous. Almost always, the essence of what appears anomalous turns out to entail evidence for how phenomena we've habitually designated as separate and separable appear, instead, highly interconnected. The variables that seem particularly to require investigation entail things like sometimes startlingly negligible effects of separation across space and time, the extent to which subjective states of an observer have critical import for determining the nature of whatever is eventually observed, or the impact of empathy on what ends up being observable—empathy either between the elements of observation themselves, or between observer and observed.

I'll briefly describe one such anomalous finding, obtained in studies that are distinguished by their apparent methodological soundness as well as by their stubbornly inexplicable results.

In a series of experiments with chicks and rabbits, René Peoc'h (1995) has repeatedly demonstrated that animals appear capable of influencing the movements of robots programmed for random movement. An overview of Peoc'h's work was recently published by Peter Fenwick (1996), neuropsychiatrist at London's Maudsley Hospital, under the engaging title, "Chickens Don't Lie." He started by describing Peoc'h's early work with chicks:

> A mechanical robot was programmed to receive a code from a random number generator inside it, which instructed it to make random movements. It was put in an experimental area in which chickens were about to hatch. On hatching, the chicks imprinted on the robot and treated it as their "mother," following it in its random walk. After three days of living with the randomly moving robot the chicks were taken away and in their absence the movements of the robot were recalibrated to show that it was still moving randomly. A chick was then reintroduced to the experimental area in a cage so that it was able to see the robot, but not follow it. It was observed that the movements of the robot became less random; it spent more time close to the chick than it did elsewhere in the area (1996, p. 12).

Fenwick went on to describe Peoc'h's work with rabbits:

> A rabbit placed in a cage beside a randomly moving
> robot becomes frightened. The robot then spends more
> time in the area furthest away from the rabbit's cage....
>
> Even more fascinating was an experiment where the rab-
> bit, once it was familiar with the robot, was starved for
> two days. Food was then placed on top of the robot... the
> robot [was then observed] to make more movements
> towards the rabbit and to spend more time near the rab-
> bit's cage....
>
> Two young rabbit kittens who were litter mates and had
> been brought up together for six months were put into
> separate rooms. A blood pressure transducer was placed
> on an ear of each rabbit. If one rabbit was frightened so
> that its blood pressure fell, a similar fall was seen in its
> sibling. However, if the two rabbits were not siblings and
> had not been brought up together, the effect did not
> occur.... (pp. 12-13).

Fenwick concluded:

> The effects are strong, and the question of cheating by
> the subjects (always raised to discount parapsychological
> effects) appeared to be ruled out. Chickens don't cheat.
> One explanation for these effects is that there is an
> underlying psychic field, the nature of which has yet to
> be defined...What is clear is that if this work is confirmed
> then interconnectedness of mind would be a reality (p.
> 13).

Some version of a field effect like that hypothesized by
Fenwick has been suggested by a number of investigators in their
attempts to account for apparently anomalous effects of minds on
each other, on animals, and on machines. Among the most developed have been the ideas of biologist Rupert Sheldrake (1981,
1988, 1994, 1995), who has hypothesized that the morphogenetic
fields which shape developing forms of plants and animals are:

responsible not only for morphogenesis, but also for the organization of instincts and behavior, for mental activity and for the co-ordination of individual organisms within societies. The generic name for these organizing fields is morphic fields. I postulate that these fields have an inherent memory, given by a process called morphic resonance, involving the influence of like upon like through space and time (in Lorimer et al., 1999, pp. 70-71).

Through what Sheldrake calls the hypothesis of formative causation, he suggests that morphic fields help establish the structure of all self-organizing systems from the simplest to the most complex: molecules, crystals, cells, tissues, organisms, and—most radically—even societies of organisms. They represent a field not yet accounted for by physics and they have an intrinsically evolutionary nature. Beginning with years of work in cell and plant biology, and then proceeding to studies of animal behavior and human learning, Sheldrake has marshaled impressive experimental evidence to suggest that his hypothesis of formative causation may account for a number of commonly accepted findings regarding apparently evolutionary aspects of biological systems which no other theory has yet managed to explain (things like the commonly reported "100th monkey effect" in which labs across the world simultaneously produce identical new discoveries with no identifiable explanation of the various coincidences involved).

In terms of mind-machine interactions, the Princeton Engineering Anomalies Research Laboratory has produced some of the most extensive and carefully controlled experiments to date. The PEAR Lab was established by Princeton's School of Engineering and Applied Science in 1979 for the sole purpose of applying rigorous scientific study to the interaction of human consciousness with random physical processes. Its founder, Robert G. Jahn (1996), described the Lab's original studies as follows:

The basic protocol of these experiments requires human operators to attempt to influence by anomalous means the output of various simple machines, each of which involves some sort of random physical process. These devices are electrical, mechanical, fluid dynamical, optical or acoustical in character...the operators, seated in front of these machines but in no physical contact with them, using whatever personal strategies they wish, endeavour to produce statistically higher output values, lower output values, and baseline or unaltered output values, over interspersed periods of pre-stated intentions....

All told, some fifty million experimental trials have been performed to this date, containing more than three billion bits of binary information...Anomalous correlations of the machine outputs with pre-stated operator intentions are clearly evident. These take the form of shifts of the distribution means that are statistically replicable, and quantifiable in the range of a few parts in ten thousand deviation from chance expectation, on the average. Over the total data base, the composite anomaly is unlikely by chance to about one part in a billion....

From this huge array of empirical indications, it seems unavoidable to conclude that operator consciousness is capable of inserting information, in its most rudimentary 'objective' form, namely, binary bits, into these random physical systems, by some anomalous means.... (1996, pp. 33-34).

At this point, literally hundreds of experiments have been conducted in labs across the world that have produced anomalous findings similar to the ones obtained by Peoc'h, Sheldrake and the PEAR Lab (see Radin, 1997, and Lorimer et al., 1999, for a summary). As clinicians interested in how the mind works as well as the nature of its limitations and capacities, I believe we ignore careful consideration of those experiments to our cost. I think it likely that results of those studies stand mightily to alter our understanding of precisely the phenomena which daily most interest us—things like the effects of empathy, the nature of intuition, or the basis of unconscious communication. In fact, I'll put it even more strongly: *if what appears to happen in the studies I have described happens in our offices, our ordinary definitions of clinical facts and our conventional understanding of clinical process may exclude some exceedingly critical variables* (Mayer, 1996). Observations like the ones I've summarized are, in my view, exactly the kinds of observations which will enable us to push the envelope on our own thinking in ways that will ultimately provide powerful and needed enrichment to our psychotherapeutic endeavors.

CONCLUSION

I'm suggesting that the view of reality and mind which is starting to emerge from a number of fields outside psychoanalysis is ascribing increasing importance to two things that have been intrinsic to psychoanalytic thinking from its inception. The first is the power of mind to affect our experience of reality and even the nature of reality itself. The second—which is what led analysts to locate object relations at the heart of human development and transference as the vehicle for psychological change—is the quintessentially relational, intersubjectively determined nature of what we call reality.

However, while I think it's fair to say there's no field of endeavor in which the power of mind and the relational nature of reality have been more emphasized than in psychoanalysis, I would say that psychoanalytic thinkers have, in recent years, been slow to recognize the dramatic implications of their own basic premises. So, while we've developed the observational instruments as well as the conceptual frameworks which could allow for continuing radical elaboration of those premises, I believe we've lost sight of our radical edge. As we've worked to help heal individuals, I believe we've remained with a thrust that was indeed radical for Freud, but has us at this point lagging behind other disciplines. It may be that the demands on knowledge currently being articulated by those outside our field will be exactly what can put us back where Freud left us, and remind us of how radically our particular sphere of knowledge can inform both knowing and how we go about knowing.

So that's the promise. If we can tolerate the efforts I earlier described to simplify and demystify what we're doing as psychoanalysts and psychotherapists, I think we'll be creating myriad opportunities to clarify how our method works. In the process, I think we'll find we're entering vast new areas of complexity—not, as I put it earlier, the complexity of obfuscation, but something more like the complexity inside Blake's grain of sand. We'll perceive, I think, in our simplest and most straightforward interactions with patients, the extraordinary complexity of the connectedness that permits the psychotherapeutic process to change people. We'll come, I believe, to see how communicative processes we've subsumed under labels like intuition or projective identification emerge from qualities of connectedness between patients and their therapists that will challenge our usual ideas about how space and time divide us as strongly as the anomalous observations I just described.

I began by suggesting that the hundred years since Freud have had us looking at the tip of the iceberg in assessing the ways our two basic psychoanalytic assumptions—the centrality of love and our pervasive unconsciousness—operate to determine how people live. As we augment our understanding of the therapeutic process in the various ways I've been suggesting, I think we'll be expanding both our understanding of love and our understanding of unconscious mental capacities to a degree we've so far barely anticipated. I think we're likely to find ourselves with a vastly enriched sense of human possibility as a result. Helping people develop the implications of that possibility so they can live better lives will be our challenge as psychotherapists.

REFERENCES

Abram, D. (1996). *The spell of the sensuous: perception and language in a more-than-human world*. New York: Pantheon Books.

Bader, M. (1994). The tendency to neglect therapeutic aims in psychoanalysis. *Psychoanalytic Quarterly, 63*, 246-270.

Bernfeld, S. (1985). The facts of observation in psychoanalysis. *International Review of Psycho-analysis, 12*, 342-351. (Original work published 1941).

Bernstein, J. (1999). The politics of self-disclosure. *Psychoanalytic Review, 86*, 597-607.

Berscheid, E. (1999). The greening of relationship science. *American Psychologist, 54*, 260- 266.

Bertoft, H. (1996). *The wholeness of nature: Goethe's way toward a science of conscious participation in nature*. Hudson, NY: Lindisfarne Press.

Dossey, L. (1995). How should alternative therapies be evaluated? *Alternative Therapies in Health and Medicine, 1*, 8-10, 79-85.

Dossey, L. (1999). *Reinventing medicine: Beyond mind-body to a new era of healing*. San Francisco: Harper.

Eisold, K. (1999). The rediscovery of the unknown: An inquiry into the essential work of psychoanalysis. Presented at the Annual Spring Meeting of Division 39, The American Psychological Association.

Fenwick, P. (1996). Chickens don't lie. *Network: Journal of the Scientific and Medical Network, 62*, 12-13.

Grossman, L. (1994). On coming to an agreement about the nature of treatment. *Canadian Journal of Psychoanalysis, 2*, 203-221.

Harman, W. (1998). *Global mind change: The promise of the 21ˢᵗ century*. San Francisco: Berrett-Koehler.

Harman, W. & Clark, J. (1994). *New metaphysical foundations of modern science*. Sausalito: Institute of Noetic Sciences.

Jahn, R. (1996). Information, consciousness and health. *Alternative Therapies in Health and Medicine, 2*, 32-38.

Jahn, R. and Dunne, B. (1987). *Margins of reality: The role of consciousness in the physical world*. New York: Harcourt Brace

Jovanovich.

Jahn, R. G. (1988). Physical aspects of psychic phenomena. *Physics Bulletin, 39,* 235-237.

Jeans, J. (1943). *Physics and philosophy.* Cambridge: Cambridge University Press.

Keller, E. (1983). *A feeling for the organism: The life and work of Barbara McClintock.* New York: W. H. Freeman & Co.

Lipman-Blumen, J. (1996). *The connective edge: Leading in an interdependent world.* New York: Jossey-Bass.

Lorimer, D., Clarke, C., Cosh, J., Payne, M., & Mayne, A. (Eds.). (1999). *Wider horizons.* Colinsburgh, Scotland: Scientific and Medical Network.

Mayer, E. (1996). Subjectivity and intersubjectivity of clinical facts. *International Journal of Psychoanalysis, 77,* 709-737.

Peoc'h, R. (1995). Psychokinetic action of young chicks on the path of an illuminated source. *Journal of Scientific Exploration, 9,* 223-229.

Pert, C. (1997). *Molecules of emotion.* New York: Simon & Schuster.

Radin, D. (1997). *The conscious universe.* San Francisco: Harper Edge.

Renik, O. (1996). The perils of neutrality. *Psychoanalytic Quarterly, 65,* 495-517.

Renik, O. (1999). Playing one's cards face up in analysis: An approach to the problem of self-disclosure. *Psychoanalytic Quarterly, 68,* 521-539.

Salk, J. (1983). *Anatomy of reality: Merging intuition and reason.* New York: Columbia University Press.

Sheldrake, R. (1981). *A new science of life.* London: Blond and Briggs, Ltd.

Sheldrake, R. (1988). *The presence of the past.* London: HarperCollins.

Sheldrake, R. (1994). *The rebirth of nature.* Rochester, VT: Park Street Press.

Sheldrake, R. (1995). *Seven experiments that could change the world.* New York: Riverhead.

Skolimowski, H. (1994). *The participatory mind: A new theory of knowledge and of the universe*. London: Penguin Books.

Sperry, R. (1981). Changing priorities. *Annual Review of Neuroscience. 4*, 1-15.

Turner, F. (1991). *Tempest, flute, and Oz: Essays on the future*. New York: Persea Books.

Wheatley, M. (1994). *Leadership and the new science: Learning about organization from an orderly universe*. San Francisco: Berrett-Koehler.

Wheeler, J. A. (1974). The universe as home for man. *The American Scientist*, November/December.

CHAPTER 13

REFLECTIONS OF A GROUP ANALYST

MALCOLM PINES, M.D.

I was born in 1925 at my parents' home in Whitechapel, a Jewish immigrant area in London's East End, a mile or so from the docks and in the shadow of the London Hospital, a major teaching hospital. This was where immigrants landed as the Jewish immigrants did in the 19th and early 20th centuries, followed by immigrants from the Indian subcontinent. Our house, a substantial three story brick building, was surrounded by Sephardic and Ashkenazic synagogues, with a "Mission to the Jews" (to convert them to Christianity) thrown in for good measure. At the entry of the house there was a pathway with a swinging metal gate and a bench to the side, and children used to play on this swinging gate. My brother, sister, and I considered it to be our property, but so did the local schoolchildren whom my father used to chase away when they became too noisy. There would often be patients sitting on the bench waiting to enter the house where my father, a general practitioner, had his surgery. The waiting room was the front room of the house on the ground floor and though it could hold up to 20 persons seated, there were at times so many more that the queue extended through the front hall into the street.

My parents had immigrated to Britain in 1921, first from Russia and then from Belgium. The Pines family name was well known in the Russian and Polish community, therefore my father quickly established himself and built up a busy practice. It was his Uncle Leon, who had gained medical distinction as a renowned ophthalmic surgeon and had private clinics in Warsaw and Bialistock, who trained my father, Noe, as his assistant. My mother, Miriam Rebecca Jaschunsky, also qualified in medicine at the University of Dorpat, now Tallin in Estonia, a Baltic university largely staffed by German academics. It was unusual for a Jewish girl from a bourgeois family to study medicine in pre-World War I Russia. My father came from an intellectual Jewish background, a typical mixture of rabbis, scholars, and merchants, whereas my mother's family was comprised of successful storekeepers in the small town of Ostrow, in White Russia.

Higher education was difficult for Jews in Tsarist Russia, only the cleverest children could progress to higher education. Both my father and his elder brother Inia competed successfully for this higher education. Inia became an electrical engineer and remained in Moscow throughout his lifetime. My father, born in Moscow, received his medical education at the University of Kiev and qualified in about 1910. Throughout World War I he served in the Russian Army, first as a field doctor and then at the Battle of Tannenberg and later as a surgeon, receiving many decorations both from the Russians and from the Belgians, for he had also been attached to a Belgian regiment serving on the Russian front. He was proud to be a "Chevalier de la Couronne Belge," similar to the French Legion d'Honneur, and always wore the small ribbon in his buttonhole. I well remember his pride in walking in the parade with the Jewish Ex-Soldiers past the Cenotaph in Whitehall to commemorate the armistice that ended World War I.

My parents met and married at the end of the War and settled in Ludsk, then in Russia now in Poland, where my sister

Dinora was born. They set up a medical clinic but, with the coming of the White Russians during the Russian Civil War, my father was taken hostage several times so they decided to leave for Belgium where my paternal grandfather was already living in Antwerp. Since Belgium offered no opportunity to continue his career as an ophthalmic surgeon, they then moved to England. My sister Dinora, after whom our London house was named in stained glass over the front door, is now a distinguished psychoanalyst and I believe we are one of the few siblings in the psychoanalytic community.

As to my parents' temperaments, my father was energetic, irascible, full of self-confidence, and had a very wide range of knowledge of medicine and many other branches of learning. My sister tells how when she asked if we could have an encyclopedia, he replied, "You do not need one, all you have to do is to ask me!" He was not able to achieve his ambition of practicing solely as an ophthalmic surgeon and physician for he was required to take a higher degree in surgery. This was unlike the system in Russia and continental Europe where, if you qualified as a Doctor of Medicine, you were entitled to enter into any branch of medicine or surgery. My father, however, would not compromise with what he considered an unfair system. Thus, he was partly frustrated in his career and had to earn his living as a general practitioner, but continued to practice ophthalmology both privately and in the Department of Ophthalmology of the London Jewish Hospital where he ran the department single-handedly during World War II.

Almost all of my father's patients had to submit to an examination of the retinal fundus—and this included my future wife! I well remember him telling me that it is only on the retina that we can see the structure and function of the vascular system and look inside the living human body. I dedicated my paper "Reflections on Mirroring" (Pines, 1998b) to my father for, as a psychotherapist, I intend to see and understand the structure and function of a person's mind. The word retina means "network" and as a group analyst I am an observer of the network of human communications. Though my father would have wished my career to be in bodily medicine, when I decided to become a psychiatrist and psychoanalyst he agreed to support me in this and helped to pay for my analysis, which at that time cost two guineas per session.

My parents' marriage was often turbulent. My mother longed for her Russian parents and family and for several years would not speak English, therefore, my sister Dinora's first language was Russian. My elder brother, Arnold, two years older, became an excellent chest physician. He died mountaineering just before he was 60 years old. He was sensitive, clever, very athletic, and strong-willed, which brought him into opposition with my father who punished him excessively for his obstinacies. Learning from this, I was more hidden in my opposition, becoming evasive and slightly delinquent, stealing small sums of money until inevitably this was discovered and I was severely punished. As the youngest with two older successful siblings, I had inevitably to cope with rivalry and feeling less capable, and strove to find ways to differentiate myself from them.

To complete this family story, my father had a number of coronary thromboses from his 60s onwards, dying during one such episode at home in his early 70s having summoned me at night by telephone to his assistance. I injected intravenous aminophyline and called for aid, but he did not recover. In later years, my mother had several episodes of agitated depression, painful to witness. She had several hospitalizations and was given ECT at home without either anesthetic or relaxant. I had to assist at this, which I did with some horror. In my later psychiatric career I gave many ECTs in hospitals with well-trained nursing assistance and always with anesthesia and relaxants. Mother also suffered cardiovascular disease and was discovered dead at home from a ruptured aneurysm.

As are Jewish families, we were close-knit, obedient to the authoritative father, and ambivalently close to the submissive and depressive mother. We were not conventionally orthodox and only went to synagogue on the high and holy days. But the environment both at home and in the area in which we lived was deeply Jewish. There were street markets where the language was mainly Yiddish with many kosher butchers and bakers. I can recall the marches of Oswald Mosley and the Fascist Blackshirts through the East End from 1936 onwards and saw riots in the nearby streets.

I was brought up with English housekeepers and nannies, which established English as my native language. No doubt this influenced me in my choice of a non-Jewish English wife. The understanding of both Jewish and non-Jewish mentalities has been essential to my work as a psychotherapist and my school experiences were clearly important to this understanding. I went daily to the City of London School, a minor public day school (in Britain public equals private!) where, though there were many other Jewish boys, the majority were Christian (currently there are many Muslims and students of other faiths as well). On the outbreak of the War in 1939, when I was 14, the whole school was evacuated to the country to share the buildings of a famous and very Christian public school, Marlborough College, founded for the education of sons of the clergy. It was in this setting that I observed the very different personalities and characteristics of the British upper class, a significant gain in information.

At school I was educated in the languages and humanities, but because of the War my father insisted that I study medicine and thereby be exempt from military service until completing my studies. I felt that I should volunteer for military service, but was persuaded differently by him. I therefore left school at 17 to study the basic sciences in London and well remember V1 and V2 bombs, and sheltering at times under the reinforced table in the cellar in what were called "Morrison Shelters."

I was fortunate in being accepted at Cambridge for the first years of medical studies, anatomy, physiology, biochemistry and pathology. I lived a privileged undergraduate life, even in wartime, soaking up the atmosphere and tradition of the ancient university. It was there that I first began to read psychology and psychoanalysis and became fascinated with the subject. I finished medical education in London at University College Hospital, well known as a center of medical scientific research, qualifying in 1949. By then I had already decided on a career in psychiatry.

I persuaded my father to help pay for an analysis, applied at the Institute of Psycho-Analysis and, to my great surprise, was provisionally accepted. I was only in my early 20s and, I later realized, much too young to enter into analysis. I would have been better off facing the normal difficulties and pleasures of a medical student's life. My initial interviewers were John Bowlby, then a Major in army uniform, and Sylvia Payne who had been a distinguished President of the Psycho-Analytic Society. I began analysis with Adrian Stephen, the younger brother of the famous writer Virginia Woolf, at 1 Upper Harley Street not far from University College Hospital. His wife Karin was also a psychoanalyst. Adrian and Karin were persuaded by Ernest Jones in the 1920s to study medicine before becoming psychoanalysts, whereas James and Alix Strachey were allowed to go straight to Vienna.

I had to find ways of getting away from the hospital for my analytic hours and I therefore missed many medical student life experiences. This represented a collusion of the analytic situation with some avoidant defenses that I had developed in childhood. Adrian Stephen was already quite ill when I started analysis with him and died some 18 months later. I was at first intimidated by his impressive height, 6 feet 5 inches, by his gentle reticence, and, of course, by my own sense of peril in beginning the immersion into the world of the unconscious. His death was in some ways a release and I could then concentrate my energies on study, work, and ordinary life.

I qualified and then worked in Sheffield, a provincial university town where I had good training experiences in medicine. Returning to London through the Sheffield connection, I was fortunate to be accepted to the postgraduate medical hospital at Hammersmith and at my second attempt succeeded in becoming a member of the Royal College of Physicians, a higher degree in medicine necessary for a career as a specialist. This was the step my father had not taken and he was proud of my success. This qualification secured an entry to the Maudsley Hospital, the postgraduate center for psychiatry in London then under the fierce direction of Dr. Aubrey Lewis, later Sir Aubrey.

PSYCHIATRY

The Maudsley was at the forefront of British psychiatry. The famous 19th-century psychiatrist, Henry Maudsley, had left a substantial bequest to found a modern hospital for the early treatment of mental disorders and made it a condition that only patients who voluntarily consented to treatment be admitted. Under its previous directors both clinical expertise and research evidence were emphasized. Basic science and research departments were created—neuropsychiatry, neuropathology, neurochemistry, genetics, psychology (where Eysenck reigned)—and psychotherapy had always been represented. Completely new to psychiatry, my first position was in Aubrey Lewis' professorial unit and rigorous indeed it was. Lewis could reduce strong men and women to tears by pointing out their errors and weaknesses in history-taking and general psychiatric competence. I thrived on the challenge and insisted at times on the psychodynamic aspects of my patients. Lewis was sufficiently impressed to suggest that I take up a career in academic psychiatry, but the condition for this was to discontinue analytic training, which I refused to do. After that he showed no particular interest in me, though he did congratulate me when I was the first person to be awarded a distinction in the Academic Diploma of Psychological Medicine that he had newly created.

Maudsley registrars considered themselves an elite brotherhood and sisterhood, and friendships and connections formed there remained strong in subsequent years. My position in general psychiatry remained respected even after I had become a psychoanalyst, and this helped when later I took part in establishing a secure place for psychotherapy in the training of general psychiatrists and developing psychotherapy as a specialty within psychiatry.

What influences impressed me and remain with me from my Maudsley days? My first consultant was Brian Ackner, brilliant of mind, well aware of his physical and mental attractiveness and somewhat narcissistic, attributes that he utilized in both his teaching and treatment. He enjoyed working with hysterical women. He encouraged my psychodynamic approach and supervised my treatments, though he did not have psychotherapeutic training himself. Tragically, some years later, he had a manic depressive illness and committed suicide in the outpatient department of the Maudsley. James Anthony, the collaborator with S. H. Foulkes in group analysis, was Reader in Child Psychiatry and helped me with the treatment of an autistic boy, encouraging me to treat his defecations as gifts! But the most lasting and deepest experiences were with my peers and those somewhat older. Amongst those was the brilliant Henri Rey who uniquely combined a fervent belief in Kleinian psychoanalysis with Piagetian developmental psychology and had a thorough knowledge of electroencephalography and neurochemistry. Another friend was Murray Jackson, then a Jungian who later became a Kleinian analyst, partly influenced in this direction I believe by my psychoanalytic approach. David Clark, a considerable innovator in social psychiatry, was a few years my senior.

It was while I was at the Maudsley that I resumed my psychoanalytic training. I was recommended to Foulkes as a training analyst for the Anna Freud Group. He was then a consultant psychotherapist at the Maudsley. I knew little about splits between Melanie Klein, Anna Freud, and the existence of the Middle Group but I was advised by Karl Abraham's daughter Hilda not to become a Kleinian. I began my analysis with Foulkes in what was a slightly delinquent manner for both of us, in that I began my sessions on the couch in his consulting room at the Maudsley Hospital until he found a time at his private consulting room. Amongst his other analysands were James Anthony and Alan Parkin who later became a distinguished leader of Canadian psychoanalysis. At the time I knew little about Foulkes or his pioneering work in group analytic psychotherapy (Pines, 1976). My wish was to train as a psychoanalyst, but evidently I have followed his career in being both a psychoanalyst and a group analyst. More on this later.

Within an academically rigorous and challenging atmosphere that was skeptical of the theory and practices of psychoanalysis—Eysenck was professor of psychology and taught me basic psychology—we few psychoanalytic devotees had to defend our convictions, a good training in academic debating. Healthy skepticism is necessary for a balanced view in the cultish worlds of psychoanalysis and group analysis, so I have the Maudsley to thank for maintaining my interest in debate and research.

S. H. FOULKES

Michael Foulkes, as he was known later on in life, was the only son in a Jewish family that was well integrated into the German community in Karslruhe as agricultural traders. He served in the German army during World War I as a telephone operator and then qualified in medicine at Frankfurt. He became a psychiatrist and for two years was an assistant to Kurt Goldstein at his Institute for the Study of Brain Injuries where he assimilated the findings of Gestalt psychology. He went to Vienna for psychoanalytic training where his analyst was Helene Deutsch.

Vienna in the mid to late 1920s was a very active psychoanalytic community where the influence of Wilhelm Reich was significant. Foulkes became a close friend of Robert Waelder. He returned to Frankfurt as Director of the outpatient clinic at the newly established Institute of Psychoanalysis, which was directed by Karl Landauer. Undoubtedly he was exposed to the Frankfurt sociologists who occupied the same building as the psychoanalytic institute: the psychoanalysts included H. Meng, Erich Fromm, and Frieda Fromm-Reichmann; the sociologists Adorno, Horkheimer, Marcuse, Karl Mannheim, and Norbert Elias. Elias and Foulkes certainly influenced each other. Foulkes reviewed Elias' (1939) great work *The Civilizing Process* in the *International Journal of Psycho-Analysis* before World War II. Through Elias, Foulkes began to integrate sociologic theory with psychoanalytic theory. He left Germany for England in 1933 and joined the British Psycho-Analytical Society. After wartime service as a psychiatrist, he became a training analyst for the Anna Freud Group and it was in that way that I became a member of that group. Later I belonged to both the Contemporary Freudian Group, as it is now called, and the "Independent" group of nonaligned psychoanalysts who do not wish to belong to either the Klein or the Freud groups.

I conducted seminars for the Institute of Psycho-Analysis on sexuality and more significantly on some American contributions on psychoanalysis focusing on Erikson (1965), Loewald (1980), and Lichtenstein (1977). Erikson's focus on the psychosocial, Lichtenstein's on identity, Loewald's on therapeutic process, all struck me as demonstrating a wider grasp of the complexities of human nature than I encountered in England. There was a natural progression towards self-psychology by which I do not mean only the Kohutian school. Sociologists and psychologists have contributed greatly to a concept of self such as in the writings of William James (Wilshire, 1984), George Herbert Mead (1934) and contemporary writers. Also in recent years I have found the writings of Mihail Bakhtin (Holquist, 1990), a Russian philosopher, of great interest. Bakhtin developed a "dialogical" approach to human development and intercourse which is particularly relevant to the face-to-face work of group analysis.

GROUP ANALYSIS

Group Analysis, about which I have written extensively, takes human beings to be fundamentally social. Each one of us is a nodal point in a social network, which is a concept that Foulkes took from Goldstein's emphasis that neurones form a neural network. In health, neurones are nodal points in the network, but in neurologic illness they become focal points of disturbance. We live our lives participating in dynamic psychological networks—families of origin, social networks of school, work, and culture. Therapeutic groups establish dynamic networks in which individuals can re-establish connection with parts of themselves that they have lost through repression, projection, and other processes. While this innovative theory of Foulkes provides an extremely useful basis for practice, it has shown itself to be in need of revision and amplification. As group analytic teaching has reached many centers beyond London, this revision is in progress. Group analysis is taught and practiced in Scandinavia, Switzerland, Germany, Italy, Croatia, Slovenia, and Spain.

FOULKES AND BION

Both Foulkes and his contemporary Wilfred Bion developed their ideas during World War II, though Bion did not train as an analyst until after the war. Bion's work (see Pines, 1987, 1992, 1998) led to the "Tavistock" tradition with its almost exclusive emphasis on "the group as a whole" approach. By contrast the Foulkesian approach allows the conductor to focus on individuals as well as on the group, a flexibility that makes patients feel more comfortable, which increases the therapeutic potential of the group situation. Bion's understanding of psychotic process has had a considerable influence on psychoanalysis whereas Foulkes' is little known. However, as "relational psychoanalysis" develops there are clear convergences between this aspect of psychoanalysis and group analysis.

THE CASSEL HOSPITAL AND T. F. MAIN

Returning to my odyssey, I decided to leave the world of general psychiatry to specialize in psychotherapy. This meant leaving the Maudsley and taking up an appointment at the Cassel Hospital under its charismatic director Thomas Forrest Main, always known as Tom. The Cassel Hospital had been founded after World War I for the treatment of "shell shock in the officer classes of the British army" (Pines, 1998a). The money was provided by members of the famous German-Jewish Cassel family who were bankers and friends to King Edward VII during his many years of waiting as Prince of Wales to succeed his mother Victoria on the throne. The Cassel became progressively psychoanalytic in orientation and many psychoanalysts were employed there as they did their training. Tom Main had a brilliant career in army psychiatry. He collaborated with Foulkes and his colleagues at Northfield Military Hospital and re-entered civilian psychiatry determined to create a "therapeutic community," a term he had originated at Northfield. The Cassel was to be a hospital where psychoanalysis would be combined with an understanding of the dynamics of the hospital community.

I spent more than 10 years at the Cassel while completing psychoanalytic training and after, and it was there that I achieved my first Senior Consultant position. Main, who taught me psychosocial medicine, was a brilliant seminar leader and supervisor. He inspired his staff, both medical and nursing, with "the positive side of ambivalence," a favorite phrase of his, and his writings were inspiring, particularly his famous paper "The Ailment" (Main, 1989). But his very brilliance created a challenge and an imbalance for many of us and I had to leave to find my own place.

I took up a position as Senior Lecturer in Psychotherapy at St. George's Hospital Medical School under another brilliant man, Professor Arthur Crisp. Not a Maudsley man, he was determined to develop his hospital, St. George's, as a major force in British psychiatry and, in my opinion, succeeded to a large measure. He wanted a psychotherapist to change the inpatient unit from traditional and organically oriented to psychodynamic, within the constraints of the unit that had to cater to both acute and chronic patients, to research interests in the eating disorders of anorexia and bulimia, and to the effects of modern stereotactic neurosurgery sometimes used successfully in the treatment of intractable obsessional neuroses and depressions.

For some five years I had an exciting time introducing small and large group meetings to the unit, supervising doctors, psychologists, and nurses and taking part in the innovations in inpatient psychiatry celebrated in Lionel Kreeger's (1975) *Large Group* monograph. I made two subsequent moves in my teaching career, first back to the Maudsley Psychotherapy Department and finally to the Tavistock Clinic. At the Maudsley, I taught both individual and group psychotherapy to the bright, sometimes enthusiastic, often skeptical young psychiatrists. After the retirement of Aubrey Lewis, he was succeeded by Sir Dennis Hill who had a good understanding of psychoanalysis and was married to a psychoanalyst. Hill changed the atmosphere of the Maudsley from

Lewis' dominance to a more collaborative style which recognized the eminence of his younger colleagues. By this time there were many powerful "barons" and "empire builders" within the Maudsley and the institution became somewhat fragmented, which is probably an inevitable phase in a rapidly developing institution.

My final destination in the National Health Service was the Tavistock Clinic, which held a pre-eminent position in British psychiatry as a psychotherapy training institution. For many years it was under the direction of J. D. Sutherland, another wartime convert to psychoanalysis and therapeutic community. Whereas Foulkes taught at the Maudsley, Bion, and later Henry Ezriel, taught at the Tavistock Clinic and there was a rivalry between these institutions. Their approaches to group psychotherapy somewhat replicated the Kleinian and Freudian divisions as described in *The Freud-Klein Controversies* (King & Steiner, 1991). At the Tavistock, my charge was to reintroduce an interest in and practice of group psychotherapy that had been lost after the enthusiasm of the immediate post-war years. The research carried out by David Malan (1976) had showed the relative ineffectiveness and unpopularity of the Bion/Ezriel approaches for patients whereas Foulkes' group analysis had increasingly been recognized as both effective and economic. However, the task was difficult. All the trainees were undergoing personal analyses as part of psychoanalytic training and the majority were strongly influenced by the Kleinian school. It was difficult to motivate them both to understand and adequately to practice group psychotherapy and to believe that the work could be done by the patients themselves rather than through the interpretations of the therapist.

During this time, the 1970s, I became deeply involved in trying to understand and to treat borderline patients both in individual and group psychotherapy and came to grips with both Kohut's and Kernberg's innovative approaches. I made my own synthesis of these and was fairly successful in my treatments though I had a very difficult and prolonged encounter with a patient through which I had to come to terms with and understand the very powerful countertransference involvements with these patients.

FAILURE IN THE COUNTERTRANSFERENCE

Writing from the perspectives of the end of the century, I can see how advanced we are now in our understanding of the forces that lead to countertransference enactments. In the past three decades we have begun to appreciate the prevalence of childhood sexual and emotional abuse, how these lead to dissociative states and complex post-traumatic syndromes. Had I had that knowledge in the early 1970s, I believe that I could have held to the boundaries of the analytic situation with a young woman patient whose problems I now see more clearly as having emerged from such a complex traumatic syndrome. The traumata were re-enacted in the analysis, the roles of victim and abuser shifting between us. My involvement with the patient led to a partial break-down in my marriage, family, and professional life. The outcome was damaging to all, the patient, myself, those close to me both personally and professionally. The love and support given by my wife and children enabled me to survive the trauma. My efforts at reparation to my patient were inevitably inadequate and the painful consequences of the events of 25 years ago continue to reverberate even today.

Much has been written in recent years about these difficult countertransference situations. The work, for example, of Glen Gabbard and Eva Lester (1996) has clarified events that I had no adequate framework for. Their concept of "masochistic surrender" by the therapist to the patient has resonated for me, as has Michael Tansey's (1994) descriptions of dissociative states in his patient, which were in some ways much like those I experienced with my patient, but which he was able to master within himself, thus keeping his analytic perspective on the situation—something I was not able to do. Though I had been able to help colleagues and trainees with difficult countertransference situations, I could not do that for myself and did not accept for myself imperative need for further personal therapy.

In what now amounts to almost 50 years of experience in psychiatry and psychotherapy, this has been an isolated incident, but it is one that continues to sadden me. I feel it necessary to include this in my autobiographical sketch, so that it should more fully reflect my life experience and I ask indulgence of the reader to forebear from drawing conclusions about my life as a whole, though I do understand that reading this is inevitably a disturbing experience.

MY CAREER IN PSYCHOANALYSIS AND GROUP ANALYSIS

I had by this time already joined Foulkes in the Group-Analytic Practice that he had founded with James Anthony after the war. We established a quite large and quite successful practice from which the Institute of Group Analysis has developed as demands for training increased.

I was over 40 when I published my first paper, written for a conference on sexuality (Pines, 1968). It was a discussion of the research of Masters and Johnson. As I well remember, it was then that I felt for the first time the pleasure of speaking to an attentive and appreciative audience. Over the years I became confident in my ability to maintain listeners' interest and did this by entering into imaginative dialogues with the audience. I also became a skilled chairperson; a chairperson who can stimulate and maintain a dialogue between speakers and audiences makes a significant contribution to a meeting. I can attribute this confidence and ability to having participated in many large groups, which have been a feature of group analytic work over the past 20 years. These groups may consist at times of several hundred persons, if the facilities for sight and hearing are adequate, but more often may be of 50 to 150 persons. The European group analytic tradition is to include large groups in all of our workshops and conferences, thereby allowing for participation by all and allowing the emergence of unconscious dynamics.

Many of my articles have been written as contributions to conferences and demand has stimulated thought and research into a variety of topics: therapeutic process, healing, shame, mirroring, dialogue, self-psychology, psychoanalysis, and group analysis. I enjoy the immersion into a subject and have, when time allowed, spent many hours in libraries where I have enjoyed chasing up lines of conceptual development. I have a strong historical inclination and have enjoyed setting temporary work as foreground against the background of earlier work.

I did not seek to become a training analyst in the Institute of Psycho-Analysis. I disliked the institutional politics and did not wish to live the enclosed life of a training analyst. Rather than fit myself to the procrustean bed of psychoanalysis, I took an active part in the development of group analysis both nationally and internationally.

While Foulkes was alive, the Group Analytic Society became larger and stronger and I joined the Group Analytic Practice that had been started by Foulkes, Anthony, and Patrick de Mare after the war. Of my founding colleagues, only de Mare and Robin Skynner are still alive, although the latter has suffered a severe stroke. We were called on to start providing training in group analysis and some years later several of us established the Institute of Group Analysis as a separate teaching entity from the Group Analytic Society and the Group Analytic Practice.

These were turbulent and exciting years and we have had considerable success in our training programs culminating in our Qualifying Course that leads to membership of the Institute of Group Analysis. This involves personal group analysis in a straightforward patient group for at least three years. I am proud of the quality of teaching that we provide and the quality of our graduates.

MY EXPERIENCE OF PSYCHOANALYTIC TRAINING

I was not particularly impressed with the quality of the training provided at the Institute of Psycho-Analysis in London in the 1950s. Tensions between the Kleinians and the non-Kleinians were still high, Anna Freud had retreated to the Hampstead Child Psychotherapy Clinic and, as students, we were divided into three camps: Kleinians, Freudians, and the Middle Group led by

Michael Balint, Winnicott, and others. The viewpoints seemed narrow though I was impressed by Balint's wider vision and gained much from participating in the workshop on short-term psychotherapy that he organized with the staff of the Cassel Hospital and the Tavistock Clinic, work later written up by David Malan (1963). My supervisors were Mrs. Hedwig Hoffer and Charles Rycroft. I found Mrs. Hoffer intimidating and not very helpful whereas Rycroft was interesting to talk with but not particularly helpful clinically. Paula Heimann impressed me as a seminar leader with her fine attention to detail and her capacity for looking deeply into the material presented.

Bion led us in some seminars on psychosis, which at that time I was little able to learn from. Bion used to come into the seminar room, sit silently for a while, while we students became tense and anxious at the quality of his silence, which was deep and dark. He invited us to consider with him the meaning of the delusions and hallucinations of patients he was working with at the time. Many years later I had the opportunity to treat a former patient of Bion's in a group and she told me that, although she found him intimidating at times and that he would lose his temper with her, there were moments when he would give interpretations that made her feel very much lighter and better inside.

My Development as a Psychoanalyst

Martin Grotjahn, with whom I had a lively correspondence, was a Berlin-trained psychoanalyst who moved towards group analysis in the last quarter of his life. From the depth of his knowledge of the history of psychoanalysis he viewed the contemporary scene with quizzical humor and contributed thoughtful, short, wise essays to the journal *Group Analysis*, accompanied by witty, incisively drawn cartoons. He had a dictum: "When young psychoanalysts talk to each other, they talk about their patients; in midlife, they talk more about money; in old age they talk mostly about themselves." Grotjahn wrote mostly about himself and drew a witty cartoon entitled "my favorite patient" in which he was shaking hands with the mirror-image of himself. I now know these stages from my own life (Pines, 1985, 1998b). As a younger analyst I held to a strict line, relatively distant, technically correct as I viewed it—"equidistant from id, ego, and super-ego" as Anna Freud had laid out.

I went to Anna Freud for supervision in her father's house in Maresfield Gardens, together with four or five other young aspirant analysts of her "B" group. Umberto Nagera, Moses Laufer, and Ernst Freud were part of the group. Anna Freud's supervisory style was to be a quiet, attentive listener, sitting in her armchair by the lit fireplace that was glowing in winter. Her forte was offering comments about the patient's psychic structure and she was relatively disinterested in the technical issues such as the experience of countertransference. I respected her clarity and the quiet authority with which she offered her ideas. We greatly looked forward to 9:45 p.m. when Paula, the housekeeper who had accompanied them from Vienna, came in with her tray of coffee, strudel, and whipped cream!

Over the road at her child therapy clinic, Anna Freud imposed high standards and was reputed to read all the weekly and monthly reports made by students about her patients. It was here that Umberto Nagera, Joseph and Anne-Marie Sandler, and others produced their research, such as the Hampstead Index that enabled clinicians to pool their experience and thereby elaborate theoretical concepts. Anna Freud had a distant relationship to the British Psycho-Analytical Society because of the strong representation of the Klein group. I remember many "scientific" Wednesday evening meetings, where the communications from both Anna Freud's and Klein's followers were more politically than clinically "correct." Years later, in a paper "What Should a Psychotherapist Know?" (Pines, 1998c), I argued that therapists should know how to give "incorrect" interpretations, since precise and correct interpretations are not possible; they belong to a concept of psychoanalysis as a precise knowable science, which it is not, and which drives out the vital ingredients of responsiveness, intuition, sympathy, and empathy, without which psychoanalysis loses its heart.

Gradually I was drawn to the "Independent" group of which Michael Balint and Donald Winnicott were the leaders. They were very different characters: Balint, brilliant, provocative, charismatic, Hungarian; Winnicott, sensitive, somewhat remote, thinking through his ideas as he spoke, very English. Balint headed a research team in short-term psychotherapy in which I participated that led to David Malan's well-known book on short-term psychotherapy.

I became friendly with John Klauber whose early death robbed our society of a wise, humane leader. Prior to his medical and psychoanalytic training he had been a historian, a discipline that deeply informed his psychoanalytic outlook.

I followed Heinz Kohut's work almost from its beginning, finding it profound and illuminating. Kohut offered a vision of the vital importance of self-object relations, the matrix of self-psychic development that resonated with Foulkes' group-analytic theory of network and matrix. Kohut's recognition of the impact of historical circumstances on psychic development meshed with my own outlook, which has been deeply influenced by the work of the sociologist Norbert Elias, with whom Foulkes had worked in Frankfurt, later in London. This interest then spread to the American psychologists who had richly contributed to ideas of self and society: Baldwin, Cooley, and especially Mead and his school of symbolic interaction. This naturally led me to those American analysts who are socially and historically sensitive: Karen Horney, Erich Fromm, Harry Stack Sullivan, Heinz Lichtenstein, Erik Erikson, and most significantly Hans Loewald whom I studied deeply. He impressed me with his background in philosophy and his wide comprehension of psychoanalysis, and the need for the analyst to love his or her work and through the work to love the patients.

PRACTICE AND PUBLICATIONS

I retired from the National Health Service at the age of 63 having combined part-time hospital and teaching work with building up a private practice in individual analysis and group analysis. Having always kept a foot in both camps, I had to try to make my own synthesis of the theoretical bases of individual analysis and group analysis, a subject which I have treated at length in several papers. What group analysis has contributed is the experience of working with many more patients than I could have encountered as an individual analyst and being witness to the great capacity that patients have to understand both themselves and their fellows in the setting of a group analytic group. The theory base of group analysis must differ significantly from psychoanalysis in its "one body" form, modified though this has been by the development of Object Relations Theory. Group analysis respects the primary social nature of the human being and Foulkes' works laid down a good framework for both our theory and our practice. This framework still remains to be filled in by the research and experiences of his successors. It has been exciting to follow the research into the parent-infant relationship, which supports this basically social view of the human being. Over the years the work of Spitz, Mahler, Loewald, Lichtenstein, Stern, Emde, Kohut and his followers have all affirmed this basic sociality.

I have always taken a considerable interest in the historical background to psychoanalysis; psychoanalysis as figure against the ground of historical changes in the culture of western society. Foulkes was considerably influenced by the sociologist Norbert Elias who showed how the western personality has developed and altered under the pressure of social developments. With the rise of the state monopoly of violence, individuals have had to learn to restrain their aggression and to internalize both their own individual urges and their relationship to the increasing power of the state. In this way we can see the dynamic changes in the structure of personality over historical time with the rise of the superego, which represents both the fantasy and the reality of forces that both administer punishment and provide protection from the violence of others. All these psychic structures—ego, id, and superego—are malleable by these historical forces, which group analysis has taken more account of than has psychoanalysis, though there are some exceptions to this. In recent years I have been much influenced by developments in both self-psychology and relational psychology approaches that are compatible with the basic tenants of group analysis.

For some years now, I have also been interested in and influenced by the Russian philosopher of language Mihail Bakhtin. His approach to language as a dialogue, as utterances that seek responses, is central to my view of the human being as an entity that seeks out a responding world rather than being driven by hypothetical instinctual forces. The concept of dialogue is at the heart of group analysis, more clearly so than at the heart of psychoanalysis, though I have no doubt that the psychoanalytic situation itself is a dialogical situation par excellence.

I have tried to make some synthesis of the fields of knowledge that we need for an adequate understanding of psychotherapy, but the rate of accumulation of knowledge makes this a task that is beyond the capacities of any one individual and we must always settle for a partial understanding. The temptations of certainty have to be resisted and we must remain aware of all the depths of hidden knowledge previously revealed and those yet to be revealed.

INTERNATIONAL ASSOCIATION OF GROUP PSYCHOTHERAPY

Soon after 1945, international meetings were organized to bring together pioneers and enthusiasts for group psychotherapy, which had been greatly developed during World War II. From these early meetings, an International Council for Group Psychotherapy was formed: the leaders were Jacob Moreno, the charismatic founder of psychodrama who challenged psychoanalysis, Sam Slavson, who pioneered a psychoanalytic approach to groups in the U.S. and who founded the American Group Psychotherapy Association, Joshua Bierer, an Adlerian who had started the movement to extend hospital psychiatry into day and night hospitals, and finally Foulkes. The International Association of Group Psychotherapy (IAGP) originated from this Council and its main activity was to hold three-yearly international meetings. Moreno was president, Bierer and Foulkes vice presidents, but

Slavson soon withdrew. Foulkes, after Moreno and the psychodramatic movement dominated the scene, also began to lose interest. The turning point was at the Zurich Congress in the early 1970s when Moreno was dying and dearly wanted the International Association to take on new life and bring together these competing interests. I went to represent Foulkes and group-analysis and met with the dying Moreno who seemed sincere in his intents. Therefore, I became active in the International Association of Group Psychotherapy and served later as president for three years and organized a successful Congress in Copenhagen in 1980. I have seen the IAGP develop into a creative force in world psychotherapy and psychiatry and am well satisfied with my having helped in this. Through IAGP I have traveled extensively in Europe, North and South America, Australia, Japan, Taiwan, Hong Kong, and Israel, and encouraged the local developments.

After Moreno's death, the organization was basically in the hands of Samuel Hadden, Jay Fiddler, and myself. Sam was a good president for our transition, a good parliamentarian who drew clear lines of responsibility and accountability. Jay and I organized the program for the next congress in Philadelphia on a shoestring. This meeting gave new life to the organization and here I pay tribute to Jay as president, treasurer, and secretary, roles he accomplished with his quiet tact and efficiency, always with humor and dignity.

We determined that IAGP should have its proper international identity and not be a satellite of the powerful American Group Psychotherapy Association (AGPA). I am glad that we achieved this and that the relationship between the two organizations has been cordial. Prominent members of AGPA have served as presidents and officers and their administration has always given IAGP respect and support.

IAGP has succeeded in bringing together group therapists from all five continents: meetings in Latin America, Yugoslavia, and Scandinavia have stimulated the growth of group therapy in these regions. I helped innovate regional conferences, first in the Pacific rim, Australia and Taiwan, countries where group therapy is gaining support.

American Group Psychotherapy Association

The highly professional AGPA is a major force in group psychotherapy and I have taken upon myself the task of informing its members of group analysis as understood and practiced in Britain and of which most North Americans are uninformed. Our American colleagues in group psychotherapy are empiricists and less interested in group analysis as an alternative epistemology with its own theory basis, which is the emergence of the person from the social matrix. American group psychotherapy to a considerable extent originated from Slavson's overadherence to psychoanalysis, transposing psychoanalysis of the individual to the group situation. There is also considerable interest in the "group as a whole" approaches that follow from both Bion and Kurt Lewin. Psychodrama has survived the death of Moreno and continues to flourish.

I have taken part in many meetings of this organization that manages to retain a cheerful friendly atmosphere. I have appreciated the privilege of conducting groups in the Institute and teaching in the Institute program, thereby maintaining and developing a collegial bridge between Europe and North America. This traffic is two-way and I and my colleagues who have also been to AGPA have been greatly stimulated by our experiences there.

Work Abroad

In 1947, soon after the end of World War II, Danish medical students invited British counterparts to Copenhagen. We were thrilled to leave England and cross the North Sea, to escape the food rationing and austerity of bombed and damaged London for the cheerful Danish capital. It was then that I fell in love with Denmark, and with a beautiful, talented Danish girl. I was very happy 20 years later to be invited to teach group analysis in Copenhagen through Ebbe Linneman and Lise Rafaelsen. For several years a group of London group analysts traveled four times or more a year to conduct training groups and give seminars and supervision to our Danish colleagues who eventually created their own Institute of Group Analysis. We followed this with a training course on the supervision of individual psychodynamic psychotherapy. A few years later I was invited to Norway to initiate a group analytic training course, which similarly has been highly successful. In the smaller countries one can sense how group analytic training and therapy have influenced the psychiatric system throughout the country, deepening the impact of psychodynamic and psychosocial medicine.

Some years later we also organized trainings in the former Yugoslavia. Sadly, our work there, though it led to an enthusiasm for and training in group analysis in Slovenia, Serbia, and Croatia, did nothing to help prevent the disintegration of that short-lived and artificial nation state, nor did I anticipate the disastrous violence that was soon to erupt. It is a particular nostalgic pleasure to recall the summer schools of psychotherapy in Dubrovnik, the beautiful ancient city on the Adriatic.

My enthusiasm and enjoyment of foreign travel and work is undoubtedly linked to my family's European heritage and to my familiarity with different languages, which I heard in my home and in foreign travels in childhood. I have a strong reaction against insularity but inevitably, as something of an outsider, have some envy of those who do not seem to need to stray beyond their own intellectual, emotional, and physical boundaries.

HISTORY AND PSYCHOANALYSIS

Partly as a result of my work for the Publications Committee of the Institute of Psycho-Analysis, where I was exposed to the growing literature on the problems of the translation of Freud into English, my interest increased in the historical background of psychoanalysis, of Freud's Vienna, and of his own cultural origins and attitudes. I have addressed these issues in a number of papers and I found a particular interest in comparing how psychoanalysis took root in England with its Vienna, Berlin, and Budapest counterparts. My analysis with Adrian Stephen, a member of the famous Bloomsbury Group, led to a personal interest in how that group of Cambridge and London non-Jewish intellectuals had taken to psychoanalysis and helped in its development. James and Alix Strachey and Adrian and Karin Stephen were significant members of the Bloomsbury Group and Ernest Jones clearly resented that he was not accepted by them, coming as he did from a Welsh Nonconformist middle-class background as opposed to their free thinking upper middle-class orientation. This interest in the history of psychoanalysis naturally led to my involvement with the International Association for the History of Psychoanalysis (Pines, 1989).

I think it will be easy to understand that the European origins of my family, my Jewishness, my training at the Maudsley, my analysis with Stephen and Foulkes, all have contributed to my involvement in a wider range of activities than most "pure" psychoanalysts. For instance, I was the editor of the *International Library of Group Psychotherapy and Group Process* in which have appeared both original volumes in English and translations from French and German and shortly Italian. I greatly enjoy this opportunity to appreciate the work of the psychoanalytic and group analytic community as a family who live, as do or did members of my own family, in widely distributed networks but who still retain a sense of connection—in group analytic terms, a foundation matrix.

ON BEING BOTH A PSYCHOANALYST AND A GROUP ANALYST

Psychoanalysis is a very closed profession. An analyst spends so much of his or her working day intensively involved with a succession of single patients; the impact these experiences have upon the psychoanalytic community is something I have addressed on my paper "Dissent in Context: Schisms in the Psychoanalytic Movement" (Pines, 1998d). Psychoanalysis as a profession holds many psychological and social dangers for both analyst and patient: the social isolation, the peculiar intimacy, the constant exploration of transference and countertransference. The effects show in the constant rivalries within the psychoanalytic community, in the power of training analysts, the problems of unresolved transferences, and the organizational dynamics within psychoanalytic societies and the international psychoanalytic community, which are not addressed.

For these and other reasons, I believe that all psychoanalysts should participate, or should have participated, in personal group psychotherapy and group dynamic situations, for these act as counterbalances. A psychoanalyst in a group situation is exposed as a person and also bears witness to the capacities of persons who are not trained in psychoanalysis to make creative use of the therapeutic situation, a needed and humbling observation. This does not mean that group analytic societies and institutions do not also have many psycho-social problems. They do, but they attempt more fully to recognize and to deal with these problems. The atmosphere of group analytic meetings is on the whole more cordial and open than I have met in psychoanalytic meetings and we have less of a tendency to idealize and to follow sectional leaders.

EXPERIENCE AND AGING

I have come to see psychotherapy, individual and group, as a way of releasing healing potentials. Toward the end of his life, Winnicott stated that psychotherapy does not consist of giving apt or clever interpretations; rather it is a process of giving back to the person what they have brought with them, a process of receptive and sensitive dialogue for which a reliable and careful setting is essential. I remember that Winnicott wrote that his purpose in making interpretations is to show the patient that he has failed to understand, by which I believe he means that patients and analysts are constantly engaged in trying to reach for understanding, paradoxically succeeding through their failures. It is the honest attempt to understand that reaches the patient and can bridge the gap between two minds. The essence of group analysis lies in the formation of the matrix, a network of communication established through the mental and emotional history of the group, through its failures and successes in achieving understanding and communication.

The sociologist Norbert Elias gave us a precious heritage with his description of the civilizing and decivilizing processes. He gave us a historical perspective on the evolution of personality, connecting the processes of sociogenesis and psychogenesis. We find ourselves through our belonging to chains of interdependency, which extend from family into society. Foulkes and Elias have shown us how we are permeated to the core by these colossal forces of society, which are within us, not without. Language, religion, education, social class all make their imprints, forces which psychoanalysis is used to, and still to some extent regards as instinctual givens. Loewald has shown us how the instinctual is a deeply social process, that id, ego, and superego formations are created between infants and caregivers from the moment of birth onwards, and probably prenatally. The old English word "connexity" has been revived to denote these chains of interdependency. The word "connect" derives from the Latin "con-nectere," to tie or join together. The older English word "connexity" denotes as interdependency, which derives from the intrinsic interconnectedness of self (Mulgan, 1997).

WORK IN HAND

On reaching my mid-seventies, I, like many psychotherapists, find myself still active and still apparently needed! I have a busy individual and group analytic practice, continue to edit the journal *Group Analysis* and to edit a series of books. I have renewed my interest in both neuropsychology and the psychoses, fields which are rapidly developing in new understandings. Another interesting development was initiating and working out with colleagues the possibility of a new degree course established jointly between the Institute of Group Analysis and the Department of Social Psychology at the London School of Economics, provisionally entitled "Clinical and Organizational Aspects of Groups." This movement into the academic world is both stimulating and demanding, part of the increasing involvement that psychotherapists are engaging with the universities, which in the United Kingdom has not happened to any great extent so far.

In conclusion, a few personal remarks. My wife and I met when she was nursing and I was a doctor in a general medical ward. Her warmth, practicality, and good humor have been essential components to my professional life. Perhaps too much of my life has been given over to work, partly from economic necessity, but also because of a curiosity to explore the many pathways that opened up through this dual career as a psychoanalyst and group analyst. I have three children: my daughter trained as a historian, then became a social worker, and is now also a counselor. My elder son has a brilliant career as a molecular biologist and clearly has inherited my father's and brother's scientific capacities; the younger son has an interesting career in films and television. Between them they represent a healthy balance of the arts and sciences and I am well pleased. Though I suffered a coronary thrombosis of some severity some fifteen years ago, I look forward to further years of activity as a therapist and teacher, though with age comes the wisdom to appreciate how limited our knowledge is and how much remains for future generations to uncover. I found these sayings of Confucius with which I end, a very comforting and fitting conclusion to this first essay in autobiography:

> *At fifteen, I set my heart on learning; at thirty I took my stand; at forty I came to be free of doubts; at fifty I understood the Law of Heaven; at sixty my ear was attuned; and seventy I followed my heart's desire without overstepping the line.*

Confucius, *The Analects*

REFERENCES

Elias, N. (1939/1994). *The civilising process*. Oxford: Blackwell.

Erikson, E. (1965). *Childhood and society*. Harmondsworth: Penguin.

Foulkes, S. H. (1938). Norbert Elias' *The civilising process*. [Review of the book *Selected Papers: Ch. 6*.] *International Journal of Psychoanalysis, 19,* 263-266.

Gabbard, G., & Lester, E. (1996). *Boundaries and boundary violations in psychoanalysis*. New York: Basic Books.

Holquist, M. (1990). *Dialogism: Bakhtin and his world*. London: Routledge.

King, P., & Steiner, R. (Eds.). (1991). *The Freud-Klein Controversies, 1941-45*. London: Routledge.

Kohut, H. (1971). *The analysis of the self*. New York: International Universities Press.

Kreeger, L. (Ed.). (1975). *The large group: Dynamics and treatment*. London: Constable.

Lichtenstein, H. (1977). *The dilemma of human identity*. New York: Aronson.

Loewald, H. W. (1980). *Papers on psychoanalysis*. New Haven: Yale University Press.

Main, T. F. (1989). *The ailment and other psychoanalytic essays*. London: Free Association Books.

Malan, D. H. (1963). *A study of brief psychotherapy*. Mind and Medicine Monographs. London: Tavistock.

Malan, D. H. (1976). A follow-up study of group psychotherapy. *Archives of General Psychiatry, 33*, 1303.

Mead, G. H. (1934). *Mind, self, and society*. Chicago: University of Chicago Press.

Mulgan, G. (1997). *Connexity: How to live in a connected world*. London: Chatto & Windus.

Pines, M. (1968). Human sexual response—a discussion of the work of Masters and Johnson. *Journal of Psychosomatic Research, 12*, 39-49.

Pines, M. (1976). The contributions of S.H. Foulkes to group-analytic psychotherapy. In L. Wolberg & M. Aronson (Eds.), *Group therapy: An overview* (pp. 9-29). New York: Straton Intercontinental.

Pines, M. (1985). Mirroring and child development. *Psychoanalytic Inquiry, 5*, 211-231.

Pines, M. (1987). Bion: A group-analytic appreciation. *Group Analysis, 20*, 251-262.

Pines, M. (1989). On history and psychoanalysis. *Psychoanalytic Psychology, 6*, 121-135.

Pines, M. (Ed.). (1992). *Bion and group psychotherapy*. London and New York: Tavistock/Routledge.

Pines, M. (1998). *Circular reflections: Selected papers on group analysis and psychoanalysis.* London & Philadelphia: Jessica Kingsley.

Pines, M. (1998a). A history of psychodynamic psychiatry in Britain. In M. Pines (Ed.), *Circular reflections: Selected papers on group analysis and psychoanalysis* (pp. 183-208). London & Philadelphia: Jessica Kingsley.

Pines, M. (1998b). Reflections on mirroring. In M. Pines (Ed.), *Circular reflections: Selected papers on group analysis and psychoanalysis* (pp. 17-39). London & Philadelphia: Jessica Kingsley.

Pines, M. (1998c). What should a psychotherapist know? In M. Pines (Ed.), *Circular reflections: Selected papers on group analysis and psychoanalysis* (pp. 131-149). London & Philadelphia: Jessica Kingsley.

Pines, M. (1998d). Dissent in context: Schisms in the psychoanalytic movement. In M. Pines (Ed.), *Circular reflections: Selected papers on group analysis and psychoanalysis* (pp. 103-116). London & Philadelphia: Jessica Kingsley.

Tansey, M. J. (1994). Sexual attraction and phobic dread in the countertransference. *Psychoanalytic Dialogues, 4,* 139-152.

Wilshire, B. W. (1984). *The essential William James.* Albany: SUNY Press.

CHAPTER 14

PERSONAL AND PROFESSIONAL LIFE

OWEN RENIK, M.D.

I might summarize the development over time of my think-ing as an analyst by saying that I believe I've become clearer about, and come to pursue more directly and explicitly, the purposes that originally determined my choice of career. I'll try to explain what I mean in a bit more detail.

When I was eight years old, my mother fell ill with a severe case of myasthenia gravis. At the time, treatment for myas-thenia was rudimentary, and her condition deteriorated rapidly. Our family life shattered, and I was devastated by my powerless-ness to save either my mother or myself from the appalling loss. As I grew into my teenage years, I realized that the real catastrophe had been not so much my mother's physical debility *per se* as her psychological reaction to it.

So I had reason to be impressed, from an early age, by the power of psychological symptoms, and to be strongly motivated to find ways to achieve psychological symptom relief. No surprise, then, that I eventually decided to pursue a profession devoted to trying to help people feel better—specifically, to trying to help people be able to deal with their circumstances, whatever those might be, with maximum satisfaction and minimum distress.

Some psychoanalysts come to their profession out of academic, rather than clinical, interest. They are scientists, concerned first and foremost not with healing, but with studying the human mind, and they are attracted to psychoanalysis because it seems to them the best available psychological theory. I am not one of these. My orientation has always been completely therapeutic: I have tried to cure myself by curing others. Psychoanalytic theory only interests me as a guide to effective clinical practice. I was never comfortable with Freud's cautions against therapeutic zeal. Psychotherapeutic zeal always came naturally to me. Not too long ago, I wanted to participate in a workshop at Commonweal, the alternative medical institute. The application form asked, "What percentage of your patients suffer from life-threatening illnesses?" I answered, "If by 'life,' you mean breathing in and out, five percent. If by 'life,' you mean a meaningful experience characterized by a great deal more pleasure than pain, ninety-five percent."

I do think it is possible to practice clinical analysis without prioritizing therapeutic benefit as an outcome measure, and many analysts do so; but this approach to the clinical analytic encounter is very different from my own. It also has the obvious liability of being at odds with the ambitions most patients bring to the treatment situation. People who come to see psychotherapists want to be helped to feel better. Ordinarily, they don't aspire to the examined life for its own sake; they just want symptom relief. Therefore, an analyst who conceptualizes and measures the effectiveness of what he or she does in terms separate from symptom relief ("psychoanalytic goals," as opposed to "therapeutic goals") is likely to be operating with an objective in mind very different from the objective that most of his or her potential analysands will have in mind.

My own focus on symptom relief as the aim of clinical analysis, while it certainly originates in my personal history, seems to me to be consistent with the needs of the great majority of patients. Over time, I have found myself increasingly alienated from conceptions of psychoanalysis as a rarified pursuit, suitable only for a select group of patients. Clinical analysis practiced on that basis, I think, threatens to deteriorate into a proselytizing activity—or worse, into a pyramid scheme promulgated through training institutions.

As it turns out, I learned that the determinants of my decision to become a psychoanalyst, and of my therapeutic orientation, had even earlier roots than I realized when I first made my career choice. I had been aware since childhood of the catastrophic impact upon me of my mother's illness and her psychological response to it; but it wasn't until much later, when I was a psychoanalytic candidate, that I discovered that my mother, long before she had fallen ill with myasthenia, had suffered a postpartum depression so severe that it had been necessary for me to be sent to live with relatives for several months when I was about a year and a half old. My parents had never spoken about the episode afterward. I had no conscious knowledge of the experience. In my own memory, for many years, it had been screened by various later periods of exile related to my mother's physical illness. In the course of my personal analysis, however, I became curious about certain inexplicable contradictions I noted concerning the details of what I recalled of being unable to live at home as a child. I actively questioned my father about when I had been sent away and what had happened. In response to my confrontation, he revealed to me for the first time the history of my mother's psychiatric problems prior to her myasthenia.

I was, of course, in some ways upset and in other ways relieved by what I had uncovered: upset because learning about my parents' denial of the sad events made me deeply disappointed and resentful; and relieved because the information I now had allowed me to make sense of and eventually free myself from certain longstanding symptoms. As regards my professional development, though, the details of what had obviously been all along an unconscious memory of early trauma showed me how a therapist's personal psychology participates in the cure. The realization came in a very dramatic way, having to do with the fact that by the time I discovered this early chapter of my own history, I had already written and published a report of the following case (Renik, 1981).

*   *   *   *   *

The patient was a young man who was terribly hemmed in by obsessions and compulsions of all sorts. He spent the better part of every day preoccupied with intrusive nonsense thoughts or executing various rituals. After two years or so, our analytic work together had gotten to the point at which we were able to understand that these activities served to prevent him from being aware of violent, sadistic fantasies that would come to his mind and disturb him very much. This timid and inhibited man was inwardly boiling with rage, often in response to apparently trivial events. A female co-worker would close a window he had opened and he would imagine grinding his heel into her face.

The question for us had become why he was so prone to fury, especially to fury at women; and here we were stuck. He had certain grievances toward his mother, and we had gone over these. Something in his attitude toward me seemed relevant, a demandingness that was only thinly covered over by ingratiation and compliance; but the transference elements involved remained elusive. We just had not made much headway in clarifying his chronic anger.

There were sometimes claustrophobic aspects to the situations that seemed to provoke him, and his associations suggested that resentment toward a younger sibling *in utero* might be playing an important genetic role in generating his sadistic fantasies. He had a dream in which he was swimming around in a pond, urinating, thus killing some young corn that was growing on the bottom. The dream, in particular, made quite an impression on him. He felt it confirmed the idea that he might have been hostile to the arrival of a younger sibling, and he ransacked his mind—with characteristic obsessive thoroughness—about his feelings toward his six-year-younger sister, trying to dredge up memories of her birth, of his mother's pregnancy and his reactions, etc. It all yielded very little.

This man had trouble sleeping, and from time to time made use of a mild sedative that he got from his internist. When he first described taking the pills, I made some comment about medicating his anxiety instead of analyzing it, such that he firmly associated me with the idea that renunciation was in order. In fact, he came to take the pills less and less, and would look to me for approval about his progress in this regard. It was not a major point of investigation, but I did have the chance from time to time to remark that not using the pills seemed to be something he felt he was doing at least as much for me as for himself. Of course, I encouraged him to look into his fantasies about my investment in the matter.

On one such occasion he came in and announced that he had not taken any sleeping pills for a month. As usual, I did not congratulate him, and as usual he complained about this. In the course of exploring his reactions to this familiar situation, he moaned that it was like being weaned from the breast, I couldn't realize how difficult it was. I made the following comment to him: "It's as if you feel like the only person who was ever weaned from the breast."

Now I think the content of this interpretation was valid, and, as I will describe in a moment, it had very productive results. My interpretation called his attention to a particular fantasy, based on an implicit denial of the facts of life. It related to attitudes of entitlement and a sense of injustice that was a central feature of his transference to me. All of this was potentially useful information, and conveying it to the patient was consistent with good analytic technique.

However, I remember the state of my feelings at that moment very clearly. The general context was my frustration with the treatment seeming bogged down and my exacerbated impatience with this man's hyperintellectual style and underlying whiny complaints. I had been going to save him when many before me had failed. But now, after a successful initial phase of analytic work that confirmed our mutual idealizations, we were each feeling disappointed in the other. Against this general background of resentment toward the patient, I was feeling sorry for myself; and when he essentially claimed that nobody knew the trouble he felt, my reaction was to review some of the more difficult periods in my own past and to ask myself who this guy thought he was, telling *me* about suffering...

Out of this not very admirable set of sentiments what I said to him was not entirely kindly meant, and therefore was not put as gently as it might have been. My empathy with him was harnessed to my own emotional needs at least as much as to my analytic functioning. Far from realizing that my own grandiose self-pity had been provoked by a similar state in the patient, and fashioning a constructive interpretation on the basis of self-analysis, I had competitively contended with him for first place in a suffering contest—although I did use truth as my weapon, and I remained within the realm of observation, both of which were important constraints.

The patient was *struck* by my interpretation (pun very definitely intended). He blinked and paused fractionally, obviously feeling the hostility I had expressed; but he did not verbalize any reaction to this aspect of my remark; and I, out of continuing denial of my countertransference motivation, did not address his avoidance. Instead, what happened was that the patient took my interpretation at face value and began to associate to the content of it. He thought about the fact that his own son had been weaned from the breast some years earlier. Compliantly, the patient reflected that what I had said about his not being unique had been true.

However, despite the patient's effort to keep his sense of injury by me out of conscious awareness—and despite my tacit collusion with his effort—his warded-off reaction broke through, and in a form that made it possible to elucidate his transference even while consciousness of my countertransference enactment was being avoided by both of us. As he spoke about recognizing that others had, indeed, been weaned from the breast, the patient made a slip, substituting the name "Gary" for his son's name. When he claimed to know no one named Gary, I suggested it couldn't have come from nowhere and that he seemed reluctant to associate to "Gary." He shook his head and said, "No, the only Gary I can think of is the younger brother my parents told me about that was stillborn when I was a year and a half old." (!) He couldn't believe he had never mentioned it before. Obviously, it was relevant to so much that we had explicitly puzzled about together over two years of analysis. When he had been assiduously searching his memory for experiences about the birth of a sibling that might illuminate the origin of his sadistic preoccupations, his mother's pregnancy with Gary, and the subsequent stillbirth, had never come to mind.

From here, our work led to retrieval of early childhood memories that had not previously been consciously available to him. After the delivery of his stillborn brother his mother had suffered a severe postpartum depression. A dream revealed the patient's childhood understanding of his mother's depression. In the dream, his mother was squatting and had a miserable, dejected expression. Something was terribly wrong. A long lip of bleeding flesh drooped from between her legs. He had a strong urge to go toward her to help, but at the same time he dreaded touching her.

Fantasies about stillbirth, his mother's genitalia, and the loss of body products by excretion all had become confused and condensed in the child's mind into an impression that his mother was depressed because she had lost something important. This impression resulted in a conflict between the child's wish to substitute himself for what was missing in order to make his mother once more loving and lovable, and his fear of having to sacrifice himself to restore her loss. In fact, throughout our sessions he had been expressing this conflict in his reports of the many dreams in which he would be irresistibly drawn toward a boiling sea or into the eye of a storm. The conflict was revived during his latency when his mother would, for ill-defined reasons, join him in bed, and he could feel the warmth of her body close to his.

The patient's mother's depression had been sufficiently severe that he had been sent away to live with an aunt for six months. Early experiences of rejection and abandonment had been eclipsed in his memory by positive images of the aunt in whose care he had been placed. There had been a kind of tacit collusion with the aunt throughout his childhood, beginning during the time his mother had been disabled. His aunt totally idealized him and was unconditionally accepting, in return for which he did not contradict her fantasy that he was actually her son. Part of the patient's transference to me was an expectation that he could recreate the kind of collusion he had with his aunt. One aspect of his reaction to my interpretation, consciously passed over but revealing itself through the slip, was that I was refusing the deal. I was insisting on being an angry, rejecting mother instead of a gratifying aunt in order to punish him for the hostility and demands toward me that lurked beneath his surface good-patient pose. The childhood theory had been that his devastated mother had sent him away because his resentment of the frustrations he had to endure during her pregnancy and his jealous rage toward little Gary *in utero* had caused the stillbirth.

As these concerns emerged and their origins were clarified, the patient's attitude toward women changed. He became less angry, and his preoccupation with sadistic fantasies diminished correspondingly. He developed more comfort in his sexual life. For a time, he was tremendously excited by cunnilingus, and noticing this, realized that he was counterphobically overcoming a longstanding horror and disgust toward the female genitalia. Frank confusion about women's anatomy came to light. His sleep difficulty essentially disappeared and he discontinued sedative use altogether.

Eventually, I did take up with the patient his disavowal of my real lapses, and the way he avoided thinking about the possibility that I could be angry at him and act on that feeling. His need to cling to an idealizing transference fantasy of mutual uncritical adoration and his need to avoid conscious disappointment in me became significantly less driven, though the amelioration was somewhat limited by his fear of re-experiencing what must have been an overwhelming infantile rage and despair.

*   *   *   *   *

Imagine how I felt some years after this treatment had taken place when I learned about the events surrounding my own mother's postpartum depression. I immediately thought back to my patient, and recognized that the self-pity and competitiveness that had motivated the hostile, but productive interpretation I had made to him—crucial to the success of his analysis, as it turned out—had arisen from a repressed traumatic memory of mine that had been uncannily similar to my patient's repressed traumatic memory. When I had asked myself who this guy thought he was, telling *me* about suffering, I hadn't been conscious of the most important reason for my resentful self-righteousness: I knew exactly what he was talking about because I had gone through it too! My retrospective realization set in motion a line of thought that ultimately led me to the conclusion that countertransference enactment, so-called, is the raw material of all psychoanalytic technique, good and bad (Renik, 1993).

Another important fact of my personal and professional development is that I'm an only child. My father had to supplement the small income from his civil service position by working a second job in the evenings and on weekends, so he wasn't around very much. As a result, when my mother became incapacitated, I was left on my own a lot. I grew up with not as much support, and also with not as much accountability, as might otherwise have been. In other words, I got used to operating, for better or for worse, according to my own rules. Among the complicated consequences of my childhood situation is that I've always found it pretty easy to go my own way: I've never been much of a joiner, and therefore, I've never had much of a need to rebel, either. I think this tendency toward field independence, so to speak, has shaped the trajectory of my analytic career.

Irwin Hoffman (1994) wrote a paper a few years ago in which he described analysts' need to "throw away the book." I discussed that paper when Irwin gave it at our Institute in San Francisco, and I disagreed with his assumption that a conflict between ritual and spontaneity is inevitable and universal among analysts. Since then Irwin and I have continued our goodwilled and fruitful argument.

In my opinion, Irwin generalizes incorrectly from his own experience. He was a *yeshiva bucher*: he grew up with the book. Therefore, he had to throw it away in order to formulate his own ideas. We might say that in his childhood, Irwin had a lot of support, but also had to contend with an excess of accountability. On the other hand, my own situation, as I've mentioned, was exactly the opposite: I was, if anything, too much of a law unto myself. Coming to psychoanalysis with my character, I never adopted the book in the first place; therefore, I never had to throw it away. It was more my style to read the book, take what I liked, and let the rest go, as I went along.

I think that there is a relation between this style and the place I have found myself occupying within the analytic community. Lew Aron (Aron & Mitchell, 1999), introducing an article of mine that was included in a volume on contemporary psychoanalytic thinking, described my position this way:

> *Renik's controversial writings have been particularly influential not only because of his compelling prose, but also because, unlike the vast majority of the contributors featured in this collection, Renik speaks with the prestige deriving from his position of power in the mainstream psychoanalytic establishment. Ironically, in the very act of critiquing the analyst's authority, Renik draws on his own institutional authority as Editor of the highly esteemed* Psychoanalytic Quarterly, *and as Program Chair of the American Psychoanalytic Association. These powerful institutional positions have magnified the radical edge of Renik's proposals* (pp. 407-408).

I agree with Lew's assessment of the way my particular psychoanalytic voice has been socially constructed. The question arises, then (and I have been asked it many times): How did someone who has strongly criticized the orthodoxy of official psycho-analysis get to lead the committee that arranges the scientific activities at the semi-annual meetings of the national organization? How did an author who has challenged the basic theoretical and clinical concepts with which the *Psychoanalytic Quarterly* has long been associated come to be that journal's editor?

An important part of the answer, of course, concerns the integrity of the people who gave me those jobs. The presidents of the American Psychoanalytic Association who appointed and re-appointed me program chair were very well aware of my views. They believed that the organization needed to become more inclusive and less self-satisfied. Similarly, many of the members of the *Psychoanalytic Quarterly's* Board of Trustees, at whose pleasure I serve, may disagree with me about psychoanalysis in important ways; but they have always been willing to let our differences be argued out in the free marketplace of ideas, and have consistently supported me as editor.

Another important factor, though, has to do with my non-*yeshiva bucher* character. Certain features of traditional, mainstream psychoanalytic thinking have always seemed, and continue to seem, useful to me. At the same time, I consider an analyst to be irreducibly subjective in every aspect of his or her clinical activity. Therefore, while it is true that I find longstanding technical principles like analytic anonymity, neutrality, and abstinence to be misguided and counterproductive, it is also true that the concept of compromise formation is basic to the theory of motivation that underlies and directs my clinical work; and when I listen to patients, my thinking is organized by cognitive structures involving the idea of defense elicited by unpleasurable affect (see Renik, 1990). Accordingly, I'm sometimes identified as a "relational" analyst, and I'm called an "ego psychologist" as well. Both labels are accurate. As a result, I'm situated psychoanalytically in the way that Lew described—and happy to be!

I mention this aspect of my psychoanalytic development—that I've wound up being able to use an establishment platform to propose anti-establishment ideas—because I feel that here, too, I've taken a journey that has led me ultimately to pursue more clearly and directly the original purposes that brought me to psychoanalysis. Like many people, I was drawn to psychoanalysis because of its originally radical spirit; and, also like many people, I was disappointed by the conformism I found, once I entered the ranks of the profession. It's not surprising that my fairly extensive psychoanalytic organizational involvement has convinced me of the stultifying effects of organization upon psychoanalysis.

I don't want to be misunderstood as espousing a naïve kind of individualism for psychoanalysts. I realize the crucial importance to individual analysts of having a psychoanalytic community. There is a grave danger for the analytic practitioner of becoming isolated. However, my clinical experience over the years has convinced me that for most patients, the core of psychological suffering centers around an inability to identify and use freedom. In order to help with this problem, an analyst has to be able to identify and use his or her own freedom; and my impression is, unhappily, that use of an analyst's personal freedom is not facilitated in psychoanalytic organizational life. On the contrary, psychoanalytic organizations tend to be conservative and to stifle the individuality of their members.

To my mind, then, an analyst's task in relation to colleagues involves participation in the analytic community in such a way as to oppose the destructive effects of the undeserved authority that is often granted psychoanalytic institutions; and that is what I have tried to do. Similarly, I think that in clinical work, an analyst's task involves participating in the treatment relationship in such a way as to oppose undeserved authority granted to the analyst by the patient. My own work, in recent years, has been increasingly directed toward the problem of how to develop a more truly collaborative psychoanalytic treatment relationship (Renik, 1997). This has involved critical review of a number of longstanding principles of psychoanalytic technique (Renik, 1995, 1996).

If psychoanalysis is to be a systematic, therapeutic discipline, a science of healing, I think it is of the utmost importance that we define clinical psychoanalysis in terms of *outcome*; and that symptom relief, as experienced by the patient, be the fundamental measure of success. It makes no sense to me to define clinical psychoanalysis in terms of *technique*, as is often done when organizations establish and impose official "standards" (the patient comes at least four times a week; the couch is used; the basic rule of free association is followed; etc.). Defining psychoanalysis in technical terms ritualizes method and establishes the analyst in a position of false expertise. In science, we expect technique to evolve and we need to retain an experimental attitude toward it. I think Lacan was right when he said that each individual analyst must reinvent analysis for himself. I would extend that dictum to say that each analytic couple must reinvent clinical procedure for itself.

Any number of clinical experiences in which I've observed innovative psychoanalytic techniques producing successful psychoanalytic results have led me to believe that a misguided psychoanalytic orthodoxy developed over the years concerning the matter of technique. My conclusion is that in each and every treatment, technique should be formulated from an empirical and experimental perspective: procedure has to be negotiated collaboratively between analyst and patient, according to case-specific needs. One of the most instructive, formative encounters of this kind, for me, was the following (Renik, 1999b).

* * * * *

Some time ago, a woman in her early 30s came to see me, complaining that she felt like she was falling down a well and couldn't do anything about it. That was all she could say about her distress. I tried to get her to elaborate, explaining why it would be helpful for her to say anything at all that came to mind about her experience, but to no avail. "I just feel like I'm falling down a well, and I can't do anything about it," she repeated. She remained very concrete in her statements, though she clearly understood what I meant when I talked to her about her use of metaphor.

In fact, I couldn't help her speak spontaneously about very much at all. For the most part, she responded only to questions from me, and then usually after a significant pause. Sometimes her silence lasted long enough that I wondered whether she intended not to answer, or had become distracted; but eventually she would speak, and what she said was invariably to the point. It was apparent that she took time to consider and carefully choose her words. Any number of efforts on my part to explore with her the reasons for what was obviously a drastic caution on her part were in vain.

Slender and pale, she sat quite still in her chair, her drawn features composed in a grave expression. There was no doubt of her suffering and her desire for help. She took our dialogue quite seriously, but she was determined to participate in it in her own way. Was she paranoid? It certainly seemed so. Did she have a thought disorder? Not in the sense of any difficulty with abstract thinking or concentration, at any rate, though she very well might have been delusional. I found her poignant and appealing. Something about her intelligent and purposeful vigilance, extreme as it was, gave me the sense that I might be able to help her gain some relief through an understanding of her suffering, if I could find a way to negotiate a partnership with her.

Over several sessions, I questioned her about her problem and what had led up to it, and tried to gain an impression of her history. There were definite limits to what she was willing to reveal; and I soon learned that when she decided to go no further on a given topic, it was pointless to try to make her reticence a subject for investigation. The following picture emerged.

The eldest of five, she had been raised in relative affluence on the East Coast. Her father was a very successful businessman and her mother a socialite. The parents were preoccupied with their own interests. She had never felt close to either of them, nor to her younger brother and sisters. When she graduated from high school at 17, she left home to live independently and had been completely out of contact with her family ever since. She would say no more about her childhood.

She had taught herself to type, and after leaving home supported herself largely through office work. She was evidently a very efficient secretary and had no trouble finding jobs. She moved a number of times—at one point, she spent a year in Alaska because she wanted to see what it was like to live in a less developed place—and wound up in the Bay Area, where she decided to go to college. She majored in classics, and graduated from university *summa cum laude*. She then went on to a prestigious law school, finishing second in her class. She chose the law because she liked solving logical problems. She thought of becoming a criminal attorney since she felt it was important for people to have their rights—an obviously significant sentiment about which, unsurprisingly, she would say nothing further.

I had the impression that throughout her travels, she had remained socially quite isolated, spending much time in solitary pursuits. I did get a glimmer, though, of a few carefully selected, often quite odd relationships with other people. One of these was with a brilliant, eccentric, young philosophy-student-turned-car-mechanic, with whom she eventually moved in, and, during her first year of law school, married. The two shared several passionate intellectual interests, including archeology. They spent vacations visiting Indian ruins in this country and in Central and Latin America.

They fought a great deal. Her husband didn't like it when she talked about law school. He also insisted that he should be able to bring his lovers, male and female, to their home. Her resentment of his infidelity led to her complete withdrawal from their sex life, which had previously been active, though she claimed not to have enjoyed it. At the time she first consulted me, they had arrived at an arrangement in which her husband conducted his affairs outside the home and didn't tell her about them. She remained sexually inactive and steadfastly refused her husband's overtures, which had become relatively infrequent.

It seemed to me that her very unusual, and in many ways quite unsatisfying, marriage was of the greatest importance to her. Even when she was most bitterly critical in her descriptions of her husband, she never mentioned a thought of leaving him. When I asked her about this, she would say, "We're married." I inferred that the relationship was a crucial anchor for her.

It was upon graduation from law school, six months prior to our first visit, that the feeling of falling down a well had begun. I learned that despite her great academic success, and her successful history of employment as a secretary, she had found herself completely unable to look for a legal position. She had not made a single phone call to set up an interview since graduation. Recently, she had begun to go out less and less for any reason. Increasingly, she dreaded leaving her apartment.

My patient was clearly nursing an acute, fulminating agoraphobia. The onset of it suggested that, whatever else was involved, she was intensely conflicted about working as a lawyer. Though I knew really very little about this young woman, I was quite struck by how much importance she seemed to place on her very few, almost irrevocable commitments. A career in law, for which she had worked long and hard, was one; her marriage was another. Taking my cue from her mention in passing that her husband didn't like it when she talked about law school, and given that she portrayed him as extremely narcissistic, competitive, and controlling, I wondered whether she might be struggling with the fear that she would be forced to give up her husband or her profession—either way an insupportable loss. At the end of a session, I said something about this possible dilemma to her, connecting it with her feeling that she was falling down a well and couldn't do anything about it.

Next hour, my patient said that she had made some phone calls and was starting to set up employment interviews. She had also gone out shopping for new clothes. This considerable alleviation of her symptoms was reported very straightforwardly, without significant affect. "I'm happy about it," she stated simply and flatly when I inquired into her manifest lack of feeling about the dramatic change. She did not relate it to what I had said to her the previous hour about a possible conflict with her husband. "I guess so," was her answer when I asked if she thought there might be a connection.

On her way out, she surprised me by pausing at the door, turning, and saying—still in the same serious tone—"How about giving me a hug?" Somewhat taken aback, I replied, "I don't think that's really the best way I can help you. Let's talk about it next time." My tone was friendly, if anything a bit gently reassuring, since I was concerned she might be hurt by a refusal on my part that we had no chance to discuss.

This took place on a Friday. On Monday (we were meeting five times a week) she came in, sat down, and asked angrily, "Why did you yell at me?" She explained she was referring to the exchange at the door. I tried to invite her to explore her own ideas about why I might have yelled; but of course her position was, "I haven't got the faintest idea, that's exactly why I want you to tell me." I tried to explain that, in my view, I hadn't yelled. I tried to suggest various anxieties, wishes, etc., on her part that may have disposed her to experience me as yelling. I tried many things, but none of them accomplished much.

After this turn of events, she said even less during our meetings, spending much of her time in tight-lipped silence. Nothing I could do seemed to affect the situation. "Tell you everything that comes to my mind? Why on earth would I want to do that?" she asked derisively. At the same time, she reported that she was moving ahead in her job search. Whatever it was that was going on between us, it seemed to be having a beneficial effect on the rest of her life, so I decided to be patient.

However, as weeks went by, although she continued to progress on the career front, things seemed to get worse and worse during the hours. "I'm a group of particles that will fly apart. I need to be inside you. But you don't want me to be inside you. You're afraid I'll devour you." These thoughts came out a bit at a time. Needless to say, there was no question of further exploration of them. Her fury mounted. Each time she reached into her handbag, I half expected her to produce a .375 magnum—or at the very least, a tape recorder.

My concern steadily increased. I thought there was a real possibility that something dramatic could eventuate. Whatever the therapeutic benefits, some kind of malignant experience of me seemed to be escalating, and I could find no way to address it. I tried to talk to her about what seemed to be happening. She just became more and more desperate to have something from me that I didn't know how to provide, and more and more enraged at me for not providing it. I wondered whether, since she was evidently unable to consider relinquishing her painful attachment to me, it might be in her best interests for me to sever it. At the same time, I worried that if I did that, she would feel herself a rejected, devouring monster and be utterly devastated.

Finally, one day I said to her: "You know, as we've discussed, I really don't know how to help you. I've explained the ways I usually work with people that I've found to be useful, and they don't make sense to you. I know what you say you want from me; but I don't really understand it, and I haven't been able to make it happen. I worry that by continuing to see you, I'm preventing you from getting into a treatment that might be helpful; I worry that I may even be making you worse. On one hand, you seem to be getting on better with looking for a job than you were before we started; and if our meetings are helpful to you, even if it's in a way I don't understand, I'm happy to continue. But on the other hand, our relationship is causing you tremendous pain, and it seems to be getting worse. Sometimes I think it might be best for you to stop, and that you're unable to yourself, so maybe I should call it off from my end. It's a real dilemma, and I'm not sure how to proceed." To all of this, she said, predictably, nothing.

She came in the following session, however, carrying a large stack of spiral-bound notebooks. "I thought these might be useful to you in helping you make your decisions," she announced as she offered them to me. Taken aback by this most unexpected gesture, I took them and looked through them. Each line on each page of each book was filled with her small, neat handwriting. What the notebooks contained was a complete record of all our meetings—not only of everything she had said and I had said, reconstructed after each session, but of all the thoughts that had passed through her mind during her silences. I thanked her at length for bringing me the books, and acknowledged how meaningful and important it was that she had decided to let me see them. I told her I wanted to read them all, but it would probably take me awhile to do it.

During the hours that followed, she frequently asked me if I had finished reading the notebooks yet, and I would reply that I was working on it. As I did make my way through the notebooks, I found that there were no real surprises in what I read. The thoughts that had filled her silences, I saw, were essentially extensions of what she said to me: the same complaints, anxieties, perplexities, and resentments.

Finally I finished. When I returned the notebooks, I said to her, "I'm very glad you gave me these. In a way, I didn't find anything new. The thoughts you didn't tell me during our meetings seem to me very much in line with the ones you did tell me. After reading everything you wrote, I still don't know how to help you, or if I can help you. But there is one very important thing I did learn from your notebooks: It's clear to me that no matter what my actual intention or how carefully I explained it to you, if I were to unilaterally end the treatment, you would be sure it was because I want to get rid of you, because I don't want you to devour me. That's not the case; I don't want you to think that. So I'm making you a promise here and now: Unless you make it impossible for me to continue by breaking up the furniture or something like that—I'm never going to terminate our meetings on my own initiative."

A small smile crossed her face. After that, her mood in the hours lightened, and she began talking a bit more freely. In time she told me how when she was a child her parents would go off for month-long vacations without warning, leaving it to a babysitter to inform the children when they arrived home from school; how her father sometimes stroked her "little titties," as he called them, when he came into her room to say good night; how conditions of neglect and arbitrariness sparked bitter rivalries among all the siblings; and many other details of what seemed to have been an erratic and abusive upbringing. As always, there remained limits to what she was willing to discuss about the things she disclosed. Meanwhile, she was able to find a position as an associate in a law firm, and to realize after a year that it was not a good situation and leave it for a different one. She brought her professional problems up for us to talk about—again, within limits that she established without explanation.

Eventually we came into conflict over my policy about cancellations. I charge for all unfilled missed visits that cannot be rescheduled. She considered this unfair—not a justifiable way of doing things that she simply didn't like, a different opinion than hers to which I had a right, but manifestly, unequivocally unfair. I saw that her point of view was not going to change. She might have submitted, but she clearly felt she shouldn't have to. I told her I thought I had a perfect right to do things my way and that I disagreed with what I regarded as her self-righteousness, but that our relationship was more important to me than either the principle or the money. I suggested that we compromise. She agreed, proposing that she not be responsible for absences she told me about two weeks or more ahead of time. I accepted this arrangement.

Her career proceeded well. Eventually, she found a job she liked a lot. She came to be highly regarded by both her associates and her clients. Along the way she discussed with me such problems as sometimes feeling over-identified with the criminal defendants she represented, and how this interfered with her work. Also, things were changing significantly in her marriage. She had an affair with a colleague, terminated it, and began to confront her husband more directly and constructively with her dissatisfactions. Her husband stopped being unfaithful. They began to forge a more effective day-to-day relationship and resumed having sex.

One day, after we had been working together about two years, she came in and announced, "I can't see you." I asked her what she meant (we met vis-à-vis), but she replied only, "I can't see you when you're looking at me." Expectably, further analysis proved impossible. "What do you think we should do?" I asked eventually. "Well," she said, "I think you should face away from me so I can see you." "Sorry," I replied, "I'm not willing to do that." "Why not?" she asked. "Because I don't like working with people when I can't see them," I explained. "How do you think I feel?" she responded. I told her I was sure she didn't like it either.

I was very sympathetic, but I just wasn't willing to do what she wanted. She told me that wasn't fair. I said maybe not, but I just wasn't willing. She kept coming to our appointments, though she obviously didn't like the conditions. After a few days of growing discomfort on my part, I said, "Okay. I'm willing to face off to the side and not look at you every other session. How does that sound?" She thanked me, and from then on, that's how we proceeded.

Later, she reported that she had re-contacted her family and was beginning to have regular visits with them. She described her mixed feelings toward her affectionate but disorganized and irresponsible mother, and her conflicts in dealing with her brilliant, interesting, and exploitive father. Her social circle widened and I began to hear more about the details of her friendships. She brought forward various ideas about me and feelings toward me. Upon occasion, we were able to relate these to longstanding concerns originating in prior relationships.

At a certain point, she again became preoccupied with her experience of me as rejecting. This time she was less furious, and more able to advance her complaint as something to be discussed. Specifically, she said she didn't feel like talking to me because she never got a response to anything she said. I found this particularly puzzling, as I told her, because my own experience was of prizing her sparse communications and of always responding immediately, usually in the hope of helping her say more. Apparently, our views were different, and we didn't seem to be able to get very far in understanding why. We kept on trying to clarify what was happening; but as the months went by, things remained pretty much the same. She didn't feel she got anywhere talking to me about her difficulty in talking to me.

Apparently, we had reached an impasse. She didn't like what was happening, but she didn't want to stop seeing me. She just wanted me to change. She was beginning to have the feeling of falling down a well. Once again, I worried that it made no sense to continue our meetings; and once again felt at the same time that it would be a mistake for me to terminate. I told her that I was in the same dilemma as before. (Also not for the first time, I went to colleagues for consultation about the case. I received a great deal of sympathy and encouragement, but no enlightenment about how to proceed.)

She wouldn't talk to me about myself because she believed I was unable to listen, but she didn't want to give me up. An idea occurred to me: what about finding her someone else to talk to about me and our relationship? I asked her if she might want to see a second therapist to discuss what was going on with us. She thought it was a good idea and asked me to suggest someone, which I did. Actually, she saw a number of therapists whom I recommended—all women, at her request—for anywhere from one session to three months, until finally she found someone who really worked for her. She settled into a schedule of seeing me three times a week and the other therapist once a week or every other week. This dual therapy continued for the rest of the time we worked together.

Our treatment lasted for two more years, until her husband, who had now returned to graduate school, found a teaching position in another city. When she left, she was planning to try to have a baby. She had always felt that it was pointless to bring a child into the world, but as a result of many issues we discussed together, her attitude changed. Over the years since I last saw her, I have received a number of postcards telling me—always laconically—that things are okay.

*   *   *   *   *

The reason I found this clinical experience so instructive was that it forced me to come to terms with the observation that if I defined psychoanalysis in terms of *outcome*, the treatment was a successful psychoanalysis—symptom relief was dramatic and far-reaching, associated with a revised understanding of self, others, and relationships—whereas, if I defined psychoanalysis in terms of *technique*, the treatment could hardly have been less psychoanalytic. The very fact that an excellent outcome could be obtained through procedures so at variance with standard ones in and of itself suggested to me unavoidably that at least some of our assumptions about the mechanism of action of clinical psycho-analysis and therefore about optimal psychoanalytic technique were questionable. How certain can we be, I had to ask myself, for example, that solicitation and investigation of free association is the only, or even the most expeditious, means by which to help a patient achieve therapeutic benefit through greater self-aware-ness? It didn't seem to be required in this case. In any number of conspicuous and dramatic ways, our way of proceeding violated received psychoanalytic wisdom concerning the need to reflect rather than enact, and the importance of maintaining "the frame."

Most of all, my negotiations with my patient and their consequences made me realize the importance of establishing a treatment relationship in which there is active and full collabora-tion between analyst and patient. It was only because I was facing the relatively unusual dilemma of feeling locked into a situation in which I hadn't the least idea how to proceed (the patient wouldn't cooperate with my methods, but I was afraid that stopping the treatment would be more damaging than continuing) that I accepted my patient as a completely co-equal collaborator. Previously, I had often invited and seriously considered a patient's ideas about how best to work together. I thought of myself as a rather open and flexible analyst. But now I had to realize that my invitations had always been for the patient's input about how best to work together within limits dictated by *my* methodological assumptions. This was the first time that I had ever undertaken to collaborate with a patient on devising the fundamental technique we would use—and I had only done it because I couldn't think of anything else to do under the circumstances!

Having arrived at the subject of collaborative technique, I'll conclude this account of the history of my thinking as an ana-lyst by turning toward the future. In my opinion, advances in psy-choanalytic clinical practice now depend upon our capacity to con-ceptualize a more active role for the patient than has been indicat-ed by our generally accepted theories. It seems to me that we are required not to relinquish our claims to expertise, as some colleagues who are threatened by contemporary developments sometimes misguidedly believe, but to review and redefine the nature of psychoanalytic expertise: we are experts in establishing and maintaining an investigative partnership, rather than experts about what goes on in the minds of our patients.

Part and parcel of the evolution of our conception of analytic technique will, I believe, involve acceptance of the crucially constructive role of what has been called (although it is a problematic term) self-disclosure by the analyst. My own clinical approach has come to be that I try, as best I can, to play my cards face up in analysis (Renik, 1999a). I think of analytic treatment as proceeding via the establishment of an ordinary and practical, but extraordinarily candid, relationship between analyst and patient. Willingness to tolerate a certain measure of disconcerting exposure to scrutiny by the other is required from both parties. The trajectory of my personal and professional life, past, present, and future, continues in the direction of increasing conviction that I and my patients—not to mention friends and loved ones!—are best served if, rather than aspiring to transcend my personal motivations, I make every effort to make my own view of them explicitly available and to take responsibility for them.

REFERENCES

Aron, L., & Mitchell, S. A. (Eds.). (1999). *Relational psychoanalysis: The emergence of tradition.* Hillsdale, NJ: Analytic Press.

Hoffman, I. Z. (1994). Dialectical thinking and therapeutic action in the psychoanalytic process. *Psychoanalytic Quarterly, 63*, 187-218.

Renik, O. (1981). Distraction as an obsessive-compulsive strategy. *Bulletin of the Menninger Clinic, 45*, 409-427.

Renik, O. (1990). Comments on the clinical analysis of anxiety and depressive affect. *Psychoanalytic Quarterly, 59*, 226-248.

Renik, O. (1993). Countertransference enactment and the psychoanalytic process. In M. Horowitz, O. Kernberg, & E. Weinshel (Eds.), *Psychic Structure and Psychic Change*, pp. 137-160.

Renik, O. (1995). The ideal of the anonymous analyst and the problem of self-disclosure. *Psychoanalytic Quarterly, 64,* 466-495.

Renik, O. (1996). The perils of neutrality. *Psychoanalytic Quarterly, 65,* 495-517.

Renik, O. (1997). El poder del paciente. *Revista de Psicoanalasis, 54,* 137-147.

Renik, O. (1999a). Playing one's cards face up in analysis: an approach to the problem of self-disclosure. *Psychoanalytic Quarterly, 68,* 521-539.

Renik, O. (1999b). Psychoanalysis defined in terms of outcome rather than technique. Unpublished.

CHAPTER 15

THE INDIVIDUAL IN CONTEXT

EDWARD R. SHAPIRO, M.D.

I write this chapter from the office of Robert Knight, Otto Will, and Daniel Schwartz, former medical directors of the Austen Riggs Center. With my appointment in 1991, the title changed to Medical Director/CEO. The addition reflects a generational shift in psychiatric institutional roles from overseeing the treatment of the individual (the medical director) to managing an organization for treatment (the CEO). In institutions providing psychotherapy, the transformation of institutional life in the last decade in this country has required an increasingly focused attention on the institution as a whole in order to respond adequately to the individuals within it.

I always knew that dynamic psychotherapy was a powerful instrument for understanding the individual. I once believed that it existed in its own right, with its own development as a method. Now, given the socially supported managed care assault on psychotherapy, I no longer believe that psychotherapy can continue to exist without attention to the social institutions that support it. Like all tools, psychotherapy exists in a social context. Organizations, which have always been social holding spaces for this kind of treatment, are no longer secure. This has influenced the practice of psychotherapy.

The Austen Riggs Center today is one of the few psychiatric institutions devoted to the intensive psychoanalytic psychotherapy of disturbed patients. It stands for a set of values that are under massive social attack: the importance of the individual, the need for reflective space to understand individual and collective irrationality, the power of a community of examined living for the study and treatment of irrationality, and the willingness to authorize the competent aspects of disturbed patients by providing them with a completely open setting for treatment.

The question I was asked by the editors was how I got to this place and what my professional experience might illustrate about the changes in our field during my career. My response, of course, is filtered through my own conceptualizations. In this chapter, I try to find a way to be self-reflective without being too self-indulgent. Most individuals are lucky to have one or two significant ideas in their careers. My own learning is about the intermingling of individual and context (Shapiro & Carr, 1991). I have devoted my professional career to an integration of psychoanalytically oriented psychotherapy with an awareness of the impact of the context on the individual's internal life. I will use my personal and professional development to offer a view of the evolution of the field.

FAMILY CONTEXT

I was the third son born to first generation American-Jews from Russian and Ukrainian immigrant grandparents. Three generations back, my ancestors included a rabbi who hid from the Tsarist police in the basements of St. Petersburg while teaching the Talmud, and a liquor store owner in the Ukraine. My maternal grandfather ran a small hardware store in a Black ghetto under the elevated train in Dorchester. Though trained as an engineer, my father ran a small interior decorating shop in Boston. Shortly before my birth, my mother decided to go to Portia Law School in Boston, at a time when most women did not have careers. She graduated, but decided not to practice law, and became a grammar school secretary. The relevant bits of this lineage for my professional life include preserving the tradition against opposition, managing in a strange context, and pushing the traditional frames.

My parents lived in my mother's parents' home through the childhoods of my two older brothers. My mother told me that she had decided to have me—ten years after my middle brother—as a way to convince my father to move us away from her parents and into her own home. My conception was, therefore, formed in the context of tightly managed aggression about separation. That was my family task—to represent more dependency and demand than could be managed with limited resources, to work through the containment and management of feelings about separation, and to move my parents toward home ownership. These conflicted family dynamics have been part of my work with adolescents and families, and are part of my everyday work life.

My oldest brother—15 years older—was pushed through Harvard College by the war, and graduated from medical school at 19, going to the Menninger Clinic to study psychiatry, when psychoanalysis was at its height of popularity. When he became a psychoanalyst in Boston, and then a training analyst, I was fascinated. A powerful memory from my preadolescence was a visit to my brother's Cape Cod home by Dr. Paul Myerson (who later became chief of psychiatry at Tufts). Paul was prematurely white-haired, and I remember him telling my brother about his excitement about something he had just learned from a patient. I thought, "How could such an old man be so excited about learning?"

EDUCATION

At Yale, I studied Russian language and literature. During the summers of 1960 to 1963 (including the period of the Cuban missile crisis), I traveled for months with the Yale Russian Chorus to the Soviet Union, spending hours on street corners talking with Russians, visiting their homes, feeling the impact of totalitarianism. Graduating a year early, I was not accepted at the medical schools I applied to because they were aghast at my wish to travel prior to matriculation. I took a year off to wander through Eastern and Western Europe. At Stanford Medical School, I was awarded a master's degree in anthropology, receiving grants to study government medicine and witch doctors in Tobago, West Indies. I returned to Boston to finish medical school at Harvard, taking an internship in medicine followed by a residency in psychiatry at the Massachusetts Mental Health Center.

"Mass Mental" was dominated by two Harvard professors: Jack Ewalt, the superintendent, and Elvin Semrad, the clinical director. Jack was a Texan, who kept a gun in his desk drawer. His screening interview for residents was to ask what kind of car we drove, and to interpret our phallic narcissism—of which he had an abundance. He was a masterful leader and politician, and, as Commissioner of Mental Health in Massachusetts, made sure the old state hospital was well supported for learning. He was a powerful man, and we all had deep ambivalence about him.

Elvin Semrad was the guru for several generations of psychiatry residents. He had an amazing gift of talking directly to the most disturbed, psychotic patients. In discussions with him, we watched the most incoherent, bizarre people transformed into humans suffering in deeply moving ways from painful life experiences. Semrad's capacity to evoke clarity, depth, and feelings from such patients was electrifying for us, illuminating his dictum: "Your textbook is the patient." He encouraged us not to read, but to learn from our patients.

One of our tasks was to work with a patient at Boston State Hospital. I was assigned a chronic schizophrenic woman, who had been hospitalized since I was in the third grade. On my first visit, she chased me down the corridor throwing her feces at me. When I presented her to Semrad, I had prepared a list of interventions, including a sheltered workshop, behavioral treatment, and medication. Semrad's response—in front of my fellow residents—was, "You obviously don't have the heart for this kind of patient." I was devastated, but in response, I sat with that patient several times a week for the next three years. I learned a great deal from her about her life and her illness.

My first year of residency was in the Day Hospital, where we worked with severely disturbed patients who went home every night. We carried the anxiety of their freedom and I learned to rely on the head nurse, who spoke simple Boston English to these patients and understood their struggles. She was aggressive and direct, but her deep links to these patients were palpable. In my third year, I was appointed chief resident on one of the inpatient wards, and was responsible for a group of first-year residents. This was my first experience of teaching/administration. I was charged by Ewalt and Semrad to "clean up" an in-grown, incestuous system, writing my first paper about the experience of developing an interdisciplinary team to address the transition from long-term hospitalization to the community (Shapiro, 1974). My residency years at Mass Mental produced a group of prominent researchers and administrators, including Steven Scharfstein (currently CEO of Sheppard Pratt), Thomas McGlashan, chief of psychiatry at Yale, Alan Schatzberg, chief of psychiatry at Stanford, and John Gunderson, professor of psychiatry at Harvard Medical School, and prominent researcher on borderline pathology. Ewalt and Semrad had stimulated our ambitions.

PSYCHOANALYTIC TRAINING

Our basic training was psychoanalytically oriented, and, in my second year of residency, I entered the Boston Psychoanalytic Institute as a candidate. My training analyst was Avery Weisman (Weisman, 1965). Two events stand out from our work together. The first had to do with Dr. Weisman's barely noticeable stutter, about which I never said a word. At one point in the analysis, feeling his presence behind me, I said, "It's like the sword of Damocles." At least, that's what I thought I said. In fact, I said, "It's like the sword of Demosthenes." Dr. Weisman repeated my phrase with a questioning tone, and I felt embarrassed that

I had gotten it wrong. I asked, "Isn't it Demosthenes? Who's Demosthenes?" He said, "Look it up!" When, to my astonishment, I read that Demosthenes was the Greek orator who had cured his stuttering by holding stones in his mouth, it taught me about the unconscious, transference, and my conflict about aggression toward the father.

The second event occurred as I was exploring my father's death. He had died five years before, while I was on the road driving to Stanford, and my family had been unable to reach me. I missed his funeral, and I had not visited his grave. In the analysis, I was fantasizing about Dr. Weisman's death and wondering if I would go to his funeral. He quietly said, "You'd better!" I experienced this comment as my father's voice coming from the grave and telling me he wanted me to be there. It awakened my deep grief and I became the mobilizer for my family's placing a long overdue stone on my father's grave. I understood then the way that transference is both current and past, real and evocative, recreating the past in a transformative way (Weisman, 1972).

In my training, psychoanalysis was the preeminent method for understanding the individual's internal life. My own experience in analysis was intensely absorbing, and I was devoted to grasping its methodology from teachers who had found an extraordinary way to listen to people. The dynamics of the outer world paled by comparison. In the face of this compelling method, families seemed largely irrelevant. During my residency training, I largely agreed with Freud's notion that families could be understood as "external resistances to treatment."

My institute education was dominated by a generation of training analysts who had survived the split of the Boston Institute. I had heard of the politics of the split as an adolescent, listening to my brother's group of rebels who had protested the controlling voice of the earlier generation of European trained analyst-teachers: Greta and Edward Bibring, Helen Tartakoff, Ives Hendrick, Malvina Stock, Helene Deutsch. The contentious issue was their slowness in appointing new training analysts. Helen Tartakoff had said to the younger group, "We are trying to appoint new training analysts, but we just can't find any who are qualified!" This led to open rebellion. The older group left to start the Psychoanalytic Institute of New England (PINE). My brother's group was aiming to liberalize the institute, opening it to new voices and ideas. Nonetheless, my institute training was primarily classical and Freudian.

My candidate group was composed entirely of psychiatrists; other disciplines were either excluded or compelled to accept dramatically limited (nonclinical) roles. Medical psychoanalysts led all the departments of psychiatry, and served as models for careers as psychoanalysts. I read Freud, and learned about ego psychology. The focus was on uncovering the internal dynamics of the individual, the nature of unconscious conflict, and the mechanisms of defense. We did not read Winnicott, Klein, or Jung. Anyone interested in projective identification was referred to as a "Crypto-Kleinian," and discounted.

National Institute of Mental Health

I had won an appointment in the Public Health Service during the Vietnam War, and was deferred through my training to go to the National Institute of Mental Health (NIMH) after my residency. I was assigned to the Adult Psychiatry Branch, Section on Personality Development, where I met Roger Shapiro, my section chief in the Adolescent unit. He and John Zinner were studying the relationship of family experience to personality development. They had inherited the unit from Murray Bowen and Lyman Wynne, who had hospitalized whole families of schizophrenics and written brilliantly about family dynamics and "pseudo-mutuality." Roger introduced me to Erik Erikson's writing on adolescent identity (Erikson, 1956) and Wilfred Bion's work on groups (Bion, 1961). I immersed myself in these perspectives and those of Winnicott.

Roger and John had written a brilliant paper about projective identification (Zinner & Shapiro, 1972), opening a new perspective on family dynamics. They illuminated a way to hold onto psychoanalytic theory and an interpretive tradition, while moving outside of the boundaries of the individual. Originally formulated by Melanie Klein (1946) as an intrapsychic process involving the infant-mother relationship, projective identification had been further developed by Kernberg (1966) as one of the underlying mechanisms for object relationships. The recognition that the child develops by identifying aspects of the self as "good" and projecting "bad" aspects into another while maintaining an unconscious link to those projections allowed a deeper examination of affective links between people. Grasping this dynamic opened the role of the other as "good enough" container, metabolizer, and stabilizer of the child's negative projections. The parental task is to tolerate the projected aggression without excessive retaliation or withdrawal. With this containment, the child is able to reinternalize these projections through identification and integrate an increasingly coherent sense of self without fearing the potential destructiveness of his aggression. These ideas offered a new view of child development, a mechanism of family interaction, and a way to conceive of some of the processes of psychotherapy.

The NIMH setting was a completely open unit for borderline adolescents where the individual was in four-times-weekly psychotherapy and the entire family was in weekly conjoint family therapy. This was a different structure from my formal training, where families were parceled off to the social workers. Here, I was the individual therapist and also worked with a colleague as co-therapist for the family. Roger Shapiro was my intellectual mentor. He taught me the possibility of building an interpretive dialogue with both patient and family that illuminated both intrapsychic and interpersonal dynamics. This was the era of available research money. We had endless resources, fascinating clinical cases, and time to write. Each intensive psychotherapy and family treatment was recorded and transcribed, and family meetings were observed behind one-way mirrors. We pored over transcripts for hours, searching for illuminating dynamic material.

My tenure at NIMH coincided with Otto Kernberg's ground-breaking work on borderline dynamics and object relations theory (Kernberg, 1966, 1975) and his intense debate with

Heinz Kohut (1971) about the nature of narcissism. These were heady times in psychoanalysis, where classical theory was being stretched and new perspectives were opening for interpretive work with severely disturbed patients. Psychoanalytic meetings were packed, and institutes were highly desired learning centers. I transferred as a candidate to the Washington Psychoanalytic Institute, where I audited two years of classes.

Both Kernberg and Kohut's work illuminated the work with disturbed patients. Though neither theorist addressed these connections, their theories provided links between individual and family dynamics. I began to apply the ideas to the interpersonal dynamics I was seeing. David Berkowitz, John Zinner, Roger Shapiro, and I developed a writing group, producing a group of papers that applied the thinking of Kernberg and Kohut to the family dynamics of disturbed adolescents [most of these papers are collected in Scharff, 1989]. I sent my first paper, a case study (Shapiro, Zinner, Shapiro, & Berkowitz, 1975), to Dr. David Reiss, the acting chief of the Adult Psychiatry Branch at NIMH. He sent me back a seven-page single-spaced response, analyzing my thinking, providing the historical antecedents, and laying out my next ten years of research. It was one of the most generous mentoring acts I had ever experienced, and I was grateful to have been taken so seriously. As Dr. Reiss pointed out, I was learning how internalized multi-generational family dynamics contributed to parental ability to discern the actuality of their children, and how these unconscious distortions affected the personality development of the child.

Though our training had introduced us to countertransference, the prevailing notion was that such reactions were problems to be taken to the therapist's individual analysis. At NIMH, I began to learn more deeply how patients communicate to their therapists through projective identification, and how countertransference could be used—through what Erikson called "disciplined subjectivity" (Erikson, 1958)—to learn about these unconscious family communications.

One clinical experience significantly changed my thinking. I was working with a borderline adolescent girl in a family where the father's fragile self-esteem was maintained by an unconscious family agreement to see him as only good, generous, and responsive. This unipolar perception was what Roger called a "defensive delineation" (Shapiro, 1966), requiring the other side to be carried by another family member. In this case, my adolescent patient was seen by family members as rapaciously demanding and "bad." Neither adolescent nor father could be perceived in this family with their human complexity.

In one family meeting, I watched the parents and siblings irrationally collude to insist that my patient's perceptions about her father's unavailability could not possibly be true. She had a choice: to agree with her family's insistence and remain a family member at the cost of giving up her differentiated experience. Or, she could insist on her own perspective and feel abandoned by them. In an individual therapy meeting later that same day, I found myself replicating the family dynamic in astonishing detail, in a way that engaged both my own neurosis and the patient's transferences (Shapiro, Shapiro, Zinner, & Berkowitz, 1977). I had unwittingly become my patient's family, driving her crazy. Only my having participated in the family work allowed me to grasp my own repetition and help my patient gain perspective on this event. I had learned in my training that transference was derived from early childhood experience, internalized. But what I was seeing were transference distortions that both fit the reality of the contemporary family and evoked corresponding reactions in me. Were we all regressing to fit the patient's need to remember and repeat critical aspects of her childhood? And if so, how could such combined irrationality be understood? And, in relation to what? The day I grasped this uncanny repetition, I thought, "I know what I want to do with my career." I wrote three papers about this one case (Shapiro, 1978a; Shapiro, et al., 1975; Shapiro, et. al., 1977).

I was learning how the family functioned as an irrational group, with each member unwittingly contributing to the picture. I saw how this unconscious collusion both fit the dynamics of each individual and contributed to a fixed and recognizable family dynamic. I was seeing how a group could regress in relation to a task, and began to see the family's task as helping each individual (parent and child) master the relevant developmental stage. The congruence of this understanding with Erikson's speculations about the interdependence of generations (Erikson, 1950; Shapiro & Fromm, 1999) lay beyond my recognition at this point. I began to see the value to the regressed family of an observer who could hold and articulate an outside perspective, allowing each member of the family to grasp his or her individual regression and join with other family members in more competent interpersonal work.

I was learning a more sophisticated way of thinking about families and child development than the blaming "schizo-phrenogenic" mother formulations of the previous generations. I began to see the kind of recognition that children require from their parents and the ways in which unconscious conflict within family members and within the family group precludes the possibility of such recognition.

McLean Hospital

The pressures from biological psychiatry were building, and NIMH was beginning to close its dynamic research. As the unit closed, I turned back to Boston and applied for a job at McLean Hospital. Shervert Frazier, psychiatrist-in-chief, asked me what I most wanted to do. When I told him I wanted to recreate the NIMH unit, he found $100,000 for construction costs and we built the Adolescent and Family Treatment and Study Center (AFTSC), a program that I directed for 15 years. While I completed my analytic training at the Boston Institute, the AFTSC developed a pragmatic clinical approach for severely disturbed adolescents and families derived from the NIMH research. The growth of this program was part of a renaissance at McLean, in which Frazier authorized a broad range of approaches to treatment and encouraged an atmosphere of mutual respect and learning. McLean was a wonderful place to work, with young psychiatrists and psychologists beginning their careers with ideas, resources, and diverse experiences, including psychoanalysis, behavioral treatment, psychopharmacology, child and adolescent treatments, and the study of trauma. Frazier was "letting a thousand flowers bloom."

In my second year at McLean, my medical school mentor, John Nemiah, by then the editor of the *American Journal of Psychiatry*, asked me to write a review article on borderline personality development (Shapiro, 1978b). Writing this piece under John's vigorous editing allowed me to integrate a range of theories into a coherent perspective. Several years later, I wrote a paper "On Curiosity: Intrapsychic and Interpersonal Boundary Formation in Family Life," in which I introduced the concept of pathological certainty, a notion that captured what I was learning about child development and family process (Shapiro, 1982).

At the Adolescent and Family Treatment Unit (AFTU), in addition to the intensive (three times weekly) individual psychotherapy for the adolescent, and weekly family and couples meetings, we developed a weekly multiple family meeting for over 50 people (Shapiro & Kolb, 1979). This was a relatively unstructured meeting, focusing on authority, with powerful moments of joining between parents and children in different families. We studied family group contributions to adolescent suicide (Shapiro & Freedman, 1987), and furthered the exploration of the ways in which multigenerational conflict is transmitted through the parents to be lived out in the characters of the adolescent children.

I also began a decade-long 10-month seminar on human development for residents and postdoctoral students. Over time, Judith Jordan, [see her chapter in this book] and I developed the seminar into a process-content format, where one of us would hold the didactic focus, while the other attended to the group dynamics. We regularly found that the dynamics of the class—particularly in relation to the group transference to the teachers—played out the developmental themes we were studying. It was a compelling methodology, most effective when we were able to negotiate the methodology with the class and they could join in the interpretive as well as cognitive learning.

TAVISTOCK GROUP RELATIONS LEARNING

McLean gave me my first experience of real administration. I was a program director and learning about the difficulties of managing a multidisciplinary group in relation to a sub-task of a larger organization. I found it difficult to focus entirely on the work, given the institutional irrationality. My NIMH mentor, Roger Shapiro, had for years been directing experiential conferences in the Tavistock tradition on the dynamics of organizations. I signed up as a member of a residential conference, and began a second period of intense learning, similar to the countertransference learning I'd had at NIMH. In the relatively unstructured atmosphere of an experiential conference on leadership and authority, I found myself unwittingly constructing a group with the same dynamics as the one I was developing at McLean. I could see the ways in which my own irrational process contributed to the group's difficulties. For the second time in my career, I was stunned by the way in which the dynamics of projective identification recreated and illuminated group, individual, and system-wide phenomena. I saw my own character evoking projections from others that shaped the ways in which I and they were able to work. I found the experience as stimulating and powerful as my own analysis.

I returned as a member to a two-week-long Tavistock conference at Leicester, England, and joined the Washington-Baltimore Center of the A. K. Rice Institute. Over the next decade, I helped found the Boston Center of the A. K. Rice Institute, served on the Institute's National Board of Directors, directed a National Scientific Meeting, and served both as director and staff member of over 30 experiential conferences in this country and Europe, using the learning in my adolescent program and in my writing (Carr & Shapiro, 1989; Shapiro, 1987; Shapiro & Carr, 1991). I also began to develop a private practice as an organizational consultant, working with hospitals, law firms, and businesses. I was deepening my recognition that the boundary around the individual, so definitely established in early psychoanalytic theory, was more permeable than we had learned. The inner world and the outer world were in dynamic interaction (Shapiro, 1997a).

At one of the group relations conferences, I served on the staff with a young cleric from England, A. Wesley Carr (currently the Dean of Westminster Abbey), who came more directly out of the learning of the Tavistock Institute for Human Relations in London. We developed a friendship and found a powerful connection between his understanding of the larger social meaning of institutions (through his life in the Church of England) and my understanding of the individual development in the family and organizational context. In the middle of my tenure at McLean, I invited Wesley to consult to my program (Shapiro & Carr, 1987). This required him to enter an unfamiliar professional space and, by mobilizing a new role beyond our friendship, help our system uncover its organizational dynamics. We subsequently wrote a book together, called *Lost in Familiar Places: Creating New Connections between the Individual and Society* (Shapiro & Carr, 1991). Wesley and I worked out a methodology for interpreting irrationality in organizational life and used it to trace individual development in its social context. We formulated an approach for grasping the effect of others on the self in any context through a process of negotiated interpretation, in which one listens for how the other is right and tries to make sense of the connections.

In our thinking, interpretation simply means discovering links between otherwise disconnected aspects of experience by placing them in a context. Our interpretive stance uses three components: individual experience, organizational role, and organizational task. It suggests that taking seriously one's experience in role and listening to that of others in linking organizational roles can allow for negotiated interpretation of the organization. This approach allows individuals to locate themselves in a role within a particular social context and, through that role, discover a way to relate to the larger society. The need to interpret the experience of being lost in familiar places seems increasingly important in a society where dislocation, lack of reflective space, and disruption of those social institutions that manage dependency (the family, religion, health care) have created an increasing isolation and atomization of the individual.

After I had run my McLean program for 15 years, Shervert Frazier left his position as psychiatrist-in-chief. His departure marked the transformation in the field from a central focus on dynamic psychiatry to the preeminence of the biological and behavioral, and a related shift around the financing of health care. The next administration of McLean was characterized by a massive accommodation with managed care as the external health care world became transformed. It was no longer possible to provide long-term intensive treatment with any degree of security. And, the organizational structure of the hospital shifted toward massive top-down decision making, with increasingly less delegated authority. I continued my analytic practice and became the director of Psychosocial Training and Consultation at McLean, while I looked for a way to continue my work.

The turmoil of the institutional transition coincided with turmoil in my personal life. A teacher of mine from the Boston Institute, Anton Kris, invited me for lunch at his home because he was worried about me. When he asked me how I was, I told him. He became my second analyst, illuminating for me the earlier issues that lay behind my first psychoanalysis. Kris understood these issues (Kris, 1976, 1982, 1984), and he took a different stance toward his work with me from the one I had been familiar with. As an analyst, his personality was not obscure: he took clear positions, argued his perspective, and illuminated my vulnerability, previously denied aggression, and unconscious self-criticism. I began to see the personal and family background for my interest in adolescents and families. One of the important differences between this psychoanalysis and my first one was that I was now conscious of my symptoms: I needed him. Our work together opened a previously sealed area of my character, one my family, friends and colleagues were more familiar with than I. In one of Dr. Kris' papers, he quotes a patient to whom he offered psychoanalysis, who said, "I don't want an analysis, I want someone to help me!" He was not afraid of this kind of dependency—and he allowed me fully to face it in myself. One by-product of this psychoanalysis, was that I learned that it was possible as an analyst to be fully present without losing an interpretive role. This shift in the stance of the analyst was an important change in the practice of psychoanalysis. A more personal consequence was my marriage to Donna Elmendorf, Ph.D., and our creation of a late-in-life son, Joshua, who joined my first son Jacob, named after my father, and my stepson Zachary as the third son of a complex new sibship.

THE AUSTEN RIGGS CENTER

In Stockbridge, Massachusetts, the Austen Riggs Center was in transition, with pressures to eliminate long-term treatment. I was interested in the Center both because of its traditions of providing intensive psychotherapy and my interest in applying my organizational learning to a setting where I could be in charge. The trustees selected me as the next director. In the year prior to my arrival, I established a process with the Riggs' patients, staff, and trustees to articulate a mission that both held onto the traditions of Riggs and joined the priorities of the rapidly changing external world. Facing the fiscal transformation of health care, we decided to develop a spectrum of settings to maximize patients' resources and give them the longest opportunity for intensive psychotherapy in a community of examined living. We brought together business people and clinicians with patients and families to help them both manage and interpret the individual meanings of their resource limitations. We discovered that a major problem our patients had in maximizing their resources for treatment was that they got lost in irrational interpretations about those resources (e.g., family dynamics of need, guilt, and separation or confusions between financial limitations and limitations of emotional resources). Taking the space to address both management and interpretation allowed for a more rational approach (Shapiro, 1997b).

The open setting at Riggs is a powerful intervention. The most disturbed patients, some coming from locked wards and seclusion rooms, negotiated their way into the open setting by facing their ultimate responsibility for their lives. Riggs' 80 year tradition supports our admissions contract where patients are told that if the need is for clinicians to save their lives, Riggs is not the appropriate place. If, on the other hand, patients will take their own responsibility (with the help of their families) for their lives, we will help them with their treatment. This clear boundary evokes major anxiety from patients accustomed to turning themselves over to caretakers. Over time, it mobilizes the patients' competence, helping them to face the limitations of their resources and shape a community of examined living so that they can learn about the communicative meaning of their behavior (Shapiro, 1999). When the Center celebrated its 75th anniversary in 1994, we held an international conference on "The Inner World in the Outer World," bringing together distinguished psychoanalysts from around the world to consider this open boundary (Shapiro, 1997b). Our thinking led us to create the Erikson Institute for Education and Research at the Austen Riggs Center, designed to bring clinicians and nonclinicians together to develop a common model for making sense of individual and social dynamics.

In the eight years of my tenure at Riggs, we have brought families fully into the Center, developed a contextual focus for the treatment (the mission is now "The study and treatment of the individual in context"), and recognized the way the therapeutic community provides our patients with a way to externalize their characterological difficulties in a community of examined living. Our patients experience themselves in a kind of theater-in-the-round. They see what they evoke in others and hear from others what they need to discover in themselves. This relentless feedback helps them to develop a language for the psychotherapy that supports the work in an outpatient setting. Riggs has moved from a long-term hospitalization program to a more flexible spectrum of care, where patients are more fully in charge of their resources and treatment. The Erikson Institute at Riggs is becoming a way to bring other disciplines into the Center to develop an interdisciplinary language with which we can export the learning from our clinical work with patients back to the disturbed world that has helped to produce them.

APPLICATION TO THE WORLD OF PSYCHOTHERAPY

As the editors anticipated, I see the changing world of psychotherapy through my own lenses: conceptual, organizational, and political. The initially autocratic European stance toward psychoanalysis in this country was met by an equally autocratic American medical establishment that took control of psychoanalytic organizational life. The tradeoffs were straightforward: high standards, rigorous control, and economic power resulted in rigidity, suppressed innovation, and exclusion of brilliant minds from other fields (Eisold, 1998). The field must sustain a professional culture that supports the use of the tools of psychoanalysis for transforming the individual's relationship with himself. However, it must preserve the flexibility that allows new perspectives and findings from the psychoanalytic encounter to develop and transform the professional culture.

Despite its rigid internal and external control, the psychoanalytic establishment had little impact on the burgeoning development of psychotherapy practice. Practitioners with little or no training operate in most of the big cities, articulating only marginal connections with psychoanalytic ideas. The development of the psycho-biological revolution came simultaneously with the articulation of very focused cognitive-behavioral approaches to psychotherapy.

When intensive political pressures for managing the health care system emerged in the late 1980s, psychoanalysis was the least prepared. Managed care, limitations of finances, tight oversight, and threats to confidentiality attacked its foundations. Those treatments aimed at the "quick fix" were approved. Psychopharmacology, cognitive-behavioral treatment, and manualized therapies rapidly pushed uncovering treatment to the side. Psychoanalysts could no longer so easily fill their practices.

At the millennium, the medical hegemony in psychoanalysis has disappeared and people from all disciplines are coming in for analytic training. Candidate classes in many institutes are full, despite the shortage of analytic patients. Insurance will not pay for this form of treatment, particularly without adequate statistical evidence for its efficacy. I believe that classical, Freudian psychoanalysis in this country is likely to be limited to training cases and the wealthy.

But there is a renaissance of applications of psychoanalytic thinking: in literature, sociology, anthropology, history, and organizational consultation. The power of the unconscious will not be obliterated by the current focus on the manifest. The recent political preoccupation with the sexual behavior of President Clinton provides evidence for the ongoing interest in unconscious motivation. As the world becomes more interdependent, the need for a negotiated interpretive stance is increasingly necessary. Individuals, disoriented by rapid change, look for meaningful connections with others. Though advances in brain chemistry will continue to allow individuals to better manage their affects and thinking, the freedom that comes with psychoanalytic understanding will remain a fundamentally coveted value in our culture.

The shifts I have made in my own thinking relate to these larger transformations. Initially convinced that a relatively neutral analyst could deeply grasp the secrets of the individual's unconscious, I gradually learned how the personality of the observer influenced the data. From there, it became easier to shift to examining the next series of bounded contexts: the couple, the family, the group, the organization, and the larger society. Now, when I see individuals in treatment, particularly the more disturbed and traumatized ones, I also see around them the larger context. The context does not replace the individual; broadening the focus allows a more comprehensive understanding of the individual. For example, when I see a patient who is dissociating, unable to integrate herself, and communicating through behavior, I quite frequently see more than her aggressive conflicts. I begin to hear about the divorced, angry parental marriage that she internalized, the generations of conflict behind them, the treatment systems that worked with the patient, parents, and resources without talking to each other, and the larger society with its rapid social changes and lack of reflective spaces.

I suspect that the psychoanalytic stance, and those treatments that attend to transference, resistance, and the unconscious, will spread, and the learning will be applied to other aspects of social life. With some naïve optimism, I continue to hope that discovering a shared context for experience—the outcome of a negotiated interpretive stance—will be valued in this new millennium.

REFERENCES

Bion, W. R. (1961). *Experiences in groups and other papers*. London: Tavistock.

Carr A. W., & Shapiro, E. R. (1989). What is a "Tavistock" Interpretation? In A. W. Carr & F. Gabelnick (Eds.), *Proceedings of the International Symposium* (pp. 53-58). Washington: A. K. Rice Institute.

Eisold, K. (1998). The splitting of the New York Psychoanalytic society and the construction on psychoanalytic authority. *International Journal of Psychoanalysis, 79*, 871-886.

Erikson, E. H. (1950). *Childhood and society*. New York: Norton.

Erikson, E. H. (1956). The problem of ego identity. *Journal of the American Psychoanalytic Association, 4*, 56-121.

Erikson, E.H. (1958). The nature of clinical evidence. *Daedalus: Journal of the American Academy of Arts and Sciences, 87*, 4, 65-87.

Kernberg, O. (1966). Structural derivatives of object relationships. *International Journal of Psychoanalysis, 47*, 236-253.

Kernberg, O. (1975). *Borderline conditions and pathological narcissism*. New York: Jason Aronson.

Klein, M. (1946). Notes on some schizoid mechanisms. *International Journal of Psychoanalysis, 27*, 99-110.

Kohut, H. (1971) *The analysis of the self*. New York: International Universities Press.

Kris, A. (1976) On wanting too much: the exceptions revisited. *International Journal of Psychoanalysis, 57*, 85-95.

Kris, A. (1982). *Free association*. New Haven and London: Yale University Press.

Kris, A. (1984). The conflicts of ambivalence. *Psychoanalytic Study of the Child, 39*, 213- 234.

Scharff, J. S. (1989). Foundations of object relations family therapy. New York: Aronson.

Shapiro E. R. (1974). Using the team concept to change a psychoanalytically oriented therapeutic community. *Hospital and Community Psychiatry. 25*, 353-362.

Shapiro, E. R. (1978a). Research on family dynamics: Clinical implications for the family of the borderline Adolescent. *Adolescent Psychiatry, 6*, 360-376

Shapiro, E. R. (1978b). The psychodynamics and developmental psychology of the borderline patient: A review of the literature. *American Journal of Psychiatry, 135*, 1305-1315.

Shapiro, E. R. (1982). On curiosity: intrapsychic and interpersonal boundary formation in family life. *International Journal of Family Psychiatry, 3*, 69-89.

Shapiro, E. R. (1987). Interpreting irrationality. In J. Krantz (Ed.), *Irrationality in social and organizational life* (pp. 1-9). Washington, DC: A. K. Rice Institute.

Shapiro, E. R. (Ed.). (1997a). *The inner world in the outer world: Psychoanalytic perspectives*. New Haven and London: Yale University Press.

Shapiro, E. R. (1997b). The boundaries are shifting: Renegotiating the therapeutic frame. In E. R. Shapiro (Ed.), *The inner world in the outer world: Psychoanalytic perspectives*. New Haven and London: Yale University Press.

Shapiro, E. R. (1999). A holding context for psychotherapy impasse. *American Journal of Psychoanalysis* (in press).

Shapiro, E. R. (2000). Institutional learning as Chief Executive. In L.. Gould, L. Stapley, & M. Stein, (Eds.), *Applied experiential learning: The group relations approach*. New York: Psychosocial Press.

Shapiro, E. R., & Carr, A. W. (1991). *Lost in familiar places: creating new connections between the individual and society*. New Haven and London, Yale University Press.

Shapiro, E. R., & Freedman, J. (1987). Family dynamics of adolescent suicide. *Adolescent Psychiatry, 14*, 191-207.

Shapiro, E. R., & Fromm, M. G. (1999). Erik Erikson's clinical theory. In B. J. Sadock & H. I. Kaplan (Eds.), *Comprehensive textbook of psychiatry*, New York: Williams and Wilkins.

Shapiro, E. R., & Kolb J. E. (1979). Engaging the family of the hospitalized adolescent: The multiple family meeting. *Adolescent Psychiatry, 7*, 322-342.

Shapiro, E. R., Shapiro, R. L., Zinner, J., & Berkowitz, D. A. (1977). The borderline ego and the working alliance: Indications for individual and family treatment in adolescence. *International Journal of Psychoanalysis, 58*, 77-87. (Reprinted in J. Scharff [Ed.], *Foundations of object relations family therapy*, New York: Aronson, 1989.)

Shapiro, E. R., Zinner, J., Shapiro R. L., & Berkowitz D. A. (1975). The influence of family experience on borderline personality development. *International Review of Psychoanalysis, 2*, 399- 411. (Reprinted in J. Scharff [Ed.], *Foundations of object relations family therapy*, New York: Aronson, 1989.)

Shapiro, R. L. (1966). Identity and ego autonomy in adolescence. In J. Masserman (Ed.), *Science and psychoanalysis* (pp. 16-24). New York: Grune and Stratton.

Weisman, A. D. (1965). *The existential core of psychoanalysis*. Boston: Little-Brown.

Weisman, A. D. (1972) *On dying and denying: A psychiatric study of terminality*. New York: Behavioral Publications.

Zinner, J., & Shapiro, R. L. (1972). Projective identification as a mode of perception and behavior in families of adolescents. *International Journal of Psychoanalysis, 53*, 523-530.

CHAPTER 16

RECLAIMING THE DISAVOWED: THE EVOLUTION OF AN INTEGRATIVE POINT OF VIEW

PAUL L. WACHTEL, PH.D.

I f there is a single thread that unites the various ideas I have worked with in forming my views about psychotherapy, it is perhaps that of reclaiming the disavowed or ignored. On one level, reclaiming the parts of themselves that they have cast aside is most fundamentally what I work to help my patients accomplish. On another, the effort to bring back and look again at what has been disregarded is also part of the larger context of that work, the guiding vision, on many levels, of what life, society, and honest intellectual work are about.

    As I reflected on the progress of my thinking in the course of writing this chapter, this theme of reclaiming—and, importantly, reintegrating or giving a place to—the disavowed or cast aside echoed again and again. It defines my vision of the essence of psy-choanalysis, which remains in the center of my clinical and theo-retical thinking. It clarifies at the same time why I have repeatedly felt the need to go outside and beyond psychoanalysis, as I have attempted to reclaim and reappropriate what psychoanalysis has overlooked and neglected. And in a different way, it defines as well my vision of the good society and my interest in applying psychoanalytic and psychological insights to the task of social renewal; that vision centers on reintegrating into the social main-stream those who have been disregarded and creating the condi-tions in which they, in turn, can reappropriate their own rights and potentials.

Origins

I grew up in a relatively poor family in a lower middle class neighborhood in the Bronx—or, as I sometimes prefer to put it, in the shadow of Yankee Stadium. (For many years, despite rather average athletic skills, my fantasy life centered on playing baseball for the Yankees or basketball for the Knicks. I suppose it is a measure of my finally reaching maturity—or is it of resigna-tion?—that I no longer, as I stroll the streets of New York, dream of a Faustian bargain in which I trade all the books I have written for an unstoppable jump shot.)

Ours was a loving home (I think actually a *genuinely* lov-ing home). But it was also a home marked by rather limited engagement in the world of ideas or in the social and political events that occupy so much of my adult consciousness. My par-ents were good and kind people, but their interests were largely defined by the boundaries of the family. I am always surprised when people assume I grew up in an intellectual household. I think what they are likely picking up is the intellectual *hunger* that has stayed with me from the very absence of such stimulation in my childhood years.

Perhaps the narrowness of my parents' interests accounts, in part, for my longstanding concern with not permitting myself to be defined by the boundaries or restrictions that have characterized the intellectual communities to which I have belonged—why, while remaining committed to a psychoanalytic point of view, I questioned many of psychoanalysis's key assumptions (e.g., Wachtel, 1997); why, though continuing to be fascinated by psychology and committed to looking at the world psychologically, I felt a need to go beyond the confines of a psychological perspective and incorporate social, economic, historical, and philosophical considerations in the work I did (e.g., Wachtel, 1983); and why, while remaining strongly a man of the left and a believer in the struggle for racial justice, I found it important to challenge the cant that I felt was constricting progressive discourse on race and limiting its impact (Wachtel, 1999). In each instance—psychoanalysis, psychology, progressive politics—I remain strongly committed to my "family of origin," but I seem to be continually trying to "reform" the family, to induce it to be more open to the way the world looks from outside its circumscribed confines.

UNIVERSITY YEARS

I began my studies as a physics major at Columbia, but over time realized that I was far more interested in the dynamics of personality (and of society) than in the dynamics of particles. A paper I wrote for a freshman humanities course—a course delayed until my junior year because I had had to take so much math and physics—had a decisive influence. It was a personality portrait of Alceste, the lead character in Moliere's play, *The Misanthrope*. The excitement of probing the hidden motivational wellsprings that revealed a paradoxical dynamic underlying Alceste's behavior was intense and exhilarating. Going largely on instinct—I had not yet taken a single psychology course—I found myself discovering talents and passions within myself of which I had hardly been aware. I have ever since had a great love for all the works of Moliere.

Finally, after almost completing the major in physics, I decided at the end of my junior year to switch to psychology. I arranged to take an exam in introductory psychology in the fall and studied the material over the summer so that I could take primarily psychology courses in my senior year and fulfill the requirements for the major. The change was liberating, but I chafed a bit under the narrowness of the Columbia psychology department at that time. In general, my educational experience at Columbia was broad and intellectually exhilarating; in many ways, it felt like it was at Columbia that I was "born." But the psychology department in those years was so narrowly focused on a Skinnerian vision that, still relatively naive, I actually wondered if the fact that so many psychology books were catalogued in the library under the call letters "BF"—Skinner's initials—reflected obeisance to his enormous influence.

In contrast, the psychology department at Yale, where I did my graduate study, seemed a virtual cornucopia. The Institute of Human Relations, an effort to bring together the ideas of Hullian learning theory, psychoanalysis, and the perspectives of sociology and anthropology, was no longer a functioning institution by the time I arrived—although the building in which the department was housed still bore its name—but the intellectual legacy of that extraordinary collaboration still could be strongly felt. A number of my professors were simultaneously steeped in psychoanalysis and in the research tradition of American psychology, and I not only got to learn psychoanalytic theory in a depth that was unusual in American graduate schools but to view it in a way that did not isolate (or exempt) psychoanalytic thought from the research tradition.

Two faculty members in particular were mentors to me at Yale, each providing me with something different and essential. Sid Blatt took me under his wing and introduced me to the tradition of psychoanalytic ego psychology—to the work of Erikson, of Anna Freud, of Hartmann, Kris, and Loewenstein, and especially of David Rapaport. (I still recall with fond amusement borrowing Sid's copy of Rapaport's *Organization and Pathology of Thought* and wondering why he had bothered to underline it, since he had underlined virtually *every* passage, rendering the markings incapable of emphasizing any.) Seymour Sarason, also very much a mentor, became a model for me of the application of psychological thinking to the larger issues of our society. In my various efforts over the years to bring to bear my clinical and my social concerns (especially in *The Poverty of Affluence* [Wachtel, 1983] and *Race in the Mind of America* [Wachtel, 1999]), Seymour was always very much in my mind as I proceeded.

I stayed at Yale for my internship, where I continued to work with Sid Blatt, who had moved over to the psychiatry department, and also found enormously valuable the opportunity to participate in clinical seminars with Ernst Prelinger and with Roy Schafer.

Perhaps the most obvious influence of my Yale years on the approach I eventually developed was that of John Dollard and Neal Miller, who were both at Yale during the time I was a graduate student there. I had more contact with Dollard, who was in fact my very first psychotherapy supervisor, but the impact of both of their writings (especially, but by no means exclusively, *Personality and Psychotherapy* [Dollard & Miller, 1950]) is clearly and strongly evident in the direction my own work took.

POSTDOCTORAL TRAINING AND THE BEGINNINGS OF A NEW DIRECTION

When I left Yale, I thought of myself as primarily a proponent of psychoanalytic ego psychology, and that was the perspective I brought to bear both in my clinical work and in my research. But the seeds of a rethinking of that perspective were already there, and in a few years that rethinking was to lead me in directions that I could never have anticipated. I had encountered relatively little discussion of either Horney or Sullivan in graduate school (although John Dollard had had an interest in Horney's thinking, especially in her examinations of the ways that people perpetuate in the present difficulties that may have had their origins years earlier). But I had been attracted to and intrigued by their ideas, and wished to learn more about them, along with deepening my understanding of and ability to use the more mainstream psychoanalytic perspective. I therefore decided to seek psychoanalytic training in the postdoctoral program at New York University.

NYU's postdoctoral program appealed to me because, unlike most psychoanalytic training programs, it was not committed to a single theoretical viewpoint but had, as part of its *raison d'etre*, a commitment to including a wide range of theoretical perspectives. Although I did not yet know that I would devote much of my career to developing an integrative approach to psychotherapy that drew upon the widest possible range of perspectives and methods, it seems that, even at that early stage of my professional development, I already had an interest in encountering diverse viewpoints and in not being hemmed in by orthodoxy.

As it turned out, NYU both did and did not fulfill my expectations. On the one hand, I did get to take courses with teachers ranging from Erich Fromm (whose anti-authoritarian message turned out to be taught in a surprisingly authoritarian manner) to classical Freudians to Sullivanians and existentialists. On the other, the program eventually split into "tracks," which vitiated somewhat the true exchange of ideas. The experience was, all in all, a positive one—I now teach in the program—but it was also a lesson in how difficult it is to sustain a real dialogue on issues that cut as close to the quick of human experience as do those of psychoanalysis and psychotherapy.

For me, however, the experience in the postdoctoral program promoted both the maturing of my clinical practice and a keener sense of the questions and contradictions I wished to address. My identity as I entered the program was poised somewhere between that of the psychoanalytic ego psychology I already knew fairly well and the interpersonal perspective I wished to learn more about. My pursuit of ego psychology, it turned out, was more central in the research aspect of my career in those years, while my clinical thinking was increasingly influenced by the interpersonal point of view. My overall professional identity continued to be strongly psychoanalytic (including the interpersonal perspective within the psychoanalytic umbrella). I sought in my clinical work to promote insight, to analyze the transference, to be alert to signs of resistance and conflict, and to interpret the patient's behavior and experience in the "neutral" manner I had been taught was most respectful of the patient's autonomy and most effective in promoting meaningful and enduring change. Although my viewpoint now places all of these activities in a somewhat different theoretical context, and although my work now includes a variety of other aims and activities as equally central, I continue to pursue all of those aims, with the exception of the last. I still value highly some of the considerations that *led* to the idea of neutrality, but as I shall explain below, I now view the concept of neutrality per se as highly problematic and as associated with aspects of clinical practice that are counterproductive and even at times inhumane (Wachtel, 1987, chapter 11; Wachtel, 1993).

Throughout my postdoctoral training, I made a point of choosing supervisors who represented a range of theoretical viewpoints. The experience was enriching, but it was also challenging and, at times, even troubling. I respected each of these supervisors, and hence could not readily dismiss one for the sake of aligning myself with another. Yet some of what supervisor A emphasized was derided by supervisor B, and some of what supervisor C said made the work superficial was precisely what supervisor D said deepened the work. I struggled to reconcile these differences, to find what way of working seemed best *for me* and, I realized more afterward than at the time, to develop an overarching theoretical view that could put their different viewpoints together in a way that was fully attentive to their varied insights and observations.

A First Encounter with Social Learning Theory and Behavior Therapy

If the experience of attempting to reconcile the conflicting views of my postdoctoral psychoanalytic supervisors was the content that generated my interest in the integration of different points of view, the catalyzing event was my encounter with Walter Mischel's book, *Personality and Assessment* (Mischel, 1968). Mischel, then a professor at Stanford and a leading figure in the field of social learning theory, had written a book that was a provocative challenge not only to psychoanalysis but to any approach to studying personality that emphasized traits and characteristics manifested across a wide range of different situations. Mischel's book was virtually unknown among psychoanalysts, but it had a great impact among academic psychologists in the field of personality. It was much discussed as well at NYU's Research Center for Mental Health, where I had gone as a research associate and research assistant professor in 1969, shortly after Mischel's book was published.

The Research Center, under the leadership of George Klein and Robert Holt, was at the time perhaps the foremost center in the United States for psychoanalytically-oriented basic empirical research and a rare venue where academic psychology and psychoanalysis, both pursued with rigor, converged. In connection with my activities at the Research Center, I was invited to participate in an APA symposium on Mischel's book, and the position I was expected to take in the symposium was clearly on the "anti" side. As it turned out, the symposium was never held (I no longer recall why), but it turned out to be one of the most significant forums in which I had ever participated—even if only internally. For in preparing for my anticipated presentation, I had to study in some depth the social learning viewpoint and the behavior therapy approaches associated with it. Until that point, what I knew about behavior therapy was what most people in psychoanalytic circles knew (or thought they knew)—that it was a superficial, rather mechanical approach, manipulative and morally questionable, and certainly not worthy of very much attention. I also knew (or thought I knew) that even when behavior therapy produced results, these were of short duration and usually led to symptom substitution or worse. Within a very short time, however, my views on these matters were to change rather significantly.

In studying Mischel's arguments and the research underlying them, and in learning more about the actual practice of behavior therapy and the results obtained, I discovered several things that surprised me. First, behavior therapy was not the straw man I had been led to believe it was by my teachers (or, more accurately, by the ideological currents in which they and I were both immersed). Rather, it was an approach that was rapidly evolving and demonstrating increasing clinical sophistication and effectiveness. Second, and even more surprising, it gradually became clear to me—at first in a vague and intuitive way and increasingly on the basis of careful examination of assumptions, evidence, and the various options for understanding and conceptualizing key clinical observations—that behavior therapy was not as antithetical to or incompatible with psychoanalysis as I (and virtually everyone else on both sides of the divide) had assumed. Indeed, it increasingly seemed to me that behavior therapy filled a gap that I had begun to perceive in the psychoanalytic approach and that behavior therapy was strong where psychoanalysis was weak and vice versa. Putting them together, I began to think, might be both possible and valuable.

THE BEGINNINGS OF CYCLICAL PSYCHODYNAMIC THEORY

In pursuing further this initially intuitive perception, I had to articulate for myself more clearly the key assumptions of the psychoanalytic approach and to examine whether there might be an alternative way to conceptualize the observations on which psychoanalytic views were based. In thinking about why—aside from guild considerations or the simple antipathy to the unfamiliar—psychoanalysts would be opposed to the utilization of behavioral methods, it became clear that a central (if not always spelled out) conceptual foundation of the opposition was what I came to call the "woolly mammoth" model that was at the heart of much of psychoanalytic thought, both clinically and theoretically.

Very early in the development of psychoanalysis, when Freud was still thinking in terms of the repression of actually occurring childhood traumas, rather than in terms of wishful but conflicted fantasies, he referred to the "remarkable freshness" of the memories he had recaptured. The "wearing away" that characterized ordinary memories, so that the recollection was but a pale shadow of the actual experience, did not seem evident in this realm; the same affective intensity accompanied the memory of the long-ago event as was experienced at the actual time of the trauma. In the phenomena now labeled PTSD, of course, this persistence of intensity seems to occur even without repression. It would take us too far afield to discuss here the implications of contemporary observations on this disorder for Freud's early conceptualizations. More germane to the issue I wish to highlight here, when Freud (1897/1985) revised his understanding of what these memories actually represented—viewing them as frequently reflecting wishes and fantasies rather than actual traumas—he retained the same essential conceptual structure: the repressed wishes and fantasies, too, were thought to be preserved in their original form, rather than undergoing the modifications more typical of our thoughts and feelings as we grow up.

I labeled this model the "woolly mammoth" model (Wachtel, 1977) because it called to mind the image of the woolly mammoths that explorers occasionally find buried in the deep freeze of the arctic like a steak in our home freezer, so well preserved that their meat could literally be eaten by anyone with a taste for archaic cuisine. It was the idea that "infantile" or "archaic" (Paleolithic?) psychic remnants remain preserved in the recesses of the psyche—even while the rest of the personality continues to grow and change in response to new experiences—that seemed to me the substantive core of the opposition to utilizing behavioral interventions. (I say "substantive" core because, as noted above, a good part of the opposition is not directly traceable to specific theoretical considerations but to aesthetics, the sense that behavior therapists are "them" or "other," or issues of economic competition and professional identity.) If the real issues that maintain the patient's difficulties have to do with psychological structures and processes lying beneath a layer or barrier that renders them impervious to the ordinary processes of change, decay, or diminution of affective intensity that affects material "above" the barrier, then a method directed to "the surface" is likely to have little impact on the real sources of our problems (and to be, in a very literal sense, superficial).

Originally, my explication of this model was focused on the classical and ego psychological versions of psychoanalytic thought (Wachtel, 1977). There the preserved infantile features were largely centered around the drives and the fantasies associated with them. But in expanding my explorations of psychoanalytic modes of theorizing and their implications (Wachtel, 1997), I found that "woolly mammoth" theorizing characterized as well the fundamental structure of most object relations and self-psychological versions of psychoanalytic thought. These theories, too, posit a part of the personality that does not "grow up," that is split off and preserved in its original, "archaic" form, yielding not only fixations but "developmental arrests." These theories tend to emphasize "preoedipal" rather than "oedipal" influences, but the basic assumption survives the differing content and emphasis— the personality can be characterized as stuck at some early developmental "level."

In certain ways, the "woolly mammoth" model did account well for the phenomena observed in psychoanalytic practice. "Primitive" or "infantile" or "archaic" psychological inclinations did seem to emerge in the course of psychoanalytic work, and on first inspection it did appear that they had more to do with the circumstances of childhood than with the realities of the person's current life. But the model's seeming explanatory power came at the price of ignoring other phenomena that were equally important.

To begin with, although Mischel's account was incomplete in the opposite direction (see Wachtel, 1973a, 1973b), his emphasis on the variability of people's behavior from situation to situation is well taken. A moment's reflection on how we are with our friends, with strangers, with our bosses, with our spouses, with our children, and with our parents will make it clear that not only do we behave very differently in these different settings, but the way we *feel* about ourselves, our basic sense of identity, of competence or incompetence, of shyness or boldness, can vary quite substantially as well. There are people with whom we feel funny, interesting, and uninhibited, and people with whom our entire sense of well-being, adequacy, or vitality seems to disappear. An account in which the actual experiences of daily living are mere surface phenomena is insufficient to account for our acute respon-

siveness to the variations daily life presents. Giving such prepon-
derant weight to presumed unchanging structures from early
childhood leads either to ignoring or downplaying the variability—a serious error both clinically and theoretically—or to ad hoc
accounts that do not enable any consistent understanding of the
sources of that variability.

Also insufficiently addressed by the woolly mammoth
model is the success achieved—with little or no evidence of symptom substitution—by a variety of well-documented behavioral
interventions. By the logic of the woolly mammoth model, behavior therapy *should not* attain the results it does; it *should* be just a
superficial balm that leaves the essential dynamics untouched. But
although there are numerous reasons why simply *replacing* the
psychoanalytic approach with a strictly behavioral regimen would
be a very great loss (see, for example, Wachtel, 1982a, 1982b, 1997),
it is now clear that behavior therapy (or, in the variant that is more
common these days, cognitive-behavior therapy) yields clinical
results far more profound and substantial than psychoanalysts
had predicted. It is difficult to maintain that the predictions of the
traditional psychoanalytic model about the clinical results of
behavioral interventions stand up to the evidence.

Overcoming Anxiety and the Process of Working Through

As I further reflected on the negative perception of behavior therapy by psychoanalytic writers, it became apparent that this
attitude was also due to a false conflating of behavior therapy with
suggestion. The idea that "taking away symptoms" was a superficial and at best temporary expedient, and that symptom substitution was the likely result, derived historically from the clinical
experience of using hypnosis in a superficial and essentially
prepsychoanalytic way. It was very largely hypnosis that psychoanalysis replaced as a clinical tool, and it was hypnosis that—
implicitly or explicitly—remained the primary image of nonpsychoanalytic therapies for most psychoanalysts. Freud's famous
comment about a psychotherapy for the masses that alloyed the
"pure gold" of psychoanalysis with the base metal of suggestion is
a prominent instance of this implicit frame of comparison.

In fact, even the use of hypnosis rarely embodies any longer the approach that psychoanalysts have implicitly envisioned as the invidious nonpsychoanalytic therapy. Contemporary uses of hypnosis tend to incorporate the insights of psychoanalysis and to employ an approach that bears little resemblance to the kinds of suggestion that psychoanalysis replaced a century ago. Suggestion, to be sure, is a central feature of such therapies, as it is in behavior therapy, *and as it is in psychoanalysis.* Psychoanalysis has been the therapeutic approach that attempts most radically to replace or transcend suggestion, but it is by no means devoid of a rather large helping of that essential therapeutic nutrient (see Wachtel, 1993, chapter 9, for an extensive discussion of the role of suggestion in psychoanalysis and of Freud's lifelong struggle with the demon of suggestion). But behavior therapy—like psychoanalysis—is a good deal more than just suggestion, and analysts err very markedly when they fail to appreciate that behavior therapy does not "take away" symptoms but rather *treats* them.

Indeed, one of the key considerations that heightened my interest in integrating a behavioral dimension into psychoanalytic work was the recognition that what behavior therapy addressed most of all was the "working through" dimension of therapeutic work, the dimension that, in my view, psychoanalysis had named but not really developed sufficiently. The problem, it increasingly seemed to me, was that psychoanalysis as a method of clinical practice and as a theory of therapeutic change had still not sufficiently assimilated Freud's by now decades-old rethinking of the role and nature of anxiety, a rethinking that had enormous implications—or should have had—for how the clinical practice of psychoanalysis is undertaken.

In the early years of psychoanalysis, Freud had viewed anxiety as primarily a discharge phenomenon, a consequence of the buildup of unsatisfied or undischarged drive tension resulting from repression. But in *Inhibitions, Symptoms, and Anxiety*, Freud (1926) concluded that anxiety was more a cause of repression than a consequence. This was a potentially momentous shift because on several occasions Freud had stated quite explicitly that repression was the cornerstone of psychoanalysis. But if anxiety underlay repression, then anxiety was even more fundamental, and Freud had, in essence, shifted the very cornerstone of psychoanalytic theory and practice. If repression—not knowing something about ourselves—was the fundamental basis of our psychological difficulties, then insight—knowing ourselves better, undoing the repression—was the key to therapeutic change. The overarching emphasis on insight, from this vantage point, made sense, as did the dismissive attitude toward the therapeutic value of behavioral interventions such as systematic desensitization or flooding. However successful such methods might be at diminishing anxiety, such reduction of anxiety, from the vantage point of the earlier theory, seemed of only fleeting importance in comparison to the cardinal goal of promoting insight.

Once it was recognized, however, that anxiety was the fundamental cause of our psychological difficulties, then the overriding goal of therapy can be seen to shift. *Becoming less afraid* becomes even more important than attaining insights. From this vantage point, the new, more active methods to diminish anxiety that accrued from the clinical and conceptual approach of behavior therapy could be seen as operating closer to the heart of the clinical process and thus as much more likely to make a useful contribution. Indeed, full understanding of the implications of the revised theory of anxiety points to an appreciation of a substantial convergence in their final common pathway, as it were, between these behavioral methods and the "interpretations" that have been the most venerable interventions in traditional psychoanalytic approaches. Both, in fact, promote change via *exposing* the patient to that which he or she has fearfully avoided (Wachtel, 1997).

FROM WOOLLY MAMMOTH TO VICIOUS CIRCLE

The considerations offered thus far indicate some of the reasons I became interested in the possibility of integrating behavioral measures into my psychoanalytic work and why I was encouraged that such a course made sense. But a major task remained if such an integration was to proceed on a theoretically coherent basis and not lose touch with the clinical phenomena that psychoanalytic work had unearthed. A comprehensive theory had to incorporate both the observations at the heart of the psychoanalytic point of view and the observations that anchored the rather different vision of behavior therapists and social learning theorists. (It would also, I realized before long, have to incorporate important elements of the third major psychotherapeutic approach to appear in this century, family therapy. This dimension of the cyclical psychodynamic viewpoint, however, was not developed until some time later, and I will discuss it below.)

In pursuing the task of melding these varied observations into a coherent theoretical synthesis, the woolly mammoth model—whether explicit or implicit—was a significant impediment. It created in essence an almost impenetrable barrier between psychoanalytic and behavioral or social learning visions—with psychoanalysis emphasizing aspects of the personality that have been split off from the mainstream of psychological development so that they are preserved in their original form and cannot grow up or change with new experiences, and social learning theory emphasizing the ways our behavior and experience change with changing circumstances and contingencies. In wrestling with these competing visions, each partially valid but limited, the key conceptual move derived from a closer examination of just what keeps the seemingly infantile, primitive, or archaic features locked in. What emerged was an emphasis on *vicious circles* as the key element maintaining the connection between past and present and the conceptualization I came to call *cyclical psychodynamics.*

Consider, for example, the following example, described in *Psychoanalysis, Behavior Therapy, and the Relational World* (Wachtel, 1997), which contributed to the reconceptualization I am describing here:

> *I had been working for a while with a man who was rather severely suspicious and mistrustful of others. Not surprisingly, he saw me in a similar light, interpreting almost everything I did as designed to thwart and frustrate him. Knowing that he had experienced his father as being brutal and aggressive, and*

believing that my own efforts, even when momentarily frustrating to him, were primarily in his interest, I interpreted his reactions to me essentially as transference phenomena. I viewed his constant complaints of others' hostile and spiteful reactions to him in a similar light. There seemed to me a paranoid cast to his thinking that distorted others' actions to look like intentional affronts.

It thus came as a source of considerable enlightenment to me one day to recognize, in the course of a discussion of a possible appointment change, that in the guise of an effort to "understand" the request before deciding whether to try to fulfill it, I had really been provoking and frustrating this man. His perception of me as in conflict with him was, I had to recognize, correct, and my perception of him as distorting my innocent behavior was largely incorrect. I began to reflect on this, and recognized that on a number of occasions in the past I had acted similarly toward him. Further (I would still maintain), this kind of covertly spiteful, ungiving attitude was not at all typical of how I usually am with my patients.

My view of the troubling pattern in this man's life changed markedly after this experience. I reconsidered my view that his perception of others as spiteful and thwarting was a distortion, and wondered instead if they, like me, had reacted to something about him by really wanting to get in his way, annoy him, and so on. I shared with him my recognition of how I had acted with him, how it differed from my usual behavior with patients, and what I thought it meant about how we ought to proceed. Our attention then turned toward examining, in much sharper detail, his behavior in the period just prior to the "offenses" by others of which he complained. Aided particularly by my attention to what he had been doing that had provoked my own unhelpful reactions, we were able to gain much greater clarity about what the sequences that characterized his difficulties in living were really like, and therapeutic progress increased considerably (Wachtel, 1997, pp. 141-142).

There will be readers, I am sure, who will view this example simply as an instance of countertransference that could have been avoided if only I had been "better analyzed." Countertransference, to be sure, is always a part of the clinical process, but as I have discussed in detail elsewhere (Wachtel, 1993, 1997), the view of countertransference that regards it as always an error or failing on the therapist's part, as a departure from a desired state of neutrality, can be a serious impediment to effective clinical work—and indeed, can be a motive for the therapist to hide from herself the emergent countertransference feelings she is experiencing. In my own view, what this vignette primarily illustrates and the reason it represents a significant moment in the shaping of my view of the clinical process and of personality development—is that tendencies in the patient that are readily viewed as internal and derived from the past are in fact frequently maintained by real experiences in the present. This does not mean ignoring the role of the past; the pattern of suspicion, hostility, and actual mistreatment under discussion here was indeed a product of the patient's early experiences, including the experiences with his father mentioned above. His behavior, to be sure, was in response to the circumstances he was encountering in the present, but not in any simple sense that elevates the immediate situation over character or life history (see Bowers, 1973; Magnusson & Endler, 1977; Wachtel, 1973a, 1973b). The situations we encounter are very largely of our own making and choosing. The consistency we may observe in personality derives in large measure from the consistency in what we evoke from others. Many of the most important "independent variables" in our lives are not so independent at all; they are themselves a product of our behavior toward the other.

This does not mean that everything is in our control or is our responsibility. Many of the events in our lives simply "happen to" us. But, in the realm of interpersonal behavior that plays such a significant role in our lives—and especially in the issues that are of concern in psychotherapy—the circumstances we encounter are dynamic and reciprocal; how other people act toward us depends a great deal on how we act toward them. At the same time, the attitudes and expectations from which our behaviors toward them derive are in large measure a product of our previous experiences with them, our experiences with people we perceive as similar, and the earlier experiences which contributed to shaping our grounding assumptions about people. Stated differently, the situations we consistently encounter are virtually a definition (simply from a different vantage point) of what our "personality" is—something about *us* that is manifested rather consistently through our lives. One person brings out the hostile side of most people he meets, while another brings out the cooperative and fun-loving side of the same people. They are a different "stimulus," a different "independent variable" for the two people.

Returning then to the observations that underlie the woolly mammoth conceptualizations, the cyclical psychodynamic approach takes those same observations and places them in a larger context. From the cyclical psychodynamic vantage point, the seemingly infantile or archaic psychological structures or inclinations persist not because they are split off and locked up in a part of the psyche inaccessible to the input of new experiences—not that is, *in spite of* the person's ongoing experience—but *precisely because* of that experience. The problematic, and indeed often unconscious, proclivities *seem* out of touch with adult experience because we generally do not examine that adult experience in sufficient detail. Instead, we implicitly assume, to borrow Heinz Hartmann's (1939) phrase, that everyone is functioning in a roughly similar "average expectable environment." In fact, however, the emotional texture and relational subtleties of the environment we encounter—not just how we *interpret* or idiosyncratically *distort* the meanings on the basis of our past experiences, but the real details of what transpires—differ in crucially important ways for each person. While the concept of an average expectable environment may be useful for understanding the evolutionary processes that underlie the *general rules* of functioning that characterize us as a species, attention to such an abstraction leads us severely astray in understanding the uniqueness of individual personality or the particular skews in development that underlie neurosis.

No one lives in an average expectable environment. Each person's world of interpersonal interaction—who he or she encounters over the thousands of interactions that make up the day and how precisely they behave (even how they give an emotional tone to the simplest acts such as saying hello, giving change at the checkout counter, and so on) is as unique and emblematic as a fingerprint. When we look closely at the continuing back and forth between internal states and structures and ongoing experience, what we find is that the details of each fit together in lock and key fashion.

In essence, then, our internal states—the conflicts, wishes, fears, and assumptions that underlie our behavior—lead us to act in ways whose consequences tend to reaffirm those same conflicts, wishes, fears, and assumptions. The patient noted above, for example, was in one sense maintaining anger, suspicion, and fear of affectionate or trusting behavior that was implanted, as it were, in childhood. But in another sense, he was simply responding to the daily reality of his life. The pattern *started* very early, but it is *maintained* by its consequences in the present. The suspicion and hostility he manifests today is more directly the product of what happened yesterday than of what happened years before, and it will in turn bring forth results that will be the source of *tomorrow's* suspicion. (Elsewhere [e.g., Wachtel, 1991a, 1997] I have discussed this process as requiring others as "accomplices" in our neuroses, and have suggested that the therapist can gain a more effective understanding of the patient's difficulties by examining how the patient draws others in to play—usually unwittingly and unconsciously—such an accomplice role. I shall return to the notion of accomplices below.)

The person's present way of life is not simply the *product* or *expression* of his underlying dynamics. It is the ongoing *source* of those dynamics as well. The dynamics of personality are bi-directional, leading not just from inside to outside but from outside to inside as well. As a consequence, interventions directed toward the manifest patterns in the patient's life, or toward any of the emotional reactions in the present that are a part of the continuing replication of his internal/external dilemma, are not superficial band-aids that bypass the deeper dynamics at the heart of the neurosis. Rather, these interventions have the potential to engage the true heart of the neurosis, which lies not "inside" or in the past but in a self-replicating way of life that links the past and present to the (likely but not inevitable) future.

THREE CAVEATS

Three caveats are essential at this point in order to assure that the reader understands the point of view that guides the above discussion: (1) the pattern is not inevitable; (2) the influence of situations is not direct and automatic, bypassing the psychological structures of concern to psychoanalysts; (3) behavioral interventions alone, unintegrated with psychodynamic understanding, are often insufficient.

With regard to the first caveat, the behavior deriving from the individual's conflicts and assumptions is *likely* to evoke certain predictable responses from others, but those responses are not inevitable. If, over a period of time, the other person were to respond in ways that went counter to the first person's expectations, this would provide an opportunity for the pattern to change. Indeed, as I will elaborate shortly, that is a critical element at the heart of successful psychotherapy.

Turning to the second caveat, however, part of what makes unlikely the kind of salutary outcome that breaks the maladaptive pattern is that we do *not* respond directly or automatically to "the situation." The situation that influences our behavior is the situation *as perceived*, and the way we perceive it is very significantly a product of our expectations, the ways we have coded previous experiences, the defensive needs that require us to notice certain things and not to notice others, and so forth. Although psychoanalysts have often overemphasized this "internal" source of behavior and experience, using it virtually to ignore the crucial impact of what really is transpiring, it is indeed the case that the individual's pre-existing psychological structures play a powerful determining role. Even Mischel emphasized this (1973a, 1973b), especially after being criticized for having offered an extreme situationism (Bowers, 1973; Magnusson & Endler, 1977).

In essence, the above two considerations point to a kind of race against time, with the stake being either change or the perpetuation of a maladaptive pattern. In initial encounters with another person, the patient is at least as likely to encounter behavior that is counter to his neurotic expectations as to find them confirmed. The new person, not having a history with the patient, is likely to begin behaving according to the expectations and habits generated by his own life history rather than to immediately fall into a complementary "accomplice" role. Were the new person to persist in relating to the patient in this fashion, it would provide an opportunity for change; new behavior from the other would feed back to modify the patient's expectations and eventually to establish a different, more adaptive, internal and external transactional pattern. But because the patient is likely to see the interaction through his own filters, he is not likely to notice very readily that his expectations have been disconfirmed. Or, to describe the process more precisely, he is likely to *interpret* the events in his own idiosyncratic fashion. Consequently, he is likely to continue responding in his habitual way, and thus to increase the likelihood that even if the other is not initially inclined to act as an accomplice, he or she eventually will. And if that does happen, then the pattern gets locked in again, based on the apparent "confirmation" of the baleful expectation. On the other hand, if the patient's expectations begin to change in response to the other's counteranticipated behavior before the other's behavior begins to change in response to the patient's, then a process of *change* can accelerate, as the new behavior evokes new expectations which evoke more of the new behavior, and so on. Again, this is what often happens when psychotherapy is successful.

But, as any practicing clinician knows, the process of change is enormously complicated, and rarely proceeds in a smooth or continuous path. "Two steps forward and one step back" is usually about as good as it gets. And this is where the third caveat comes in. Even at times in the treatment of relatively simple symptoms, and almost always when the work concerns more complex issues of relationships or the sense of self, the phenomena that psychoanalysis depict as "resistance" come into play. I have met few practicing behavior therapists who have not acknowledged, in conversations about clinical work, that such phenomena arise and who have not observed that patients frequently do not do—or do in oddly counterproductive ways—what the behavior therapist believes would prove helpful. (In referring to "practicing behavior therapists," I am making a distinction between behavior therapists who engage substantially in clinical practice and researchers or university faculty members with a behavioral or cognitive-behavioral orientation whose ideology remains pure precisely because it is rarely muddied by the complexities of substantial clinical work.)

The label "resistance" for these phenomena is usually not very helpful (see Wachtel, 1982b, 1993); but the phenomena themselves are pervasive, and unless they are addressed, the therapeutic work is likely to be compromised. They may be addressed in a variety of ways, but psychoanalysis, as an approach that has especially highlighted these phenomena and organized its clinical thinking around them, is a particularly rich source of ideas in this regard.

The psychoanalytic perspective also alerts us to another consideration crucial to effective clinical functioning: in the circular processes described above, it is not just *assumptions* that the individual brings to bear and in turn has maintained or even strengthened by what transpires. *Desires* are crucial as well. The *conflicts* that so crucially structure neurotic patterns of living, and that lie at the heart of the resistances that impede therapeutic progress, are fueled by our continuing to desire the very outcomes that we also fear. Psychoanalysis has been virtually unique in its emphasis on unearthing and articulating the often surprising desires that lie underneath or alongside the more conventional and socially acceptable wishes that are typically assumed in cognitive-behavioral work (see, for example, Wachtel, 1997, pp. 125-131).

To fully incorporate these psychoanalytic insights into the more integrative work undertaken from the cyclical psychodynamic model, however, one further consideration is essential to address: desires, too, are transactional. The desire may seem infantile or archaic, but just like the assumptions that both generate and are generated by the repeated transactions of our daily lives, desires, too, are both cause and effect. The nature of what we strive for, even if outside of awareness, contributes powerfully to shaping the actual encounters in which we find ourselves. But those encounters, with the stimulation, gratifications, and deprivations that they bring, in turn shape the nature of our desires, contributing on still another level to the cyclical perpetuation of longstanding patterns in the present. Without understanding both the conflicted desires that unconsciously contribute to these patterns *and* the way those desires are repeatedly fueled by ongoing experience, our ability to do therapy most effectively is impaired.

Put differently, the internal processes are not simply cognitive, and the transactional process is not simply that of the self-fulfilling prophecy, however important that process remains. Also central to the perpetuation of the pattern are powerful affective and motivational influences which have been the particular province of study of the psychodynamic approach.

THE ACTIVE—AND REAL—PSYCHOTHERAPIST

As my further thinking about these various issues has evolved since the original publication of *Psychoanalysis and Behavior Therapy* (Wachtel, 1977), a number of new themes have emerged as elaborations of the ideas discussed thus far. In certain ways, many of these are elaborations of Harry Stack Sullivan's (1953) view of the therapist as a "participant observer." With the development of a broader, "relational" version of psychoanalytic thought (see, for example, Aron, 1996; Mitchell, 1988, 1993; Wachtel, 1997, especially chapter 15), the implications of this point of view have been extended, though not always with sufficient acknowledgement of Sullivan's seminal contribution. Current psychoanalytic discourse includes quite considerable discussion of the differences between "one-person" and "two-person" models. The cyclical psychodynamic approach fits clearly within the relational and the two-person visions of psychoanalytic thought, but its openness to influences from outside the psychoanalytic camp altogether has taken it in somewhat different directions.

My ideas about the nature of transference, for example, and the importance of considering what is *really* happening in the transaction paralleled in significant ways those of Merton Gill (e.g., Gill, 1982, 1983, 1984), yet in certain important respects we took these ideas in quite different directions. We were both members of the Rapaport-Klein Study Group, which met annually in Stockbridge, Massachusetts, and I had numerous opportunities to exchange thoughts with him about the implications of our shared views on transference. I remember those conversations fondly, if with a bit of chagrin. Although Merton always conveyed a palpable respect for my thinking, my interactions with this brilliant, witty man with the deep, booming voice often brought out in me a residual boyish self-consciousness I had long outgrown in most of my other interactions. Part of this response, to be sure, reflected the fact that Merton, a full generation older than I, was someone whose work I had read admiringly while still a student; but I suspect that among the more significant determinants was the combination of my affection for him and his strong aversion to sentimentality. In any event, although we each understood the other's logic, we never could come to an agreement on the implications of the ideas that we shared. Merton retained a commitment to *analyzing* as the key, even if analyzing in a way that acknowledged what the psychoanalytic mainstream had long denied. I saw the same appreciation of the inevitable real impact of the analyst or therapist as pointing to the possibility of continuing to employ what is valuable about transference analysis—especially its emotional immediacy and the direct access of the analyst to what is transpiring in relation to the patient's experience—and at the same time incorporating other useful interventions as well.

As I saw it, since the patient was *always* responding in part to what the therapist has actually done—whether the therapist is answering a question, not answering a question, giving advice, not giving advice, interpreting, being silent, or whatever—then intervening via the measures that behavior therapists had shown to be effective was just one more possible way for the therapist to behave. In *all* of these instances, the patient's own contribution still has very considerable room to be expressed. Just as one patient might see the therapist's silence as comforting or competently professional, and another might experience the same behavior on the therapist's part as depriving, hostile, or reflecting the therapist's not knowing what to do, so too might the same range of subjective judgments be apparent in the face of the therapist's deciding—or not deciding—to employ systematic desensitization to address a patient's phobia. The implication I drew from the view of transference largely shared by Gill and myself (e.g., Gill, 1982, 1983, 1984; Wachtel, 1981, 1982a, 1993) was that since a valid and comprehensive analysis of transference includes the therapist's behavior as a part of what determined the patient's experience—and then proceeds to explore with the patient why, of all the possible ways he or she might have experienced the event that transpired, this was the one that felt to him or her most compelling—it is possible to retain the virtues of transference analysis even while adding the complementary virtues of active interventions such as those of behavior therapy.

Behavior therapy, however, was by no means the only source of useful active interventions designed to break the vicious circles in which people get caught. As I was completing work on *Psychoanalysis and Behavior Therapy* (Wachtel, 1977), it became clear to me that many of the ways I was reconceptualizing psychological disorder bore considerable resemblance to the views of family therapists. They too were thinking in terms of circular rather than linear processes, and employing active interventions to break up the troubling pattern. Since my understanding of family therapy at that point came mainly from my wife, Ellen, who was completing family therapy training at the Ackerman Institute, it seemed natural to explore the interface between my evolving psychodynamic view and the approaches of family therapists via a collaboration with her (Wachtel & Wachtel, 1986). (It was no small additional virtue that I got to be the co-author of our book even though she did the lion's share of the writing.)

THE THERAPIST'S LANGUAGE AND A MORE SEAMLESS INTEGRATION

The most central concern of my thinking about psychotherapy in the last decade has been the exploration of what psychotherapists actually say and the implications of various ways of conveying to the patient the therapist's understanding of the patient's experience and dynamics (Wachtel, 1993). In teaching clinical psychology graduate students, I found that what most intrigued them—and, I was interested to learn, most set their experience with me apart from their experiences with other teachers and supervisors—was my interest in the (not infrequent) times when they thought they understood the patient reasonably well but could not find the right words to express their understanding to the patient. "How can I say that in a way that will be helpful?" became a kind of leitmotif through the practicum courses I taught, and I began to recognize how little such questions were addressed in the psychotherapy literature or in most training programs.

As I explored these issues further, I became aware of a closely related theme that wove itself insistently through my explorations of therapists' language: The conceptualizations and terminology that dominate our field are highly invidious, and there is a premium in many therapists' training and ongoing thinking on unearthing pathology (and the deeper the better). The result is what Wile (1984) has called "accusatory interpretations."

My own thinking about the language therapists use began with a similar concern, and I explored a variety of ways in which therapists can be subtly and unwittingly—but nonetheless significantly—accusatory (Wachtel, 1993). Examining this issue in both interpretations and the process of inquiry, I then considered how the therapist's comments could instead build on the patient's strengths and help to amplify them and create a positive momentum for change. In recent years, my interest in these matters, and my conviction that they are insufficiently appreciated as the often crucial difference between therapeutic success and failure, has led to still further changes in my way of working. Over time, my work has become more "seamless" (Wachtel, 1991b). The behavioral or systemic dimensions of the work are less readily identifiable as "doing something different"; they are woven right into the manner of offering interpretations and even of listening. From the beginning of my integrative experiments, I moved comfortably back and forth between modalities—for example, capitalizing on the opportunities for transference exploration afforded by introducing behavioral measures and making such exploration a regular part of my use of such measures. But as I further sharpened my use of language as the medium of what is, after all, the "talking cure," I found that comments that advanced the cause of deepening the patient's experience of him- or herself and of his or her affective life could also have, at the very same moment, elements of support, of providing structure and direction that encouraged new adaptive action, and so forth (Wachtel, 1993). This evolution fostered exploration of the role of attribution, suggestion, self-disclosure, and the relation between reframing and interpreting. It led as well as to an examination of the continuing dialectic in psychotherapy between the need to respect and affirm the patient's experience and the need to help the patient to *change* his or her way of seeing things in crucial ways.

In all of these explorations, my concern was to root the discussion very concretely in what therapists actually say. If one operates from a relational or two-person model, it seemed to me, then it no longer is acceptable to hide behind vague allusions to "interpreting the negative transference" or "interpreting the oedipal dynamics." The therapist's contribution is crucial, and the impact of what she says and how she says it must be central to our understanding of the process of change. Because *Therapeutic Communication* (Wachtel, 1993) is probably the most detailed and concrete examination available of what therapists actually say in the course of therapy—and of what ways of communicating our understanding help and what ways impede—it seems to me likely that this work will end up as my most enduring and broadly applicable contribution to the field.

SUPPORTS AND INSTITUTIONAL CONTEXTS

This account of the development of my thinking and practice would be incomplete without mention of two especially important sources of support in an effort that, at least in its early years, went very much against the grain of dominant ideas. One of those sources has been the doctoral program in clinical psychology at the City University of New York, where I have taught since 1972. I doubt that there is a brighter or more talented group of students in any clinical program in the country, and I have benefited enormously from their probing questions, intellectual curiosity, and emotional openness. Many of my ideas have been developed in the course of elaborating them in the courses I have taught there.

A second, more recent—but by now reasonably long-standing—source of support and encouragement has been the Society for the Exploration of Psychotherapy Integration (SEPI). I was one of the founders of SEPI when it began in the early 1980s, and I have been centrally involved in SEPI ever since. SEPI has offered two benefits in particular that have aided enormously the process of exploring ideas at the interface of different traditions. First, SEPI has provided a home for those of us whose identity includes a strong inclination toward integrative thinking. Many of us continue to belong to organizations representing our original orientations—in my case, psychoanalysis—and continue to find those ties very meaningful. But there is no other place where I can not only exchange ideas with therapists from orientations other than my own but share a sense of *common identity* with them. As someone whose theoretical vision strongly emphasizes the importance of context, I do not underestimate the importance of this institutionalized integrative context in my life and in my work.

The second major contribution that SEPI has made to facilitating the task of developing still further the integrative vision that guides my work is the unique atmosphere that pervades the organization. SEPI meetings are remarkably free of the narcissistic stance-taking that is so common at other professional meetings. To a truly surprising degree, people come to SEPI meetings at least as much to listen to and learn from others as to demonstrate their own ideas. The panels at SEPI meetings are generally not debates or displays but genuine and meaningful exchanges, and the more informal contacts in the hallways of SEPI meetings have had a similar quality. SEPI has afforded me the opportunity to develop close friendships with colleagues from around the world, and the exchanges I have subsequently had with them—both in their countries and closer to home—have contributed valuably to broadening and extending my point of view.

EXTENDING THE INSIGHTS OF PSYCHOTHERAPY TO SOCIETY AT LARGE

I began this chapter by identifying as a common thread in all my work the reclaiming of the disavowed. Clinically, that has meant helping people to reappropriate those parts of themselves that they have felt a need to hide or push away. Theoretically, it has meant reclaiming the observations and understandings that have been rejected or ignored because they come from a clinical or research tradition that is viewed as "other." I wish, in this final section, to highlight one more way in which the theme of respecting and re-including the excluded is especially important.

It is, of course, not just ideas or even parts of the self that are excluded; *people* and *groups of people* are as well. The United States is a society that was founded on a severe contradiction— ideals of liberty and a reality of slavery. Though slavery was abolished more than a century ago, we are living still with the results of that contradiction. The inequalities that continue to divide us socially and economically rend us psychologically as well, creating pain, conflict, anxiety, guilt, and self-doubts in differing ways in different segments of our divided national community. The healing of that pain and that rift cannot be achieved without attention to the real injustices and inequalities that persist in both blatant and subtle ways. But these changes, in turn, are unlikely to be achieved without an understanding of the conflicting and often disavowed feelings that contribute to maintaining them.

Race in the Mind of America (Wachtel, 1999) is my effort to contribute to breaking the vicious circles that keep us locked in antagonism and mistrust. Like my earlier efforts at applying psychological insights to social analysis (e.g., Wachtel, 1983), *Race in the Mind of America* builds on the analysis of vicious circles I first developed for understanding the clinical situation. It is my hope that in extending the cyclical psychodynamic perspective into the realm of racial division and social injustice, I can contribute in some measure to resolving what has been our society's most intractable dilemma.

PSYCHOTHERAPY AT THE MILLENNIUM

It remains, finally, to comment on the theme that the editors of this volume have set as the framework for the stories each of us has to tell. What will psychotherapy look like in the new millennium? Perhaps the only certainty is that there will be surprises that we have not anticipated. But there are at least issues that can be discerned as likely to shape the direction of the field in significant ways. Perhaps the most pressing questions we face are not about the theory or practice of psychotherapy per se but about values. What kind of society do we want to be? Where do we choose to invest our resources? What do we regard as the fundaments of a good life?

Our answers to these questions, I believe, have been rooted in a basic misunderstanding of our material and psychological circumstances. Despite frequent charges that we are a society too obsessed with the psychological, too concerned with our "selves," our "relationships," our narcissistic calculus of hurts and anxieties, I believe that the opposite is closer to the truth. Our culture leads us to define the good life very largely in material terms and—even more significantly—to misunderstand tragically the ways that our pursuit of continuing growth in material product actually undermines the sense of well-being it is thought to promote (Wachtel, 1983). The psychological toll of our competitive, market-oriented way of life is immense, and it is compounded by the ways that we are seduced into attempting to assuage our discontents by still more of the same wrong solution. The latest instance of this is the intrusion of so-called managed care into the relationships between caregivers and people in need of care. "Bottom line" values lead us, in essence, to conclude as a society that spending more on boats, computer games, and extra-large "family rooms"—and hence less on such matters as psychotherapy—is the path toward the good life. But large family rooms in which the actual family is in tatters bring small compensation, especially when a good part of why the family is in tatters is the stress resulting from having to earn the money to purchase the newly standard amenities.

Psychotherapy has never been a value-free, technical activity. We have more to heal, I believe, than a discrete set of "disorders." Part of what we must work to heal, indeed, is the very value system that is represented by the clerks and accountants who increasingly serve as the gatekeepers for who receives psychological services. To be sure, addressing the suffering that results from the "officially" recognized disorders that are embodied in each shifting version of the DSM should remain a high priority. So too should the effort to relieve that suffering more rapidly. There is certainly nothing inhumane about brief psychotherapy when it represents more rapid relief. But no one with eyes to see can claim that the managed care movement is primarily about faster relief of suffering. If is about limiting the *dollars spent* on relieving suffering (whether that suffering be psychological or physical). And it is rooted in the premise that the dollars are better spent elsewhere.

The future of psychotherapy, I believe, lies not just in improving our techniques but in examining our values and our assumptions. If psychotherapists continue tacitly to accept the value system of the corporation, to accommodate to a world in which they are "providers" or "venders" and in which "empirical validation" of their work is speciously tied to so-called manuals and to committee-designated lists of disorders (see Messer & Wachtel, 1997), then the future of psychotherapy is rather dim. It will continue to provide a useful service, but its real potential for human betterment will lie fallow. If, on the other hand, the new century sees a renewed vigor in the role psychotherapists play as explorers of the sources of satisfaction and dissatisfaction in living, if the techniques we have developed are applied not just to "disorders" but to the enhancement of experiencing, empathy, and relatedness in everyday life, then the prospects are far more promising. In recent decades, our entire society has been seduced by the siren values of the marketplace. Psychotherapy, as I see it, is potentially a domain in which those very values can be challenged and their impact on our lives clarified. Important members of our profession once aimed that high (see, for example, Jacoby, 1983). As the new century dawns, perhaps we can muster the vision and courage to do so again.

REFERENCES

Aron, L. (1996). *A meeting of minds: Mutuality in psychoanalysis.* Hillsdale, NJ: The Analytic Press.

Bowers, K. S. (1973). Situationism in psychology: An analysis and a critique. *Psychological Review, 80,* 307-336.

Dollard, J., & Miller, N. (1950). *Personality and psychotherapy.* New York: McGraw-Hill.

Freud, S. (1897/1985). *The complete letters of Sigmund Freud to Wilhelm Fliess.* J. M. Masson (Ed.). (pp. 264-266). Cambridge: MA: Harvard University Press.

Freud, S. (1926). Inhibitions, symptoms, and anxiety. *Standard Edition.* London: Hogarth Press, 1959, pp. 87-172.

Gill, M. M. (1982). *Analysis of transference.* New York: International Universities Press.

Gill, M. M. (1983). The interpersonal paradigm and the degree of the therapist's involvement. *Contemporary Psychoanalysis, 19,* 200-237.

Gill, M. M. (1984). Psychoanalysis and psychotherapy: A revision. *International Review of Psycho-Analysis, 11,* 161-179.

Hartmann, H. (1939). *Ego psychology and the problem of adaptation.* New York: International Universities Press.

Jacoby, R. (1983). *The repression of psychoanalysis.* New York: Basic Books.

Magnusson, D., & Endler, N. (Eds.). (1977). *Personality at the cross-roads: Towards an interactional psychology*. Hillsdale, NJ: Laurence Earlbaum Associates.

Messer, S. B., & Wachtel, P. L. (1997). The contemporary psychotherapeutic landscape: Issues and prospects. In P. L. Wachtel & S. B. Messer (Eds.), *Theories of psychotherapy: Origins and evolution* (pp. 1-38). Washington, DC: American Psychological Association.

Mischel, W. (1968). *Personality and assessment*. New York: Wiley.

Mischel, W. (1973a). Toward a cognitive social learning reconceptualization of personality. *Psychological Review, 80*, 252-283.

Mischel, W. (1973b). On the empirical dilemmas of psychodynamic approaches: Issues and alternatives. *Journal of Abnormal Psychology, 82*, 335-344.

Mitchell, S. (1988). *Relational concepts in psychoanalysis*. Cambridge: Harvard University Press.

Mitchell, S. A. (1993). *Hope and dread in psychoanalysis*. New York: Basic Books.

Sullivan, H. S. (1953). *The interpersonal theory of psychiatry*. New York: Norton.

Wachtel, E. F. & Wachtel, P. L. (1986). *Family dynamics in individual psychotherapy*. New York: Guilford.

Wachtel, P. L. (1973a). Psychodynamics, behavior therapy, and the implacable experimenter: An inquiry into the consistency of personality. *Journal of Abnormal Psychology, 82*, 324-334.

Wachtel, P. L. (1973b). On fact, hunch, and stereotype: A reply to Mischel. *Journal of Abnormal Psychology, 82*, 537-540.

Wachtel, P. L. (1977). *Psychoanalysis and behavior therapy*. New York: Basic Books.

Wachtel, P. L. (1981). Transference, schema, and assimilation: The relevance of Piaget to the psychoanalytic theory of transference. *The Annual of Psychoanalysis*, Vol. 8 (pp. 59-76). New York: International Universities Press.

Wachtel, P. L. (1982a). Vicious circles: The self and the rhetoric of emerging and unfolding. *Contemporary Psychoanalysis, 18,* 273-295.

Wachtel, P. L. (Ed.). (1982b) *Resistance: Psychodynamic and behavioral approaches.* New York: Plenum.

Wachtel, P. L. (1982c). What can dynamic therapies contribute to behavior therapy? *Behavior Therapy, 13,* 594-609.

Wachtel, P. L. (1983). *The poverty of affluence: A psychological portrait of the American way of life.* New York: Free Press.

Wachtel, P. L. (1987). *Action and insight.* New York: Guilford.

Wachtel, P. L. (1991a). The role of "accomplices" in preventing and facilitating change. In R. C. Curtis & G. Stricker (Eds.), *How people change* (pp. 21-28). New York: Plenum.

Wachtel, P. L. (1991b). From eclecticism to synthesis: Toward a more seamless psychotherapeutic integration. *Journal of Psychotherapy Integration, 1,* 43-54.

Wachtel, P. L. (1993). *Therapeutic communication: Knowing what to say when.* New York: Guilford.

Wachtel, P. L. (1997). *Psychoanalysis, behavior therapy, and the relational world.* Washington, DC: American Psychological Association.

Wachtel, P. L. (1999). *Race in the mind of America: Breaking the vicious circle between blacks and whites.* New York: Routledge.

Wile, D. B. (1984). Kohut, Kernberg, and accusatory interpretations. *Psychotherapy, 21,* 353-364.

CHAPTER 17

THE PATH TAKEN
ALLEN WHEELIS, M.D.

A profound sense of unworthiness drove my choice of profession, both as psychoanalyst and as writer, a motivation beginning in childhood when I was taught by my father—an authoritarian and very convincing teacher—that I was, in his often repeated phrase, "a lowdown no-account scoundrel." That was the wound of my childhood. Throughout my life, often without recognizing it, I have been seeking to redeem myself, to acquire a worthy identity. My work as a physician, then a psychiatrist, then a psychoanalyst, all ostensibly to help other people, was in its origin a trying to cure myself. That motivation drove also my wish to be a writer. Both were attempts to do something that would make me loved. If loved enough, I would be cleared of the childhood indictment. Of course, that effort was futile; no accomplishment, however great, can neutralize the childhood wound, and no experience of being loved can silence the unconscious identity of worthlessness.

My entire life experience has taught me that such a wound is very hard to heal; I have fought my demons to a draw but not much more. In adolescence I was isolated and friendless. I was eager for friends, but too shy to reach out to them. I began to read the great novels, *Look Homeward Angel, Anna Karenina, The Magic Mountain*. I felt closer to the characters in these books than to the people around me. I understood them, knew that they would understand me. I began to associate myself, also, with the authors of these wonderful books. Gradually, I began to think that perhaps I could myself write such a book. A plot began to unfold in my mind, and presently I decided to drop out of college to write a novel. I left Baton Rouge where I had been living with my uncle and studying at Louisiana State University and went to San Antonio, Texas, where I had grown up. I took a room in the YMCA, five dollars a week, which left the same amount for food. I found that I could live on this, and began to write my novel. To appease my mother, I agreed to go back to college after a year whether or not the novel was completed. I made this promise easily, confident that by that time my literary career would have accrued such promise that I would never have to make good on this commitment. I settled into a solitary life and began to write.

The central idea of the novel was that carnal love brings about the death of spiritual love: if lovers would only love continently their love would last forever. I wrote all day, every day, seven days a week. Having no money for pleasure or for vice, I worked also late into the night. The months passed, the pages accumulated, and the manuscript grew thicker. Nearing the end, I read it through and found it to be good. Then I developed insomnia. Night after night, no matter how tired I might be, I could not sleep. I became exhausted, unable to write. A refrain would go through my mind—"I've got to sleep because if I can't sleep I can't write and if I can't write I can't finish the novel and I have to finish the novel." Sitting at my desk, I would rest my head on my left hand and would wake up to hear my head hitting the desktop. I would lie on the bed and would be seized by a frenzy of agitation and restlessness. I'd take a shower and try again. I would go out to run, hoping to replace my sick exhaustion with normal fatigue, would lean against a building to rest and recover consciousness with legs buckling, slumping to the ground. I turned for help to a family doctor who had taken care of my father. He thought the trouble was infected tonsils and I agreed to have them removed. After a couple of weeks, with much pain and bleeding, I had recovered, but still could not sleep. I was getting sick and didn't know where to turn. I would have to go back to see this doctor again. But just then I was overtaken by a wave of common sense and told myself, "Don't be a fool. Don't be a fool *again*. You *knew* that tonsillitis was not causing this insomnia. Why did you let him butcher you?"

I went to the public library, looked under insomnia, nothing; under sleep, *The Sleeping Beauty*; under psychology, I found a lot and began to read. I found nothing on the first day, or the second, but on the third day I came upon an idea that seemed like a psychological tool, the case history of a young man who had developed paralysis of his right arm for which no cause could be found. He went from doctor to doctor without benefit, until he came eventually to someone who inquired into his life as well as his symptom: He was deeply religious, a student of divinity, planning to become a minister, and had for some months been in intense conflict about masturbation. Now here was a stunning idea: something experienced as an affliction, something alien and unwanted, something perhaps even life-threatening, may nevertheless be created by the sufferer as a solution to an inner problem. Could I be doing that? Could my affliction be self-created? Could it be that although I *believe* I want to finish the novel, actually I do not want to? Why? I felt myself reaching deep for the answer. *Perhaps because if I did I would have to acknowledge that it was a failure.* Suddenly a rush of insight, I could see the entire scenario: if I couldn't sleep, I would get sick, would lose weight, tuberculosis would be suspected, I would be sent to a sanitarium like Hans Castorp in *The Magic Mountain*. Nothing would be found, confusion, uncertainty, months of bed rest, and in the course of all that turmoil, I would never have to acknowledge that my novel was no more than a sentimental account of a hypersensitive boy, written by an immature author. Back at the YMCA I sat down to a bit of writing of a different kind. "Dear Mama, You were right; I was wrong. I am not ready yet to write the novel I had in mind. It's almost finished but I'm not going to finish it because I know now it is not good. I am going back to college." Then I went to bed and fell sound asleep.

I went then to the University of Texas and took a bachelor's degree in 1937 with a major in literature. Following graduation, I became a student of economics, due to the influence of a remarkable and charismatic teacher, Clarence Ayres. At the same time I was also writing plays and acting in amateur theatricals. From 1936 to 1938, I was the director of the Austin Little Theater, living at starvation level. My salary was $100 per production and there were five productions a year. Each play ran for three nights a week for two weeks. It was during these years that I found myself studying Freud and Adler. I could have found an additional job to make extra money, but was writing plays in every spare moment. By this time I was married and was beginning to feel acutely how precarious was the career I seemed to have chosen. I decided that I should find a way to make a living first, and then arrange some way to write. So I went to medical school, because medicine was the tradition in my family. My father and grandfather, and all of my grandfather's brothers were physicians, and I knew that as a physician I could do useful work and also make a living. I arrived in New York City with my wife on September 1, 1939, with a scholarship to Columbia University, College of Physicians and Surgeons, the day the German armies invaded Poland and began World War II.

My most admired and revered teacher was Robert Loeb, Professor of Medicine. He had not much use for psychiatry or psychoanalysis, and urged me to become an internist; so by the time I graduated I had no idea of becoming a psychiatrist. My wife had been supporting me throughout medical school, and I felt much indebted to her. I wanted to intern at the Peter Bent Brigham Hospital, and Loeb offered to make it possible, but it paid nothing, and my wife would have had to continue to support me. In order to take over this responsibility, I became an intern at Chelsea Naval Hospital, much to Loeb's dismay. As it turned out, this proved to be an extraordinarily good internship. The attending staff was made up of members of the medical faculties of Harvard and Boston University and, because it was war-time, they were now staffing the Naval Hospital. In 1944, after the internship, I was assigned to the marines and sent overseas. Just by chance I didn't go to Iwo Jima. I did go to Okinawa, but was in a reserve division that didn't land. Much of every day I was free. I began writing another novel and decided that the medical specialty with the most relatedness to literature was psychiatry. By the time I was discharged from the navy, in the late spring of 1946, I knew I wanted to be a psychoanalyst.

During the post-war years, psychoanalysis was at the zenith of its prestige as a therapy and as a theory. I wanted to go to the newly formed psychoanalytic institute at Columbia University, and was accepted, but the appointment paid nothing, and I now had a wife and two children to support. Again I approached Robert Loeb. He shook his head ruefully at my being so stubbornly on the "wrong track," but sent me to his friend Lawrence Kubie. I trudged down to #8-1/2 East 81st Street and met the remarkable man, told him I wanted training in both psychiatry and psychoanalysis, and at the same time had to make a living. He picked up the phone, called Karl Menninger—such was his dramatic way—and said I was coming. Within hours I was on a train. In Topeka I was given a battery of psychological tests by David Rapaport, was interviewed, and was accepted.

In Topeka, 1946 to 1947, I became acquainted with the choleric and bombastic Karl Menninger, the quiet, school-masterish Robert Knight, the Talmudic logician David Rapaport, and the reserved, ambitious Roy Schafer. Also present and much in evidence were Merton Gill and Margaret Brenman with their project in hypnotherapy. Erik Erikson was a visiting lecturer coming every month or so.

Robert Knight was our most admired and respected teacher, and when early in 1947 he announced his forthcoming departure to become medical director of the Austen Riggs Foundation in Stockbridge, Massachusetts, it was felt as a tremendous loss in Topeka. It was a great surprise and a great honor when, a month later, he asked me to come with him. I happily accepted. The same offer was made to Sam Tabbat who was already in analysis with Robert Knight. Roy Schafer came too.

In September of 1947, the four of us from Topeka arrived in Stockbridge, where Ed Howard had been the acting director. Two psychiatrists, two residents, and one psychologist—that was the entire staff from 1947 to 1948. It was a time of very hard work, all of the cases being worked up and presented by me or by Tabbat, with case conferences three times a week. An exciting and pivotal year, my life tilting ever further away from my Southern origins. I applied to and was accepted by the New York Psychoanalytic Institute. That involved the making of special arrangements for classes on Saturday mornings. At the same time I began a training analysis with Bob Knight, for whom I continued to have great admiration. He had an openness of mind and a modesty about what he knew that was not widespread among psychoanalysts of that time.

In 1947 and the years that followed, Riggs was kept full of patients by referrals from Lawrence Kubie in New York. Many of them were young people, college students. Most of them were very disturbed, character disorders or, as we called them then, ambulatory schizophrenics. We saw a lot of these patients get better, including the very sick ones. My understanding of therapeutic action was the commonly accepted model of insight, *emotional* insight, facilitating change. We also saw a lot of these patients who had got better get worse again after they went home. Many would come back.

It was a therapeutic community; and the clinical improvement was a consequence not simply of the four times weekly psychoanalytic psychotherapy, but of the supportive context, the holding environment, protective nursing, and ancillary group activities. A sense of community was established, and had enormous therapeutic effect. The imaginative and supportive activities program had been created by Joan Erikson and by a number of artists whom she engaged as instructors, such as Bill Gibson.

It was a turning point in my life to be in this small intimate professional setting with people whom I so much respected, and to have the experience of being myself in analysis, and beginning to take courses in analysis. I drove to New York every Saturday, leaving Stockbridge around five or six in the morning to arrive for a nine o'clock course. The arrangements were made for me and for two other candidates who also lived at some distance from New York. The three of us would meet in New York and would have four or five hours of training over the course of Saturday. Heinz Hartmann, Lawrence Kubie, Ernst Kris, Rudolf Loewenstein, Annie Reich, and Kurt Eissler were our teachers. There were no lecturers or formal case presentations, we simply met and talked with mentors.

While I flourished in this training, I experienced also the beginnings of a lasting distress at the dogmatic tone of psychoanalysis, of the certainties it offered on such scant evidence. It was too sure of itself, presumptuous in its claim to an inside line on truth, and in its reductive dismissal of other avenues of knowing. I was becoming skeptical. The culture was in flux and psychoanalysis was being accorded the potential of salvation, a promise that we—both as individuals and as a society—might rise above the conditions of life as we had known it to something better and finer. I didn't believe it. I was becoming a doubter, everywhere finding incompatibilities and incongruities, baroque conjectures blithely asserted as facts. I felt myself becoming a maverick, apostate to the dogma being offered. I never liked this position, never announced it, never claimed it; but as my psychoanalytic training progressed, I felt increasingly isolated from teachers and colleagues. They seemed, as the years passed, to know more and more, while I was knowing less and less. I was moving to the periphery of psychoanalysis. I never wanted to be a rebel, have never wanted to establish a school of thought that would challenge psychoanalysis. Psychoanalysis was simply losing credibility for me without my having anything credible to offer in its place. I had only skepticism.

While Robert Knight was a true believer, he had grown up in the Midwest in an atmosphere of pragmatism and empiricism, and had been a school teacher, so his practice of psychoanalysis was leavened by a kind of American common sense, unlike some of the European immigrant psychoanalysts who were doctrinaire and sectarian. I never lost respect for him. He gathered around him a remarkable staff—Merton Gill, Margaret Brenman, David Rapaport, Joseph Chasell, Erik Erikson, Roy Schafer, and David Shapiro. Riggs became an internationally acclaimed center for psychoanalysis.

My own analysis lasted the two years that was then the minimum requirement of the New York Psychoanalytic Institute. There was no finality about its ending. I had never felt it to be necessary therapeutically, I was simply fulfilling a requirement. "This is not a complete analysis," Knight reported to the Education Committee, but "it suffices to meet training requirements." There was still current in those days the preposterous concept of a *complete* psychoanalysis.

Robert Knight looked for and found for me suitable cases for analysis, and those analyses were supervised by Robert Knight, Erik Erikson, and Joseph Chasell. I got into trouble with the New York Psychoanalytic Institute because a segment of the Education Committee felt that the cloistered situation at Riggs was "incestuous," and that a training analysis between staff members should not be allowed. I squeaked by and was graduated in 1951.

It was at this time that my first writing appeared. While I had written a lot of fiction and drama, none had been published. "Flight from Insight" appeared in the *Journal of the American Psychiatric Association* in 1949. Soon thereafter my first work of fiction, the story, "Goodbye, Mama," was published in *The New Yorker*.

During the years 1951 to 1953, I was, for the first time in unmediated contact with what it means to be an analyst, with what one can do and achieve. It seemed to me that psychoanalysis had been tremendously oversold to—and overbought by—a culture bereft of God but still hungry for salvation. I was disillusioned. The harvest it garnered seemed rather little compared to what had been promised. Out of that feeling of disillusionment, I wrote "Vocational Hazards of Psychoanalysis" (1957), mournful in tone because I was lamenting a loss of faith. Knight liked the paper and thought it should be published. Two or three days later, however, he called me into his office and said that, though he couldn't ask me *not* to publish it, Margaret Brenman, to whom he had shown it, felt it might bring discredit to the institution. He left it for me to decide. I thought his position was tactful and generous: he didn't want to censor or exclude the paper, but did let me know that he had become uneasy about its being published. I deferred to what I knew he wanted. Two or three years later, in San Francisco, with no longer any connection to Riggs, I again submitted the paper to Robert Knight, who was the American editor for the *International Journal of Psychoanalysis*. He accepted it and it was published in 1957. That paper then became a chapter in what was my first book, *The Quest for Identity*.

Following my move to San Francisco, I wrote two theoretical papers, "Will and Psychoanalysis" (1956), and "The Place of Action in Personality Change" (1950). They were offered as contributions to psychoanalytic theory, but were in fact efforts to nudge psychoanalytic theory in a different direction, according more place to conscious intent, conscious learning, and conscious behavioral attempts to change. I was moving closer to William James and John Dewey and the pragmatic psychologists, Thorstein Veblen and C. E. Ayres, and I realized after writing these two papers that I was now so far away from mainstream psychoanalytic theory that I couldn't comfortably contribute to the field. As a consequence, I moved more and more towards literary expression. And then I found myself riding two independent and willful horses, addressing psychological issues and at the same time trying to make literature. Such has been the distinguishing characteristic, as well as the burden and the bane, of my professional life—part writer of literature and part psychological thinker. My books contain narrative fiction along with theoretical inquiry. My first book, *The Quest for Identity* (1958), was made up of chapters of inquiry into the social psychology of American life interspersed with chapters of personal narrative illustrative of social change.

As a psychotherapist I have been an independent. Only in the first two or three supervised analyses could I be said to have followed a proper Freudian protocol with proper Freudian assumptions. Thereafter I have used everything I know, in whatever ways compassion and empathy and respect might suggest, to understand and to help my patients. Of theory I do not believe much. My bedrock beliefs are that people can change and that one person can help another.

Nothing can be falsified in psychoanalysis. Kohut cannot displace Klein. Freud wanted to be, not only right, but right in such a way as would prove others wrong. In this he fails. We all fail. Freud makes his appeal—and a very powerful appeal it is—not by being preemptively right about anything, but by offering a vision of human life that makes sense of our experience. But it doesn't make complete sense, nor exclusive sense. No one is drummed out, no view is exorcised. Jung makes his appeal in the same way. And Rank and Sullivan and Horney and all the rest. A chorus of contending voices, each with a catchy tune, and each claiming to be the one true theme. How we are to make sense of our lives is not something that some great genius can get straight once and for all, but an ongoing task of interpretation in a changing field.

REFERENCES

Wheelis, A. (1949). Flight from insight. *American Journal of Psychiatry, 105,* 915-919.

Wheelis, A. (1950). The place of action and personality change. *Psychiatry: Journal of Interpersonal Processes, 13,* 135-148.

Wheelis, A. (1951). Goodbye Mama. *The New Yorker.* October 13, 1951.

Wheelis, A. (1956). Will and psychoanalysis. *Journal of the American Psychoanalytic Association. IV,* 285-303.

Wheelis, A. (1957). Vocational hazards of psychoanalysis. *International Journal of Psychoanalysis, 37,* 171-184.

Wheelis, A. (1958). *The quest for identity.* New York: Norton.

CHAPTER 18

BACK TO THE FUTURE
JOSEPH J. SHAY, PH.D. AND
JOAN WHEELIS, M.D.

We hope that the preceding chapters have offered a clearer understanding of where psychotherapy has been in the past century, especially in the last 50 years, and how it has changed. Embedded within these personal odysseys is not only the history of psychotherapy but also clues to its future trajectory. As much as we now know, we also know that we do not yet possess the answers we are seeking. The currents that have carried us to our modern understandings have not brought us to the end of the journey, but they have transported us to a place of greater clarity. While we have not yet discovered the DNA of psychotherapy, we are searching. Our contributors have spent their lives engaged in this process of searching, of examining or transforming our earlier paradigms, a process described by Kuhn (1962/1996) as "intrinsically revolutionary... [and] seldom completed by a single man and never overnight" (p. 7).

While the reader can draw his or her own conclusions about whether and how the paradigm has shifted, we offer three central observations about the structure of psychotherapy that emerge from our reading of these chapters. We follow these observations with predictions about some likely paths the field of psychotherapy will take.

WHAT DO WE KNOW?

After a century of presumed progress, it is extraordinary—discouraging to some—that we know so little for certain.

While we have highlighted, in our introductory chapter, convergences among our contributors, it is also clear that as a whole they do not wear the same lenses to view the psychotherapy universe. We have not yet created a manual of "truths" shared across orientations, and we have not yet agreed upon even a single North Star to guide us. In attempting to distill the wisdom of our contributors, there are, however, three indisputable conclusions we can offer. While they will seem simple and obvious, and certainly not original, we can hold them as the current "truths" upon which new understandings will be fashioned.

First, *psychotherapy is not psychotherapy is not psychotherapy.* While we all know roughly what we mean by psychotherapy, namely, two (or more) people in a room having a serious conversation about the problems of one of them, the nature of this conversation, and of the experience that accompanies it, vary widely across therapists. To witness, for example, Edward Shapiro (see chapter 15) in one office and Arnold Lazarus (see chapter 8) in another illuminates this point. Witnessing is worth a thousand words. We have hundreds of models of therapy, hundreds of thousands of practitioners working within these models, and millions of interventions offered by these practitioners, with many of these interventions only marginally, if at all, within the models they espouse. Every therapist—every therapist—knows this to be true. As Renik (1998) says, let's get real.

Second, *a patient is not a patient is not a patient.* All therapists know, as well, that patients arrive in the office at different ages, with different issues, at different developmental stages, with different goals, at different levels of crisis, with different ideologies of change, of different genders, with different cognitive capacities, and even—to be inclusive but not to be crass—with different financial resources. This "truth" of difference has been submerged for much of the history of psychotherapy, perhaps because it might have paralyzed the progress of the field to have been identified too soon. The inevitable ramification of this idea of difference is that psychotherapists must, of necessity, gear their understandings and their interventions toward the particular person before them in the room. Fortunately, the first observation above—that psychotherapy is not a unitary process—can dovetail beautifully with this second.

The third observation flows logically from the first two, and has also been experienced by all therapists and essentially confirmed by our contributors. As much as we have struggled with the issue, *we do not yet understand the nature of the change process.* If psychotherapy is not a unitary phenomenon, and if patients are notably different, then it would seem to follow that the change process may not be unitary either. The nature of change cannot be easily or cleanly separated from *what* (which focus) is to be changed in *whom* (which patient), or *when* (at which point in one's life), *how* (which model), or *by whom* (which therapist).

Where, then, are we going?

PREDICTIONS FOR THE FUTURE

It is a verity that no one can predict the future. As Yogi Berra famously said, "Prediction is very hard, especially when it's about the future." Nonetheless, based on what we have learned from our contributors as well as our own perspective, we have some thoughts about where the field of psychotherapy is likely to go. Our selection of epigrams at the start of this book points to the direction of our predictions, namely, that what lies ahead will build on what has gone before, will periodically circle back to some of the very positions left behind, and will also be, at times, completely original. Moreover, the future of psychotherapy will predictably interact with the future of other developments in society. As the millennium turns, there are revolutions occurring in the computer world, the biomolecular world, and the quantum physics world (Kaku, 1997). Changes in the social, economic, and political spheres will also predictably affect the changing shape of psychotherapy, as will movements toward the integration of knowledge itself (e.g., Wilson, 1998).

What paths might this take? First, integrative models of therapy are on the verge of gaining hegemony and will do so, largely because of the general recognition of the three observations offered above. One size of psychotherapy cannot fit all, so different sizes are going to be tried. Initially, this will occur in an eclectic ("mix-and-match") way until we develop a deeper understanding of what works best for whom (e.g., Beutler & Clarkin, 1990; Norcross & Goldfried, 1992; Prochaska, 1995).

Conversely, a significant minority of therapists, viewing this move toward integration as a slide toward dilution and imprecision, will want to preserve some of the older forms in purer fashion. Partly, they will be driven in this direction because their careers are tied to particular forms, partly because they see a salvageable baby in the bathwater, and partly because history tells us that movement in one direction often occasions a dialectic pull in the opposite direction. The tension between these two forces will occasion significant advances in our thinking as increasingly sophisticated research paradigms result in our being compelled to discard particular, albeit cherished, disproven ideas.

Second, psychotherapists of all disciplines will be thinking more about biology. Research into the human genome, neurophysiological processes, and biological pathways of behavior and thought will provide rich material for therapists to consider in trying to understand the mind, the body, and behavior.

Third, a growing number of therapists will pioneer interventions that make use of computers and the internet and other technologies not yet developed. We will see more therapy occurring outside of an office setting, and, as a result, learn more about which qualities of the relationship are necessary for change. "Virtual" therapy may become a commonplace term.

Fourth, psychotherapy will no longer ignore society's changing demographics. By 2050, when almost half of the United States will consist of people of color (Tomes, 1998), multicultural psychotherapy will be far more influential. Current psychotherapeutic models are entirely unprepared for this shift in demographics.

Fifth, in the next hundred years we will develop a more refined understanding of the nature of change. As above, it will be clear that *change is not change is not change*. More specifically, we will separate change into various components, among them, the nature of change, the agents of change, the conditions of change, the mechanisms of change, and the biology of change. And then, we will put these components back together into a unifying model of change. The poetry of psychotherapy and the science of psychotherapy will each be given a prominent place in this unification.

Sixth, as psychotherapists more closely examine the nature of change, we will increasingly turn to Eastern cultures for whom change (impermanence) is central to religious thought and practice (e.g., Nakamura, 1964/1985). Buddhist philosophy, for instance, will continue to make significant inroads into psychotherapeutic models (e.g., Epstein, 1995).

Finally, historical analyses of psychotherapy will continue to examine psychotherapeutic endeavors of the time in the context of what has gone before. In that history, we today are the "before." Some of these efforts will ask how, at the turn of the millennium, intelligent professionals could have held some of the beliefs we hold today. Historians of psychotherapy will ask, how did we get here and where are we going?

> *We shall not cease from exploration.*
> *And the end of all our exploring*
> *Will be to arrive where we started*
> *And know the place for the first time.*
> *"Little Gidding," T. S. Eliot*

REFERENCES

Berger, P. L., & Luckmann, T. (1967). *The social construction of reality: A treatise in the sociology of knowledge.* Garden City, NY: Anchor Books.

Beutler, L. E., & Clarkin, J. (1990). *Selective treatment selection: Toward targeted therapeutic interventions.* New York: Brunner/Mazel.

Consumer Reports. (1995, November). Mental health: Does therapy help? 734-739.

Epstein, M. (1995). *Thoughts without a thinker: Psychotherapy from a Buddhist perspective.*

Frank, J. D. (1973). *Persuasion and healing* (2nd ed.). Baltimore: Johns Hopkins University Press.

Kaku, M. (1997). *Visions: How science will revolutionize the 21st century.* New York: Anchor Books.

Kuhn, T. S. (1996). *The structure of scientific revolutions* (3rd ed.). Chicago & London: University of Chicago. (Original work published 1962)

Nakamura, H. (1985). *Ways of thinking of Eastern peoples: India, China, Tibet, Japan.* Honolulu, HI: East-West Center Press. (Original work published 1964).

Norcross, J. C., & Goldfried, M. R. (Eds.). (1992). *Handbook of psychotherapy integration.* New York: Basic Books.

Prochaska, J. O. (1995). An eclectic and integrative approach: Transtheoretical therapy. In A. S. Gurman & S. B. Messer (Eds.), *Essential psychotherapies: Theory and practice* (pp. 403-440). New York: Guilford Press.

Renik, O. (1998). Getting real in analysis. *Psychoanalytic Quarterly, 67,* 566-593.

Schnog, N. (1997). On inventing the psychological. In J. Pfister & N. Schnog (Eds.), *Inventing the psychological: Toward a cultural history of emotional life in America* (pp. 3-16). New Haven and London: Yale University Press.

Seligman, M. (1995). The effectiveness of psychotherapy: The *Consumer Reports* study. *American Psychologist, 50,* 965-974.

Tomes, H. (1998, December). Diversity: Psychology's life depends on it. *APA Monitor,* p. 28.

van den Berg, J. H. (1961). *The changing nature of man: Introduction to a historical psychology.* New York: Norton.

Wilson, E. O. (1998). *Consilience: The unity of knowledge.* New York: Knopf.

NAME INDEX

A

Abraham, H., 289
Abraham, K., 289
Abram, D., 269
Abramovitz, A., 170
Ackerman, D., 176
Ackerman, N., 192
Ackner, B., 288
Adams, J., 74
Adler, A., 396
Adler, G., 250
Adorno, T., 290
Alarcon, R., 51
Alexander, F., 36, 37
Anderson, H., 230
Anthony, J., 289, 296, 297
Aron, L., 60, 225, 321, 381
Arsenian, J., 192
Ayres, C., 396, 401

B

Bader, M., 258
Bakhtin, M., 291, 302
Baldwin, J., 48
Baliat, M., 297, 299, 300
Bandura, A., 175
Banks, A., 139
Bart, P., 137
Bass, A., 6
Bass, E., 1
Bateson, G., 108
Bateson, M. C., 54
Begley, S., 4
Belar, C., 203
Benjamin, J., 83
Bennett, M. J., 27, 35
Berg, I., 113, 114
Berger, P., 5, 216

Bergholz, S., 72
Bergin, A., 188
Berk, S., 203
Berkowitz, D., 263, 345, 346
Bernfeld, S., 256, 270, 271
Bernstein, J., 261
Berschied, E., 266, 267
Bertoff, H., 269, 271
Bettelheim, B., 100
Beutler, L. E., 175, 405
Berwick, D. M., 34
Bibring, E., 342
Bibring, G., 72, 73, 74, 99, 104, 342
Bickerton, D., 6
Bierer, J., 302
Bion, W., 292, 294, 309, 343
Biren, J., 146
Bishop, H., 129
Blake, W., 278
Blatt, S., 10, 362, 363
Bolan, R., 84
Boszormenyi-Nagy, I., 193
Bowen, M., 190
Bowers, K.S., 375
Bowlby, J., 287
Boyd-Franklin, N., 60
Bozarth, J.D., 175
Brenman, M., 397, 400, 401
Brodie, H.K.H., 129, 130
Brooks, G.R., 198
Bruner, E., 68
Bruner, J., 13, 211
Buber, M., 253
Budman, Gabrielle, 27, 28
Budman, Shari, 27, 35
Budman, Simon H., 11, 12, 13, 18-45
Budman, Susan, 23, 28, 35
Buie, D.H., 243, 246, 249, 250
Butler, S., 35

C

Campbell, L. E., 228
Carr, A.W., 213, 338, 349, 350
Catherall, D.R., 224
Chase, T., 129
Chasell, J., 400
Chevron, G., 34, 226
Cienfuegos, A., 61
Chiauzzi, E., 35
Clark, A., 111
Clark, D., 289
Clark, J., 269
Clarke, C., 269
Clarkin, J., 406
Cohen, L., 46
Coles, R., 211
Collins, J., 29, 30
Collins, L., 46
Colman, K., 192
Comas-Díaz, L., 11, 12, 46-66
Cooley, C.H., 300
Corsini, R.J., 167, 168
Cosh, J., 269
Crisp, A., 243
Cummings, N. A., 3, 34, 201
Cushman, P., 122

D

Davis, L., 1
Davison, G.C., 173
Dawes, R. M., 182
deMare, P., 297
Dean, R., 11, 12, 67-95
Deck, A., 146
DeLeon, P.H., 3
Demby, A., 27, 28, 36
Demos, J., 2, 5

Deutsch, F., 99
Deutsch, H., 290, 342
Dewey, J., 401
Dicks, H.V., 217
DiClemente, C. C., 36
Doering, C., 129
Dollard, J., 363
Dossey, L., 269, 272
Doyle, G., 196
Dumont, M., 122
Duncan, B., 52
Dunne, B., 269

E

Eisold, K., 261, 354
Eissler, K., 399
Elias, N., 290, 300, 301, 307, 308
Elmendorf, D., 352
Emde, R., 301
Endler, N., 375, 379
Epstein, M., 407
Epston, D., 90, 110
Erikson, E., 70, 148, 211, 291, 300,
    343, 345, 347, 362, 397, 398, 400
Erikson, J., 398
Ewalt, J., 340, 341
Eysenck, H., 2, 188, 288, 290
Ezriel, H., 294

F

Fairbairn, W. R. D., 76, 217
Fanon, F., 48
Faros, P. F., 192
Fay, A., 176
Feldstein, M., 27, 34, 136
Fenby, B.L., 86
Fenichel, O., 147

Fenwick, P., 273, 274
Ferenezi, S., 256, 265
Fiddler, J., 303
Fiedler, F. E., 1
Fishman, H., 223
Fleck, S., 52, 53
Fleck-Henderson, A., 89
Foege, W. H., 203
Foley, G. M., 226
Foulkes, S. H., 10, 289-294, 297, 301, 303, 306, 308
Framo, J., 225
Frank, J. D., 1
Frank, K. A., 225
Frank, R., 203
Frazier, S., 347, 350
Freedheim, D. K., 2, 56
Freedman, J., 348
Freedman, L., 76
Freeman, J., 3
Friere, P., 50
French, T., 36, 37
Freud, A., 99, 289, 297, 299, 362
Freud, E., 299
Freud, Sigmund, 2, 5, 7, 10, 11, 12, 26, 41, 72, 97, 98, 127, 149, 212, 244, 256, 257, 278, 305, 312, 343, 368, 371, 396
Freud, Sophie, 10, 11, 12, 13, 96-125 (See also Loewenstein, S. F.)
Freudenberger, H. J., 2
Fromm, E., 265, 290, 300, 364
Fromm, M. G., 347
Fromm-Reichmann, F., 6, 237, 290
Futcher, J., 146

G

Gabbard, G. O., 225, 294
Garfield, S., 188
Gartrell, N., 11, 12, 13, 126-146
Gergen, K. J., 230
Gergen, M. M., 230
Gerson, M. J., 225
Gibson, W., 398
Gilden, L., 23
Gill, M. M., 382, 383, 397, 400
Gilligan, J., 122
Gladwell, M., 6
Glass, G.V., 189
Goffman, E., 107, 108
Gold, M., 27
Goldenberg, I., 191
Goldfried, M.R., 1, 173, 406
Goldner, V., 223, 225
Goldstein, K., 290
Goleman, D., 4, 157
Goodfield, J., 268
Goodson, W., 136
Goolishan, H. A., 230
Gottman, J., 223
Gray, B., 192
Greenberger, D., 140
Griffith, E. H., 57
Grotjahn, M., 298
Guerney, B., 194
Gunderson, J., 341
Guntrip, H., 76
Gurman, A., 11, 18, 31, 36

H

Hadden, S., 303
Haley, J., 192, 222, 228
Hall, M., 140, 146
Hamilton, G., 74
Hamilton, J., 139
Hare-Mustin, R., 223
Harman, W., 269, 271
Harris, J. R., 6
Hartmann, H., 362, 377, 399
Healy, D., 237
Heimann, P., 298
Held, B. S., 182
Hendrick, I., 236, 342
Hendryx, J., 129
Herman, J., 134, 136
Herman, S.M., 186
Hersch, C., 191
Hill, D., 290
Hill, S. S., 2
Ho, M.H., 60
Hoffer, H., 298
Hoffman, I., 320, 321
Hoffman, L., 223, 230
Hollis, F., 74
Holquist, M., 291
Holt, R., 366
Horkheimer, M., 290
Horney, K., 256, 264, 300, 363, 402
Howard, E., 398
Howard, G.S., 60

J

Ja, D. Y., 62
Jackson, D., 192
Jackson, M., 289
Jacobsen, F. M., 53, 54, 55, 56

Jacoby, R., 390
John, R. G., 269, 271, 275
Jalali, B., 58
James, H., 251
James, W., 291, 401
Jaschunsky, M. R., 283
Johnson, J. R., 228
Johnson, L., 74
Johnstone, B., 203
Jones, E., 287
Jordan, J. V., 11, 12, 132, 147-166
Jung, C., 5

K

Kaku, M., 405
Kantor, D., 218, 219, 221
Kaplan, A., 11, 132
Kaplan, H. S., 224
Kaschak, E., 140
Kassan, L. D., 9
Katz, J., 129
Keeney, B., 109, 193
Keller, E., 268
Kellner, H., 216
Kelly, J., 196
Kernberg, O., 149, 213, 294, 344, 345
Ketcham, K., 1
King, P., 294
Kinnier, T., 135
Klauber, J., 300
Klein, G., 366
Klein, M., 76, 99, 213, 289, 299, 343, 382
Kleinman, A., 62
Klerman, G., 34, 35, 191
Knight, R., 357, 397, 398, 400, 401
Kohut, H., 80, 149, 294, 300, 301, 344, 345

Kolb, J. E., 348
Kolodny, R., 129
Koocher, G. P., 2
Kopecky, G., 197, 198
Kopp, S., 26
Kraemer, H., 129
Kramer, P., 1
Kreeger, L., 293
Kreitzberg, C. B., 174
Kris, A., 351
Kris, E., 362, 399
Krokoff, L. F., 223
Kubie, L., 397, 398, 399
Kuhn, T. S., 5, 6, 403
Kundera, M., 196
Kwee, M. G. T., 180
Kwee-Taams, M. K., 180

L

Laing, R.D., 214
Laird, R.A., 195
Lamb, M., 196
Landauer, K., 290
Landes, A., 180
Langer, 19-21, 38
Laufer, M., 299
Lazare, A., 192
Lazarus, A. A., 2, 10, 11, 12, 13, 167-186, 404
Lazarus, C. N., 176
Lehr, W., 219
Lester, E., 294
Levant, R. F., 11, 187-208
Levy, B., 192
Lewin, K., 304
Lewis, A., 287, 288, 293
Lichtenstein, H., 291, 300, 301
Lightsey, J., 238

Lindsey, G., 28
Linneman, E., 304
Lipman-Blumen, J., 267
Lo, B., 36
Localio, R., 136
Loeb, R., 396, 397
Loewald, H., 291, 300, 301
Loewenstein, R., 362-399
Loewenstein, S. F., 96, 101, 107, 109, 110, 111, 112 (See also Freud, Sophie)
Loftus, E., 1
Loiselle, J., 196
Loriaux, L., 129
Lorimer, D., 269, 275, 276
Luborsky, L., 189
Luckmann, T., 5
Luepnitz, D. A., 112
Lykes, B., 51

M

Macht, L., 192
Magausson, D., 375, 379
Mahler, M., 301
Main, T. F., 292, 293
Malan, D., 26, 294, 298, 300
Maltas, C., 11, 12, 209-235
Maltsberger, J. T., 10, 12, 236-252
Mann, J., 36, 80
Mannheim, K., 290
Marcuse, H., 290
Masters, W., 129, 296
Maudsley, H., 288
May, R., 5, 7
Mayer, E. L., 10, 11, 12, 253-281
Mayne, A., 269
McClelland, D., 191
McClintock, B., 268

McCracken, J., 82
McGill, D. W., 60
McGinnis, J. M., 203
McGlashan, T., 341
McWhirter, E., 135
Mead, G. H., 291, 300
Meahi, P., 182
Meissner, W., 213
Memmi, A., 42, 55
Meng, H., 290
Menninger, K., 397
Merry, J., 36
Messer, S., 389
Metha, A., 135
Meyer, A., 5
Miller, G., 191
Miller, J. B., 11, 132, 134, 152, 154,
    155, 156
Miller, N., 363
Miller, S., 114
Milliken, N., 136
Minrath, M., 52
Minuchin, S., 110, 111, 192, 222, 223
Mischel, W., 365, 366, 378
Mitchell, S., 225, 304, 381
Mohammed, Z., 195
Monelli, C., 61
Moreno, J., 302, 303
Morrison, A., 109
Mosbacher, D., 139, 146
Mosher, R. L., 194
Mosley, O., 286
Muir, R. C., 214
Mulgan, G., 308
Murphy, G., 171
Murray, H., 148
Myerson, P., 339

N

Nagera, U., 299
Naiburg, S., 66
Nakamura, H., 407
Nelson, W., 196
Nemiah, J., 80
Norcross, J. C., 2, 36, 56, 175, 406

O

O'Brien, P., 137
Ogden, T. H., 240
Olarte, S., 136

P

Padesky, C., 140
Padilla, A., 54
Parkin, A., 289
Patterson, C. J., 138
Payne, M., 269
Payne, S., 287
Penn, P., 223
Peoc'h, R., 273, 276
Perry, S., 104
Pert, C., 272
Peterson, D. R., 182
Pfister, J., 2
Pierce, C., 191
Piercy, F., 195
Pines, A., 285
Pines, D., 283
Pines, I., 283
Pines, L., 283
Pines, M., 10, 11, 12, 282-311
Pleck, J., 134
Pollack, W. S., 198
Prelinger, E., 363

Prochaska, J. O., 36, 42, 406
Putnam, J. J., 99
Putnam, M., 99

R

Rabinovitz, J., 196
Radin, D., 276
Rafaelsen, L., 304
Ramos-McKay, J., 50
Rank, B., 99
Rank, O., 99, 402
Rapaport, D., 362, 382, 397, 400
Reder, P.A., 111
Reed, N., 139
Reich, A., 399
Reich, L., 192
Reich, W., 290
Reiss, D., 10, 345
Renik, O., 10, 11, 12, 13, 225, 261,
    312-336, 404
Rey, H., 289
Rhodes, M., 92
Rhue, T., 129
Richmond, M., 74
Rodas, C., 139
Rogers, C., 5, 191
Rogers, W., 191
Rosen, R.C., 176
Ross, M., 203
Roth, S. A., 86
Rothblum, E., 146
Rotter, J.B., 175
Rounsaville, B. J., 34, 226
Rowe, R., 191
Rycroft, C., 298

S

Salk, J., 268
Sampson, H., 36, 254, 256
Sandler, A.M., 299
Sandler, J., 299
Sarason, S., 10, 362, 363
Sasserath, V. J., 174
Satir, V., 192
Schafer, R., 230, 397, 398, 400
Scharff, D. E., 221
Scharff, J. S., 221, 345
Scharfstein, S., 341
Schatzberg, A., 341
Schnog, N., 2, 3, 6
Schon, D.A., 84
Schwartz, D., 337
Seligman, M., 12, 183, 202
Selvini-Palazzoli, M., 222, 223
Semrad, E., 10, 236, 237, 238, 241,
    242, 245, 250, 340, 341
Shapiro, E. R., 10, 11, 12, 213, 337-
    358, 404
Shapiro, R., 10, 213, 343, 344, 345,
    346, 349
Shay, J., 1-17, 66, 217, 403-408
Sheinberg, M., 223
Sheldrake, R., 274, 275, 276
Shlien, J., 191, 192
Shneidman, E., 244
Sholomaskas, P., 226
Shon, S., 62
Shorter, E., 2, 3, 6, 7
Sifneos, P., 36, 80
Silverstein, L., 198
Singer, B., 189
Skinner, B.F., 5, 211, 362
Skolimowski, H., 267, 271
Skynner, R., 215

Slavson, S., 304
Smith, M. L., 189
Socarides, C., 134
Soldz, S., 36
Spark, G.M., 193
Sparks, C., 139
Spence, D., 68
Sperry, R., 269
Spitz, R., 301
Sprenkle, D. H., 193
Sprinthall, N. A., 194
Standal, S.W., 167, 168
Stanton, A., 237
Stechler, G., 225
Steenbarger, B. N., 36
Steinglass, P., 222
Steiner, R., 294
Stephen, A., 287, 305, 306
Stephen, K., 287, 306
Stern, D. B., 85, 301
Stiver, I., 11, 132, 152, 154, 156
Stock, M., 342
Stone, E., 60
Strachey, A., 287, 306
Strachey, J., 287, 306
Strickland, B., 51
Sullivan, H. S., 164, 168, 237, 265,
    300, 363, 381, 402
Surrey, J., 11, 132
Sutherland, J. D., 294
Sutton, P. M., 193
Suzuki, S., 39
Swenson, C., 82
Szasz, T., 1

T

Tabbat, S., 398
Talmon, M., 2

Tansey, M., 295
Tarshis, L., 196
Tartakoff, H., 342
Tharoor, S., 62
Thiemann, S., 136
Thomas, J. L., 34
Tomes, H., 406
Toro, G., 129
Turner, C., 51
Turner, F., 271

U

Ullman, L., 173

V

Valenstein, E. S., 237
van den Berg, J.H., 4
Vandenbos, G. R., 3, 4, 56
Veblen, T., 401
Villapiano, A., 35
Vorenberg, J., 74

W

Wachtel, E. F., 225, 383, 384
Wachtel, P. L., 10, 11, 12, 13, 225,
    359-392
Waelder, R., 290
Waldfogel, D., 82
Walker, G., 228
Wallach, 19-21, 38
Wayne, S., 192
Weingarten, K., 86
Weisman, A., 341, 342
Wertlieb, D., 28
Weiss, J., 36
Weiss, S. R., 109

Weissman, M. M., 34, 52, 226
Wheatley, M., 267
Wheeler, J., 267
Wheelis, A., 11, 12, 393-402
Wheelis, J., 1-17, 403-408
Whitaker, C., 192
White, M., 90, 110
Wile, D., 384
Will, O., 337
Williams, T. A., 180
Williamson, D., 190
Wilshire, B. W., 291
Wilson, E. O., 405
Wilson, G.T., 183
Winer, R., 227
Winnicott, D., 76, 297, 299, 343
Wisneski, M. J., 27
Wolpe, J., 10, 168, 169, 170, 171, 173
Woolf, V., 287
Wynne, L., 343

Y

Yalom, I., 196

Z

Zinner, J., 213, 227, 343, 345, 346

SUBJECT INDEX

A

absence of action of therapist, 225
abuse of children, 156
abuse of patients, 136
accusatory interpretations, 384–385
actions of therapist, 225
acute disconnections, 154–155
Adolescent and Family Treatment
    Unit (AFTU), 213, 214
advice to students, 115–120, 204
advocacy, 133
affect, behavior, cognition (ABC) tri-
    modal approach, 176
affect containment, 247
affective links, 344
agoraphobia, 168
AIDS, 87–89
ambivalence, 156
American Foundation of Suicide
    Prevention, 243–244
American Psychiatric Association
    (APA), 133–135, 136
amygdala hijack, 157
analysts. *See* clinicians
analytic gain, 258
anger, 243, 244
anonymity, analytic, 322
antidepressants, 138
anti-purism theme, 11
anxiety, 371–372
anxiety as discharge phenomenon,
    371–372
arch-behaviorism, 172
arrogance of practitioners, 151

assessments, elements of thorough,
    176–179
associations for group therapy,
    302–304
assumptions, individuals', 380
assumptions about people, 255–266
attitude, 164–166
autistic children, 100
auto-euthanasia, 244
average expectable environment, 376
aversion, 248

B

BASIC I.D., 175, 177–178
behavior, interpersonal, 375–376
behavioral change, 139, 225
behavioral health products, 33–34
behavior as predictor of response,
    378
behavior therapy, 170, 366–367, 370
beliefs, unconscious, 272
bereavement in children, 104
Biological Modality, 178
blaming the victim, 50, 150
blank screen therapists, 26
Boston University Fatherhood
    Project, 195–196
boundary establishment, 353
boundary violations, 137
brain functioning, 162
breadth of training, 171, 183
brief therapy, 11, 113, 138. *See also*
    time-effective therapy
British object relations theory, 213

C

case-specific needs, 324
centrality of relationships, 161
change
  behavioral, 139, 225
  nature of, 406–407
  participants in, 163–164
  process of, 379–380, 405
  promoting, 372
"character armor," 225
character disorders, 246
characteristics of observers, 268
childhood wound, 393
children
  abuse of, 156
  autistic, 100
  bereavement in, 104
  child guidance culture, 105
  dysfunctional child guidance
    model, 105–106
  parentified, 97
  schizophrenia in, 108
chlorpromazine, 237
chronic disconnection, 154–155
circular versus linear processes, 383
classical theory, 72–73, 368
client-centered therapy, 5, 130, 193
"clients" versus "patients," 5
clinical intuition, 84, 254–255, 262
clinicians
  arrogance of, 151
  of color, 51
  countertransference as error of,
    375
  early training of, 4
  erotic responses to clients,
    247–248
  exploitive, 136–137

homosexuality in, 83–84
interpretive role of, 352
language of, 384
multiple, 227
numbers of in the U.S., 4
as participant observers, 381–382
personal psychology of, 314–315
professional concerns of, 6
psychoanalysis of, 251
reasons for becoming, 97
self-disclosure by, 103, 116, 159,
  334
subjectivity of, 225
tasks of, 242
therapeutic alliance, 323
cognitive-behavioral modalities, 140,
  172, 354, 380
cognitive therapy, 171–172
collaboration, 86, 227, 260, 334
collectivism, 62
common ground, emerging, 225
communality, 115
communities, therapeutic, 353
community mental health approach,
  122
compassion, 164–166
complementary medicine, 269
condemned isolation, 155
conditioning therapy, 168
confidentiality, 354
conflict, 219, 380
congruence, 194
conjoint treatment, 221
connectedness, 79, 265–266, 272
connections, unseen, 267
Connective Era, 267
connexity, 308
conscience, 215

consciousness and physical world, 270

constructivism, 84–85, 229

constructivist family treatment, 86

containment of affect, 247

context, 49, 60

Control Mastery Theory (CMT), 36–39

contstructionist focus, 89–90

conversational principles, 257, 258

conversations about course of therapy, 260–261

corrective relational experience, 160

countertransference
 anger in, 243
 avoidance of, 375
 dealing with, 345
 erotic responses to clients, 247–248 |
 ethnocentric, 56
 failure in, 295–296
 hate in, 243
 irruption, 241
 universality of, 243

countertransference enactment, 320

critical incidents, 166–167

criticism by clients, 118

cross-cultural practice, 92

cultural diversity, 62–63

cultural issues, 51–52, 92

cultural stories, 60

cyclical psychodynamics, 373–374

D

decivilizing processes, 307–308

defenses, 214, 224, 244, 249

defensive delineation, 346

delayed gratification, 135

deliberate psychological education, 194

demographics, 406

desires, 215, 380, 381

Diagnostic and Statistical Manual (DSM), 4, 129

Dialectical- Behavior Therapy (DBT), 6

dialogue concept, 302

discharge phenomenon, 371–372

disciplined subjectivity, 345

disconnection, 154–155, 157, 162–163

distortion, 249, 376

diversity, cultural, 62–63

divorce process, 228

donor insemination (DI), 138–139

drama, 119

dyads, inter-ethnocultural therapeutic, 56

dysfunctional child guidance model, 105–106

dysfunction as representative of problems of living, 194

E

early psychotherapeutic thought, 2–3

Eastern concepts, 62

eclecticism, 170

educative functions of therapists, 248

effectiveness research, 202

egalitarian relationships, 133

ego-dystonic homosexuality, 130

ego psychological versions of psychoanalytic thought, 368–369

electroconvulsive treatment (ECT), 237

emerging common ground, 225
emotional holding, 248
emotionally isolated individuals, 114
empathic attunement, 156
empathic failure, 79
empathy, 130, 153, 271
empowerment, 137
enactment, countertransference, 320
enfolding of the observer, 271
erotic responses to clients, 247–248
Ethics Hotline, 121
ethics violations, 136
ethnic/racial/gender identity development, 60
ethnic transference issues, 56
ethnocultural liberation paradigm, 55
ethnocultural psychotherapy, 54–61
evolution of personality, 307–308
examined living communities, 353
existential analysis, 7
existential approach, 5
experiential schools of therapy, 195
experiments, chicks and rabbits, 273–274
exploitive therapists, 136–137
Eye Movement Desensitization Reprocessing (EMDR), 6

F

family communications, 345
family myths, 55–56
family systems therapy, 222
family therapy
    internal conflicts, 214
    as major approach, 373
    Minuchin's videotape of, 110

pioneers of, 192–193
structural/strategic, 111
Fatherhood Project, 195–196
fear in countertransference, 243
fears, exposing patient to, 372
feedback loops, 222
feedback on client's effect on therapist, 117–118
feminism, 113
flashbacks, 31
flexibility, 11, 25–26, 38, 74
flight into health, 31
focus of treatment, 39
folk healers, 49–50
follow-up investigations, 174
formative causation, 275
founders of schools of therapy, 11
frames of reference, 162–163
functioning, general rules of, 376
future of psychotherapy, 40–41,
    61–63, 181–182, 200–203, 388–390,
    405–407
fuzzy thinking, 262

G

gender identity development, 60
genuineness, 153
goal-oriented treatment, 140
goals of narrative theory, 113
good enough clinical encounters, 97
group analysis, 291–292, 301
"group as a whole" approach, 304
group psychotherapy, 109–110
group therapy associations, 302–304
growth, clinical, 93–94
growth-fostering relationships, 161

H

Hampstead Index, 299
hate in countertransference, 243, 248
health care facts, 203
historical background to psycho-
    analysis, 301–302, 305–306
historical schools of therapy, 195
HMOs, 27, 161–162. *See also* man-
    aged care
holism, 50
homework, 38–39
homophobia, 127
homosexuality, 83–84, 128, 129, 130
honesty, 118, 262
hostility, 377
humanistic approach, 5
humility, 164–166
hybrid mixtures of modalities, 41
hypnosis, 371

I

identity, sense of, 369–370
identity development, 60
imipramine, 237
impasses, 157
individual mode of psychic func-
    tioning, 214
infantile features, 368–369
"injustice collection," 122
Innovative Training Systems (ITS),
    33–34
insight, 139, 372
insight-oriented modalities, 140, 246
insulin shock treatment, 237
integrative models, 405–406

integrative thinking, 386
interconnectedness, 62
interdependency, 308
inter-ethnocultural therapeutic
    dyads, 56
interpersonal behavior, 375–376
interpretations
    of behavioral methods, 372
    giving "incorrect," 299
    idiosyncratic, 376, 379
    negotiated, 350
    of reality, 229–230
intersubjectivity, 161
interventions, "unpsychoanalytic,"
    225
intrapsychic defenses, 213
intrapsychic phenomena, 68
intuitive process, 84, 254–255, 262
investigative methodologies,
    267–268
involuntary hospitalization, 249
irrationality, 350
isolation, emotional, 114, 153

K

knowing-in-action, 84

L

language, 85, 108, 384
leaders in the field, 4–5
learning theory, 170
lesbians, 129
life as theater metaphor, 108
limit-setting, 249
linear versus circular processes, 383

lobotomies, 237
long-term treatment, 74
loving the patient, 247
low income clients, 74

M

major tranquilizers, 237
male emotion socialization process, 198
malice, 248
managed care, 93, 201–202, 337–338, 354
manuals, 183
marriage, 216–217
masochistic surrender, 295
medication. *See* psychopharmacology
memories, 367
mental health professionals. *See* clinicians
mentors, 34, 345
methodologies, 267–268, 350
Milan school, 86
mind-brain relation, 269
minimum sufficient network (MSN), 215, 227
minority clinicians, 51–52, 56
misguidedness, recognizing, 255
modeling process, 119–120
models
    dysfunctional child guidance, 105–106
    integrative, 405–406
    Newtonian physics as treatment, 151–152
    one-person, 381–382
    psycho-educational, 110, 194
    relational, 152–154, 385

of schools of therapy, 195
solution-focused, 113–114
stages of change, 36
tripartite, 195
woolly mammoth, 367–369, 373
modes of theorizing, 369
monocultural clinical approaches, 52
morality, 101
morphic fields, 275
morphogenetic fields, 274–275
motivation, 255, 322, 355
multicultural psychotherapy, 406
multidirectional partiality, 193–194
Multimodal Life History Questionnaire, 180
multimodal therapy, 174–180
multi-therapist systems, 227
mutual acceptance of other's projections, 217
mutual disconnection, 157
mutual empathy, 156, 159, 160–161
mutuality, 152, 153, 260
mystification, 256, 261–264
myths, 55–56, 163–164

N

narcissism, 217
narcissistic deficiencies, 246–247
narratives, 68, 90, 92, 113
narrative theory, 113
National Collaborative Study of Depression, 189
National Longitudinal Lesbian Family Study, 139
nature of change, 405
nature of reality, 277
negotiated interpretation, 350
neobehaviorism, 172

neutrality, 86, 322, 375
New Age therapists, 182
Newtonian physics as treatment
    model, 151–152
nodal points, 291
nonjudgmentalism, 130
normality, 229–230
normalization, 118
normative male alexithymia, 197

O

objectivism, 84
object relations theory, 76, 213, 217,
    301, 344
observation, 256, 266, 270–271
observers, 268, 355
100th monkey effect, 275
one-person models, 381–382
one-person psychology, 265
openness to surprise, 13
opportunity theory, 117
oppression, 50–51, 60, 137, 163
outcome measures, 324, 333
outcome research, 180

P

parental roles, 190, 344
parentified children, 97
parents, malevolence against, 111
participation in treatment, 25–26
participatory observation, 270–271
partnership between events and
    observers, 271
pathological certainty, 348
pathologizing of women, 151
pattern maintenance, 377, 381

PEAR Lab, 275–276
pedagogy of the oppressed, 50–51
perceived situations, 378
perceptions, unconscious, 272
Personal Development Program, 194
personality, 307–308, 355, 376,
    377–378
personal psychoanalysis, 251
personal psychology of therapists,
    314–315
Person-Centered orientation, 175
physical world and consciousness,
    270
positive psychology, 12
positive reframes, 223
postmodernism, 84, 85, 112, 182, 228
postmodern skepticism, 231
post-positivistic beliefs, 91
post-structuralism, 85
post transition analysis stage, 56
post-traumatic stress disorder
    (PTSD), 25, 137, 367–368
practitioners. *See* clinicians
predictable responses, 378
"prescribing" the symptoms, 223
privatization, 121
problem identification, 177
procedure, negotiating the, 324
process of psychotherapy, 307–308
professional boundary violations,
    137
profit motives, 121, 161–162
projection, 118, 217
projective identification, 213, 224,
    240, 343–344
protective strategies, 156
"psychache," 244
psychic functioning, 214

psychoanalysis
  behavioral dimensions in, 371
  countertransference as raw mate
    rial of, 320
  historical background to, 301–302,
    305–306
  as a profession, 306
psychoanalytic goals, 313
psychoanalytic method, 266
psychoanalytic project, 257–258
psychoanalytic thinking, 265
"psychoarcheological" explorations,
  171
psycho-biological revolution, 354
psychodrama, 304
psychodynamic orientation, 3, 116
psycho-educational model, 110
psychogenesis, 308
psychological functions, 215
psychology, redefining, 202–203
psychometricians, 181
psychoneuroimmunology, 272
psychopharmacology
  antidepressants, 138
  chlorpromazine, 237
  considering use of, 224
  imipramine, 237
  major tranquilizers, 237
psychotherapists. *See* clinicians
psychotherapy
  effects of, 189
  goals of, 158
  what we mean by, 404
psychotherapy instruction in training programs, 6

Q

qualities, relationship, 220

questionnaires, 180

R

racial identity development, 60
racism, 83
rage reactions, 249
reality, 229, 268–269, 277
reality testing, 247, 249
reciprocity, 114
reclaiming the disavowed, 387
recovery strategies, 137
redefining psychology, 202–203
reflexivity, 84
reframing, 223
regressed families, 347
regret, 135
re-including the excluded, 387
relatedness, 261–262
relationality, 267
relational model, 152–154, 385
relational psychoanalysis, 292,
  381–382
relational resilience, 155–156
relationship-enhancing moments,
  118
relationship qualities, 220
relationships
  building client/therapist, 72
  centrality of, 161
  connectedness, 265–266
  between consciousness and
    physical world, 270
  as core of psychological growth,
    151
  development of transference, 221
repetition of situations, 376
repression, 371–372
resistance phenomena, 380

respect, 164–166
responsibility, 353
responsiveness, 299–300
role models, 133
role of observer, 268
rules, 116, 376

S

sadism, 248
safety strategies, 155
schizophrenia, 108, 237
schizophrenogenic families, 6, 111, 347
schools of therapy, 194–195
science of relationality, 267
"scientific revolution," 6
self-adjustment stage, 56
self and other stage, 56
self-awareness, 271
self-control, 215
self-development, 194
self-disclosure, 103, 116, 159, 334
self-in-relation theory, 132
self-psychology, 78
sense of self, 247
separate self, 162
separation, 152
serial work, 93. *See also* time-limited therapy
sexual exploitation of patients, 136
sexual problems, 224
shame
    clinician's experience of, 77–78
    and disconnection, 153
    role of, 196–197
    sources of, 197, 200
    of therapists, 163–164
short-term treatment, 138

siblings of autistic children, 100
social context of psychotherapy, 338
social dangers of psychoanalysis as profession, 306–307
social workers, 181–182
societal sources of disconnection, 162–163
Society for the Exploration of Psychotherapy Integration (SEPI), 386–387
sociogenesis, 307–308
solution-focused models, 113–114
spiritual components of psychotherapy, 50, 61, 179
stages of change model, 36
stock taking, 172–173
strength perspective, 12, 115
structure/process schools of therapy, 195
studies
    chicks and rabbits, 273–274
    comparative, 189
    conversational patterns, 24
    National Longitudinal Lesbian Family Study, 139
    PEAR Lab, 275–276
    treatment outcomes, 180
subjectivity, 225, 270
success, 324
suggestion, hypnotic, 371
suicidal patients, 243–244, 244–245
suicidal process, 245
supervisor-student relationship, 119–120
supportive-evocative psychoanalysis, 25–26
supportive psychotherapy compared to insight oriented, 246
surprise, openness to, 13

survival strategies, 155
suspicion, 377
symptoms, 222, 223, 313–314, 370
systematic thinking, 254–255
systemic family treatment, 86, 223–224
systems theory, 108

T

"talking cure," 385
"Tavistock" tradition, 292
technical eclecticism, 170, 175
technique, 324, 333
technology in behavioral change approaches, 41
testimony, 60–61
"testing" of the therapist, 37–38
testosterone levels, 129
theoretical base of group analysis, 301
theoretical integration, 175
theories
    British object relations, 213
    classical, 72–73, 368
    Control Mastery Theory (CMT), 36–39
    goals of narrative, 113
    learning, 170
    modes of theorizing, 369
    motivation, 322
    narrative, 113
    object relations, 76, 213, 217, 301, 344
    opportunity, 117
    rigid adherence to, 161
    self-in-relation, 132
    systems, 108
theorizing modes, 369

therapeutic alliance
    connectedness in, 79
    healing power of, 161
    understanding the, 36
    weakening of the, 244
    work occurring within the, 77
therapeutic communities, 353
therapeutic gain, 258
therapeutic goals, 313
therapeutic impasses, 157
therapeutic zeal, 313
therapists. *See* clinicians
time-effective therapy, 18, 36, 39
time-limited therapy, 93, 140
"Top Secret" tasks, 196
traditional medicine, 269
training, 6, 182
transactional process, 381
transference
    as aid to observation, 256
    analysis of, 383
    compared to projective identification, 213
    development of transference relationship, 221
    distortions, 346
    ethnocultural, 56
    nature of, 382
    transformative nature of, 338
transpersonal defenses, 224, 227
transpersonal mode of psychic functioning, 214
trauma, 156, 157. *See also* post-traumatic stress disorder (PTSD)
traumatic disconnection, 157
treatment modalities, 38, 60–61, 140
trimodal approach, 176
tripartite model, 195